T0321744

Cybersecurity Issues, Challenges, and Solutions in the Business World

Suhasini Verma
Manipal University Jaipur, India

Vidhisha Vyas
IILM University, Gurugram, India

Keshav Kaushik
University of Petroleum and Energy Studies, India

A volume in the Advances in Information Security, Privacy, and Ethics (AISPE) Book Series

Published in the United States of America by
IGI Global
Information Science Reference (an imprint of IGI Global)
701 E. Chocolate Avenue
Hershey PA, USA 17033
Tel: 717-533-8845
Fax: 717-533-8661
E-mail: cust@igi-global.com
Web site: http://www.igi-global.com

Library of Congress Cataloging-in-Publication Data

Names: Verma, Suhasini, 1976- editor. | Vyas, Vidhisha, 1980- editor. |
  Kaushik, Keshav, editor.
Title: Cybersecurity issues, challenges, and solutions in the business
  world / Suhasini Verma, Vidhisha Vyas, and Keshav Kaushik, editors.
Description: Hershey, PA : Information Science Reference, [2023] | Includes
  bibliographical references and index. | Summary: "This book centers on
  the basics of cybersecurity innovation alongside the methods and
  strategies for organizations to adopt, allowing readers to have a more
  profound comprehension of cybersecurity in the business world"--
  Provided by publisher.
Identifiers: LCCN 2022024503 (print) | LCCN 2022024504 (ebook) | ISBN
  9781668458273 (hardcover) | ISBN 9781668458280 (paperback) | ISBN
  9781668458297 (ebook)
Subjects: LCSH: Data protection--Economic aspects. | Database
  security--Economic aspects. | Computer security--Economic aspects.
Classification: LCC HF5548.37 .C934 2023 (print) | LCC HF5548.37 (ebook)
  | DDC 658.4/78--dc23/eng/20220526
LC record available at https://lccn.loc.gov/2022024503
LC ebook record available at https://lccn.loc.gov/2022024504

This book is published in the IGI Global book series Advances in Information Security, Privacy, and Ethics (AISPE) (ISSN: 1948-9730; eISSN: 1948-9749)

British Cataloguing in Publication Data
A Cataloguing in Publication record for this book is available from the British Library.

All work contributed to this book is new, previously-unpublished material. The views expressed in this book are those of the authors, but not necessarily of the publisher.

For electronic access to this publication, please contact: eresources@igi-global.com.

Advances in Information Security, Privacy, and Ethics (AISPE) Book Series

Manish Gupta
State University of New York, USA

ISSN:1948-9730
EISSN:1948-9749

MISSION

As digital technologies become more pervasive in everyday life and the Internet is utilized in ever increasing ways by both private and public entities, concern over digital threats becomes more prevalent.

The **Advances in Information Security, Privacy, & Ethics (AISPE) Book Series** provides cutting-edge research on the protection and misuse of information and technology across various industries and settings. Comprised of scholarly research on topics such as identity management, cryptography, system security, authentication, and data protection, this book series is ideal for reference by IT professionals, academicians, and upper-level students.

COVERAGE

- Privacy-Enhancing Technologies
- Access Control
- Telecommunications Regulations
- Electronic Mail Security
- CIA Triad of Information Security
- Network Security Services
- Internet Governance
- IT Risk
- Computer ethics
- Security Classifications

IGI Global is currently accepting manuscripts for publication within this series. To submit a proposal for a volume in this series, please contact our Acquisition Editors at Acquisitions@igi-global.com or visit: http://www.igi-global.com/publish/.

Titles in this Series

For a list of additional titles in this series, please visit: www.igi-global.com/book-series

Handbook of Research on Technical, Privacy, and Security Challenges in a Modern World
Amit Kumar Tyagi (Vellore Institute of Technology, Chennai, ndia)
Information Science Reference • © 2022 • 474pp • H/C (ISBN: 9781668452509) • US $325.00

Applications of Machine Learning and Deep Learning for Privacy and Cybersecurity
Victor Lobo (NOVA Information Management School (NOVA-IMS), NOVA University Lisbon, Portugal & Portuguese Naval Academy, Portugal) and Anacleto Correia (CINAV, Portuguese Naval Academy, Porugal)
Information Science Reference • © 2022 • 271pp • H/C (ISBN: 9781799894308) • US $250.00

Cross-Industry Applications of Cyber Security Frameworks
Sukanta Kumar Baral (Indira Gandhi National Tribal University, India) Richa Goel (Amity University, Noida, India) Md Mashiur Rahman (Bank Asia Ltd., Bangladesh) Jahangir Sultan (Bentley University, USA) and Sarkar Jahan (Royal Bank of Canada, Canada)
Information Science Reference • © 2022 • 244pp • H/C (ISBN: 9781668434482) • US $250.00

Methods, Implementation, and Application of Cyber Security Intelligence and Analytics
Jena Om Prakash (Ravenshaw University, India) H.L. Gururaj (Vidyavardhaka College of Engineering, India) M.R. Pooja (Vidyavardhaka College of Engineering, India) and S.P. Pavan Kumar (Vidyavardhaka College of Engineering, India)
Information Science Reference • © 2022 • 269pp • H/C (ISBN: 9781668439913) • US $240.00

Information Security Practices for the Internet of Things, 5G, and Next-Generation Wireless Networks
Biswa Mohan Sahoo (Manipal University, Jaipur, India) and Suman Avdhesh Yadav (Amity University, India)
Information Science Reference • © 2022 • 313pp • H/C (ISBN: 9781668439210) • US $250.00

Global Perspectives on Information Security Regulations Compliance, Controls, and Assurance
Guillermo A. Francia III (University of West Florida, USA) and Jeffrey S. Zanzig (Jacksonville State University, USA)
Information Science Reference • © 2022 • 309pp • H/C (ISBN: 9781799883906) • US $240.00

Handbook of Research on Cyber Law, Data Protection, and Privacy
Nisha Dhanraj Dewani (Maharaja Agrasen Institute of Management Studies, Guru Gobind Singh Indraprastha University, India) Zubair Ahmed Khan (University School of Law and Legal Studies, Guru Gobind Singh Indraprastha University, India) Aarushi Agarwal (Maharaja Agrasen Institute of Management Studies, India) Mamta Sharma (Gautam Buddha University, India) and Shaharyar Asaf Khan (Manav Rachna University, India)
Information Science Reference • © 2022 • 390pp • H/C (ISBN: 9781799886419) • US $305.00

701 East Chocolate Avenue, Hershey, PA 17033, USA
Tel: 717-533-8845 x100 • Fax: 717-533-8661
E-Mail: cust@igi-global.com • www.igi-global.com

Table of Contents

Chapter 15
Abubakar Bello, Western Sydney University, Australia
Alana Maurushat, Western Sydney University, Australia

Detailed Table of Contents

Chapter 1

    Smita Mahesh Pachare, Symbiosis Skills and Professional University, India
    Sunita Bangal, Indira Institute of Management, Pune, India

In this chapter, the authors aimed to investigate cyber security, information security, and privacy in the context of the fintech ecosystem in India with real-time cases and examples. In the chapter, basic framework for cyber security is discussed along with an iterative process with actions under consideration. This chapter is aimed at providing a brief overview of cyber security in the fintech ecosystem. The nature of cyberattacks faced by organizations on digital payments channels with real-time examples include cybersecurity risk – reality check, traditional threats versus latest threats, cyber forensic and monitoring technologies. The chapter will also be focused on Cyber Swachhta Kendra' (CSK), maintaining cyber hygiene in digital payment transactions, and innovative ways to security and privacy in digital payments. Preventive measures in digital payment to avoid fraud are given.

Chapter 2

    G. V. Chiranjeevi Adari, College of Engineering, Jawaharlal Nehru Technological
        University, Kakinada, India
    Ramalinga Raju Manyala, College of Engineering, Jawaharlal Nehru Technological
        University, Kakinada, India

Smart grid is based on the usage of digital devices and two-way communication between supply and utility. Even though it offers so many advantages as compared to the traditional grid, the major challenge it needs to face is cyber security. As with the advancements in IoT and related infrastructure, smart grid is more vulnerable to attacks. In order to develop the counter measures against security threats, there is a necessity to review different attacks the smart grid can be subjected to. National Instituter of Standards and Technology has identified the major cyber security R&D challenges as 1) device level security, 2) cryptographic and key management, 3) networking issues related security, and 4) system level security. In this chapter, the different issues and challenges to the R&D of cyber security as identified by European Network and Information Security Agency and National Instituter of Standards and Technology are presented. Later, the chapter also presents different digital devices and communication protocols to counteract the cyber-attacks for the smart grid.

Chapter 3

Sunny Dawar, Faculty of Management and Commerce, Manipal University Jaipur, India
Pallavi Kudal, Dr. D.Y. Patil Institute of Management Studies, Pune, India
Prince Dawar, Poornima Group of Colleges, Jaipur, India

Cybersecurity is an extremely important matter in the current business world due to increasing cyber threats. Cyber attackers have increased their cyber-attacks on almost all the business operations using various advanced techniques. All kind of business organization ranging from small scale to large organizations have been impacted. So, cybersecurity has become a necessity for all kinds of firms, and adopting the secured techniques of business transactions has become a prerequisite of the business. The authors wish to find the conceptual framework of cybersecurity, associated risks related to cybersecurity, ways for ensuring cybersecurity in businesses, emerging trends in cybersecurity, and different initiatives taken in India for ensuring cybersecurity.

Chapter 4

Edward T. Chen, University of Massachusetts, Lowell, USA

The purpose of this chapter is to understand the severity of cyberattacks and identify the importance of using cybersecurity to protect organizations from future threats. This chapter will discuss the types of attacks that can occur along with the types of security measures that can be implemented to ensure information remains protected for individuals or organizations. Information regarding cyberattacks in certain businesses, healthcare organizations, and social media will also be discussed to assess and identify the different types of cyber threats. Information from previous research studies and past data will be evaluated to identify the types of cybersecurity that can help different organizations as well as identify and prevent any future threats they could potentially encounter. Further examination of previous and future cyberattacks will also be discussed to understand how those threats occurred, where they come from, and how security can be used to combat them.

Chapter 5

Suhasini Verma, Manipal University Jaipur, India
Jeevesh Sharma, Manipal University Jaipur, India
Keshav Kaushik, University of Petroleum and Energy Studies, India
Vidhisha Vyas, IILM University, Gurugram, India

Digital transformation in financial transactions has changed the method of payment. We have witnessed a many-fold and rapid increase in the digital payment. As more individuals opt for digital payments, the potential of being exposed to cyber-attacks such as online fraud, theft of identity, and spyware or virus attacks is rising. Transaction on digital mode has led to an increase in internet-based crimes known by the term 'cybercrime'. Cybercrime is an illegal act practiced by hackers on web applications, web browsers, and websites. Secured payment is critical for any company that deals with electronic payments and transactions. One of the most vital issues confronting players in the digital payment ecosystem is cyber security. The growth of such cyber-attacks can be attributed to various reasons, including a lack of knowledge and a poor digital payment infrastructure. To safeguard against threats of cybercrime, there are various cyber security techniques. This chapter deals in understanding the causes, threats, and solutions to cyber-attacks in digital payment methods.

Chapter 6
Vijaya Geeta Dharmavaram, GITAM School of Business, India
Oly Mishra, Indian Institute of Foreign Trade, India

Know your customer (KYC) is a measure adopted by financial institutions like banks to render timely services to their legitimate customers. Cybercriminals are resorting to KYC fraud through Vishing and SMiShing attacks. Customers have been falling prey to such frauds in the name of KYC updation. The chapter proposes the application of the supervised machine learning model to detect KYC fraud related to SMS and prevent such frauds. A dataset of sample KYC fraud messages and non-fraud messages is taken to train the machine learning model. The model is trained to extract the relevant features that distinguish fraud messages from valid messages, thus detecting fraud messages. The model was tested with popular supervised machine learning algorithms. The proposed model may be made as part of a security patch in the messaging service. KYC fraud has become rampant in recent times, and the chance of an individual falling for such attacks are highest given that it is a mandatory process. Previous research studies provided generic solutions for such frauds.

Chapter 7
Amit Kashyap, Nirma University, Ahmedabad, India
Pranav Saraswat, Nirma University, Ahmedabad, India

The importance of digital technologies for social and economic developments and a growing focus on data collection and privacy concerns have made the internet a salient and visible issue in global politics. The internet has transformed how we do business and created new opportunities for cross-border trade and investment, enabling small businesses worldwide to connect with customers and suppliers in the global market. In this chapter, the author conceptualizes the digital media business in India, which utilizes the internet to create the biggest platform for commerce worldwide. The author discusses regulations that are required in the cyber law and the safe harbour rule of cyber law, which is constantly harnessed by the digital media and e-commerce companies that act as intermediaries to protect them from the actions of the end-user on their platform.

Chapter 8
Sneha Verma, Banaras Hindu University, India

In today's IT-regulated era, data is nothing less than money. It is rightly said that a person who has data can become a millionaire. That is the power of data. For business organisations, information and business-related data is like blood. If there is any shortage or leakage, it could risk the life of the business. The business information has become a part of the valuable assets of the company. Thus, information security should be given high importance in the corporate governance system of the company. For this purpose, the role of the management of the company comes into focus. The management and the board of directors work towards the success of their company; thus, it is their sole responsibility to protect the valuable assets including the confidential business information. The board needs to make decisions regarding corporate governance by keeping the information security in consideration. Thus, information security governance is the need of the hour. The present chapter focuses on the importance of the information security governance in today's information-driven world.

Chapter 9
Kush Kalra, University of Petroleum and Energy Studies, India
Bhanu Tanwar, University of Petroleum and Energy Studies, India

Cyber security policies can be defined as a formal set of rules that help regulate all the aspects of data and information exchange over the internet. These cyber policies are made with the goal to ensure the necessary regulations to protect people over cyber space and to allow a social freedom. It is necessary to maintain a balance between the two. Progress to expand the legislation to criminalize certain activities that pose as a threat to the society is rather a remarkable step for most countries. The first step is the introduction of a policy to the country. A policy is mostly used as a strategy to define different objectives and methods to address the issue of concern. Developing a policy helps the government to understand and define a required response to a problem. The battle against cybercrime cannot be solely won by introducing legislation. Certain strategies and measures that strengthen the fight against such crime and resolve conflicts are also needed.

Chapter 10
Kamalendu Pal, University of London, UK

The internet of things (IoT) is ushering in a new dawn of technological innovations in recent decades for commercial applications. The technological innovation commercial applications manifested in two forms: (1) firstly, development of industrial products and services (e.g., procurement, manufacturing, transportation, and customer service) and, secondly, digitization of business activities. In this way, regular business operation-related data collection, preservation, and analysis using digital technologies (e.g., IoT) are shaping strategic value for companies. For example, the data exchange within and among affiliated devices company works is growing, and such systems' ubiquitous nature brings them into possession of business-sensitive data and information. Hence, industries are placing immense importance on the management of security and privacy of these data to maintain smooth business continuity. Moreover, IoT-based enterprise information systems often use cryptography to maintain data security.

Chapter 11
Anand Jha, Rustamji Institute of Technology, BSF Academy, Tekanpur, India
Kirti Raj Bhatele, Rustamji Institute of Technology, BSF Academy, Tekanpur, India
Prajeesh Philip, Rustamji Institute of Technology, India
Khushi Mishra, Rustamji Institute of Technology, BSF Academy, Tekanpur, India

RESTful API-based web and mobile applications are cross-platform and can be accessed from anyplace or anytime resulting in a smoother and easier user experience. This ecosystem creates a familiar environment for business applications, especially for small businesses. However, an increasing number of such applications creates opportunities to protect passwords from various attacks. Humans choose weak textual passwords due to easiness, which may lead to the most frangible connections in the chain of authentication. The graphical password offers a better approach of authentication for web and mobile applications in the emerging business world since it uses images as input instead of alphanumeric. It also makes it difficult for the attackers to crack. This study devises a system that allows the user or client application to authenticate by tapping the right cues over a series of images that the user selects while registering in the system. The system is implemented as a web service using JavaScript technology by ReactJS on client applications and NodeJS on server end.

Chapter 12

Rajesh Yadav, GITAM University, India
Digvijay Singh, BML Munjal University, India

A few years back, it was arduous to identify cyber-security in the day-to-day activities of an organization. Writing extra code-lines was considered insignificant, and the term was considered more advanced than the current times. Most businesses were doubtful about changing their plans so that they could combat this danger as the notion of "it won't occur to me" was famous. Cyber-security is now no longer a "forbidden silo." It is considered a necessity and is no longer selective. The organization must have its security planning in such a manner that it plays an important role in its business as well as the decision-forming in the significant matters of the company. In today's scenario, organizations must have a check on their defense system to ensure security in operations. They use updated solutions and have proper information on vulnerabilities and security issues that persist at the moment. This chapter throws light on security issues in blockchain-based businesses.

Chapter 13

Nkholedzeni Sidney Netshakhuma, University of Mpumalanga, South Africa

The study aimed to assess cyber security at South African universities. The researcher will use literature to assess the state of cybersecurity at South African universities. The results from the literature review revealed poor implementation and adherence of cyber security strategy and standards by employees and students; poor cyber security awareness relative to information communication technology (ICT) infrastructures and assets; and lack of strategy and framework to implement cyber security management. The study recommends continuous monitoring and evaluation of information management systems at various South African universities with the view to assess the state. A replica of the study may be studied in other part of the world.

Chapter 14

Oluchukwu Ignatus Onianwa, University of Ibadan, Nigeria

This chapter examines Africa's strategic partnership with the Council of Europe in the development and advancement of cybersecurity on the continent. Africa is one of the continents in the world with a strong presence of information and communication technology users. Unfortunately, both government institutions and private sectors in Africa are experiencing an increase in cyber-related attacks. Different initiatives through CoE are being developed to combat the menace of cyber-attacks in Africa.

Chapter 15

Abubakar Bello, Western Sydney University, Australia

Alana Maurushat, Western Sydney University, Australia

As the threat landscape continues to evolve, users are becoming less aware, ignorant, or negligent, putting their confidential data at risk. Users easily fall prey to socially engineered ransomware attacks that encrypt and lock a computer or mobile device, holding it hostage unless a ransom is paid. The cryptoware encrypts data securely, making it almost impossible for anyone except the hacker to unlock the device. This research conducts a systematic review to identify methods for executing socially engineered ransomware attacks. Using a CRI framework, 122 studies were synthesized from 3209 research articles highlighting gaps in identifying and analyzing attack vectors, as well as the need for a holistic approach to ransomware with behavioural control as part of the solution. Human vulnerability was found to be a critical point of entry for miscreants seeking to spread ransomware. This review will be useful in developing control models that will educate organisations and security professionals to focus on adopting human-centered solutions to effectively counter ransomware attacks.

Preface

There are no mincing words that today in times of IT revolution there has been a great advancement in cyber-attack and protection techniques. In this context, cyber security, due to its technicalities and its tendencies to develop in a very short span of time, is a demanding and challenging issue. Hence, businesses need to take support from the internal information system department or an external technology company. Although businesses recognize current issues as clear and present danger, they do not understand well, what they should do and how much they should do it. Even the businesses find the issue difficult to discuss directly. Hence, cyber security is the task left to the specialized staff only and companies find it difficult to discuss the issue and initiate solutions. Cyber security needs to be positioned as a central issue among top management issues and it is a ripe time that the same need to be positioned as a business management issue rather than only an IT issue. Given the current digitization of businesses, cyber security covers the corporate activities where digital information is readily available and utilized over the entire firm. Businesses need to take cyber security as a priority task and companywide optimization.

Cyber security is the real and the businesses in this digitally transforming world are concerned about it. The threats, constant cyber-attacks and continuous history of breached data is causing alarming scenarios. The deep understanding of the challenges their profound impact and metamorphosis that information security will undergo in coming decades call for a robust diagnoses of cyber security issues, challenges faced by the business. The in depth analysis of the problems in hand will allow experts to find solutions which will safeguard them against cyber threats.

In earlier times when servers, machines and workplaces were usually placed at a static location security were strengthened using tangible machines and focused on safeguarding limited devices and machines. The security systems were built on the basis of understanding of physical external environment. Organizations focused on issues related with physical t4rsting and annual audits and assessments of devices with changes happening only once or twice in a year. However, with the changing times, the concept have renovated and paved the way for new vision of cyber spaces. With the ever changing and digitally transforming businesses and widespread adoption of cloud, the definition, threats, challenges associated with cyber world have become deeper and more defined. It is important to diagnose the matters related to cyber-crime contagion.

Cyber-attacks have become a common phenomenon in the present interrelated world. The digital transformation of majority of the business increases the volume of cyber-attacks. It is projected that by 2021, cybercrime will hit $6 trillion. More critical situation is, many of these are attacks on small businesses that do not have the gears or strategies available to safeguard themselves. Many data thefts result from phishing frauds, introducing malware into network, traffic interception and crypto jacking. Organizations are facing challenges related with hybrid cloud computing, operational security, privacy protection, security culture, etc.

The bearing and consequences of cyber security breaches are drastically different as compared to previous environments. Cyber-attacks are on large scale against commercial or public interests. A ransom ware attack against a fintech firm can result in financial disaster, on hospital can lead to loss of lives and against a university can cause career damage to many students. It is clear that the scale of risk and its potential impact are escalating fast.

The business needs to sprint to develop new innovations and solutions to adapt to this changing environment. From small start-ups to global enterprises, the line of cyber defence needs to be laid down to safeguard interest of firms, consumers and nation at large.

Training employees about contemporary tactics used by scammers can reduce the likelihood of exposing them to malicious software. Employing basic data security policies will help companies to properly handle company data and reduces the threat of internal misuse. Firms should also be vigilant about people having access to sensitive data. Control baseline, developing security culture, IT rationalization are few of the strategies, which can significantly reduce the effect of human faults on cyber security measures. While cyber-attacks remain a serious threat to firms today, there are robust solutions that can strengthen efforts to protect data and maximize value. By keeping abreast with the contemporary risks, firms can implement more effective cyber security strategies to protect themselves and their customers from unsafe data breaches and related threats.

The era of IOT, fintech, data protection and governance present a rich array of research fields which could provide possible solution to the concerns of cyber security.

There are several dangers, associated with business operating in an interconnected business, some of which are more significant than others. Malware wiping your whole system, an adversary entering your framework and changing data, an assailant utilizing your system to target others, or an adversary obtaining your credit card details and performing illegal transactions are just a few of the threats you should be aware of. Although with the best safeguards, there's no assurance that any of these events didn't occur to you, however there are actions you can do to reduce your risk. This book centres on the basics of Cyber security innovation alongside the methods and strategies for its joining with the Business. It permits the pursuer to have a more profound comprehension of Cyber security, Business, and different application regions wherein both the advances can be actualized. The book effectively provides satisfactory information about the essentials of Cyber security and Business to a typical pursuer alongside encouraging an examination researcher to distinguish some modern issue regions that rise out of the intermingling of the two advancements. Wide domains of business which are related to cyber security challenges and possible solutions made the core of this book.

The target audience of this book will be composed of professionals and researchers working in the field of Cyber security in various disciplines, e.g. researchers, academicians, scientists, advanced-level students, developers and Cyber security enthusiasts. The book will also focus youthful scientists wishing to begin investigating the possibilities of the Cyber security and business a portion of the not-yet prospected territories of research and application. Another crowd would be any analysts who are yearning in cross-discipline investigate and is searching for a solitary including reference that gives enough profundity and expansiveness to participate in utilizing ideas of Cyber security for different specialized topics he/she experts. A portion of the potential users would be reference material for graduate courses in Business, Cyber security, Artificial Intelligence, Internet of Things and so forth. It would serve unquestionably as a decent reference for the individuals who are occupied with the examination in the innovation itself and the possibilities and traps of its application in various usage spaces.

One read the chapters of the book individually, although issues and solutions in these chapters are applicable to wide variety of business domains. These chapters explore how the cyber security concerns are identified and can be applied to the specific topics and challenges of each varied business areas. Each topic chapter contains an overview of the scientific pursuits in that domain case associated with the theme objective and some practical examples and data driven insights.

The chapters in the book can be divided into different categories and domains. The chapters surveyed some of the industrial applications of cyber security systems and presented possible solutions. One of the chapters discusses different architectural issues, attack vectors, and challenges to IoT security.

Another chapter talks about issues related to privacy and security in relation to data mining technique In many data mining applications, it is not possible for parties to share original datasets with each other due to privacy concerns. To solve this problem, data mining protocols that protect data privacy have been discussed and proposed. The privacy-preserving data mining (PPDM) protocols involve rules and techniques that allow parties collaborate on the data mining applications while keeping their data private. The chapter discusses the building blocks for PPDM protocols and show some of the applications of PPDM.

An interesting chapter deals in RESTful API based web and mobile applications and how increasing number of such applications create opportunities to protect passwords from various attacks. Humans choose weak textual passwords due to easiness, which may lead to the most frangible connections in the chain of authentication. The chapter deals in the idea of graphical password which offers a better approach of authentication for web and mobile applications in the emerging business world. It uses images as input instead of alphanumeric, easier to recall and also makes it difficult for the attackers to crack. The chapter propose a system which allows the user or client application to authenticate by tapping the right cues over a series of images that the user selects while registering in the system. The system is implemented as a web service using JavaScript technology by ReactJS on client applications and NodeJS on server end.

The book contains a chapter on block chain technology which has emerged with widespread adoption in accounting and finance. With this widespread usage it gives attention to cyber threats requiring an effective implementation of cyber security as part of financial security. The witnessed cyber-attacks on this technology have demonstrated that it is not resistant to cyber threats. It is noted that the breaches have led to technical advancements which were made possible via Block chain 1.0 - 3.0. Block chain 1.0 is not completely reliable since specific currencies are linked with deceitful transactions. The Hyperledger fabric requires a modern approach for detecting the flaws and identifying vulnerabilities which are associated with the profile risk. Technological advancements have given a rise to mixer networks which are responsible for disguising transactions which adds on to the existing difficulties.

Another chapter focuses on different types of cyber-attacks arise in the power system smart Grid introducing major cyber-attacks during last 15 years across the world. It introduces the transformation from traditional grid to the smart grid followed by major causes of cyber-attacks. Since the smart grid employs huge data, the objectives of data management system are presented to the reader. A chapter on socially engineered ransom ware as an extortion crime presents a review of ransom ware prevention techniques; and an investigation of ransom ware research gaps. Ransom ware attacks are becoming more sophisticated, employing social engineering to psychologically manipulate victims to install ransom ware payloads. Socially engineered ransom ware is a challenge, and with more devices and systems connecting to the Internet of Things, ransom ware attack prevention will be the responsibility of government bodies and departments. The chapter deals in depth how the systems can be secured against such ransom ware.

Other chapters of book deals with identification of KYC fraud and techniques which can be safeguarded against such threat, a chapter on cyber-attacks on digital payments and security issues in fintech firms presents possible causes and solutions to these cyber-attacks. The book contains chapters based on data driven insights about cyber security threat in Indian Economy, in African Universities and European Council. Few select chapter increases readers interest by discussing the concerns related to governance and regulations pertaining to data and cyber security.

The book will be appealing to business professionals, students, and academic fraternity looking forward to exploring dimensions of cyber security, data governance and prevention of cyber threats and frauds. We hope the readers will enjoy the breadth of the issues covered in the book.

Suhasini Verma
Manipal University Jaipur, India

Vidhisha Vyas
IILM University, Gurugram, India

Keshav Kaushik
University of Petroleum and Energy Studies, India

Chapter 1
Cyber Security in the FinTech Industry:
Issues, Challenges, and Solutions

Smita Mahesh Pachare

ⓘ https://orcid.org/0000-0002-5173-4034

Symbiosis Skills and Professional University, India

Sunita Bangal

Indira Institute of Management, Pune, India

ABSTRACT

In this chapter, the authors aimed to investigate cyber security, information security, and privacy in the context of the fintech ecosystem in India with real-time cases and examples. In the chapter, basic framework for cyber security is discussed along with an iterative process with actions under consideration. This chapter is aimed at providing a brief overview of cyber security in the fintech ecosystem. The nature of cyberattacks faced by organizations on digital payments channels with real-time examples include cybersecurity risk – reality check, traditional threats versus latest threats, cyber forensic and monitoring technologies. The chapter will also be focused on Cyber Swachhta Kendra' (CSK), maintaining cyber hygiene in digital payment transactions, and innovative ways to security and privacy in digital payments. Preventive measures in digital payment to avoid fraud are given.

INTRODUCTION

Globally More than 85% of online buyers use at least one fintech service, a figure that is expected to rise as more people grasp and learn about contactless payments, mobile banking, online lending, online travel booking, micro-investing, and other fintech-powered money-related activities like insurance, online capital, and investment instruments, etc. The FinTech industry has become a most globalized segment of the world's economy & also among the most digitized and datafied segments among other segments and industries.

DOI: 10.4018/978-1-6684-5827-3.ch001

Presently FinTech is accountable for bringing basic changes in Global Financial Payments and investments. The rates of change specifically observed over the last two decades are summarized as ABCD systems: artificial intelligence (AI), blockchain, cloud, and data are evolving with the fund at an increasing rate. Numerous would include web and Internet of things (IoT) to this ABCD system. These changes have positive viewpoints but moreover negative ones, inside the shape of advanced threats. The FinTech industry is disquieting and becomes more challenging because of raises many risks and challenges. Financial apps are becoming gold mines for cybercriminals looking to take profitable individual and monetary information. Banks, the Payment industry, Credit, and Insurance industry, and financial institutions utilize Fintech innovation, counting through the Web & Internet, and smart devices & without strong cyber security measures, financial stability & integrity, financial efficiency, financial development, customer protection, and inclusion might be at high risk.

This chapter highlights many of the key areas of Cyber risk and challenges related to Fintech, cyber security in Fintech, and Cybersecurity solutions in the Fintech industry with real-time examples.

Financial Innovation and The Fintech Ecosystem

Traditional financial services models face difficulties in reaching customers in remote areas. Underbanked communities frequently conduct small, frequent transactions that are hampered by traditional transaction fees and commercial banking system inefficiency. Again, the financial needs of consumers differ from entity to entity and are determined by multiple factors like socioeconomic, Income level, Geographic factors, etc. FinTech is working well to address these issues. It has identified a market opportunity in serving the needs of the bottom-of-the-pyramid income segments that are usually ignored by traditional financial institutions.

FinTech is inextricably linked to financial innovation. As a result, there is a need to study the literature on financial innovation in addition to the fundamental and well-established understanding of digital innovation. Financial innovation can be considered "the act of creating and popularizing new financial instruments new financial technologies, institutions, and markets" (Lerner and Tufano, 2011). Financial innovation has changed into three categories – new products and services, new production processes, and new organizational forms (Frame and White, 2014). the study finds that financial innovation has a relationship to economic growth that varies depending on the variable used to measure financial innovation. The long-run, growth-driven financial innovations are confirmed, with causality running from economic growth to financial innovation. (Bara and Mudzingiri, 2016). Arnaboldi and Rossignoli (2015) argue that financial innovation drives economic growth, while others point to its dark side., The right kind of innovation and favorable conditions that may encourage banks to invest in new technologies would assist the financial system in carrying out its functions and, as a result, deliver growth.

THE FINTECH ECOSYSTEM

FinTech refers to financial services or products that are offered by using technology. It is a field that integrates finance, technology management, and innovation management. Fintech refers to a service sector that applies technology & Internet of things to improve the efficacy of the financial system. The main objective of FinTech is the development of systems for modeling, valuing, and processing financial products such as insurance, Mutual Funds, stocks, bonds, money, and contracts. Technology through financial services has a significant impact on our day-to-day lives, it provides the facilities and infrastructure for Digital payments, Digital payment Settlements also provide the essential infrastructure to the operation of the world's financial institutions. (*The Ernst & Young Tax Guide 2014*, p. 2).

Fintech service providers are considered choragus during COVID 19 pandemic. Fintech companies are increasingly active in mobile remittances, electronic payment systems, end-to-end user platforms, and cryptocurrency transactions. It has improved efficiency and catalyzed and accelerated the economy in important ways throughout the epidemic. However, they pose major security threats to consumers, service providers, and the economy as a whole.

For understanding, recognize, and contextualize the FinTech phenomenon we need to study a comparison of three major patterns or trends "FinTech", "eFinance," and "Digital Finance," from the point of view of their terminological similarities, "e-Finance" and "Digital Finance" are near-synonyms (Gattenio, 2002), but the only difference between the former three terminologies is the context. The extensive perspective and focus of digital finance are the digital transformation of the financial industry, "eFinance", on the other hand, is defined as "providing financial services and financial markets using electronic communications computing and data processing." (Allen, McAndrews, and Strahan, 2002) E-finance will empower both businesses and consumers by lowering transaction costs, accessing & accessing documents online quickly, and providing instant access to information.

To study cybersecurity in Fintech, we need to understand the collaborative and competitive dynamics in fintech innovation as well as the issues and challenges of risk management in the Fintech ecosystem. The FinTech Ecosystem is made up of many organizations. Every organization in the FinTech ecosystem works together to achieve a common goal which is the development and introduction of new technologies to improve or disrupt the traditional banking sector and improve the economic growth and social inclusion of more people.

The fintech ecosystem covers all the parties involved in the delivery of a product or service from a principal financial institution to an end-user. For example, a bank lends money to a customer by using a third-party online platform which could be a comparison or distribution or merely a lead generation platform. The list may include but is not limited to telecom operators from communication, regulators from approvals, auditing, marketing agencies from contents, and software houses from product or service development.

Fintech companies and startups aim to compete & completely replace traditional financial service providers by offering a superior experience or simply a more effective solution to existing problems. & for this, they rely on technologies to address consumer needs in Payments and payment settlements, wealth Management, Lending, Crowdfunding, Capital Market, Insurance, Financial Planning & management.

Another example is the Google Pay (Gpay) platform which acts as an additional discovery channel for many companies to create and deliver innovative new user experiences to drive adoption of their services, including buying tickets, ordering food, and paying for essential services like utility bills, shop and get access to various financial products.

The FinTech ecosystem is explained in Figure 1. According to Lee and Shin (2018), the participants in the FinTech ecosystem are FinTech startups; Government; Traditional financial institutions; Financial customers; and, technology developers.

Fintech start-ups are providing innovative and disruptive technology solutions to the FinTech ecosystem. Traditional financial institutions such as global and local banks, private equity trading, and venture capital funds can bring deep content and market knowledge to the ecosystem. The government implements and implements policies and regulatory environments that facilitate the development of the FinTech ecosystem.

Figure 1. Fintech Ecosystem

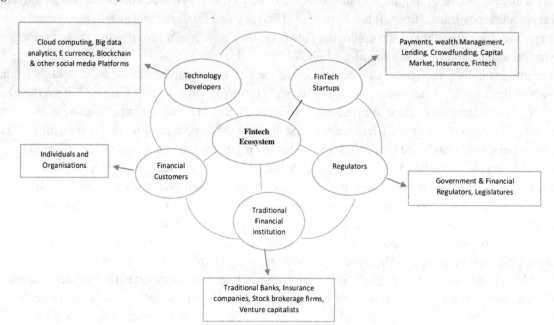

CYBER RISK

Cyber Risk is becoming a serious problem for global financial institutions. This can be described as potential exposure or potential loss as a result of a cyberattack or data breach, or damage related to the technical infrastructure. Due to the increasing dependence on smart devices, mobiles, computers, Cloud networks, programs, social media, and globally shared data, Individuals or Organizations are becoming more defenseless to cyber threats. According to Deloitte's 2019 Future Research Report, the impact of cyber risk incidents varied from real monetary costs, including financial loss due to business disruption and loss of customer trust, reputational loss, leadership changes, and regulatory fines. It ranges from monetary costs to intangible costs, Changes, and declines in company stock prices and market share. As per this report, Cyber risk is an issue that lies at the intersection of business, regulatory, and technology risks. ("The future of cyber survey 2019", 2019).

Cyber Risks in Fintech Industry

In recent years, FinTech has significantly improved traditional financial services products and services & continues to disrupt the global financial landscape. FinTech companies and startups are unique, and arguably their most important advantage is that they are not controlled or burdened by applicable laws, regulations, or systems. They are more adaptable, aggressive, and prepared to experiment and take risks.

However, their bold attitude and complete reliance on technology to provide financial services may be one of their biggest flaws. Hence it becomes a need to know about various hidden cyber risks involved in FinTech services or the FinTech industry. Figure 2 reports the number of online searches for "cyber risk" over the last three years.

Cyber risk represents a subset of a Fintech company's or financial institution's operational risk. A company's operational risk can be defined as the risk of loss due to inadequate internal procedures, failure of various corporate systems, or external events that could disrupt business operations.

Following are the listed Various cyber risks involved in the FinTech industry.

Figure 2. Number of worldwide searches for "cyber risk"
Source: Google Trends (Data assessed on 29 May 2022)

Malware Attacks

Malware term combines malicious and software, it also refers to any application that is specifically meant to harm devices, data, or individual users. Malware Attacks become more sophisticated during and after the covid 19 pandemic both in terms of malware functionality and attack vectors. This type of attack usually locks the database and system and demands a ransom. Emotet, Ursnif, Zeus, and Kronos are examples of legacy malware. All of these were originally designed as bank Trojans trying to sneak into computers and steal sensitive personal information.

In October 2021, British and Italian banks were attacked by the bank's Trojan SharkBot. This banking Trojan tricks the target into downloading malicious apps from the Google Play store, granting admin rights, collecting keystrokes, intercepting/hiding F2A SMS messages, banking and cryptocurrency. Access the currency mobile app to send money. Targets were international banks in the UK and Italy and five different cryptocurrency services around the world. The second example of a banking trojan is the Drinik banking trojan malware in September 2021 being targeted at Indian android-based financial customers. The malware stole users' data and funds using phishing techniques. The average ransomware payment rose 33% in 2020 over 2019, to $111,605 globally (Siegel, 2022).

Distributed Denial of Services

Distributed Denial of Service (DDoS) attacks are performed using the network of devices connected to the Internet. These networks consist of computers and IoT devices that are infected with malware and are remotely controlled by attackers. The purpose of these attacks is to use the targeted resources to create a denial of service. A bot means that an individual device is also called a zombie, and a group of bots is called a botnet. By 2023, the total number of DDoS attacks worldwide will be 15.4 million (Cisco, 2022).

Data Breaches

Systems that interact with financial service providers are particularly vulnerable to data breaches. Data plays an important role for banks and other financial institutions. Most banks and fintech companies allow customers to store payment data such as card details and user password details on their platforms, websites, or devices. Hackers who make online transactions and face cyber robbery can easily obtain user IDs, payment card details, and user information. Minor violations can lead to the leakage of sensitive financial data. When a data breach occurs, it loses customer trust, raises questions about the security system of fintech players, and a global data breach is the biggest challenge facing the fintech industry. The biggest risk of data being breached in Fintech is protecting data lies in mobile banking services. Personally identifiable information, and financial, and health information are greatly exposed to third parties.

A recent example of real-time data breaches is the crypto trading platform. Bitmart was hacked in December by nearly $ 200 million in a security breach caused by the theft of a private key, which primarily affected two smart chain hot wallets, Ethereum and Binance. With assets withdrawn on May 12, 2021. Data breaches were first reported in multiple locations on May 12, 2021. In July 2021, insurance technology startup BackNine released thousands of sensitive claims for data breaches hosted in Amazon's cloud, with a high percentage of sensitive personal and medical information. It was misconfigured to give everyone access to seven or more missing files inside, including the completed insurance claim. About the applicant and his family. In 2022 hackers stole the personal data of 4.5 Mn Air India passengers. MobiKwik and Juspay were also involved in data leak/breach incidents impacting over 21 Cr users. Indian petroleum refineries network faced over 90K cybercrime incidents. In 2021 the average total cost of a data breach increased from $3.86 million to $4.24 million ("Cost of a Data Breach Report 2021", 2021).

Phishing

Phishing can be done online as well as via SMS for bank transactions. Phishing attacks steal customer credentials, collect sensitive information, and an attacker can duplicate an activity in the same way as a customer. In October 2021, Russia linked the TA505 with a phishing campaign that targeted financial institutions around the world, which are being tracked as MirrorBlast with email attachments, the target is redirected to a fake OneDrive website, the compromised SharePoint, and a login request is displayed to bypass the sandbox.

APTs Against Banks

A persistent attack on a specific entity or entities to compromise their systems and obtain information from or about them is known as an advanced persistent threat (APT).

Cloud Environment Security Risk

Strong cloud security measures matter a lot for FinTech companies. Most of the Digital financial products and services in the fintech ecosystem are based on Cloud computing. Payment gateways, digital wallets, and secure online payments are part of the niche cloud computing services offered by the FinTech ecosystem. Maintaining the confidentiality and security of financial data is important and difficult for banks, financial institutions, and FinTech companies.

Cryptocurrency Related Risks

In today's FinTech world Cryptocurrencies, such as Bitcoin, Tether, Ripple, Bitcoin Cash, Ethereum, Monero, Cardano, Solana, and others, are no passing phase, empty buzzwords for investors. Cryptocurrency is decentralization of digital currencies that works without central authority and monitors transactions with low levels of regulation and overall cryptocurrency. Supported by the blockchain, it keeps customer records and enables digital payments regardless of location or time. Due to Decartelization and no Information security governance or regulation, the anonymous origin of currency global crypto Market becoming a hub for Money Laundering of assets generated through drug trafficking and other illicit activities.

Cryptocurrencies are the preferred form of exchange in the event of a ransomware attack. The actor can hide his true identity when demanding a ransom in digital currency.

In August 2021, crypto money laundering via Mixer became a hot topic. The mixer is a service that enhances anonymity by combining digital assets of many addresses and then releasing them to new destinations and wallets at random intervals.

Crypto-jacking is also a cryptocurrency cyber risk. This is the fraudulent use of someone else's computer to mine cryptocurrencies. Hackers do this through malicious links in emails that download crypto mining code to computers/devices, or by infecting websites with JavaScript code that is executed when loaded into the victim's browser.

The May 2021, Bengaluru-based eight-year-old fintech unicorn Razorpay which uses the latest technology to protect its payment information was unable to reconcile the receipts of INR 7,38,36,192 against 831 transactions resulting in a loss amounting to INR 7.38 Cr because of 'false' authorization. The company claims to enable digital payments for 200K+ businesses including Airtel, IRCTC, NSE, Swiggy, etc. With large-scale enterprises trusting the network and its payment authorization technique, the possibility of false authorization puts a dent in the company's security system. Table 1 shows the cyberattacks on FinTech Firms with an estimated loss.

Cyber Threats on Digital Capital Markets

Cyberthreats in the Digital capital market may cause manipulation of the order management system, and false or non-bidding orders, resulting in incorrect flow and corruption of the trade monitoring system, creating conditions for manipulative, illegal, and abusive trading practices. Activation of malicious automated trading strategies, increasing the risk of a quick crash can become a serious problem and challenge for digital capital Markets.

Table 1. Cyberattacks on FinTech firms with an estimated loss (worldwide)

Institution	Year	Estimated Loss
Bitstamp	Jan,2015	5.3 USD Million
Bitfinex	May,2015	0.3 USD Million
Gatecoin	May 2016	2 USD Million
DAO Smart Contract	Jun 2016	50 USD Million
Bitfinex	Aug, 2016	72.2 USD Million
CoinDash	Jul 2017	7 USD Million
Tether	Nov 2017	31 USD Million
NiceHash	Dec 2017	64 USD Million
Coincheck	Jan 2018	534 USD Million
Bitgrail	Feb 2018	170 USD Million
Coinsecure	Apr 2018	33 USD Million
CNA Insurance	March 2022	40 USD Million
AXA	May 2022	

Source: ORX News, Financial Times, Forbes,

Source: ORX News, Financial Times, Forbes,

CYBERSECURITY IN FINTECH

Cybersecurity can be explained as the processes with the help of technologies and practices designed to protect an individual or organization's intellectual property, customer information passwords or data, and other sensitive information from unauthorized access by cyber attackers or hackers. In simple words, cybersecurity means information technology security or electronic information security is the multitude of technologies, frameworks, and processes used to protect computers, servers, electronic devices, systems, data, and networks from malicious attacks, unauthorized access, technology, or device damage. It's a Practice that protects electronic or digital data from illegal or unplanned use and access, modification, or destruction. But it is becoming more critical day by day because, of the huge number of data networks, digital applications, and mobile users increasing at a gigantic rate.

With the digital transformation of finance, investments, and payments due to FinTech the financial world is more vulnerable to attacks by hackers. Cybersecurity is critical in the financial industry due to regulatory development. Not surprisingly, this is an area of focus for Financial Institutions, Fintech companies, and regulators.

Fintech products and services often make use of users' sensitive data and link with users' bank accounts for efficient online transactions so the use of cybersecurity is important for the Fintech industry. In case of a cyber-attack or a security breach, all this sensitive information is at stake. Fintech security secures such information from misuse by cybercriminals and also ensures users' trust in fintech company providers.

Cyber Security Solutions for FinTech Industry

Cyber security solutions could be categorized as a) Cyber Security solutions at the Business level or institutional level. b) Cyber Security solution at the Individual level.

Figure 3. Cyber security solutions for Fintech Industry

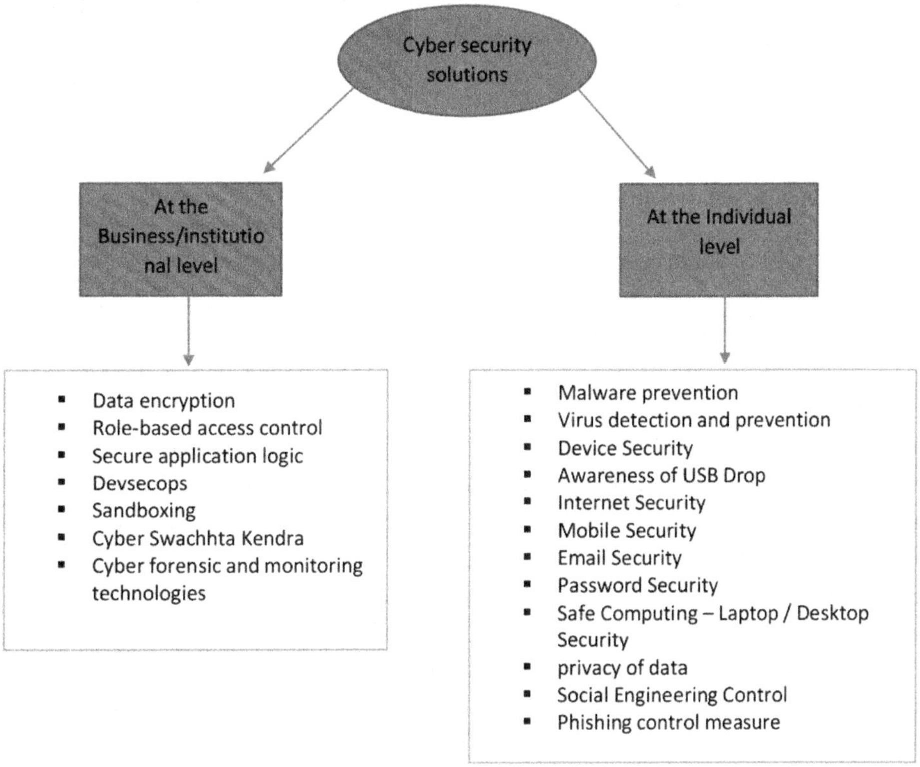

Cyber Security Solutions at the Business Level or Institutional Level

Data Encryption

Data Encryption is used to prevent malicious acts and restrict accessing sensitive data. In cybersecurity architecture, data encryption plays a vital role. Encryption encodes data and converts it into a difficult format. It can be applied to all categories of data security/protection viz. government transactions as well as personal transactions. Data encryption software is, also known as a cipher or maybe sometimes an algorithm. This algorithm develops an encryption key/scheme which theoretically can only be solved/ broken with large computation. This makes data more secure in transit and privacy is also not invaded if the key(s) are strong or complex enough to break. With the power of the data encryption algorithm data become impossible to access except for parties sharing contracts.

Role-Based Access Control

1.   On network, access, and restrictions can be imposed by Role-based access control (RBAC). As per person plays role in the organization this access control or privileges are granted. RBAC is an advanced method for access control.

2. For effective execution of their duties, Employees are allowed to access only necessary information. Factors influencing Access-based responsibility, authority, and competency. Access could be limited to tasks like viewing or modifying a file as per the job assigned to an employee.
3. RBAC helps to protect the company's sensitive data and sensitive applications from third parties and contractors.

Secure Application Logic

It is very much important to address security by businesses right at every stage of software development. Security logic has to be developed and tested at each stage of application development. The application security objective is to address software application code and data vulnerabilities:

- **Web Application Security:** The Internet has addressed web application vulnerabilities by the introduction of HTTP. HTTP creates a communication path that ensures encryption. It protects (MitM) man in the middle attacks. But not all are addressed. OWASP Top 10 are severe vulnerabilities. Many vendors devised solutions to secure web applications namely WAF (web application firewall) which prevents application-layer attacks.
- **API Security:** APIs may also suffer from vulnerabilities and these result in major data breaches. Because of this APIs expose sensitive data. This can interrupt critical operations. Some common weaknesses APIs are they suffer from are unwanted exposure of information, and weak authentication which enables API abuse. Every API has to be tested using sandboxing which could ensure security issues.
- **Cloud-Native Application Security:** As cloud computing evolved cloud-native applications are also evolved. The technologies used for implementing micro-services architecture are containers, virtual machines, and serverless platforms. While implementing this architecture, cloud-native security has become a multifaceted challenge, because these applications have a large number of moving components which transitory. Because of this, in the native environment, it becomes difficult to gain visibility for ensuring all components are secure. Businesses must have a strategy to have cloud-native application security in place.

Devsecops

Just like DevOps, DevSecOps connects three different phases/aspects of SDLC (Software development life cycle): development, security, and operations. The goal of DevSecOps is to flawlessly integrate security into continuous integration and continuous delivery process in both pre-production and production environments (Dev and Ops) DevSecOps plays important role in delivering better, more secure software faster as every phase has a role to play (Marsal, 2021).

Digital Payment

When it comes to business it would not be complete without payment (digital payment). While the industry is adapting digital platforms with greater zeal, security issues are also started attracting the attention of all. Not only do traditional or simple digital payments need to be adapted but also innovative ways need to be devised and tested for more secure transactions. Some of them are listed:

1. IoT implementation, home devices must be encrypted and secure by a Smart hardware system.
2. CVV in case of bank cards.
3. One Time Password (OTP).
4. Software encrypting passwords using cryptographic keys. ...
5. Contactless payments
6. Mobile wallet
7. Mobile point on sale. (MPS)
8. Smart Speaker payment
9. Top-rate dated security by AI/ML application
10. Use of Customers' fingerprints as a biometric measure to approve bank card purchases
11. From cards to codes
12. Biometric authentication like heartbeat analysis, iris recognition, facial recognition, vein mapping, etc.

Sandboxing

Sandbox is a standalone test environment. Users can run programs or open files without affecting the system, application, or platform on which the code is running or the user is working. Cybersecurity professionals use sandboxes to test malicious freeware/code/software. If the software is not tested against sandbox (VM) could have potentially unlimited access to all the system components, data, or resources on a network. Businesses must practice having to sandbox is implemented to protect against the malicious act of any software component (Rosencrance, 2021).

Cyber Swachhta Kendra (CSK)

FinTech firms should follow guidelines alerts issued by governing bodies or Cyber Swachhta Kendra' (CSK) from time to time. CSK The CSK is the center for malware analysis and Botnet Cleaning. It is one of the Digital India initiatives under MeitY (the Ministry of Electronics and Information Technology) which detect botnet infections in India. It also helps in cleaning notifying and securing end users' systems. The main objective is to create secure cyberspace and prevent infections.

CERT-In (Indian Computer Emergency Response Team) operates the CSK center under provisions of Section 70B of the Information Technology Act, 2000.

Cyber Forensic and Monitoring Technologies in Indian Fintech Ecosystem

FinTech firms can have a system in place to practice Cyber forensics. It is used to find evidence no matter how small it may be by gathering and analyzing information. It becomes proof of a cyber-attack. CERT-In also works on cyber forensics and sends alerts across the country.

Various Cyber Forensics Platforms available for implementation are as follows (Sangfor Technologies, Published on 13 Jan 2022)

Naive Users, Open-Source Platforms

- **Autopsy:** This is a GUI-based forensic program for analyzing smartphones and hard drives. Used all over the world
- **Encrypted Disk Detector:** This can be helpful to check support for encrypted physical disks, Bitlocker, TrueCrypt, etc.
- **Wireshark:** it is a network analyzer, it captures the network. Used to investigate network problems.
- **Network Miner:** A network forensic analyzer for MAC OS, Windows, and Linux to detect operating systems, hostnames, open sessions, and ports, through packet or PCAP file detection. It provides extracted artifacts
- **Autopsy:** it is a GUI-based digital forensic program to analyze smartphones and hard drives. Used worldwide
- **Encrypted Disk Detector:** it can be helpful to check supports for encrypted physical drives, Bitlocker, TrueCrypt, etc.
- **Wireshark:** it is a network analyzer tool, It captures the network. Used to investigate network incidents.
- **Network Miner:** A network forensic analyzer for MAC OS, Windows, and Linux to detect OS, hostname, sessions, and open ports, through packet sniffing or PCAP file. It provides extracted artifacts.

Cyber Security Solutions for Consumer / Individual Level

Malware Prevention

User Should not install third-party software, utility software, or freeware. Users must not click on any unidentified link in an email. Users must have an antivirus installed and keep it updated with the latest versions. He shouldn't disable antivirus software or proxy, these are some reasons installed.

Virus Detection and Prevention

Users should not have a myth in mind that viruses don't exist. It can be very harmful and destructive if overlooked and not adapted with proper measures. Most of the above-stated measures hold for viruses also.

Device Security

Users shouldn't keep laptops/desktops unattended or unlocked else hacker grabs the opportunity to steal organizational confidential and/or sensitive information. Hackers can share the information which will result in corporate espionage. Hackers can change their passwords. In this case, the victim will be held responsible for the act and the organization will be impacted due to the loss of information.

Awareness of USB Drop

Hacker plans to rob organizational information through infected USB. He drops USBs with implant malware on the office. The victim should not fall prey to checking the information on the USB. It should be always scanned first and then it has to be used by the user.

Internet Security

There are people always active and trying to steal organizational assets on the internet. So it is important to safeguard organizations' assets or information. There have to be policies in the organization to protect the information.

Some of the measures are as follows:

- Restricting access to sites containing offensive material, terrorism-related websites, sites distributing illegal software, hacking, and piracy-related material.
- Restricting non-business websites which will lead to the legitimate use of bandwidth for core business purposes.
- Restricting forums which engage in personal discussion, sharing, or engaging in activities like eCommerce, trading, etc.
- Under any circumstances don't bypass the proxy.

Mobile Security

The wireless intruder could be exposed to critical information, lost or stolen devices lead to treating of the entire intranet of organization, mobile viruses can take advantage of the compromised application, bluesnarfing/bluejacking create problems of stealing of data, worms may disrupt device as well as phone network.

All above-stated loopholes need to be addressed and fixed by adopting good practices and being proactive to avoid vulnerabilities before they could hit badly. Installing apps from dependable websites, installing antivirus, and maintaining digital hygiene are best practices to deal with mobile security.

Email Security

Statistics show that around 247 billion emails float every day out of which 81% are pure spam. So users have to be very cautious while clicking messages else the organization's interest may get compromised.

Password Security

Password should be of a minimum of 8 characters, it should not contain a name, NetID, or predictable patterns. It must include special characters and numeric characters. Every 45 days it has to be changed. The last six passwords should not be repeated. Businesses should also enforce this security measure along with authentication measures.

Safe Computing – Laptop / Desktop Security

There are very simple but very important measures one should, or an organization must take care of. Some of them are as follows: Businesses and users should not change OS (Operating system) settings or the hardware configuration. They can connect to any modem if it is approved by the IT Helpdesk which in turn ensures security. To prevent unauthorized access to the machine, always lock the system with password protection. Protect the machine from physical damage. Log out application and machine while leaving for an extended time. Users shouldn't enable sharing of the folder with other users on a network.

Individuals and Organizations Must Practice A Clean Desk Policy In Turn Meet The Security And Privacy Of Data

Some activities of the clean desk policy are: User should not let anyone use his laptop, he shouldn't keep any file or document unattended, and avoid sticking a password as a note on a laptop. He shouldn't keep photocopiers, fax machines, and other office equipment unattended. A document containing sensitive data must be minced before disposal. Confidential data must be in safe storage. The cabin must be locked etc.

Social Engineering Control

Users shouldn't reveal sensitive information while in a telephonic conversation, on voice mail, or on answering machines. Whenever someone is asking for confidential data whom you don't recognize always ask for their identification. Watch out for whoever reading information on your computer screen.

Phishing Control Measure

User shouldn't respond to suspicious emails, User shouldn't be fooled by scary – tactics, He shouldn't open unexpected attachments or links, and User shouldn't provide sensitive information via mail.

IMPLEMENTING A CYBER SECURITY STRATEGY

Firms should prepare themselves for cyber security risks by considering a holistic approach. Factors playing a vital role in implementing cyber security strategies are

- **Strategy-Governance-Management:** Prioritising investments, allocation of resources, and aligning security capabilities with the strategy of the firm is equally important to pay attention.
- **Emerging Trends:** Assess opportunities and security-related risks while adopting new technologies and dynamics of the business model.
- **Risks & Compliance:** Efficiently and effectively identify and evaluate and manage risk while evolving regulatory requirements.
- **Security Architecture Services Rendered:** Secure risk by design for operational disciplines and foundational capabilities

- **Threats/Vulnerability Management:** Address threats and weaknesses by anticipating changes in the risk landscape through situational awareness of internal and external factors influencing the business ecosystem.
- **Identity and Access Management:** Enable secure access. Provide integrated and secure services, processes, and infrastructure to enable appropriate control.
- **Information Privacy Protection:** Safeguard critical assets by identification, prioritizing, and protecting.
- **Incident and Crisis Management etc:** Anticipate and respond to the security crisis.

While designing a robust framework for the business ecosystem, FinTech firms should consider national as well as international standards to be followed. Adoption of these standards makes the business work globally with resilience. It safeguards nations' as well as global countries' interests as well as Some of the governing bodies and standards. Firms must be aware of and follow the ecosystem shown in the following chart.

Table 2. National and international security standards

1	Security Standards	ISO 27001:2013 Information Security	ISO 22301:2012 Business Continuity	ISO 31000:2009 Risk Management
2	International Standards / Regulations	NIST CSF NIST SP 800-53	PCI-DSS	HIPPA
3	Policies and Guidelines in India	Information Technology Act, 2000	National Cyber Security Policy	National Information Security Policy, MHA
4	Cyber Security Bodies in India	National Cyber Coordination Centre (NCCC)	National Critical Information Infrastructure Protection Centre,(NCIIPC)	CERT-In, State CERTs, Sectoral CERTs

CONCLUSION

The fintech industry is known to be a very vulnerable one. Failure to prioritize cybersecurity in the FinTech space can create serious risks for FinTech companies, financial institutions, regulators as well as customers. Not prioritizing cybersecurity in the fintech sector is a real risk that cannot be overlooked. Cybersecurity is essential for FinTech start-ups as it protects consumers, businesses, and the interests of the nation. The context is FinTech as it is subject to monetary transactions, as well as strategic business information. If cybersecurity is vulnerable, an insecure ecosystem leads to vulnerability. In the chapter discussing FinTech. Revolutionary factors and their influence on the FinTech industry. The Fintech ecosystem and key players are also covered in the chapter. The various risk factors associated with cyberthreats in FinTech are illuminated.

For any organization, to maintain and earn the trust of its customers, the CIA Triad must be regulated. Confidentiality, integrity, and availability, if done well with the holistic approach discussed in the chapter, will ensure that companies can support and protect users. Security prevents information disclosure and protects customer privacy. Integrity prevents malicious or unauthorized modification of information.

With the use of hash codes and sequential cryptography in the Blockchain system, along with decentralized structure, artificial intelligence, and machine learning (ML) algorithms for early detection of threats, Big Data is used to identify threats. Identifying cyberattack trends from the vast amount of secure data mined on endpoints are some of the new ways of working to prevent cyberthreats in the Fintech industry.

All major players in the FinTech ecosystem, including regulators, have shifted their focus from protection and prevention to rapid detection and recovery. All financial institutions and regulators are focusing their strategies more on detection, response, and remediation. They are also focused on implementing a secondary system to stay afloat in the event of a successful cyber-attack on digital financial products and services.

REFERENCES

Allen, F., McAndrews, J., & Strahan, P. (2002). E-finance: An introduction. *Journal of Financial Services Research*, *22*(1), 5–27. doi:10.1023/A:1016007126394

Arnaboldi, F., & Rossignoli, B. (2015). Financial innovation in banking. In *Bank risk, governance and regulation* (pp. 127–162). Palgrave Macmillan. doi:10.1057/9781137530943_5

Bara, A., & Mudzingiri, C. (2016). Financial innovation and economic growth: Evidence from Zimbabwe. *Investment Management and Financial Innovations*, *13*(2), 65–75. doi:10.21511/imfi.13(2).2016.07

Cisco. (2022, August 17). *What is a ddos attack? distributed denial of service.* Cisco. Retrieved from https://www.cisco.com/c/en/us/products/security/what-is-a-ddos-attack.html#~ddos-explained

Cost of Data Breach Report 2021. (2021). IBM. Retrieved from https://www.ibm.com/downloads/cas/J01XNXRO/name/05477c943ab64485.pdf

Frame, W. S., & White, L. J. (2014). *Technological change, financial innovation, and diffusion in banking.* Leonard N. Stern School of Business, Department of Economics.

Gattenio, C. A. (2002). Digitizing finance: Views from the leading edge. *Financial Executive*, *18*(2), 49–51.

John Wiley & Sons. (2013). *The Ernst & Young Tax Guide 2014.* Author.

Lee, I., & Shin, Y. J. (2018). FinTech: Ecosystem, business models, investment decisions, and challenges. *Business Horizons*, *61*(1), 35–46. doi:10.1016/j.bushor.2017.09.003

Lerner, J., & Tufano, P. (2011). The consequences of financial innovation: A counterfactual research agenda. *Annual Review of Financial Economics*, *3*(1), 41–85. doi:10.1146/annurev.financial.050808.114326

Marsal, J. (2021, July 20). *What is DevSecOps? And what you need to do it well.* Dynatrace. Retrieved from https://www.dynatrace.com/news/blog/what-is-devsecops/#:~:text=DevSecOps%20is%20the%20seamless%20integration,any%20specific%20technology%20or%20techniques

Principles for Financial Market Infrastructures. (2012). BIS. Retrieved from https://www.bis.org/cpmi/publ/d101a.pdf

Siegel, B. (2022, January 24). *Ransomware payments up 33% in Q1 2020.* Coveware. Retrieved from https://www.coveware.com/blog/q1-2020-ransomware-marketplace-report

The future of cyber survey 2019. (2019). Deloitte. Retrieved from https://www2.deloitte.com/content/dam/Deloitte/us/Documents/finance/us-the-future-of-cyber-survey.pdf

ADDITIONAL READING

Agbo, C. (2021, August 6). *Bank Customers Get N89bn Refund on Failed Transactions in 9 Years – CBN.* 21st Century Chronicle. Retrieved from https://21stcenturychronicle.com/banks-customers-get-n89bn-refund-on-failed-transactions-in-9-years-cbn

Al Duhaidahawi, H. M. K., Zhang, J., Abdulreza, M. S., Sebai, M., & Harjan, S. A. (2020). Analysing the effects of FinTech variables on cybersecurity: Evidence form Iraqi Banks. *International Journal of Research in Business and Social Science, 9*(6), 123–133.

Blackmon, W., Mazer, R., & Warren, S. (2021). *Nigeria Consumer Protection in Digital Finance Survey. Innovations for Poverty Action.* Retrieved from https://www.poverty-action.org/sites/default/files/Nigeria-Consumer-Survey-Report.pdf

CBN, Stakeholders Launch Cybersecurity Campaign #NoGoFallMaga. (2021, July 20). Punch. Retrieved from https://punchng.com/cbn-stakeholders-launch-cybersecurity-campaign-nogofallmaga

Digital Security Risk Management For Economic And Social Prosperity. (2015). OECD. Retrieved from https://www.oecd.org/sti/ieconomy/digital-security-risk-management.pdf

FinTech Futures. (2018, March 5). *Infographic: The incredible growth of fintech.* Retrieved from https://www.bankingtech.com/2018/03/infographic-the-incredible-growth-of-fintech/

Idris, A. (2020, July 1). *Why Some of Nigeria's Worst Cyberattacks Are Not Reported.* Tech Cabal. Retrieved from https://techcabal.com/2020/07/21/why-some-of-nigerias-worst-cyberattacks-are-not-reported

Kryparos, G. (2018). Information security in the realm of Fintech. In R. Teigland, S. Siri, A. Larsson, & A. M. Puertas (Eds.), *The Rise and Development of FinTech: Accounts of Disruption from Sweden and Beyond* (pp. 43–65). Routledge. doi:10.4324/9781351183628-3

Miller, M. H. (1986). Financial innovation: The last twenty years and the next. *Journal of Financial and Quantitative Analysis, 21*(4), 459–471. doi:10.2307/2330693

Phadke, S. (2020). *FinTech future: the digital DNA of finance.* Sage Publications Pvt. Limited. doi:10.4135/9789353885687

Stevens, T. (2018). Global cybersecurity: New directions in theory and methods. *Politics and Governance, 6*(2), 1–4. doi:10.17645/pag.v6i2.1569

Chapter 2
Cyber Security in Smart Grids:
Role of Digital Advanced Devices

G. V. Chiranjeevi Adari
https://orcid.org/0000-0002-7895-407X
College of Engineering, Jawaharlal Nehru Technological University, Kakinada, India

Ramalinga Raju Manyala
College of Engineering, Jawaharlal Nehru Technological University, Kakinada, India

ABSTRACT

Smart grid is based on the usage of digital devices and two-way communication between supply and utility. Even though it offers so many advantages as compared to the traditional grid, the major challenge it needs to face is cyber security. As with the advancements in IoT and related infrastructure, smart grid is more vulnerable to attacks. In order to develop the counter measures against security threats, there is a necessity to review different attacks the smart grid can be subjected to. National Instituter of Standards and Technology has identified the major cyber security R&D challenges as 1) device level security, 2) cryptographic and key management, 3) networking issues related security, and 4) system level security. In this chapter, the different issues and challenges to the R&D of cyber security as identified by European Network and Information Security Agency and National Instituter of Standards and Technology are presented. Later, the chapter also presents different digital devices and communication protocols to counteract the cyber-attacks for the smart grid.

INTRODUCTION

Smart Grid is the Most promising technology at present as Entire country is adopting smart Grid technology in the power sector to enhance the functionality of power delivery. The goals of smart grid are to reduce energy consumption and reliability of supply with reduction in the cost of power generation facilitating two-way communication. One of the major objectives is the adoptability to consumer requirements and any changes in the characteristics of power supply. Since smart Grid uses high level communication, its security is a major issue of the concern at the time

DOI: 10.4018/978-1-6684-5827-3.ch002

Centre for Strategic and International Studies (CSIS) | Washington, D.C. lists cyber incidents since 2006 under its strategic technologies program. Most of these attacks are mainly targeted the data theft. In power systems the cyber-attacks are increasing in recent years. Similarly, A Survey on Power System Blackout and Cascading Events: Research Motivations and challenges, energies, MPDI lists the cascaded power blackouts across the globe. According to it, out of total power outages, only 6% are planned outages, 26% are due to faulty equipment or human errors and about 20% are due to unknown reasons (Haes Alhelou et al., 2019). As per the historical events the following are the major power system blackouts in last twenty years.

This chapter Focuses on different types of cyber-attacks arise in the power system smart Grid introducing major cyber-attacks during last 15 years across the world. Introduces the transformation from traditional grid to the smart grid followed by major causes of cyber-attacks. since the smart grid employs huge data, the objectives of data management system are presented to the reader. The components and functionalities in smart Grid are explained followed by brief classification of cyber-attacks. The smart grid employs the most of advanced devices, their role is very essential and some auxiliary equipment are provided for proper operation. The framework and requirements developed by NIST are presented in this chapter ("Guidelines for Smart Grid Cybersecurity, Volume 1 - Smart Grid Cybersecurity Strategy, Architecture, and High-Level Requirements", 2014) (ENISA) recommendations for smart grid security are presented. Recommendations cyber-attack mitigation techniques are provided for reference of the user. Since the smart grid uses high level communication, the different communication protocols used are presented with their extensions also. The main intention of authors is to introduce the cyber security issues, different communication protocols and role of advanced digital devices in the smart grid cyber security.

List of Cyberattacks on Smart Grids and Blackouts:

1. **Blackout in US and Canada, 2003:** On 14 August 2003 is due to a failure of alarm system when a high-voltage power line in northern Ohio collided with some overgrown trees, causing the fault.
2. **Arizona–Southern California Blackout:** Due to failure of high voltage line on 8 September 2011, electricity redistribution took place and resulting in Arizona– Southern California blackout
3. **Iran Nuclear Facility Attack, 2010:** is due to the failure of Stuxnet system which results in targeting of SCADA and computer controller systems.
4. The Department of Homeland Security through the campaign from Russian hackers revealed that the networks of multiple US electric utilities were compromised, and attackers were in a position to cause blackouts.
5. **Ukraine Power Grid Attack, 2015 and 2016:** The attackers gained the access to the distribution grid operation and about 230000 people were affected by the blackout.
6. Recently in 2020, Mumbai blackout happened which is due to the failure of a transmission line. Several spokesmen claimed that it is due to the cyber-attack.

The traditional Power system uses circuits, wires, towers, transformers, sensors and cables. All these are interlinked to provide uninterrupted power supply. The smart Grid employs sensors, two-way communication devices, computation control system powered by artificial intelligence and require use of the internet. So, obviously, Grid will be vulnerable to cyber-attacks, data theft, data loss etc.

Supervisory control and Data Acquisition system (SCADA), a platform for transition from traditional Grid to the smart Grid, it is based on the communication and computational infrastructure of power system in achieving a secure and reliable operation. This communication infrastructure makes connection to the control centre with field devices in a manner that monitoring performance and remote control of a power system is possible. Phasor data concentrators aggregate measurements obtained by Phasor Measurement Units (PMUs). The function of communication infrastructure is also to connect control centres so as to achieve secure operation. Examples are Western interconnect (WECC), ENTSO-E is the European association for the cooperation of transmission system operators (TSOs) for electricity (ENTSO-E) etc. For this purpose, a set of applications are used and termed as Energy Management system (EMS) for efficient operation of the power system. For the purposes of on-line contingency analysis, and for decision support in which large amount of data is required, the computing resources of the computational infrastructure or EMS cannot be sufficient. And the smart grid always should expand in order to meet the requirements of ever-increasing demand. So, the smart grids need to adopt a distributed architecture and should have a provision for adoption of new technologies such as cloud computing.

The traditional Power system uses circuits, wires, towers, transformers, sensors and cables. All these are interlinked to provide uninterrupted power supply. The smart Grid employs sensors, two-way communication devices, computation control system powered by artificial intelligence and require use of the internet. So, obviously, Grid will be vulnerable to cyber-attacks, data theft, data loss etc.

The major causes of cyber-attacks are listed as follows:

1. Increased installation of intelligent electronic devices (IEDs)
2. The number of attacks increases with the number of devices in the network
3. Installation of third-party components
4. The unsecured third-party components increase the network's vulnerability to attacks.
5. Inadequate personnel training: in recent years improper training of personnel in the power sector, so obviously Risk factor is high.
6. Using Internet protocols: Certain protocols use data in unencrypted format leading to attacks.
7. Maintenance: During the maintenance, the operators disable the security systems, which can lead to an attack

Protecting the grid is a major challenge at the moment as the smart grid uses Ethernet, TCP/IP and other operating systems. So, the grid is more susceptible to attacks. Once the system is attacked, several meters functionality gone under the control of the attacker and the load balance of the system is disrupted. Hence awareness about the cyber security is a must so as to eliminate the risks. The National Institute of Standards and Technology (NIST) proposed several cryptographic methods.

Smart grid operation requires huge quantity of data requirement and storage to manage the grid. But unfortunately, the utilities due to the lack of infrastructure and data analysis skills still unable to make full use of the new smart grid data. There might be lack of skilled personnel and technologies and there are some challenges for customers' data management. The unused data will reduce smart grid opportunities, in terms of controlling consumers' energy consumption and avoiding peak loads through price benefits. Customers should be enlightened the huge quantity of data extracted from smart grid platforms. So, the consumers must be educated about how to communicate with their meters and with the different platforms in the grid so as to make efficient choices to conserve energy and save money

The major objectives data management in smart Grid Cyber security are:

1. Authentication: The user who access the data in smart grid must be provided with the credentials which will act as authenticated credentials while accessing the data.
2. Authorization: After successful authentication, the user should be given authorization (access) of the data services provided by the service provider (server).
3. Confidentiality: The information exchanged between the user and service provider must not be accessed by the attacker / any other third parties. So, it must be encrypted by any of the advanced encryption technologies.
4. Integrity: This feature ensures the user that data is not theft or corrupted.
5. Availability: the data must be available to the use on demand (Faquir et al., 2021).

The data management system employed in smart grid operation is responsible for all these objectives with proper security (Iyer, 2011).

At present millions of sensors are involved in the Smart Grid design continuously sharing the data over the network, so managing such a bulk network is a biggest challenge. Any cyberattack can take place damaging the key elements, confidentiality, and integrity, of the smart grid. The overall smart grid network is comprised of customers, communication network, and the people managing the network (decision makers and administrators). Cyber-attacks can take place at any or all three of these levels. The total Smart Grid functionality can be categorized as smart control centres, smart transmission networks, and smart substations

Components of Smart Grid Functionality

Figure 1. Smart Grid Properties

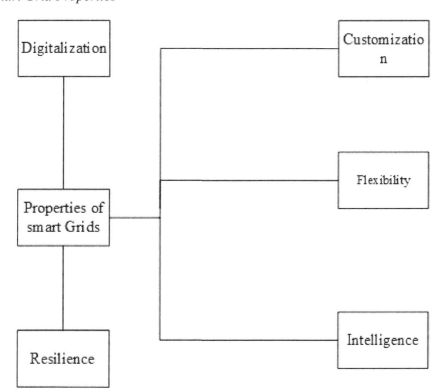

Figure 2. Smart Grid functionalities

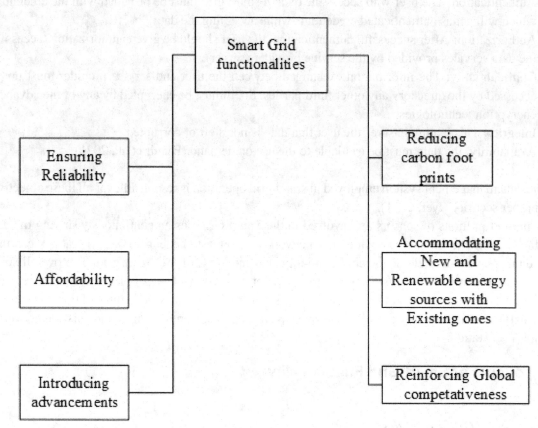

Smart Grid Constituents

Smart Control Centers

The functions of smart Control centres are monitoring/ visualization, analytical capability, controllability, interaction with electricity market (Demertzis et al., 2021).

The old and most of the existing control centres are based on the data collected by SCADA and Remote Terminal Units (RTUs). This was replaced by state measurement modules. And at present Geographical information systems (GIS) almost replaced the old systems and indicating root cause of a problem as compared against alarm based older ones. The real time online time domain analysis provides a very powerful tool for Analytical capability of the smart Grid control. The real time dynamic and adaptive techniques enable operations like separation, restoration, load allocation and sharing more controllable. Another major goal of smart grid system is to achieve high efficiency. Smart grid automatically adjusts in accordance with the market.

Smart Transmission System

Transmission networks in Smart grid involves signal processing, sensing communication, computation, advanced power electronic and digital metering to improve the efficiency. The security and quality also ensured in them. Long distance transmission uses high-capacity AC and DC facilities. Underground cables are used when the overhead lines are not possible. High temperature capability composite conductors, super conducting cables may be involved. For improvement of dynamic performance, advanced FACTS and HVDC devices can be used. To measure the line parameters and monitor the location of sensors, intelligent sensors are used. Temperature sensors, position sensors, thermal sensors, Resistivity sensors, are mainly employed for identifying faults, and failures of insulators. The operating conditions can be detected, analysed, and responded, based on these parameters, thus maintaining the reliability and security in case of the transmission.

Smart Distribution System

The equipment used in the substation in addition to be more reliable and efficient, should monitor, control, operate, protect, and maintain the substation.
    . The main functions of these smart equipment are as follows

1.   Smart sensing and measurement
2.   Communication
3.   Autonomous control and adaptive protection
4.   data management and visualization
5.   Monitoring and alarming
6.   Diagnosis and prognosis
7.   Advanced interfaces with distributed resources real-time modelling

The Role of Advanced Metering Devices

Advanced metering infrastructure refers to the Grid infrastructure connecting Meter Data Management Systems (MDMS), smart meters, communication elements among them. Automated Meter Reading (AMR) system allows meters to be read by utility personnel through wireless communication links. AMI includes Smart meters, which give periodic measurements, indicate the parameters such as RMS voltage, RMS current, phase angle, power factor, instantaneous energy consumption, instantaneous power values. Meters communication with utility MDMS over the communication network with each meter can be accessible with Internet Protocol (IP) address (Padhy and Jena, 2022).

Components of AMI

Neighbourhood Area Network (NAN)

This uses a power line communication at RF frequency about 900Mhz.PLCs are used to connect the secondary of Distribution transformer to the Consumer.

Smart Meters

Smart meters are connected to the NAN with communication interface. This interface may vary from different vendors.

Meter Data Concentrator

The function of meter data concentrator is to check and accumulate with periodic measurements by the smart meters and supporting communication with the NAN correspondingly.

Head End

Head end is the AMI's solution meter management system. It communicates with the meter concentrator with the IP address provided by the Smart Grid (Daki et al., 2017).

Figure 3. classification of AMI components

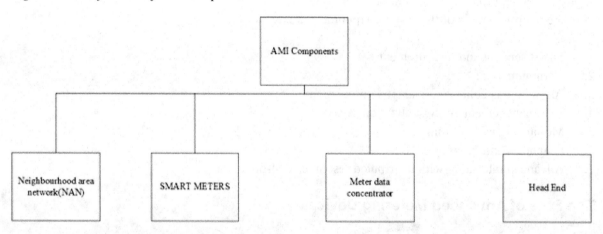

Classification of Cyber Attacks

In broad manner, cyber-attacks can be categorized as active attacks and passive attacks. In the Passive attacks, the attacker may only view the data, whereas in active attacks, the attacker can modify the data or control the receiving data by the receiver. The passive attacks can be again classified as eavesdropping attack, where the attacker can view the data packets shared from sender and the receiver and vice versa and traffic analysis attacks, where the attacker can continuously monitor the data transfer between sender and the receiver.

Active attacks are harmful compared to the passive attacks, as the attacker has full control over the data. These are classified as the replay attack, where the attacker and sender both send the data to the receiver leads to the confusion for the receiver and the masquerade attack, where the receiver keeps receiving data from the attacker even though the sender is Idle. Denial of service attack is another kind of attack in which attacker attacks the data server. The attacker can generate a number of irrelevant requests from the server and the server starts serving until all of its resources are exhausted., and due to unavailability of resources, the requests from the sender/receiver is denied (Kawoosa and Prashar, 2021).

Figure 4. Classification of Cyber attacks on the smart grid

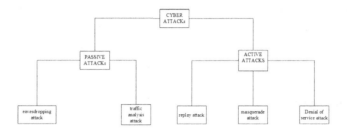

Framework Developed by NIST

The National Institute of Standards and Technology (NIST) had developed framework for Cyber security of a smart Grid, NIST suggested the following requirements for smart grids.

1. Awareness Training (SG.AT)
2. Access Control (SG.AC)
3. Audit and Accountability (SG.AU)
4. Security Assessment and Authorization (SG.CA)
5. Configuration Management (SG.CM)
6. Continuity of Operations (SG.CP)
7. Identification and Authentication (SG.IA)
8. Information and Document Management (SG.ID)
9. Incident Response (SG.IR)
10. Smart Grid Information System Development and Maintenance (SG.MA)
11. Media Protection (SG.MP)
12. Physical and Environmental Security (SG.PE)
13. Planning (SG.PL)
14. Security Program Management (SG.PM)
15. Personnel Security (SG.PS)
16. Risk Management and Assessment (SG.RA)
17. Smart Grid Information System and Services Acquisition (SG.SA)
18. Smart Grid Information System and Communication Protection (SG.SC)
19. Smart Grid Information System and Information Integrity (SG.SI) Security

Cyberattack Detection and Mitigation Techniques

Since multiple stakeholders like grid operators, electric utilities, consumers, third party service providers etc., the data management and its security is a critical task.

The framework classifies the security into three classes:

1. Communication security, which can be achieved buy key management system with end-end encryption.
2. secure computing-
3. System control security.

The detection methods earlier used in the traditional grid no longer serve at the moment. With the development of Artificial intelligence and machine learning algorithms, the smart grids are becoming smarter. In some cases, support vector algorithms can be used. With the development of telecommunication technologies and internet of things, it is possible to store the bulk data on to the cloud which will be shared to all the stack holders involved in the Grid management. The development of block chain made it very secure to protect the data as it has a property of hashing. If someone wants to change the hash value of the block, all the previous block hashes must be changed which is very complex task

Hardware-Based Security

IOT devices play the most critical role of the smart grid network. These devices must be equipped to face any cyber-attack. The hardware security problems include physical attacks, side channel analysis, and hardware malfunctions. In the physical attack, authentication system may be bypassed by the attacker. The reverse engineering methods can be used for the physical attacks. Inside channel analysis, analysing the profile features like voltage, current, frequency etc., the cryptographic keys can be found and thus leading to the. A hardware Trojan is simply any change or addition made to a circuit with the intention of causing harm. These hardware Trojans basically result in unauthorized access of private information, manipulation of circuit functioning, and reduction of circuit reliability

Some of the security systems used for smart Grid cyber-attacks are

- Physical unclonable functions
- Configurable tristate Physical unclonable functions
- Support vector machines
- Artificial neural networks
- Voltage over scaling-based authentication
- ML resistant Voltage over scaling methods

Human-Centric security approaches used at Employee Protection at Command-and-Control Centre are

1. **Multifactor Authentication (MFA):** minimizes the chance of unauthorized access. Several means can be used like SMS token, strong password, email token, hardware token authentication, phone authentication etc.
2. **Employee training:** not all the humans have same level of knowledge. So, a skilled employee operating the grid may eliminate some of the risks in the security. Proper training helps them to avoid any social engineering attacks such as phishing and ransomware.
3. **Password Strength:** setting strong passwords greatly reduce the chances of attacks. the passwords may be combination of letters, symbols, numbers, etc. password setting, and its specifications simply depend on employee and the employer.

Steps for Customer Protection are

1. Operating system protection by means of devices such as smart meters and smart inverters. And to make customers tamper –proof
2. Notifying customers every consumer plays a role in the smart grid so, notifying the energy usage and the way of usage, any deviations and time to time tariffs etc., to the consumer may reduce the chances of threats
3. Software and hardware security: besides protecting the equipment from the networks, customers should protect their devices physically by strong passwords.
4. Protection against third-party applications: Customers should check the permissions for access to application
5. Cyberattack reporting: any suspicious activity should be reported to the service provider or substation to avoid the attacks and book the culprits (Haes Alhelou et al., 2019).

Communication Protocols used in Smart Grids to Avoid Cyber Attacks

- Home area network protocol (HAN): in this the devices are connected with ZigBee and Z wave protocols
- Neighbourhood area network (NAN)-in which Devices are connected via IEEE802.11, IEEE 802.16 or IEEE 802.15.4 standards.
- Wide area network (WAN)-in which devices are connected through supervisory control and data acquisition (SCADA), distributed networking protocol 3(DNP3) and Modicon communication bus (ModBus)
- Power line communications use ModBus, DNP3, Bluetooth, Z wave, ZigBee, WiMAX IEC 61850 protocol etc.

The European Network and Information Security Agency (ENISA)- Recommendations

ENISA is a centre of network and information security expertise for the EU, its member states, the private sector and Europe's citizens. It has proposed about 10 recommendations to avoid cyber attacks in the smart grid structure. Those are listed below table.

In the following section, some common security protocols are being discussed in brief.

SCADA System

The SCADA system is based on the information from sensors and relays, which is communicated through Remote Terminal Units (RTUs) to severs and control messages from servers to relays through RTUs, and delivers control messages from SCADA servers through RTUs to relays. Information about power flow, voltage profiles and current signals is provided by Sensors. Relays are useful for control of circuit breakers and other switchgear equipment and to reconfigure the circuit on direction from RTUs. RTUs function includes Collection of measurements, Monitor the status of Relays and other equipment, and direct commands to control relays. They use wide area network (WAN) to exchange information to and from SCADA servers, which act as central processor of the SCADA system. This is depicted as shown in figure5.

Table 1. Recommendations from ENSIA

Recommendation 1	Improve the regulatory and policy framework
Recommendation 2	Foster the creation of a Public-Private Partnership (PPP) entity to coordinate smart grid cyber security initiatives
Recommendation 3	Foster awareness raising and training initiatives
Recommendation 4	Foster dissemination and knowledge sharing initiatives
Recommendation 5	Develop a minimum set of reference standards and guidelines
Recommendation 6	Promote the development of security certification schemes for products and organisational security
Recommendation 7	Foster the creation of test beds and security assessments
Recommendation 8	Refine strategies to coordinate large scale panEuropean cyber incidents affecting power grids
Recommendation 9	Involve CERTs to play and advisory role in dealing with cyber security issues affecting power grids
Recommendation 10	Foster research in smart grid cyber security leveraging existing research programmes

Figure 5. Basic SCADA System

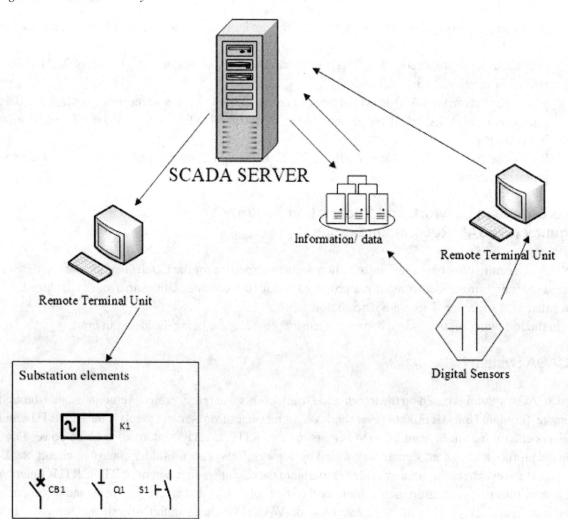

If the SCADA system uses dedicated lines for data sharing between RTUs and servers it will be more effective, but the major problem is the cost.

The communication technologies used in SCADA system includes Frequency division Multiplexing (FDM), in which each channel has a fixed non overlapping frequency range, Time division multiplexing(TDM), where channel is allocated with Recurrent fixed length time-slots. Many devices / participants can share one communication channel using Packet switching networks. The participants can communicate by variable packet lengths. In that case the technologies include x.25, Frame Relay, GPRS, Ethernet etc. in cell switched networks, fixed length packets are used. As an example, Asynchronous Transfer mode (ATM) can be cited in which data is divided into fixed length cells (Demertzis et al., 2021).

The communication infrastructure for WAN also might include, optical ground wires (OPGW) Public Switched Telephone Network (PSTN), Public Land Mobile Networks (PLMN), and satellite networks. For reliability purpose the communication infrastructure used in power systems is mostly owned by the power system operator. But at present with increasing demand, some of the equipment may also be leased to third party operators. SCADA/RTU communication protocols were independently designed by SCADA equipment manufacturers and to meet its specific needs. Due to their unique specific functions, as the demand grows, it is somewhat difficult/ impossible to combine different SCADA systems. Research is still going on in this direction. The International Electro-Technical Commission (IEC) Technical Committee (TC) published IEC 60870-5 standard in 1990 and is the foundation for today's most commonly used protocols used for RTU and SCADA server communication. European countries predominantly use IEC 60870-5-101 and IEC 60870-5-104 whereas most of the countries use Distributed Network Protocol 3 (DNP3).

IEC 60870-5

IEC 60870-5, based on Enhanced Performance Architecture (EPA) model, defines operating conditions, electrical interfaces, data transmission protocols and performance requirements. It also specifies the communication protocols for sending basic tele control messages between any two systems. EPA, the simplified version of operating systems Interconnection (OSI) model, defines three layers: physical layer, link layer, and application layer. This is shown in figure 6.

Table 2. IEC 60870-5 definitions

IEC Guideline	Functional definition
IEC 60870-5-1	physical layer, coding, bit error check, synchronization of fixed and variable data frames and formatting
IEC 60870-5-2	link layer and transmission protocols using control and address field
IEC 60870-5-3	Structure of application data units in transmission frames
IEC 60870-5-4	rules for defining information data elements
IEC 60870-5-5	Standard services (functions) of the application layer. Specific set of functions are used by the application profile.

Figure 6. EPA model layers

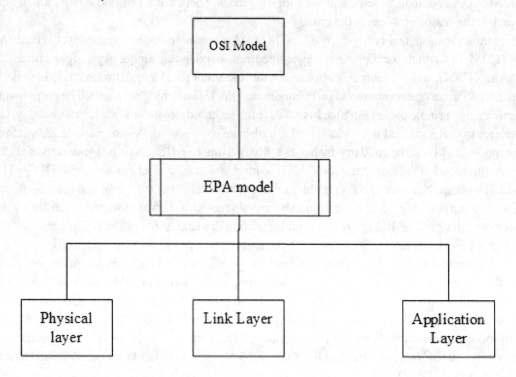

IEC 101 Standard Protocol

Published in 1995, IEC 60870-5-101 (IEC 101), IEC 101was the first IEC complete working SCADA protocol. It provides all necessary application-level functions of tele control applications. Transmission Modes IEC 101 supports balanced and unbalanced transmission modes.

The difference between these two transmission modes is that message request for exchange of data can be raised by the server only in unbalanced mode whereas both RTU and Server can initiate message requests in balanced mode.

As per IEC 60870-5-1, Addressing IEC 101 uses the FT1.2 frame format in three forms: variable-length frame format for bidirectional data transmission, fixed-length frame format for commands or acknowledgments, and a single character frame only for acknowledgments. This was depicted in previous table.

IEC 60870-5-104 (IEC 104)

To support packet switched networks IEC 101 changed and result in the form of the IEC 104 standard, in 2000. As The application layer of IEC 104 is based on IEC 101, it supports the same transmission modes as IEC 101. As Addressing in IEC 104 depends on TCP and IP as network and transport protocols, it does not impose any limitations on the physical layer and the data link layer protocols. So, addressing under the application layer is not possible in IEC 104. Reliability in IEC 104 depends on existing protocols for detection of bit transmission errors.

Figure 7. Balanced and unbalanced modes of transmission

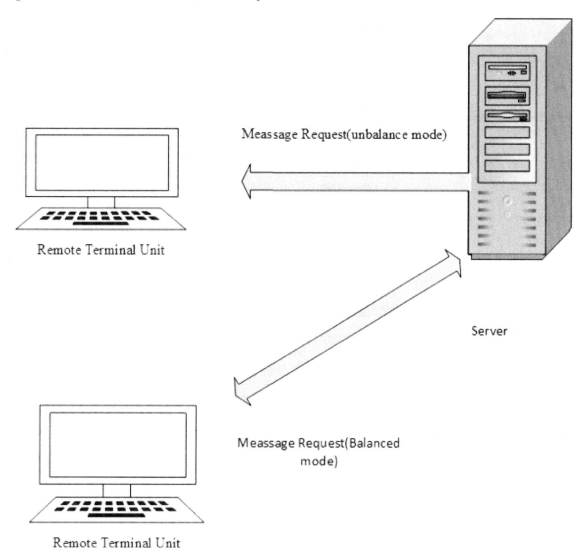

Distributed Network Protocol 3 (DNP3)

The DNP3 protocol is based on some early versions of IEC 60870-5 standards by by Harrison Controls Division in 1990s. Initially, it was developed for use in the electrical utility industry. in 1993, DNP3 became an open standard for use by the other industries and later on, IEEE adopted DNP3 as standard. DNP3 supports only balanced transmission mode (both server and client can initiate the exchange). DPN3 defines the pseudo-transport layer, between the data link layer and the application layer, to allow large data transmission by fragmentation. DNP3 protocol uses addressing based on the FT3 frame format of IEC 60870- 5-1. FT3 frame format has variable length.

Table 3. Data frame formats-addressing

	Field name	Field description
Variable length frame format	Start byte(1 byte)	Indicates start of frame
	Length(1 byte)	Length of link layer data in bytes
	Length copy(1 byte)	
	Start byte(1 byte)	Copy the start for reliability
	Link control field(1 byte)	Control functions
	Link address field(up to 2 bytes)	Device or server address
	Link user data(upto 256 bytes)	Application service data limit
	Checksum(1 byte)	Error check
	Stop byte(1 byte)	Indicates end of frame
Fixed length frame format	Start byte(1 byte)	Indicates start of frame
	Link control field(1 byte)	Control functions
	Link address field(upto 2 bytes)	Device or server address
	Checksum(1 byte)	Error check
	Stop byte(1 byte)	Indicates end of frame
Single character frame format	Acknowledgement(1 byte)	Used for acknowledgements

Table 4. DNP3 frame format

Field name	Field description	
Start byte(2 bytes)	Indicates start of the game	Fixed length header
Length (1byte)	Length of link layer data excluding CRC fields(control, address, and user data)	
Link control field(1 bytes	Control functions	
Link destination address(2 bytes)	Device/ Sensor destination address	
Link source address(2 bytes)	Device/ Sensor destination address	
Check sum(2bytes)	Error check the header	
Link user data(upto 16 bytes)		
Check sum(2bytes)	Error check the user data	
Link user data(upto 16 bytes)		
Check sum –CRC 16(2 bytes)	Error check the user data	

DNP3 provides High reliability and addressing on the data link layer. The data frame is shown in Figure 6. It is able to detect lost frames and duplication through cyclic redundancy check (CRC). The Hamming distance is 6, as compared to IEC 101 (Bailey and Wright, 2003).

Secure Extensions of IEC 101, IEC 104, and DNP3

IEC 101, IEC 104, and DNP3 needed to be upgraded as any of these do not provide the following security aspects: data confidentiality, data integrity, and data availability. Different solutions are continuously being proposed by both the Researchers and the industry to upgrade the protocols. The most prominent results are the standard IEC 62351-5 by IEC TC 57 and the standard DNP3 Secure Authentication (DNP3 SA) by the DNP Users Group. Both have been developed in parallel, and they were made compatible to each other. Both focus on the data integrity, while data confidentiality is provided only for the specific exchange purposes. IEC 62351-5 provides the security standards for IEC 60870-5 and for the derivatives, such as DNP3.

The security standards can be classified into two categories: based on the mechanism on which they are based. One group, such as IEC101, uses low bandwidth point-to-point links (IEC 101), and the other group, such as IEC 104 and DNP3, depend on the TCP/IP protocol stack.

The functionality of these two categories is presented in the Figure 8. In first category, the security Protocol uses some cryptographic algorithms via point –point low bandwidth links resulting in data integrity. In the second category, the protocols are based on Challenge response mechanism via transport security layer with message Authentication codes, result in data integrity and Confidentiality.

The SCADA infrastructure is traditionally designed to operate in an isolated manner in order to achieve secure and reliable operation assuming that no attacker has complete or detailed knowledge about the system. The isolation itself provides security. But SCADA system need to be operated incompatible with more and more sophisticated infrastructure and the need to provide additional security measures due to increasing cyber-attacks.

Inter-Control Center Communication

As Modern power systems are inter-connected in order to improve efficiency. For The proper operation of an inter-connected system, proper operation in constituent control regions is necessary. The exchange of real-time information between control centres is must. for this purpose, proprietary protocols had been proposed. The international IEC 60870-6 standard, is based on the OSI model, defines protocols for data exchange between control centres over a Wide area network (WAN). Two protocols used for the data exchange are Tele-control Application Service Element-1 (TASE.1) and Tele-control Application Service Element-1 (TASE.2). The difference is in the specification of mechanisms for message control. TASE.2 uses the Manufacturing Message Specification (MMS) for the specification and is usually referred to as the Inter-control Centre Communication Protocol (ICCP) ICCP (IEC 60870-6/TASE.2). ICCP specifies only the application layer of the OSI model, and it relies on other protocols for the underlying layers. Since ICCP cannot protect the data in exchange, IEC Technical Committee 57 specified the standards IEC 62351-3 and IEC 62351-4 depending on how lower layer protocols protect the data. IEC 62351-3 specifies security measures for end to-end security for protocols that go over TCP/IP. IEC 62351-4 specifies security measures for protocols that use MMS and provides application layer security. The end-to-end security provided by IEC 62351-3 and IEC 62351-4 protects ICCP data transfer between two ICCP hosts, one per control centre. These hosts, including databases that contain the data shared over ICCP, should be separated from the Master Local Area Network (LAN), also referred to as the control LAN, where all critical applications (e.g., SCADA server and EMS) coexist.

Figure 8. IEC 101, 104, and DNP3 Security Protocols data flow mechanism

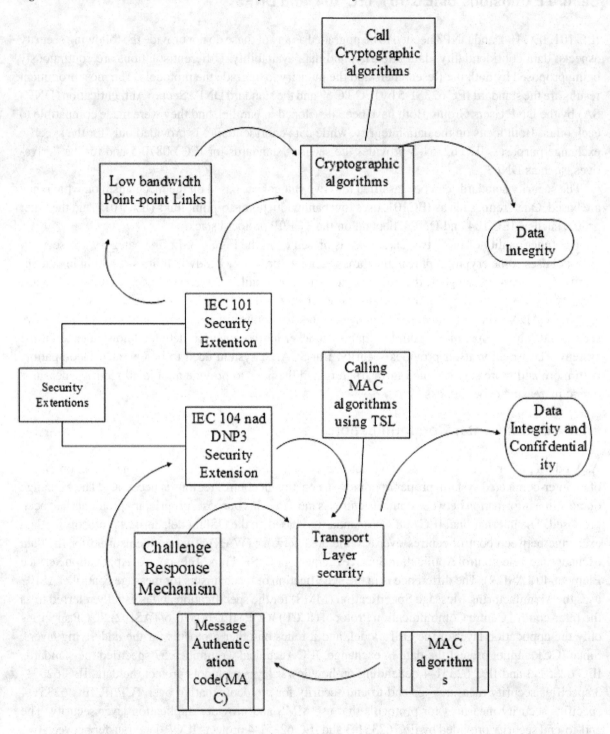

In this chapter, the the different cyber security issues in the smart grids are presented from historic timeline which result in electric power blackouts for recall. The Traditional Grid and Smart Grid is differentiated and the transformation via SCADA is presented. The causes of cyber-attacks are presented followed by the objectives of data management systems were presented. For the reader familiarity purpose, the function of smart control system, smart transmission system and smart distribution system are presented. The role of advanced metering devices and metering infrastructure were introduced. Simple classification of cyber-attacks to be faced are presented. The framework developed by NIST for detection and mitigation of cyber-attacks were presented. Widely used communication protocols and recommendations of ENISA were presented with different communication protocols. Later, and finally the reader is introduced with secure extensions of communication protocols used in smart grid security. This chapter is expected to give the basic idea for the readers who works in the area at the moment.

REFERENCES

Bailey, D., & Wright, E. (2003). *Practical SCADA for industry*. Elsevier.

Daki, H., El Hannani, A., Aqqal, A., Haidine, A., & Dahbi, A. (2017). Big Data management in smart grid: Concepts, requirements and implementation. *Journal of Big Data*, *4*(1), 1–19. doi:10.118640537-017-0070-y

Demertzis, K., Tsiknas, K., Taketzis, D., Skoutas, D. N., Skianis, C., Iliadis, L., & Zoiros, K. E. (2021). Communication Network Standards for Smart Grid Infrastructures. *Network (Bristol, England)*, *1*(2), 132–145.

Faquir, D., Chouliaras, N., Sofia, V., Olga, K., & Maglaras, L. (2021). Cybersecurity in smart grids, challenges and solutions. *AIMS Electronics and Electrical Engineering*, *5*(1), 24–37.

Guidelines for Smart Grid Cybersecurity, Volume 1 - Smart Grid Cybersecurity Strategy, Architecture, and High-Level Requirements. (2014). National Institute of Standards and Technology (NIST). Retrieved from https://nvlpubs.nist.gov/nistpubs/ir/2014/NIST.IR.7628r1.pdf

Haes Alhelou, H., Hamedani-Golshan, M. E., Njenda, T. C., & Siano, P. (2019). A survey on power system blackout and cascading events: Research motivations and challenges. *Energies*, *12*(4), 682. doi:10.3390/en12040682

Iyer, S. (2011). Cyber security for smart grid, cryptography, and privacy. *International Journal of Digital Multimedia Broadcasting*, *2011*, 2011. doi:10.1155/2011/372020

Kawoosa, A. I., & Prashar, D. (2021, January). A review of cyber securities in smart grid technology. In *2021 2nd International Conference on Computation, Automation and Knowledge Management (IC-CAKM)* (pp. 151-156). IEEE. 10.1109/ICCAKM50778.2021.9357698

Padhy, N. P., & Jena, P. (2022). *Introduction to Smart Grid (MOOC)*. NPTEL. https://nptel.ac.in/courses/108107113

ADDITIONAL READING

Abur, A. (2005, August). Distributed state estimation for mega grids. In *Proceedings of the 15th Power Systems Computation Conference (PSCC'05)* (pp. 22-26). Academic Press.

Abur, A., & Exposito, A. G. (2004). *Power system state estimation: theory and implementation*. CRC press. doi:10.1201/9780203913673

Akyol, B. A. (2012). Cyber security challenges in using cloud computing in the electric utility industry (No. PNNL-21724). Pacific Northwest National Lab.

Amin, S. M., & Wollenberg, B. F. (2005). Toward a smart grid: Power delivery for the 21st century. *IEEE Power & Energy Magazine*, *3*(5), 34–41. doi:10.1109/MPAE.2005.1507024

Armbrust, M., Fox, A., Griffith, R., Joseph, A. D., Katz, R. H., Konwinski, A., . . . Zaharia, M. (2009). *Above the clouds: A berkeley view of cloud computing* (Vol. 17). Technical Report UCB/EECS-2009-28, EECS Department, University of California, Berkeley.

Balu, N., Bertram, T., Bose, A., Brandwajn, V., Cauley, G., Curtice, D., Fouad, A., Fink, L., Lauby, M. G., Wollenberg, B. F., & Wrubel, J. N. (1992). On-line power system security analysis. *Proceedings of the IEEE*, *80*(2), 262–282. doi:10.1109/5.123296

Bobba, R. B., Rogers, K. M., Wang, Q., Khurana, H., Nahrstedt, K., & Overbye, T. J. (2010, April). Detecting false data injection attacks on dc state estimation. In *Preprints of the first workshop on secure control systems, CPSWEEK* (Vol. 2010). Academic Press.

Borden, A. R., Molzahn, D. K., Ramanathan, P., & Lesieutre, B. C. (2012, October). Confidentiality-preserving optimal power flow for cloud computing. In *2012 50th Annual Allerton Conference on Communication, Control, and Computing (Allerton)* (pp. 1300-1307). IEEE. 10.1109/Allerton.2012.6483368

Chapter 3
Cybersecurity as a Digital and Economic Enabler:
Way Forward for Developing Economies

Sunny Dawar

Faculty of Management and Commerce, Manipal University Jaipur, India

Pallavi Kudal

Dr. D.Y. Patil Institute of Management Studies, Pune, India

Prince Dawar

Poornima Group of Colleges, Jaipur, India

ABSTRACT

Cybersecurity is an extremely important matter in the current business world due to increasing cyber threats. Cyber attackers have increased their cyber-attacks on almost all the business operations using various advanced techniques. All kind of business organization ranging from small scale to large organizations have been impacted. So, cybersecurity has become a necessity for all kinds of firms, and adopting the secured techniques of business transactions has become a prerequisite of the business. The authors wish to find the conceptual framework of cybersecurity, associated risks related to cybersecurity, ways for ensuring cybersecurity in businesses, emerging trends in cybersecurity, and different initiatives taken in India for ensuring cybersecurity.

INTRODUCTION

The internet is currently transforming both social and business practices. The transition from linking computers and information to connecting people has occurred. The internet of the future could be a composition of virtualized and ascendable resources provided by service suppliers to its users. From the last decade, digital technology has altered the significance, level, capacity, and potential concerns

DOI: 10.4018/978-1-6684-5827-3.ch003

in business to the point where conventional business models and organisations have become incapable to adopt the earlier knows risky practices (Kaplan et al., 2015).

Rapid technological and service changes are significant driving and prominent worries for cyber security, demanding the reconsideration and regeneration of consistent policies for resilient liability countermeasures. Different threats have caused different types of damages to unprotected and weak information systems. Few threats concede the integrity, accessibility, or privacy of data. Financial loss is the most substantial effect of these threats, but other minor losses, such as information system devastation, can also occur. Various organisations are worried out by the ongoing question of focusing the most serious threats to their information structure assets and learning how to use the necessary tools to combat them.

It is difficult to develop an effective cyber security programme, particularly when competing organisational interests are involved. Furthermore, the evolution of social media today increases interaction, association, and online operations, not to refer to the risks that come with them. In general, it draws concerned collaborators to mitigate these risks through the development of cyber security, especially for sensitive data in information systems. It is difficult to evaluate an organization's cyber security because it necessitates the use of complex mechanisms to describe the important success considerations and indicators of the cyber security programme. However, in this critical aspect, the total amount of time passed from the experience of cutting to the discovery process is the most crucial measured to ensure the efficacy of the methods used to follow its progression (Graham et al., 2016). Cybersecurity is a series of methods, devices, and methodologies being used protect virtual space from cyber threats and cyber-attacks (Craigen, Diakun-Thibault & Purse, 2014).

Many challenges in cyber security have been addressed by cyber security community research through the revision and assessment of information visualisation methods into the area of cyber security system (Staheli et al., 2014). Cyber security threats are exploiting the increasing complexity and connectivity of new developing system infrastructures. These threats put the commerce, business, national security, and economy at various unimaginable risks. Cyber security risk has the same impact on a company's bottom line and financial risks, affecting income and pushing up costs.

Each organisation must foster an information security culture among its members to determine the level of seriousness with which security responsibilities are taken. As a result, significant organisational procedures and guidelines must be applied in order to offer information self-assurance and technical methods. These strategies must require the minimum necessities for adhering to all of the organization's privacy and security practises, as well as adhering to all of the organization's privacy and security practises, as well as following formal assemblies, protecting information, assigning access privileges, starting procedures, ensuring liability, corroborative responsibility, and following to all of the organization's confidentiality and safety practises.

IT industry deals with specific software and algorithms that help business, companies, vendors, and consumers control their economic systems and processes. In present world, FinTech has evolved to incorporate the growth and using the cryptocurrencies like Bitcoin. Regardless of the fact that several segments of information technology maintain to gain traction at present, a substantial part of IT aims on the conventional global banking segment, and India is unquestionably foremost in IT amendments globally. A feasible cybersecurity formation should endeavour to safe IoT devices. As a consequence, it must incorporate collaborative national and international forces to create guidelines, approaches, procedures, and activities that support policy tactics to cybersecurity concerns ranging from business to physical condition to enjoyment to learning to knowledge.

The IT industry has the potential to have the ultimate effect on the life phases of the world's unbanked, and it is truly a work of magical in the doing. The question of Fintech is not to improve the economic industry, but to improve the way financial services serve people. As many of our daily items can be linked to the Internet. The cybersecurity has turn out to be a key point in our everyday life cycles, and current FinTech landscape is undoubtedly challenging.

RISKS RELATED TO CYBER SECURITY

In present era of technological transformation, the Internet of Things (IoT) has become is one of the most prevalent technologies. The risks and liabilities that devices and technology face grow as they turn out to be smarter and more associated. In the last decade, the IoT has been developed extensively used in a range of industries, and many industries use it to build smarter operations. As per the report of business insider, the no. of IoT devices is likely to gain 41 billion latest by 2027. Both at home and at workplace, emerging technologies and tools like machine learning, smart devices have gained a lot of popularity for the improvement of people life.

The risks usually linked with any incident, which takes into account three security aspects: the first one related who attacks, second is related with various weakness because of which attack has happened and third is related with impact of attack (Fisher, 2014). Any act that jeopardises the confidentiality, reliability, or accessibility of data assets and systems is considered a security incident. There are several types of cybersecurity occurrences that can set an organization's or an individual's structures and associations at risk (Sun et al., 2018). Following are the various security risks which a business can face.

- Security breach refers to the act of gaining unauthorised access to a network, framework, or information, which results in an infringement of a cybersecurity.
- Malware, also known as malicious software, is any programme that is purposefully designed to harm a computer, server, client, server, or compute cluster. Malware types include worms, computer viruses, Trojan horses, spyware, and so on.
- Ransom malware, also known as ransomware, is a new designed to prevent unauthorized access people accessing their processes or personal documents, or equipment, and then requires an online comment payment to regain access.
- Phishing is a form of social manipulation in which a fraudulent attempt is made to acquire confidential material such as financial services and bank card details, account credentials, or personal information by concealing their selves as a trustable entity via an internet connected communication like email, message, or online chat, etc.
- The term "zero-day attack" refers to the threat of an unidentified security flaw for which either no patch has been published or the app developers were unsure.

As a result, all security breaches are regarded safety incidents, but not all security issues are security vulnerabilities. The banking industry has the most security vulnerabilities encompassing credit card numbers and private details, followed mostly by healthcare sector, electronic sector and the public sector.

WAYS TO ENSURE CYBERSECURITY FOR BUSINESSES

Information technology can support companies to grow into different markets but also expanding efficiency and proficiency. Companies, on the other hand, involve a cybersecurity policy to keep their personal functions, customers, and documents from evolving cybersecurity risks.

Training of Employees for Ensuring Security

Establish fundamental safety practises and guidelines for employees, such as demanding robust passwords, and develop proper Internet usage policies that describe consequences for breaching company cybersecurity strategies. Establish ground rules for how to manage and defend customer data and important crucial data.

Safeguard Data, Networks, and Computers from Cyber-attacks

The most effective defence compared to viruses, and more online risks is to utilize the most recent safety software, operating system, and web browser. Configure antivirus package to examine after each revise. Fix any other critical software informs as they happen to accessible.

Protect Internet Connection with a Firewall

A firewall is a compilation of related systems that inhibit unauthorized access to data on a personal network. Make it too sure the operational system's firewall is set on or fix free firewall software from the internet. If employees doing work from home, then make sure their home systems are firewall protected.

Make a Plan of Action for Mobile Devices

Mobile devices can present substantial security and administration challenges, particularly if they have sensitive information or have contact to the business system. To stop criminals from sneaking information though the phone is on community networks, need clients to password-keep their machines, translate their data, and fix security apps. Establish procedures for describing missing or taken equipment.

Generate backup copies of significant corporate information and knowledge

On a regular basis, copy the information on all computers. Crucial data contains word managing files, electronic databases, databases, business files, human assets files, and accounts files. Duplicate data on a regular basis, preferably weekly, and keep backup versions offsite or in the screen.

Manage Physical Computer Right to Use and
Generate Client Reports for Employees

Prevent unauthorised persons from retrieving or using enterprise workstations. Laptops are specifically exposed to theft or damage, so hold them protected up when not in use. Make it for sure that every member has their personal user account and that they use powerful passwords. Only trustworthy IT team and key employees should be accorded administrative rights.

Protect Wi-Fi Networks

If business workplace has a Wi-Fi system, then ensure its security, encryption, and secrecy. Put up wireless contact point so that it acts not transmit the system given name, also seen as the Service Set Identifier, to conceal Wi-Fi network (SSID).

Use Best Payment Card Practices

Collaboration with banks or workstations to certify the use of the most consistent and developed tools and anti-scam facilities. Extra security requirements may exist as a result of arrangements with bank or computer. Independent payment structures from other, take away safe courses, and don't deal with expenses and browse an Internet on the identical computer.

Limited Approach to Information and Control Software Installation

Allow no single employee gain access to all data structures. Employees ought to just be granted entry to the data procedures necessary for their positions and should not be allowed to connect software not including authorization.

Authentication and Passwords

Employees must utilize distinctive passwords and modify them each 3 months. Think about applying multi-element verification, which involves information other than a key to gain access. Try with vendors who manage vulnerable data, specifically financial organizations, to find out if multi-factor certification is available for account.

EMERGING TRENDS OF CYBERSECURITY IN BUSINESS

With the rise of digital insurgency comprehensive the globe, all companies, big and minor, corporates, associations, and uniform administrations are trusting on electronic organisations to achieve their day-to-day actions, creating of cybersecurity a top importance to protect information from several operational occurrences or unofficial admittance. As news of information contraventions, ransomware, and slashes develop into the standard, constant technical transformation suggests a corresponding change in cyber-security developments. Following are cybersecurity trends.

Automotive Hacking on the Rise

Latest automobiles are outfitted with automatic software that offers smooth connectivity for drivers in regions such as engine timing, cruise command, airbags, door lock, and sophisticated driver support systems. These automobiles communicate using Wi-Fi and Bluetooth technologies, which reveals them to a number of exposures and risks from hacks. With the improved use of robotic automobiles, increasing management of the automobile or utilizing microphones for spying is projected to rise in 2022. Autonomous automobiles use an still more complex system that demands strict cybersecurity protections.

Artificial Intelligence's (AI) Potential

With the introduction of AI in all market sectors, this expertise, in conjunction with machine learning, has resulted in significant variations in cybersecurity. AI has been instrumental in the development of robotic security systems, natural language managing, face recognition, and automatic threat recognition. However, it is also being used to create intelligent malware and strikes in order to circumvent the most recent data safety protocols. AI-powered warning detection systems can forecast new incidents and alert administrators immediately if there is a data breach.

The New Target is Mobile

There has been 50% increase in mobile banking attacks as per trends of cybersecurity provided in 2019 which make devices handled by hands a possible option for hacks. Individuals face greater risks as a result of our pictures, financial dealings, mails, and communications. A smartphone bug or malware could capture the notice of cybersecurity trends in 2022.

Potential Vulnerability of Cloud Computing

More and more organisations moving to the cloud, encryption techniques must be constantly monitored and maintained to prevent data leakage. Even though cloud applications such as Google and Microsoft are well-secured on their end, it is also the client end which is a substantial source of errors, harmful programs, and cyber emails.

Breach of Data

Data will proceed to be a top priority for businesses all over the world. Protecting digital data is the main objective now, whether it be for a person or company. Any small error or technical problem in system browser or applications can enable attacker to take private information.

The Internet of Things with 5G Network: A New Phase of Innovation and Risks

With the emergence and growth of 5G networks, the Internet of Things will create a latest generation of inter - connectivity (IoT). This interaction between various tools reveals them to the separate impact, risks, or an unidentified software bug. 5G design is comparatively different in the marketplace and requires considerable research to distinguish flaws in order to make the system secure from foreign threat. Each process of the 5G network could offer a spate of cyberattacks that we aren't fully cognizant of.

Integration and Automation

With volume of data increasing by the time, it is crucial that technology be executed to provide more sophisticated power over the content. Modern work requires put pressure on professionals and technicians to produce quick and effective solutions, trying to make automation more beneficial than ever before. To construct more security software in each and every facet, answerable are incorporated throughout the agile methodology. Massive and complicated web apps are much harder to secure, trying to make automation and cyber security a regarding relevant in the agile methodology.

Ransomware Targeted

Targeted ransomware is just another crucial cybersecurity fad that we can't appear dismiss. Industries, particularly in developed countries, heavily rely on specific software running their daily operations. Even if ransomware generally poses a threat to publish the accused's data unless a ransomware, it can also influence major corporations or countries.

CYBERSECURITY INITIATIVES IN INDIA

Cybersecurity assures digital technologies by securing computer programmes, connections, and statistics, as well as trying to prevent non - authorized users from gaining access data and avoiding unforeseen change or obliteration. In the Indian context, policymakers have paid reasonably little consideration to cybersecurity, to the moment the government seems to be unable to address the country's growing need for a comprehensive security equipment. In brief, India lacks proper offensively and defensively cyber resilience, which is aggravated by an absence of availability to critical mechanisms for dealing with advanced malware (Parmar, 2018). At the very same time, India is facing an urgent need to defend vital infrastructure from cybercrime, such as financial institutions, satellite communication, computer-controlled power stations, and electricity generation (Kaushik 2014).

Following are some initiatives taken in India for cybersecurity (Pande, 2017).

- Besides that, India has fewer cybersecurity programs and initiatives than other developed countries. Several of the important research suggested by the Indian government have been recommended. Furthermore, certified projects such as NCIPC i.e., India's National Critical Information Infrastructure Protection Centre and NCCC i.e., National Cyber Coordination Centre (NCCC) have been created.
- NCIPC, which has been designated as India's central board for critical data incident handling and is liable for all valuable data connectivity protection measures, including R&D projects.
- In India, the National Cyber Coordination Centre is an envisaged data protection and e-surveillance organisation. Its mission is to monitor interaction metadata and collaborate other organisations' intel gathering attempts. NCCC elements provide a cyber-attack prevention measure, cyber warfare investigations and mentoring, and so on.
- The Department of Information Technology founded the Indian Computer Emergency Response Team in 2004. The goal of developing CERT-In was to give a response to computer security in-

stances, disclose security flaws, and identify best practices in IT safety throughout nation, and is responsible for directing IT management.

- The India-US Cyber Security Discussion board was established in 2001 with the aim of safeguarding the vital infrastructure of the expertise economy. The members of the discussion board are numerous governments as well as private entities, both from India and the United States, operating under the Forum.
- NCRB (National Crime Records Bureau) will make every effort to provide Indian police with digital technologies and illegal insight so that they can quickly and successfully enforce the rules and strengthen good governance. This shall be accomplished through domestic and international police coordination level, advancement of crime investigation technology, development of IT functionality and IT enabled alternatives.
- As part of the Digital India programme, the government is establishing a centre that will identify malicious files such as "botnets" and support people in expelling such malware from their equipment. As per media reports, a 'botnet' cleaning and malware detection centre" is being founded. A botnet is a malicious software network. It has the ability to steal data and take grip of computers.
- The Indian government has stated that there's been a significant increase in cybercrime against institutions such as financial services. In India, malicious Internet activity has varied from viruses to hacking, information theft, going to spam, electronic mail, browser defacement, computer hackers' defamation, and rejection of service.

CONCLUSION

Cyberattacks on India's critical information infrastructure, such as power, banking sectors, security, and telecommunication services, have the ability to ruin the country economically and community safety. Cyber security has turn out to be a business necessity. Cyber security is involved in the whole thing we do and is constantly updated. It is becoming extremely relevant for communities to start preparing for cyberthreats that may have a negative impact on them. There were also innumerable proven instances where a community has experienced severe a harm as a result of a computer crimes incident. To determine the level of seriousness with which security responsibilities are obtained, each institution should nurture an information security policy among its participants. As a result, major operational practises and standards must be implemented to provide data security and methodology of the research. Cybersecurity threats are becoming more common. Risks that were formerly thought to be incredibly unlikely have now become more common. This trend illustrates the use of different forms of tools and methodologies in threats, as well as rising security flaws and hacker motivation. The growing influence of cyber-attacks calls for innovative, inventive, and creative solutions to mitigate the effects.

REFERENCES

Craigen, D., Diakun-Thibault, N., & Purse, R. (2014). Defining cybersecurity. *Technology Innovation Management Review*, *4*(10), 13–21. doi:10.22215/timreview/835

Graham, J., Olson, R., & Howard, R. (Eds.). (2016). *Cyber security essentials*. CRC Press. doi:10.1201/b10485

Kaplan, J. M., Bailey, T., O'Halloran, D., Marcus, A., & Rezek, C. (2015). *Beyond cybersecurity: protecting your digital business*. John Wiley & Sons. doi:10.1002/9781119055228

Kaushik, R. K. (2014). *Cyber Security Needs Urgent Attention of Indian Government*. Academic Press.

Pande, J. (2017). Introduction to Cyber Security. *Technology*, *7*(1), 11–26.

Parmar, S. D. (2018). Cybersecurity in India: An evolving concern for national security. *The Journal of Intelligence and Cyber Security*, *1*(1).

Staheli, D., Yu, T., Crouser, R. J., Damodaran, S., Nam, K., O'Gwynn, D., ... Harrison, L. (2014, November). Visualization evaluation for cyber security: Trends and future directions. In *Proceedings of the Eleventh Workshop on Visualization for Cyber Security* (pp. 49-56). 10.1145/2671491.2671492

Sun, N., Zhang, J., Rimba, P., Gao, S., Zhang, L. Y., & Xiang, Y. (2018). Data-driven cybersecurity incident prediction: A survey. *IEEE Communications Surveys and Tutorials*, *21*(2), 1744–1772. doi:10.1109/COMST.2018.2885561

ADDITIONAL READING

Clark, R. M., & Hakim, S. (Eds.). (2016). *Cyber-physical security: protecting critical infrastructure at the state and local level* (Vol. 3). Springer.

Chapter 4
The Importance of Cybersecurity for Organizations:
Implementing Cybersecurity to Prevent Cyberattacks

Edward T. Chen
University of Massachusetts, Lowell, USA

ABSTRACT

The purpose of this chapter is to understand the severity of cyberattacks and identify the importance of using cybersecurity to protect organizations from future threats. This chapter will discuss the types of attacks that can occur along with the types of security measures that can be implemented to ensure information remains protected for individuals or organizations. Information regarding cyberattacks in certain businesses, healthcare organizations, and social media will also be discussed to assess and identify the different types of cyber threats. Information from previous research studies and past data will be evaluated to identify the types of cybersecurity that can help different organizations as well as identify and prevent any future threats they could potentially encounter. Further examination of previous and future cyberattacks will also be discussed to understand how those threats occurred, where they come from, and how security can be used to combat them.

INTRODUCTION

Cybersecurity has become an incredibly important part of a day to day life in today's society. There is an enormous amount of collectible data being generated from individual's smartphone and organization's cloud and data center. All of this data is available to be exploited if not protected appropriately. Nowadays, consumers give away their personal information without even thinking twice when purchasing goods or signing up for things like credit cards and website memberships. With every click of your

DOI: 10.4018/978-1-6684-5827-3.ch004

mouse or tap on your screen, you are creating more data points that can help people learn more about you based on your Internet habits. All of this information and all of these data points are vulnerable to attack and can be used to exploit or used for personal use at the expense of others. Cybersecurity aims to prevent these attacks and keep all this information safe and secure (Fedele & Roner, 2022; Garg, 2020; Ramadan, Aboshosha, Jalawi, Alzahrani, El-Sayed, & Dessouky, 2021; Samtani, Chai, & Chen, 2022).

Information safety is of extreme importance to both consumers and businesses. People want to feel as though their information is safe. Individuals are concerned that their financial information like bank account or credit card numbers could be stolen and they would be vulnerable to identify theft, monetary theft, or credit ruin. Businesses are concerned about similar risks as well as valuable customer information or private organizational information being stolen. All of these obstacles are exceedingly difficult to overcome but can be prevented with strict cybersecurity measures put in place. Cybercrime is a global concern, as shown in recent events around the world (Stratton, Powell, & Cameron, 2017). The ramifications of these crimes on individuals and organizations cannot be stressed enough as to how devastating of an impact they can have. As technology has advanced, cybercriminals have also become that much more sophisticated in the ways that they breach different measures of cybersecurity. In turn, cybersecurity has had to also continue to advance and evolve to keep up with these cyber criminals (Janakiraman, Lim, & Rishika, 2018; Tsen, Ko, & Slapnicar, 2022; Wertheim, 2020b). This paper will examine the different methods of cybersecurity used today as well as the different cyberattacks they are attempting to stop and the effects they can have when cybersecurity is successfully breached (Culnan & Williams, 2009; Janakiraman, Lim, & Rishika, 2018; Swift, Colon, & Davis, 2020).

What Is Cybersecurity?

Cybersecurity can also be known as cyberspace security. Its term can be defined as the "'preservation of confidentiality, integrity, and availability of information in the cyberspace'" (Fisher et. al 2021). Understanding cyberattacks, learning how to respond, and successfully reacting to these threats are major steps in combating cyberattacks. Cybersecurity is becoming more and more of a threat to corporations, social media sites, personal accounts, and every other virtual program or data stored in cyberspace. It can be very dangerous for any type of attacker to hack and leak information depending on the information getting hacked (Hinz, Nofer, Schiereck, & Trillig, 2015). An organization needs to be prepared before these attacks take place. It is unknown when and if a certain type of organization will have to face a potential cyberattack. Taking measures to secure their database is the best possible way to protect their information. Understanding, and properly training employees on cybersecurity will also provide additional preparation and effectiveness in combating cyberattacks (Ayyagari, 2012; Georgiadou, Mouzakitis, Bounas, & Askounis, 2022).

Cyberspace is an infinite amount of space that can store an endless amount of information. The results provided show that the continuous growth of virtual work, virtual learning, and virtual social platforms will put the majority of people at risk of being virtually attacked. Therefore, the threats of cyberattacks will also grow and diverse types of threats will emerge with the expansion of new cyber technology. The results found that since attacks are likely to increase as technology advances, the attempt to combat them will need to be addressed promptly for each organization. Training and proper understanding of the subject will serve for better protection against cyberattacks and provide organizations with more insight into identifying and preventing possible threats (Ayyagari, 2012; Georgiadou et al., 2022).

What Are Cyberattacks?

A cyberattack is an online attack that is used against an individual or organization to exploit or steal sensitive information. There are multiple ways a cyberattack can happen and organizations need to be aware of all of them. Organizations also need to understand how certain cyberattacks will target certain organizations. No one is safe from any threats and attackers will use any method possible to get what they want. Knowing how an attack can happen and where it came from can also better assist the person or company in how to protect their organization through cybersecurity.

Many cyberattacks throughout history were purported for one reason or another, to extort people out of money or to simply damage existing computers to see if the person was capable of creating such a program. The boom in computer usage during the late '90s created a new level of need for software security. In 1999, Windows 1998 was released and there was an increased level of accessibility to computers and the Internet. Software security became more of a common thing and more security vendors were created and were actively releasing antivirus software for people to purchase to keep their computer systems safe (Fedele & Roner, 2022; Townsend, 2019; Haislip, Lim, & Pinsker, 2021).

Long gone now are the days of simple computer worms or people stealing data from your computer by peering over your shoulder and reading your computer screen. Throughout the history of cybersecurity, there have been different types of attacks that have forced the hand of people who develop cybersecurity programs to advance and evolve just to keep up. It began with The Reaper tracking down a worm leaving messages across a network and has evolved into a rapidly growing industry with more exposure and importance than ever (Hinz et al., 2015).

How Can Cybersecurity Combat Cyberattacks?

There are many problems regarding cyberattacks and cybersecurity which is why it is important to understand what it means to successfully integrate a security program that can benefit your sole organization (Tsen et al., 2022). Cyberattacks have been progressively increasing in size and therefore cybersecurity measures will need to be conducted more effectively and evaluated more frequently. Suggestions for cybersecurity protection can vary depending on the type of organization that is being run. However, a general suggestion would be that every type of organization that stores data through cyberspace should be trained in the knowledge of cyber threats and combating them. Understanding what their business is and how attackers would use their private information is also important in figuring out what security measures will need to be enacted (Ayyagari, 2012; Georgiadou et al., 2022; Spence & Bangay, 2022).

THEORIES

Organization Development Theory

Organization Development (OD) is a system-wide application that focuses on creating an effective approach to an organization (Fisher et. al 2021). The theory will allow organizations with a better understanding of cyberattacks and cybersecurity. OD is a more humanistic approach to cybersecurity as it ties culture to create a proactive approach to target cyberattacks. OD theories can provide a more prepared work environment. Organizations will learn about attacks before they could happen and remove those threats. The integration of culture change could take a while to implement but is highly effective as it is opening up a new world for the organization and its employees to see. They will be more motivated to learn, more trustworthy, and more knowledgeable about cybersecurity (Fisher et. al, 2021).

The Theory of Planned Behavior and The Cybersecurity Reporting Framework

The theory of planned behavior (TPB) can explain a person's intentions using their beliefs and attitudes (Yang et. al 2019). TPB was able to show that an organization that uses a virtual system will be affected by net perceived benefits and choose to adopt that system (Yang et. al 2019). When there is an innovative technology that will provide businesses with better opportunities, a firm is highly likely to adopt that technology. This ties to the Cybersecurity Reporting Framework. This framework is part of the AICPA (American Institute of Certified Public Accountants) and it uses three components to monitor cyberattacks. Those three components include (1) Description of the security (2) Assertion that the security entity is within proper guidelines, and (3) The AICPA's opinion of the description (Yang et. al 2019). TPB is crucial in being able to assess users' benefits and identify if the framework will be perceived as beneficial.

Routine Activity Theory

The Routine Activity theory is used to analyze criminal behavior and was used as a theoretical approach in the late 1970s to predict crimes (Govender et al., 2021). This theory is not only applied to crimes in the real world but also to crimes in cyberspace. The theory looks at three components. The first is a suitable target which means that offenders will look for attractive qualities a victim may have regarding their goals. Regarding cybercrime, attackers could be attracted to big businesses or banks with lots of money. The next is the absence of guardianship. This means that the offender will be more eager to attack if there is little security involved. The attacker will take this as an opportunity and want to breach the networking system. The third is a likely and motivated offender. This is someone who will commit a crime when they see an opportunity. That opportunity presents itself when the two complements which are a suitable target and the absence of guardianship are presented to the offender. This theory helps sum up how an offender or attacker will use certain situations to their advantage to commit a crime (Stratton, Powell, & Cameron, 2017; Swift, Colon, & Davis, 2020).

IMPLEMENTING CYBERSECURITY

Convention of Cybercrime

In 2001, the Convention on Cybercrime was signed and used as an international piece of legal protection (Horovic et. al 2021). This signing provided legality of regular use of data through virtual networks. This means that the system should be used regularly for the sole purpose of storing and using information. The information should never be taken advantage of or used against others, especially if it is private or protected data. Those who choose to steal, collect, or abuse the data they see such as attackers will face the consequences as this is a crime and will be dealt with accordingly. Cybercrime and cybersecurity are taken seriously by criminal law and are not to be taken advantage of as much private, valuable, and vital information is stored in cyberspace (Stratton, Powell, & Cameron, 2017; Wertheim, 2020b).

Implementation of Cybersecurity in Different Organizations and Businesses

There are numerous ways an organization or individual can implement and successfully use cybersecurity as there are many diverse types of security that can suit their personal needs. Bitcoin, for example, has a piece of technology that allows it to function properly which is known as Blockchain. This type of technology can be integrated into preventing attack measures and increase the effectiveness of cybersecurity, especially in financial transactions. The reason it is called Blockchain is that it stores all transactions on a block (Smith and Dhillon 2020). Each block has its data of transactions but is sorted together on a chain (Smith and Dhillon 2020). This type of technology allowed for clean and smooth business transactions through bitcoin, minimizing mistakes and errors. Applying Blockchain technology to Financial transactions would help in organizing and managing specific requirements as well as strengthen the security measures of all financial business transactions (Tsen et al., 2022; Smith & Dhillon. 2020).

On March 21, 2020, New York enacted the SHIELD Act (Stop Hacks and Improve Electronic Data Security) for businesses that "own or license computerized data" (Wertheim, 2020a). These businesses will need to follow newer and more strict requirements put in place through this Act. This Act allows businesses to learn more about cyberattacks and cybersecurity by requiring annual training as well as assessments, monitoring, testing, and data destruction. Businesses will need to destroy data that is not of significant importance after a certain time and tracking (Wertheim, 2020a). These steps can help educate organizations more about cyber threats and allow them to manage the situation without any concerns (Farahbod, Shayo, & Varzandeh, 2022).

PROBLEMS AND ISSUES

Problems and Threats Regarding Cyberattacks

There are various threats to cybersecurity which include internal and external attacks through cyberspace. These threats can be divided into four types of threats known as physical threats, human threats, data and communication threats, and operational threats. The division of those threats into these categories can open up a new view on the types of cyberattacks that occur and will allow for the proper identification of newer threats that no one has seen before. Physical threats can refer to the organization suffering from certain troubles like natural disasters, physical assault, or malfunctions for instance which the attacker uses to gain information. Human threats refer to situations occurring during the "handling, training, or monitoring [of] personnel" involving sensitive information (Zadeh et al., 2020). A good example of a human threat would be the use of trial and error to obtain a successful password. The attacker will use multiple attempts of different password combinations to try and log in to a certain account. Although it can be timely, it is highly effective. Communication and data threats are attacks through virtual software that can pose harm to an organization. Examples include Trojan horses, back doors, or viruses. Operational threats have to do with identifying weaknesses and easy access solutions in the system that can be broken through without complication. Some examples relating to these types of threats are errors in the system, abuse of the system, whether it is authorized or unauthorized access, or spoofing (Wertheim, 2019).

Four categories fall under the type of attacks or threats a person or organization can face. While the previous paragraph discussed the general sum of all potential threats, this category will discuss four common types of attacks that occur directly in cyberspace. Those attacks are flow control, injection, information leakage, and denial of service (DoS) attacks. A flow control attack uses either code injection or code reuse to change the normal controls and operations of a system to benefit the attackers' goals. An injection attack is when an attacker uses untrusted input to trick others who view this information. Malware, false data, and sabotage are used in this attack to steal sensitive information. Injection attacks are said to be one of the oldest and most dangerous attacks in cyberspace (Ramadan et al., 2021).

Information leakage attacks are the unintentional disposing of information to attackers using either side channels or an encryption key bypass. One of the most common types of attacks that fall under information leakage is phishing. Phishing attacks are used to hack or obtain information from a user or organization. Emails are forged into looking reliable or trustworthy sometimes by impersonating organizations or people (Schweigert & Johnson, 2021). When those users click this email they will get redirected to a website where they will place their information (which can vary from addresses and phone numbers to bank account numbers) which the attackers will use against them. A denial of service attack is when the attacker uses methods such as flooding, to either temporarily or permanently disrupt the system preventing users from accessing that site (Bayl-Smith, Taib, Yu, & Wiggins, 2022; Chau, 2021; Ramadan et al., 2021).

Issues in Cybersecurity

A major problem with combating threats is the lack of information and security regarding cyberattacks. There is truly little sharing and communication when it comes to organizations discussing or releasing their protective measures against cyber threats. Organizations are also likely to limit information and certain extensions on their site for extra safety without understanding how it can affect the public. Organizations need to be able to be open about their situation and also allow publicly discuss their measures for people to understand the importance of the issue at hand (Fisher et al., 2021; Spence & Bangay, 2022).

A cyberattack can affect the viability of an entire business. It is quite common for a business to misunderstand the severity of a cyberattack and not focus its attention on cybersecurity. Many believe cybersecurity to be an operational tactic instead of a strategic approach (Hepfer & Powell, 2020). Therefore, they just let IT deal with this situation instead of learning how to effectively manage it, understand it, and use it to their advantage. Many people are also very unaware of the severity of cyberattacks and because of that lack of knowledge, they do not understand how to successfully defend themselves against an attack. Cyberthreats need to be taken more seriously and dealt with more carefully to prevent potential future threats. Keeping cyberattacks hidden or concealed can affect an organization as it will show how little prepared they were for the attack as they are trying to make it appear as a minor issue. It could also prevent other organizations from learning how to deal with any threats they are facing (Farahbod, Shayo, & Varzandeh, 2022; Hepfer & Powell, 2020).

Although cybersecurity can be used to combat cyber threats, it is sometimes not effective in successfully protecting against those attacks. An organization can integrate a good defense system, however, there can still be some vulnerabilities in the system that an attacker could come across and take advantage of. Security will always be put up to ensure the system is protected but a major issue is that attackers will always find a way to get through that system.

DATA AND RESULTS

Data has shown that organizations have suffered due to cyberattacks. Due to these attacks, many organizations could potentially not only suffer from losses but also receive multiple lawsuits for those security breaches (Culnan & Williams, 2009; Garg, 2020; Zadeh et al., 2020). Facebook, for example, had been cyberattacked with 540 million records being breached by attackers. Investigation of the types of attacks that occur can help in identifying the types of cyber securities that need to be put into action for certain organizations. Vulnerabilities in the virtual cyber system of an organization can cause a weakness that attackers can target and use to hack through the organization's mainline (Swift, Colon, & Davis, 2020; Zadeh et al., 2020).

Data collected from 10-K reports were assessed and evaluated to discover what threats a cybersecurity system could face or even have (Zadeh et al., 2020). Results showed that among the four categories of the types of threats, physical threats were shown to be of the greatest risk. The data conducted also separated all information attained into different clusters based on the type of organization. This showed that each of the organizations held a different type of threat and a different level of a potential cyberattack as well. One of the clusters contained data on IT and healthcare organizations and results showed that they are more prone to physical threats therefore they focus more on combating those specific types of threats (Kwon & Johnson, 2018; Lee, 2022).

Data was collected from the CSE-CIC-IDS2018 from the Canadian Institute for Cybersecurity to understand these attacks Cyberattacks are cross-tabulated with normal traffic to identify how common attacks are. Performance metrics were also conducted to assess the 5-fold cross-validation of online classifiers. Results showed that there was a "severe class imbalance" of data from CSE-CIC-IDS2018 with a ratio of 14,429:1. The classifiers applied with random under-sampling also showed inferior performance which plays a part in the severe imbalance of the CSE-CIC-IDS2018 data (Zuech et al., 2021).

A transformation roadmap was conducted to assess IoT (Internet of Things) cybercrime risks which allowed for a better understanding of those risks and future regulations toward cyberattacks. The transformation roadmap helps transform current cyber profiles into an adaptable and more targeted risk-informed cyber profile (Graham, 2021; Radanliev et al., 2020; Xenofontos et al., 2022).

ORGANIZATIONAL IMPACTS

An organization can suffer from cyber threats. Cyberattacks can damage an organization's reputation causing many customers to leave which results in a significant loss of sales. It is important to regain the customers' trust after such an attack to ensure that they are willing to stay associated with that organization. The same applies to shareholders and anyone else involved with those organizations. Maintaining a good relationship with everyone is key to moving past an attack without the organization losing any partners or sales (Fedele, & Roner, 2022).

The healthcare system and the COVID-19 pandemic have recently imposed a large number of cyberattacks. Attackers are likely to use ransom pay against these healthcare organizations, especially during a pandemic, knowing they will pay whatever price needed to keep all their data secure (Ramadan et al., 2021). Human casualties are also highly likely to occur if attackers were to take advantage of cyber threatening those health care organizations (Gafni & Tal, 2022; Lee, 2022).

Phishing has even become more of a problem during the COVID-19 pandemic as many professional workers are now spending most of their day online. There are three types of phishing attacks which include SMS phishing, phishing emails, and phishing scams. These types of phishing occur through different online platforms. Phishing scams specifically are targeted to make people not hesitate when responding or accepting an unknown scam. During the pandemic, the ACSC (Advanced Cyber Security Center) alerted everyone of a COVID revealed fund fraud (Ramadan et al., 2021). This type of issue is dangerous and the attackers are taking advantage of a pandemic to use it for their gain. People who are willing to help out will not hesitate to donate and make a fund thinking their contribution would be of help to others. This type of attack is a criminal offense and should be treated as such since many are being harmed through a fraudulent act (Bayl-Smith, 2022; Das, Nippert-Eng, & Camp, 2022).

The U.S. Department of Health and Human Services (HHS) was also affected during the pandemic. They received a cyberattack when trying to promptly speak out about the coronavirus (Ramadan et al., 2021). This attack affected everyone since they all relied on this department to discuss and address the concerns during the pandemic. HHS servers were on overload with tons of information and requests being put through constantly for many hours (Ramadan et al., 2021). Because of this attack, current and constant monitoring of the system has been placed to ensure future threats will be prevented or detected ahead of time. HHS now uses a diverse group of people from different backgrounds (healthcare and cybersecurity backgrounds) and sectors (private and public) to respond to cybersecurity attacks on their networks (Chua, 2021; Gafni & Tal, 2022).

Although cyberattacks can leave negative impacts on everyone as a whole, cybersecurity can help everyone feel sense of relief when applying it to their systems. Security is not always going to be perfect so it will still be common for an attack to still occur. However, by constantly updating and working on the security system, attacks can be immediately targeted and stopped before severe consequences arise (Lee, 2022).

SUGGESTIONS

Cybersecurity does not only mean securing your data but also protecting the organization as a whole and its integrity. An organization needs to gain resilience against cyberattacks. Before a cyberattack, an organization must be prepared and ready to protect itself. Plans should already be put into place to properly deal with attacks. Organizations should also broaden their awareness of the issue outside their company to understand more about the issue they could face (Hepfer & Powell, 2020). A broader awareness could provide the public or other organizations with more knowledge on what is going on so they can learn from these threats and the steps the organization is taking to prevent them. This will also give the public more trust in the organization as it is making them more aware of the services the organization put into place to ensure their network is secure and the people's privacy is protected. After a cyberattack, an organization should respond to the attack and recover from it. It is always going to be difficult to recover from an attack, especially depending on the severity but the importance is getting through it and making sure nothing was lost or stolen. However, in the event something bad did happen during the attack, that organization should be prepared and ready to deal with the consequences it has left outside their business (Hepfer & Powell, 2020).

As time goes by, technology is constantly improving and updating. People are beginning to use online networks as a part of their everyday life meaning cyberattacks are also becoming more of a threat. Organizations need to be educated on potential threats and consequences that come from these attacks. Understanding and monitoring their networks would be useful in identifying possible cyberattacks and applying better cybersecurity measures (Horovic et al., 2021). Organizations need to switch from a "reactive to a proactive culture" (Fisher et al., 2021). Instead of reacting to the attacks and learning how to deal with them once they happen, it is important for organizations to constantly be learning about Cybersecurity and the attacks they can face in the future. Staying up to date on their security and protective measures will better prepare them for what is to come. Having malware put into place on computers and automatically spamming suspicious emails can help prevent or decrease these types of threats (Schweigert & Johnson, 2021; Spence & Bangay, 2022).

Cybersecurity has to be taken care of safely using physical data protection to ensure it is secure (Horovic et al., 2021). Four methodologies can be used for certain analyses regarding IoT which are: (1) risk analysis from a functional dependency (2) network-based linear modeling (3) risk impact assessment (4) goal-oriented approach (Radanliev et al., 2020). Connecting these methodologies and integrating them into an organization will help in comprehending information regarding cyberattacks. Creating a connection between IoT and cyberattacks is difficult because attacks suddenly occur. They are not predicted to happen at a certain time (Graham, 2021; Radanliev et al., 2020; Xenofontos et al., 2022).

Thousands of cyberattacks are recorded daily from all over the world leading to a state of worry for organizations (Horovic et. al, 2021). Businesses need to be aware of such threats and learn how to combat attacks. ICT systems (Information and Communication Technologies Systems) are integrated into many organizations. ICT is an integration of cybersecurity and information security, which comes from data that is stored without the use of ICT. ICT works to connect both information and cybersecurity to store all data an organization has but also keep it safe from being hacked in the future. Although some measures are in place to help prevent cyberattacks, these organizations still have little knowledge of what cybersecurity is and how to keep it updated in their network (von Solms & von Solms, 2018; Spence & Bangay, 2022).

Cybersecurity is much more complicated than cyberattacks. Therefore a complete list of the security that can be applied would be difficult and long to write out. Since there are many distinct kinds of cyberattacks, there are many different methods that can be applied to stop and prevent each of those attacks. Cybersecurity can be used in many different ways depending on the type of organization and what type of data needs to be secured. The main purpose of cybersecurity is to protect any type of data from being retrieved by potential attackers (Horovic et al., 2021). This security works to enhance and strengthen the ability to perform and store virtual data through any organizational network without the concern of information getting leaked or permanently removed.

IMPLICATIONS

As technology advances through the years, individuals and organizations will store more of their personal information allowing for more vulnerabilities and endangerment towards themselves or their organization. It is important to prevent this issue from the start rather than wait for it to occur. Taking safety measures and precautions from the start will keep attackers from gaining access to sensitive or personal information. Those who are not knowledgeable about cyberattacks have a larger target on their backs. Understanding how cyberattacks occur and how to prevent them is crucial for individuals and even organizations who want to protect their personal information. This growing issue is affecting more individuals and organizations and will only get worse through the years. Understanding how cyberattacks occur and the consequences of uploading personal information through unprotected databases will be beneficial to helping those organizations in the future (Spence & Bangay, 2022).

Cybersecurity can leave an effect on an organization's "mission, business, and programs" and the IT department. There is a great challenge in providing awareness of cybersecurity and preventing potential threats through a general understanding of the issue. No signs of these attacks have been shown to go down but actually, increase rapidly in the future (Chua, 2021).

As the years go on, there will be more Internet users. It is estimated that by 2022, about six billion users will be using the Internet meaning that the more users there are, the more cyberattacks are likely to occur It is even stated that improper measures for cyberattacks, especially in small organizations, can result in organizations going out of business. Many are unaware of the risks of threats and their severe rift therefore they are unprepared to properly combat those threats (Fisher et al., 2021; Ramadan et al., 2021).

CONCLUSION

Cyberattacks have been happening for an exceptionally long time now and are becoming progressively more common and dangerous. Virtual platforms and online work are becoming a part of everyone's everyday lifestyle. Personal or work-related data are stored online and can either be posted publicly or privately. A lot of private, personal, or professional information is saved on this universal piece of technology forever and many expect their information to remain the way they had originally uploaded it. However, there is a vulnerability in the virtual system in which many organizations and sites cannot protect themselves or their employees. Cyberattacks can happen at any time and some people are becoming more aware of. When comparing cybersecurity now versus cybersecurity in the past, it is clear that more security measures have been enacted to keep attackers away from finding their way into an account.

Organizations and individuals need to be well prepared before an attack occurs so they will know how to effectively manage the threat when it does happen. Training and educating everyone in the work environment on cybersecurity and its importance of it will be able to bring more awareness to this issue. Each organization will need to assess different techniques they can apply to their network and system. That way they will be able to identify the best method against potential attackers. It is also important for those cybersecurity measures to be constantly monitored to ensure the latest versions and securities are updated in their system.

Cybersecurity works to protect all virtual/online data from cyberattacks or hacks. This type of security is complicated and is integrated into many organizations and businesses to ensure the safety of all their information. It is important to note that cybersecurity is not one type of security that can be applied to every virtual piece of data in cyberspace to keep everything safe. Each organization differs in the level of confidentiality and level of importance, therefore, each organization will need to secure itself with the appropriate measures that best suit its needs.

REFERENCES

Ayyagari, R. (2012). An exploratory analysis of trends of data breaches from 2005-2011: Trends and insights. *Journal of Information Privacy and Security*, *8*(2), 33–56. doi:10.1080/15536548.2012.10845654

Bayl-Smith, P., Taib, R., Yu, K., & Wiggins, M. (2022). Response to a phishing attack: Persuasion and protection motivation in an organizational context. *Information and Computer Security*, *30*(1), 63–78. doi:10.1108/ICS-02-2021-0021

Chua, J. A. (2021). Cybersecurity in the healthcare industry-A collaborative approach. *Physician Leadership Journal*, *8*(1), 23–25.

Culnan, M. J., & Williams, C. C. (2009). How ethics can enhance organizational privacy: Lessons from the ChoicePoint and TJX data breaches. *Management Information Systems Quarterly*, *33*(4), 673–689. doi:10.2307/20650322

Das, S., Nippert-Eng, C., & Camp, L. J. (2022). Evaluating user susceptibility to phishing attacks. *Information and Computer Security*, *30*(1), 1–18. doi:10.1108/ICS-12-2020-0204

Farahbod, K., Shayo, C., & Varzandeh, J. (2022). Six sigma and lean operations in cybersecurity management. *Journal of Business and Behavioral Sciences*, *34*(1), 99–109.

Fedele, A., & Roner, C. (2022). Dangerous games: A literature review on cybersecurity investments. *Journal of Economic Surveys*, *36*(1), 157–187. doi:10.1111/joes.12456

Fisher, R., Porod, C., & Peterson, S. (2021). Motivating employees and organizations to adopt a cybersecurity-focused culture. *Journal of Organizational Psychology*, *21*(1), 114–131.

Gafni, R., & Tal, P. (2022). Cyberattacks against the health-care sectors during the COVID-19 pandemic. *Information and Computer Security*, *30*(1), 137–150. doi:10.1108/ICS-05-2021-0059

Garg, P. (2020). Cybersecurity breaches and cash holdings: Spillover effect. *Financial Management*, *49*(2), 503–519. doi:10.1111/fima.12274

Georgiadou, A., Mouzakitis, S., Bounas, K., & Askounis, D. (2022). A Cyber-security culture framework for assessing organization readiness. *Journal of Computer Information Systems*, *62*(3), 452–462. doi:10.1080/08874417.2020.1845583

Govender, I., Watson, B. W. W., & Amra, J. (2021). Global virus lockdown and cybercrime rate trends: A routine activity approach. *Journal of Physics: Conference Series*, *1828*(1), 012107. doi:10.1088/1742-6596/1828/1/012107

Graham, C. (2021). Fear of the unknown with healthcare IoT devices: An exploratory study. *Information Security Journal: A Global Perspective, 30*(2), 100–110.

Haislip, J., Lim, J. H., & Pinsker, R. (2021). The impact of executives' IT expertise on reported data security breaches. *Information Systems Research*, *32*(2), 318–334. doi:10.1287/isre.2020.0986

Hepfer, M., & Powell, T. C. (2020). Make cybersecurity a strategic asset. *MIT Sloan Management Review*, *62*(1), 40–45.

Hinz, O., Nofer, M., Schiereck, D., & Trillig, J. (2015). The influence of data theft on the share prices and systematic risk consumer electronics companies. *Information & Management, 52*(3), 337–347. doi:10.1016/j.im.2014.12.006

Horovic, S., Boban, M., & Stipanovic, I. (2021). Cybersecurity and criminal justice in digital society. In *Economic and Social Development: Book of Proceedings*. Varazdin: Varazdin Development and Entrepreneurship Agency (VADEA). https://umasslowell.idm.oclc.org/login?url=https://www-proquest-com.umasslowell.idm.oclc.org/conference-papers-proceedings/cybersecurity-criminal-justice-digital-society/docview/2508649367/se-2?accountid=14575

Janakiraman, R., Lim, J. H., & Rishika, R. (2018). The effect of a data breach announcement on customer behavior: Evidence from a multichannel retailer. *Journal of Marketing, 82*(2), 85–105. doi:10.1509/jm.16.0124

Kwon, J., & Johnson, M. E. (2018). Meaningful healthcare security: Does meaningful-use attestation improve information security performance? *Management Information Systems Quarterly, 42*(4), 1043–1067.

Lee, I. (2022). An analysis of data breaches in the U.S. healthcare industry: Diversity, trends, and risk profiling. *Information Security Journal, 31*(3), 346–358. doi:10.1080/19393555.2021.2017522

Radanliev, P., De, R. D., Van, K. M., Uchenna, A., Pete, B., Eirini, A., & Nurse, J. R. (2020). Dynamic real-time risk analytics of uncontrollable states in complex Internet of Things systems: Cyber risk at the edge. *Environment Systems & Decisions, 41*(2), 236–247. doi:10.100710669-020-09792-x PMID:33251087

Ramadan, R. A., Aboshosha, B. W., Jalawi, S. A., Alzahrani, A. J., El-Sayed, A., & Dessouky, M. M. (2021). Cybersecurity and countermeasures at the time of pandemic. *Journal of Advanced Transportation, 2021*, 1–19. doi:10.1155/2021/6627264

Samtani, S., Chai, Y., & Chen, H. (2022). Linking exploits from the dark web to known vulnerabilities for proactive cyber threat intelligence: An attention-based deep structured semantic model. *Management Information Systems Quarterly, 46*(2), 911–946.

Schweigert, C. T., & Johnson, R. A. (2021). Testing the susceptibility of employees to phishing emails. *International Journal of Information, Business and Management, 13*(3), 190–203.

Smith, K. J., & Dhillon, G. (2020). Assessing blockchain potential for improving the cybersecurity of financial transactions. *Managerial Finance, 46*(6), 833–848. doi:10.1108/MF-06-2019-0314

Spence, A., & Bangay, S. (2022). Security beyond cybersecurity: Side-channel attacks against non-cyber systems and their countermeasures. *International Journal of Information Security, 21*(3), 437–453. doi:10.100710207-021-00563-6

Stratton, G., Powell, A., & Cameron, R. (2017). Crime and justice in digital society: Towards a 'digital criminology'? *International Journal for Crime. Justice and Social Democracy, 6*(2), 17–33. doi:10.5204/ijcjsd.v6i2.355

Swift, O., Colon, R., & Davis, K. (2020). The impact of cyber breaches on the content of cybersecurity disclosures. *Journal of Forensic and Investigative Accounting, 12*(2), 197–212.

Townsend, C. (2019). *A Brief and Incomplete History of Cybersecurity*. https://www.uscybersecurity.net/history/

Tsen, E., Ko, R. K. L., & Slapnicar, S. (2022). An exploratory study of organizational cyber resilience, its precursors and outcomes. *Journal of Organizational Computing and Electronic Commerce*, *32*(2), 153–174. doi:10.1080/10919392.2022.2068906

von Solms, B., & von Solms, R. (2018). Cybersecurity and information security - what goes where? *Information and Computer Security*, *26*(1), 2–9. doi:10.1108/ICS-04-2017-0025

Wertheim, S. (2019). The willingness not to believe. *Certified Public Accountant. The CPA Journal*, *89*(12), 86–87.

Wertheim, S. (2020a). When is a business 'shielded' from financial harm? *Certified Public Accountant. The CPA Journal*, *90*(2), 70–71.

Wertheim, S. (2020b). Tips for fighting off cybercrime in 2020. *Certified public accountant. The CPA Journal*, *90*(3), 64–66.

Xenofontos, C., Zografopoulos, I., Konstantinou, C., Jolfaei, A., Khan, M. K., & Choo, K.-K. R. (2022). Consumer, commercial, and industrial IoT (In)security: Attack taxonomy and case studies. *IEEE Internet of Things Journal*, *9*(1), 199–221. doi:10.1109/JIOT.2021.3079916

Yang, L., Lau, L., & Gan, H. (2019). Investors' perceptions of the cybersecurity risk management reporting framework. *International Journal of Accounting and Information Management*, *28*(1), 167–183. doi:10.1108/IJAIM-02-2019-0022

Zadeh, A. H., Jeyaraj, A., & Biros, D. (2020). Characterizing cybersecurity threats to organizations in support of risk mitigation decisions. *e-Service Journal*, *12*(2), 1–34, 65–66. doi:10.2979/eservicej.12.2.01

Zuech, R., Hancock, J., & Khoshgoftaar, T. M. (2021). Detecting web attacks using random undersampling and ensemble learners. *Journal of Big Data*, *8*(1), 1–20. doi:10.118640537-021-00460-8 PMID:33425651

Chapter 5
Mounting Cases of Cyber–Attacks and Digital Payment

Suhasini Verma
Manipal University Jaipur, India

Jeevesh Sharma
Manipal University Jaipur, India

Keshav Kaushik
 https://orcid.org/0000-0003-3777-765X
University of Petroleum and Energy Studies, India

Vidhisha Vyas
IILM University, Gurugram, India

ABSTRACT

Digital transformation in financial transactions has changed the method of payment. We have witnessed a many-fold and rapid increase in the digital payment. As more individuals opt for digital payments, the potential of being exposed to cyber-attacks such as online fraud, theft of identity, and spyware or virus attacks is rising. Transaction on digital mode has led to an increase in internet-based crimes known by the term 'cybercrime'. Cybercrime is an illegal act practiced by hackers on web applications, web browsers, and websites. Secured payment is critical for any company that deals with electronic payments and transactions. One of the most vital issues confronting players in the digital payment ecosystem is cyber security. The growth of such cyber-attacks can be attributed to various reasons, including a lack of knowledge and a poor digital payment infrastructure. To safeguard against threats of cybercrime, there are various cyber security techniques. This chapter deals in understanding the causes, threats, and solutions to cyber-attacks in digital payment methods.

DOI: 10.4018/978-1-6684-5827-3.ch005

INTRODUCTION

Cybercrime is a comparatively new type of offense around the globe. Cybercrime is defined as any criminal activity that occurs on or using devices, the web, or any other technique recognized under the Information Technology Act, 2000. Criminals not only cause significant damage to society and the government but difficult to nab as well because they disguise their identities to a large extent (Patil, 2022). A variety of unlawful acts are carried out by technically proficient criminals through the internet. In a broader sense, cybercrime refers to any unlawful conduct involving a computer or the internet as a tool, a target, or both. Cyber security is the use of technology, procedures, and policies to prevent cyber assaults on systems, networks, programs, devices, and data. Its goal is to limit the risk of cyber assaults and secure systems, networks, and technology from unauthorized use. Cyber security is one of the most critical matters confronting players in the digital payment ecosystem (Jha & Kumar, 2022).

The term "cybercrime" refers to illegal behavior in which computing devices, such as smartphones, tablets, Personal Digital Assistants (PDAs), and other independent or linked computing devices are utilized as a tool or target of criminal conduct. It is frequently committed by persons with a destructive and criminal attitude for a variety of reasons, including revenge, money, or adventure According to Cybercrime Magazine, by 2025 Cybercrime will cost the globe $10.5 trillion per year. Furthermore, during the next four years, worldwide cybercrime losses are expected to climb by about 15% annually[1]. From an Indian perspective cybercrime has increased from 208,456 in 2018 to 1,402,809 in 2021[2]. The development of the digital ecosystem enables the public to access more web applications for financial transactions. The digital payment ecosystem has faced several consequences because of this quick increase and shift in end-user profiles.

Although many of the users are adopting digital payment systems some factors act as barriers to the development of digital payment systems like lack of awareness, lack of strong ecosystem for cashless payment, security concerns, cash payment preference, lack of proper digital regulations, and lack of effective grievances and redressal mechanisms. This leads to chances of getting trapped by cyber assaulters and ultimately financial losses. Assailants are adopting sophisticated, broader techniques in their cyber-attack. These include media manipulation, spyware, and espionage. Most cyber assaults are automated and try to exploit widespread flaws rather than specific websites or businesses. It is a mistake to presume that cyber attackers are uninterested in you. Cyber security is the need of every individual accessing the internet. Ensuring secured payment is an important aspect of cyber security for any company that deals with electronic payments and transactions.

The Objectives of the Study

The purpose of the chapter is to:

1. To present how the digitalization of financial transactions had cost the public.
2. To study various types of cybercrimes and the solutions through various techniques of cyber security.
3. To discuss the cybercrime rate in India and the role of regulatory bodies.

CYBER-CRIME

The Internet is one of the most influential innovations of the twenty-first century. Currently, the online world has broken down all barriers and transformed the way we communicate, play games, work, shop, make friends, listen to music, watch movies, order meals, pay bills, and greet family or friends on their special occasions such as birthdays (Al-Zahrani, 2022). As cyber threats and attacks are on the rise, cyber security is the most pressing worry. fraudsters are now using more advanced techniques to target the systems. Individuals, small enterprises, and major corporations are all affected. As a result, all companies, whether IT or non-IT, have recognized the requirement of cyber security and are working on implementing all available countermeasures.

Some definitions give a deep understanding of cybercrime. As per the Oxford Dictionary term cybercrime is "Criminal activities carried out using computers or the Internet."[3] "Cybercrime may be said to be those species, of which, a genus is a conventional crime, and where either the computer is an object or subject of the conduct constituting crime"[4] There are various ways to commit a cyber-crime and some of them are mentioned below in Figure (1).

Figure 1. Ways of cyber-crimes

- **Hacking the system:** It breaches personal security and obtains personal data.
- **Unauthorized access to systems or networks:** It's a type of hacking, an illegal action, or a criminal offense. Here, the assaulter uses someone else's account knowingly to get access to a system without the concerned person's permission.

- **Virus/worm:** Viruses or worms hack the system; it damages the system and software or stops the proper functioning of the programs.
- **Email bombing:** The hacker practices sending fake or fraudulent emails to the victims. In this, the hackers send a huge volume of emails in order to overburden the mailbox. As a result, the server crashes causing disruption to web portals' functioning.
- **Denial of service (DoS) attack:** In this, the offender attempts to render a computer or network resource inaccessible to its intended users temporarily or forever by interrupting the services of a networked host. Usually performed by sending more traffic to the target so that the ultimate users are not able to manage the system or networks.
- **Salami attack:** It is related to financial crime. In this, the hackers move step by step or take tiny steps toward financial theft. Here they make duplicates of bank accounts and withdraw a small amount of money from random bank accounts and transfer it to another account which she can access later.
- **Trojan attack:** In this, the hacker gains control over others' computer systems. Trojan horse is a type of virus that enters a system and misleads intent users.
- **Web jacking:** The hacker acquires access to and control over another genuine website.

In these forms of cyber-attacks, the hacker from a certain point begins overloading the victims' systems with different kinds of unnecessary communications and thus obstructing the legitimate data flow. Due to this, no server can access the Web or interact with other servers (Topping et al., 2021) making it accessible to use by hackers.

In the growing rate of cybercrime, devices also played a major role. Figure 2 represents the percentage of devices that are vulnerable to cybercrime in India.

Types of Cybercrime

Internal Attack

A hack on a network or computer system by someone with authorized system access is referred to as an inside attack. It's frequently done by unhappy or dissatisfied internal employees or contractors. It's possible that the insider attack was motivated by vengeance or money. Because the employee is familiar with the company's regulations, operations, IT architecture, and security system's strengths, an insider may start cyber-attacks with relative ease. This occurs when a competitive firm needs to know a firm's future strategies on specific issues majorly financial transactions. As an employee, the attacker may get strategic access to the organization and procure essential information leading to troubles and losses to the company.

External Attack

In this type of attack, the hackers are hired by internal or external persons. When a company is the victim of a cyber assault, it suffers not only financial losses but also a loss of reputation. The hacker scans and obtains data because they are not a part of the company. External attacks can be detected by carefully studying the logs generated by routers, therefore an expert network/security administrator monitors them regularly. In addition, Intrusion Detection Systems have been installed to keep an eye on any threats from abroad or foreign locations.

Figure 2. Devices most vulnerable to cybercrime

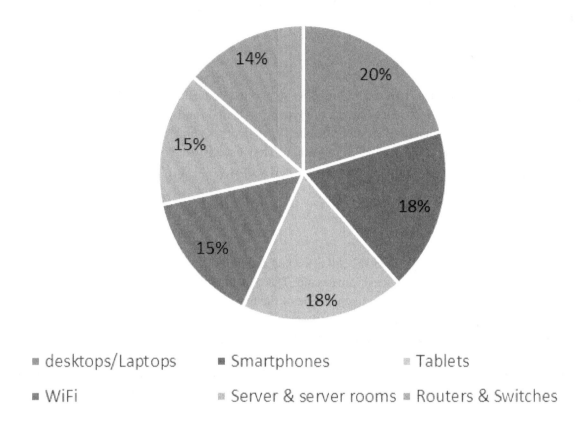

Figure 3. Types of Cyber-crime

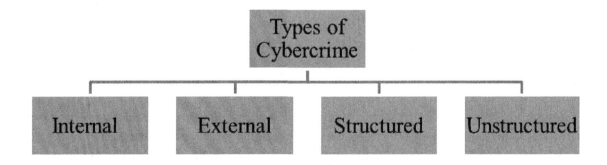

Structured Attack

These assaults are carried out by highly competent and experienced individuals who have a good understanding of the objectives behind them. They have access to sophisticated tools and technologies that allow them to gain access to other networks without being detected by their Intrusion Detection Systems (IDSs). Furthermore, these attackers possess the requisite skill to create or alter current tools to meet their objectives. Professional criminals, governments attacking other countries, politicians seeking to harm the image of a competent person or nation, terrorists, competing firms, and so on are all examples of these sorts of assaults.

Unstructured Attack

These types of hackers are less experienced and not as trained or technically professional people as compared to structured attackers. These hacks are typically carried out by unskilled individuals with no predefined motives for launching a cyber assault. Typically, these amateurs attempt to test a freely available tool on the network of a random organization. They usually use very easily available sources to attempt cybercrimes like cracking passwords and shell scripts.

CYBER SECURITY

To be protected from these cybercrimes the cell is formed and introduces a set of technologies and techniques to safeguard systems and devices from assault. These techniques define cyber security. Information security experts viewed cyber assaults to be one of the biggest threats right now (Hong & Furnell, 2021), and not managed appropriately, these attacks can cause significant losses to enterprises. Security breaches often reflect a variety of risks, human variables, mistakes, or lack of knowledge. So, "Cyber security is primarily about people, processes, and technologies collaborating to address the full range of threat reduction, vulnerability reduction, deterrence, international engagement, incident response, resiliency, and recovery policies and activities, such as computer network operations, information assurance, and law enforcement." The major techniques used in cyber security are discussed in the next section.

Techniques OF Cyber Security

Cybercrime is any unauthorized conduct that involves a system, piece of technology, or network. There are two basic sorts of cybercrime: those that target systems and others that systems unintentionally contribute to (Li & Liu, 2021). Figure 4 presents the various techniques used to reduce cyber-attacks.

Network Security

The hardware and software measures that safeguard the network and infrastructure against interruptions, illegal access, and other abuses are referred to as network security. Effective network security safeguards company assets against a variety of attacks from within and outside the company. The monitoring of cyber threats and risks linked with web browsers, websites, online applications, and networks is a major part of network security. Companies like Cisco, Palo Alto, Symantec, Fortinet, Okta, and Zscaler provide one-stop solutions for network security and keep our information safe.

Figure 4. Various techniques of cyber security

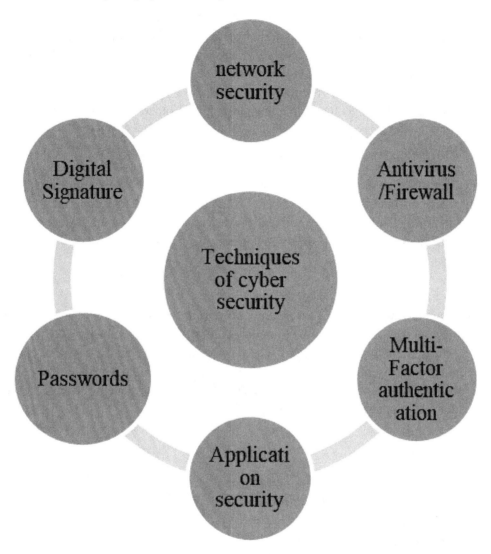

Firewall

A Firewall is a network security device that monitors, and filters incoming and outgoing network traffic based on an organization's previously established security policies. A firewall provides a safeguard to your network with an internal and external network. It monitors the network and blocks the threat and viruses to reduce the risk that might harm your network. It is useful for small and large businesses and for home networks. Antivirus software safeguards the network from harmful programs and Trojan attacks. These harmful programs damage the functioning of the devices, damage the documents and sometimes hacks the applications and leak personal details leading to larger financial and identity crimes.

Multi-Factor Authentications

Multi-factor authentication (MFA) is a type of digital verification wherein the user is getting access to the websites or software applications after successfully submitting two or more pieces of evidence to an authentication device. Two or more pieces of information can be a mobile number (OTP), password, and fingerprint. Enabling MFA reduces the risk of cybercrime because cyber attackers won't have access to the device or mobile and will not get the code that your mobile or other devices received.

Application Security

The increasing usage of online shopping through various e-commerce websites or applications has raised the risk of cybercrime or fraud. It is the process of creating, integrating, and testing security measures into applications to protect them from dangers like illegal access and alteration. Its ultimate purpose is to enhance security practices and, as a result, detect, repair, and, ideally, avoid security flaws in applications.

Passwords

Password hacking are the main source of cybercrime. Most of the persons set very easy and short passwords or sometimes set the same passwords for many other applications. It is very easy for hackers to crack these passwords. Sometimes applications send reminders to reset your password or change your password but almost all the users ignore it, this can lead users to big trouble. Cyber security experts are advised to set long and combination passwords, which must be changed frequently, and passwords must not be the same for other applications or devices.

Digital Signature

A digital signature, similar to a biometric or an extension to a digital document, certifies the validity and integrity of that document. A digital certificate is a record that verifies the identity of the bearer while also providing security.

Among all these techniques of cyber security protection from cyber-crimes, (Avizienis et al., 2004; Palmieri, et al., 2021) CIA (Confidentiality, integrity, and availability) are the three principles of cyber security for the organization. It is also known as the triangle of security. The confidentiality principle implies that only an authorized person can only access information, the integrity principle implies that only an authorized person can modify information, and the availability principle implies that the information must be provided based on certain agreed parameters (Le Nguyen & Golman, 2021). Ciampa (2012) introduced AAA (Authentication, Authorization, and Accounting) for robust cyber security. Authentication claims that all information must be original and trustworthy, authorization claims permission to access information by the authorized person, and accounting claims that all the information or event must be tracked periodically (Wang et al., 2015).

Figure 5. Common attacks with immediate actions[5]

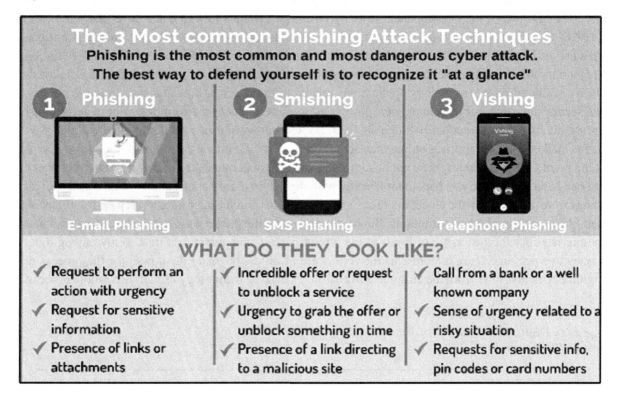

DIGITAL PAYMENT

The e-commerce era has produced new financial needs that, in many situations, existing payment systems are unable to meet. Recognizing this, practically all market participants are researching numerous forms of electronic payment systems and digital currencies along with the difficulties that surround them. With the emergence of the electronic environment, the government also initiated a campaign under the name of 'Digital India'. The main aim of the campaign was to make an economy "Faceless, paperless, Cashless. A digital financial instrument (such as encrypted credit card information, electronic checks, or digital cash) backed by a bank, an intermediary, or a legal tender facilitates financial transactions between buyers and sellers in the internet environment (Oh et al., 2006). A digital payment system converts a cash-based society into a cashless society. It includes purchasing goods and services in physical stores to sending money in and across country borders (Sarkar, 2019). The use of digital payments is rapidly growing all around the world. Since 2015, the number of non-cash payments has climbed by 60% globally. This rapid expansion has been fuelled by technical advancements and enhanced regulatory oversight (Pisoni et al., 2021). Many banks and other financial organizations are venturing into the field of digital payments because it offers interesting potential (Gupta et al., 2021). Online credit card payment systems, online electronic cash payment systems, electronic cheque payment systems, and smart cards-based electronic payment systems are the four types of electronic payment systems.

This rapid growth of adoption of digital financial transactions has been observed after the demonetization in India and COVID-19 pandemic. DT (Digital transformation) is enormously disruptive since it alters how organizations operate and distribute goods and services to customers (Subramaniam et al., 2021). DT was a major component of daily business activities for the latter three-quarters of the COVID-19 pandemic. As a result, research into the relationship between COVID-19 and DT is critical. This DT enables to develop of a digital ecosystem in an economy. This DT derived the usage of digital FinTech in ordering daily use things and many other activities to survive in this pandemic. The availability of digital-based technology applications related to the internet, big data, smart mobile phones, and secure and comfortable technological power has prompted consumers to embrace digital technology during the COVID-19 pandemic (Purba et al., 2021). Consumer transactions dominate the digital payments market, which comprises online transactions for goods and services, along with mobile payments at the point of sale via smartphone applications and online global money transfers (digital remittances). On one hand, the public was becoming friendly with digital finance or transaction because each and all things were operating on the cloud, not in cash which includes purchasing a grocery to paying a financial liability to banks and other institutions. But on another hand, the public was facing a huge financial loss by internet clicks, transferring of funds to the wrong person, and sometimes mistakenly paying more money to a person. Figure 6 represents the ecosystem of digital payment; it shows how the process of digital payments flows from the customers to customers and the technology used in this whole process.

Figure 6. Digital Payment Ecosystem
Source: KPMG report 2017

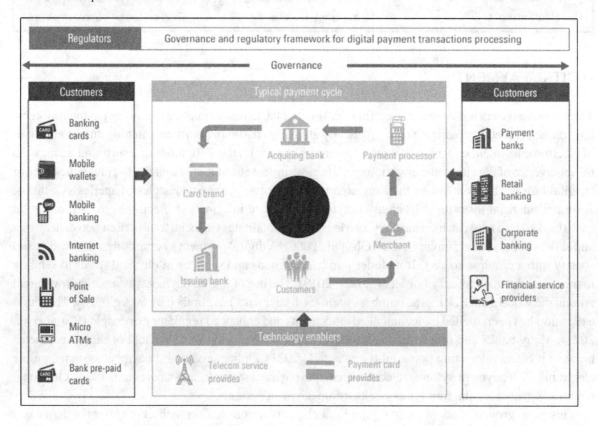

Conventional versus Electronic Payment System

In the conventional payment system only, cash was used to make a transaction because it was only the one way to do the transaction. After the involvement of banks in transaction process a new era comes into picture. The traditional payment methods involve cash credit cards and cheques. Lack of convenience, lack of security, lack of coverage, lack of eligibility, lack of instant transaction, and problems in small transactions, are the problems or limitations faced by the people while dealing with the conventional payment systems. Due to this the need for electronic payment arises. The limitation of the conventional payment process was covered by the electronic payment system (Gupta et al., 2021). With the increase in internet environment people are easy use internet and services provided on the internet. To boost the digital economy the government of India has attempted to create a favorable ecosystem for a "cashless economy" through projects such as "DigiShala," while other projects like the National Optical Fibre Network (NFON) and the Unified Payments Interface (UPI), Bharat Interface for Money (BHIM- a net-based mobile application) has aided in the faster adoption and evolution to digital payments. Electronic payment involves a digital transaction of currency between two or more parties. This method is too cheap and convenient with a very short payment processing time. This enables the customer to do online payments for shopping and many other activities also. Electronic cash, smart cards, e-wallets, credit/debit cards, and digital currency are examples of electronic payment systems. With the experience of all these facilities, the matter of security also arises as all the transactions are hosted on the cloud. So, there are a lot of chances of fraud cases. Frauds can be like duplicating customer IDs and profiles, trapping credit/debit cards, fraudulent SMS and emails to customers, fake calling on behalf of bank authorities, and sharing OTPs with family and friends. Therefore, these entire practices open door for cyber assaults and consumers suffer huge financial losses. The following data in figure 7 present the reach of the digital payment system:

Figure 7. Total number of digital payment transactions in India from FY 2018 to FY 2022 (in billions)[6]

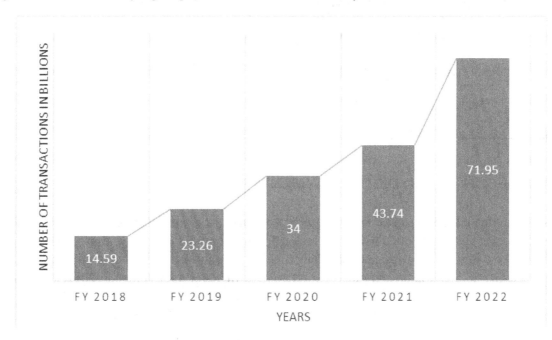

It is projected that digital payment transactions will reach $3 trillion at present to $10 trillion in value by 2026[7]. In terms of the global transaction, the value will reach US $8.49tn in 2022. China will achieve the highest cumulated transaction value of US $3497 bn in 2022[8]. Figure 8 depicts the worldwide mobile payment transactions.

Figure 8. Mobile payment transactions across the world[9]

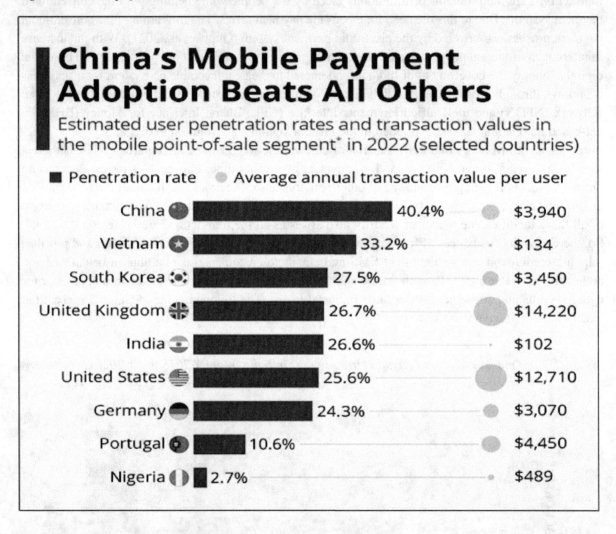

CYBER SECURITY AND DIGITAL PAYMENT FRAUD

Experts warn that there is no space for complacency as state and non-state actors attack governments and corporations alike more often with malicious malware meant to disrupt operations. According to the World Economic Forum, fraud and financial crime are a trillion-dollar business, with private companies spending $8.2 billion on anti-money laundering (AML) procedures alone in 2017. The crimes themselves have become more widespread and costly than ever before, both recognized and unreported. Several high-impact cybersecurity incidents have been reported in the last few years across industries such as healthcare, e-business, telecom, monetary services, government services, manufacturing, and hospitality, resulting in far-reaching consequences and creating cybersecurity as one of the top business risks. The threat of cybercrime is not constrained by geographical boundaries. India's corporations have been exposed to this danger in a significant way. According to the KPMG report (2017), roughly 72% of businesses have observed cyber-attacks in some form. The attacks are result of the emphasis and a strong push for digital adoption leading to phishing attacks on payment channels. The most common attacks are distributed denial of service (DDoS) and spam- a common attack vector.

As the usage of mobile phones for online transactions such as purchases, payments, and banking grew, so did the number of fraudsters who target these devices. [10]Digital payment transactions have increased fourfold in the last four years, from 3,134 crores in FY 2018-19 to 5,554 crores in FY 2020-21. A total of 7422 crore digital transactions were reported by February 28th, 2022. BHIM-UPI has emerged as citizens' favorite payment mechanism, with 452.75 crore digital payment transactions worth Rs 8.27 lakh crore completed by February 28, 2022. In line with the "new normal" of social alienation, the Covid-19 epidemic has demonstrated that digital payments offer access to healthcare using contactless payment modes like the BHIM-UPI QR code.

The percentage of fraudulent digital banking transactions made using android apps has gradually increased over the previous several years. In the last two quarters of 2021, the entire proportion of fraud perpetrated via smartphones was expected to become more than 50%. Globally personal details leaking has been the most prevalent digital payment privacy issue. According to a report published in October 2021, about 80% of persons in France fear becoming victims of online mobile payment fraud. As per a report published by CERT-In, the figure 9 depicts the increasing trend of cyber incidents in India from 2018 to 2022 (till Feb) the number of incidents was 2,08,456 in 2018 which jumped to 14,02,809 in 2021 and decreased to 2,12,487 in 2022. The reason behind the decreased number of incidents is awareness among individuals.

Organizations experience the following type of cyber-attacks on digital payment methods.

- Phishing
- DDoS (Distributed Denial of Service)
- Exploits of Vulnerability
- Spam
- Malware
- Cyber espionage
- Social engineering
- Identity theft
- Merchant Fraud

Further, the section discussed how these frauds can be avoided, crime cannot be finished by root but precautionary steps can be followed to become safe.

PRECAUTIONARY STEPS TO AVOID CYBER ATTACKS AND ONLINE FRAUD

Digital payments have grown in popularity, especially during the modern world paradigm and individuals all around the world have chosen a variety of payment options. In recent years, the expansion of digital payments has also increased in the frequency of cyber scams. The fundamental reason for this fraud's success is a lack of knowledge among individuals and businesses on how to protect their identity and money safely, particularly when fraudsters are looking for any way to make money. Anyone can be trapped in the hands of a criminal no matter literate or illiterate, rich or poor. The fraudsters hack the victim's mobile and access it remotely and stole the person's sensitive information like bank account details and OTPs. Following are some precautionary methods to ensure safe and secure digital payments to cyber attacks.

Figure 9. Cyber incidents in India from 2018 to 2022
Source: CERT-In

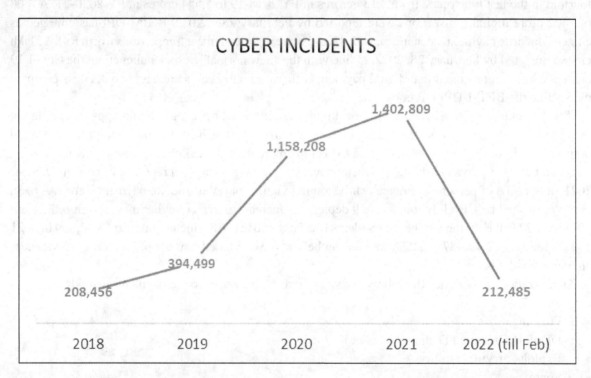

Completing KYC

Many times victims received a call from fraudsters that their KYC is incomplete, we will complete it right now on call otherwise your account will be suspended. The thumb rule to avoid such fraudulent calls is not to respond to them and never click on the link provided on SMS and emails.

Setting Passwords

The person should always choose unique passwords and must change them frequently. Make sure that the credentials for all kinds of transactions are distinct and difficult to guess. Passwords should not include names, birthdays, or other personal information. It is crucial and fundamental not to share passwords with anyone and keeping the same passwords for multiple devices.

Avoid Usage of Public Wi-Fi

When making online purchases, avoid accessing public Wi-Fi networks since they are more vulnerable to cyber-attacks, theft, and other fraudulent activities. Verified sites provide a high level of security, thus it's also crucial to utilize only reputable websites for online financial transactions.

Cross-Check QR Codes

Always double-check the beneficiary when scanning QR codes, as hackers may quickly swap a valid QR code used during transactions with a malicious QR code.

Reading Financial Statements

Remember that you read all notifications received after each payment and that you study the financial summary in detail once a week or more. If you see any discrepancies, file a ticket or approach the bank/payment platform right away.

SIM Swap Scam

Using social engineering techniques such as phishing, vishing, and smishing, the fraudster acquires the victim's banking information and registered mobile phone number. Through fake calls, they insist the victim port their old SIM to a new one as the present SIM is blocked due to some reasons. So, the person should beware of such calls and never swap a SIM, in such cases, they should directly contact the network's authorized toll-free numbers.

Above are some common tactics to be practiced by the customers to get safe from fraud. Customer data such as geographical, authentication, session, and device IP address can be stored. Machine Learning and Artificial Intelligence will play a critical role in automatically learning and identifying fraud trends (Priya & Saradha, 2021).

With discussion on cyber-attacks and precautionary steps taken to avoid these cyber-attacks have been explained in this section. Based on the review the researcher formed a model on forms of cyber security along with measures.

The above model depicts that cyber attacks can be reduced by various cyber security measures the person can adopt in their daily routine. It is advised to the public that digitalization has become a part of life and along with this there are many challenges also.

ARTIFICIAL INTELLIGENCE (AI) AND MACHINE LEARNING (ML) IN CYBER SECURITY

AI is a rapidly expanding domain of computer science that studies and develops ideas, methods, techniques, and application systems to duplicate, expand, and develop human intelligence. AI is also known as Machine Learning. We unknowingly employ a huge variety of artificial intelligence (AI) applications in daily life. like Siri, Alexa, autonomous vehicles, robotics, gaming, etc (Prasad & Rohokale, 2020). AI, deep learning, and machine learning are applied for attack detection, prediction, and intrusion detection

Figure 10. Research model
Source: Author's presentation

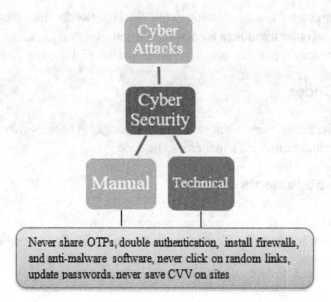

system in cyber security cases. Cybersecurity may benefit from the use of AI technologies like deep learning to build smart models for malware categorization, intrusion detection, and threat detection (Li, 2018). The detection of identifying data as normal and abnormal has been accomplished using genetic algorithms and new evolutionary neural networks, and AI algorithms help solve computer security challenges. Swarm intelligence (SI) is a strategy for picking key aspects for spotting new intrusions (Sarvari et al, 2020). Modification in machine learning results in deep learning which have three levels, input, hidden, and output level. The implication of various technologies like expert systems, intelligent agents, and techniques helps in improving the Intrusion detection system (IDS) in AI. Deep learning (DL) provides a better model for intrusion detection systems and cyber-attacks (Salih et al., 2021).

CYBER CRME IN INDIA

India has gone completely digital, therefore Internet access is now available everywhere, whether in an urban or rural setting. Everything is just a click away, whether it's social networking, e-shopping, or monetary transfers (Patil, 2022). As per the 2013-14 report of the standing committee on Information Technology, India has the world's third-largest number of internet users, with an estimated 100 million users as of June 2011, and the number is rapidly increasing. In India, there are around 22 million broadband connections maintained by 134 major Internet Service Providers (ISPs). According to the Indian Computer, emergency response Team (CERT) over 600,000 cyber-attacks were launched in 2021. The country reported 4.5 million cyber attacks in July 2020, the greatest number of attacks in the month of July.[11] The National Financial Organization of India said in March 2021 that an estimated Rs 4.46 billion had been transferred out of Bank of Maharashtra accounts as a result of a flaw in its Unified Payment Interface (UPI) application (Patil, 2022).

The Information Technology Ministry's CERT-In is the primary organization for dealing with cyber security concerns. It has been reported by CERT-In (Indian Computer Emergency Response Team) that the first two months of the year 2022 have shown more cybercrimes as compared to the whole year 2018. India recorded 2,08,456 (2018) occurrences; in 2019: 3,94,499 incidents; in 2020: 11,58,208 instances; in 2021: 14,02,809 cases; and in the first two months of 2022: 2,12,485 incidents. Further data also added that a total of 17,560 (2018), 24,768 (2019), and 26,121 (2020) websites were hacked by the criminals.[12]

REGULATION OF CYBER SECURITY IN INDIA

Informational Technology (IT) Act, 2000 recognized the importance of personal identity. This was the first time that a law was created for this purpose. This law provided to criminalize the actions against the vulnerability of public privacy (Halder & Jaishankar, 2021). The government of India has announced two initiatives: "Digital India" and "Make in India." Make in India aspires to promote investment, develop new technology, improve skill development, safeguard property rights, and establish best-in-class manufacturing infrastructure, whereas the main purpose behind Digitalized India was to transform India into an empowered society and knowledge economy. The Digital India concept includes cyber security as an integral component. The present chapter discussed some cyber security initiatives and the many agencies participating in developing a safe cyber environment in India, which is important for the Digital India program's success.

National Cyber Security Policy

The Government of India announced the National Cyber Security Policy (NCSP) 2013 on July 2, 2013, to create safe and stable cyberspace for people, enterprises, and government. The policy statement opens with a preamble that defined cyberspace and emphasizes the role of information technology in fostering the nation's economic progress. It also explains how information technology has helped India become a global player in IT solutions.

This policy aims goal of this strategy is to build a secure cyberspace ecosystem, reinforce the regulatory framework, and increase IT usage across the economy. The National Critical Information Infrastructure Protection Centre has been established to cope with cyber threats on a national and sectoral level 24x7 (NCIIPC). The strategy also intends to raise awareness of the integrity of ICT products and services and as well as to train 500,000 cyber security specialists.

Indian Computer Emergency Response Team (CERT-In)

[13]Since January 2004, CERT-In has been in operation. The Indian Cyber Community is CERT constituency. In's CERT-In is the federal entity in charge of responding to computer security incidents as they arise (Mehta et al., 2021).

CERT-In has been appointed as the national agency in charge of performing the following cyber security functions:

- Gathering, evaluating, and propagating cyber cases.
- projection and alerting occurrences of cyber security.

- Immediate actions for cyber security incidents
- Monitoring of cyber incident activities.
- Disseminate guidelines, alerts, susceptibility bulletins, and whitepapers about data security policies, protocols, and the protection, detection, and monitoring of cyber events.

Key Legislation to Strengthen the Digital Payment Ecosystem in India

- 1949: Banking Regulation Act
- 2007: Payment and Settlement Systems Act
- 2009: Pre-paid Payment Instruments in India (Reserve Bank) Directions
- 2014: Master Circular

WORLDWIDE CYBERCRIME AND LEGISLATION

Cybercrime now poses a serious threat to countries at all levels of development, impacting market participants. Law enforcement authorities and prosecutors have a significant challenge because of the evolving nature of cybercrime and the resulting skills gaps, particularly when it comes to cross-border enforcement.

- While 156 nations (or 80%) have passed cybercrime laws, the adoption rate differs by region: Europe has the greatest percentage (91%)
- Africa has the lowest (72%).
- China's Great Firewall tracks every move in cyberspace and prevents the publication of any objectionable information.
- China has a monopoly on any content that is detrimental or hazardous to the Chinese government.
- Brazil is home to the world's busiest hacker airport.
- Iran is likewise a risky place for Internet users. He also has a Crime Police squad that deals with cybercrime.[14]

CONCLUSION

The present chapter discusses cybercrime and fraud in digital payment systems. Due to digitalization, all financial transactions are taking place on the web. This scenario has given exposure to cybercrime. The chapter presents various cybercrime and the cyber security techniques to monitor them or to escape from these crimes. It highlights the shift of payment gateway from conventional to digital. The chapter presents the various regulatory bodies that regulates the cyber transaction and monitor the cybercrime across the country and the world. Many institutions like NCSP and CERT-In have worked to monitor and control these cyber frauds. The evolution of Fin-tech resulted in the development of a web-based economy. Digital payment transformed the cash-based society into a cashless scoiety. The usage of computers or electronic devices for financial transactions is attributed to an increase in cyber attacks. The major reasons and measures to avoid or get safe from these attacks are discussed in the chapter. In recent years cyber security has become vital for individuals and companies.

RECOMMENDATIONS

The chapter studies cyber-crime and cyber security in India and the world. The chapter concludes that with the increasing rate of digital transformation the public all around the world is connected with one click. This digital ecosystem has enabled customers to access A to Z on the internet. The increasing rate of internet usage in customer lifestyle has made their life very easy. Financial transactions or online money transfers to each corner of the world have reduced the hierarchy of financial transactions. Resultant to it cyber fraud or crime has taken a wide frame in the world. Now, customers are facing various cyber attacks in their life inclusive of exposing personal identification and financial losses too. These cyber-attacks have many forms and can be resolved through various techniques, as known as 'cyber security.'

Through reviewing prior literature and reports on cyber security it can be said that this issue has become very important for the economy. It is recommended to customers to always install good anti-virus software and always allow anti-virus software to protect their cloud searches. The most loopholes in cyber security are that customers never update their software, skip various information without reading, allowing everything without going through it. The customers must ensure all safety measures while surfing every site.

REFERENCES

Al-Zahrani, A. (2022). Assessing and Proposing Countermeasures for Cyber-Security Attacks. *International Journal of Advanced Computer Science and Applications*, *13*(1). Advance online publication. doi:10.14569/IJACSA.2022.01301102

Avizienis, A., Laprie, J. C., Randell, B., & Landwehr, C. (2004). Basic concepts and taxonomy of dependable and secure computing. *IEEE Transactions on Dependable and Secure Computing*, *1*(1), 11–33. doi:10.1109/TDSC.2004.2

Ciampa, M. (2012). *Security+ guide to network security fundamentals*. Cengage Learning.

Gupta, M., Verma, S., & Pachare, S. (2021). An analysis of Conventional and Alternative financing—Customers' perspective. *International Journal of Finance & Economics*, 1–11. doi:10.1002/ijfe.2541

Halder, D., & Jaishankar, K. (2021). Cyber governance and data protection in India: A critical legal analysis. In *Routledge Companion to Global Cyber-Security Strategy* (pp. 337–348). Routledge. doi:10.4324/9780429399718-28

Hong, Y., & Furnell, S. (2021). Understanding cybersecurity behavioral habits: Insights from situational support. *Journal of Information Security and Applications*, *57*, 102710. doi:10.1016/j.jisa.2020.102710

Jha, S. K., & Kumar, S. S. (2022). Cybersecurity in the Age of the Internet of Things: An Assessment of the Users' Privacy and Data Security. In *Expert Clouds and Applications* (pp. 49–56). Springer. doi:10.1007/978-981-16-2126-0_5

Le Nguyen, C., & Golman, W. (2021). Diffusion of the Budapest Convention on cybercrime and the development of cybercrime legislation in Pacific Island countries: 'Law on the books' vs 'law in action'. *Computer Law & Security Review*, *40*, 105521. doi:10.1016/j.clsr.2020.105521

Li, J. H. (2018). Cyber security meets artificial intelligence: A survey. *Frontiers of Information Technology & Electronic Engineering*, *19*(12), 1462–1474. doi:10.1631/FITEE.1800573

Li, Y., & Liu, Q. (2021). A comprehensive review study of cyber-attacks and cyber security; Emerging trends and recent developments. *Energy Reports*, *7*, 8176–8186. doi:10.1016/j.egyr.2021.08.126

Mehta, S., Sharma, A., Chawla, P., & Soni, K. (2021, May). The Urgency of Cyber Security in Secure Networks. In *2021 5th International Conference on Intelligent Computing and Control Systems (ICICCS)* (pp. 315-322). IEEE. 10.1109/ICICCS51141.2021.9432092

Oh, S., Karina, S., Johnston, R. B., Lee, H., & Lim, B. (2006). A Stakeholder Perspective on Successful Electronic Payment Systems Diffusion. *Hawaii International Conference on System Sciences (HICSS–39)*.

Palmieri, M., Shortland, N., & McGarry, P. (2021). Personality and online deviance: The role of reinforcement sensitivity theory in cybercrime. *Computers in Human Behavior*, *120*, 106745. doi:10.1016/j.chb.2021.106745

Patil, J. (2022). Cyber Laws in India: An Overview. *Indian Journal of Law and Legal Research*, *4*(01), 1391–1411.

Pisoni, G., Molnár, B., & Tarcsi, A. (2021, February). Comparison of two technologies for digital payments: Challenges and future directions. In *International Conference on Remote Engineering and Virtual Instrumentation* (pp. 478-484). Springer.

Prasad, R., & Rohokale, V. (2020). Artificial intelligence and machine learning in cyber security. In *Cyber Security: The Lifeline of Information and Communication Technology* (pp. 231–247). Springer. doi:10.1007/978-3-030-31703-4_16

Priya, G. J., & Saradha, S. (2021, February). Fraud detection and prevention using machine learning algorithms: a review. In *2021 7th International Conference on Electrical Energy Systems (ICEES)* (pp. 564-568). IEEE. 10.1109/ICEES51510.2021.9383631

Purba, J., Samuel, S., & Budiono, S. (2021). Collaboration of digital payment usage decision in COVID-19 pandemic situation: Evidence from Indonesia. *International Journal of Data and Network Science*, *5*(4), 557–568. doi:10.5267/j.ijdns.2021.8.012

Salih, A., Zeebaree, S. T., Ameen, S., Alkhyyat, A., & Shukur, H. M. (2021, February). A survey on the role of artificial intelligence, machine learning and deep learning for cybersecurity attack detection. In *2021 7th International Engineering Conference "Research & Innovation amid Global Pandemic"(IEC)* (pp. 61-66). IEEE. 10.1109/IEC52205.2021.9476132

Sarkar, M. P. (2019). Literature review on adoption of digital payment system. *Global Journal of Enterprise Information System*, *11*(3), 62–67.

Sarvari, S., Sani, N. F. M., Hanapi, Z. M., & Abdullah, M. T. (2020). An efficient anomaly intrusion detection method with feature selection and evolutionary neural network. *IEEE Access: Practical Innovations, Open Solutions*, *8*, 70651–70663. doi:10.1109/ACCESS.2020.2986217

Subramaniam, R., Singh, S. P., Padmanabhan, P., Gulyás, B., Palakkeel, P., & Sreedharan, R. (2021). Positive and Negative Impacts of COVID-19 in Digital Transformation. *Sustainability*, *13*(16), 9470. doi:10.3390u13169470

Topping, C., Dwyer, A., Michalec, O., Craggs, B., & Rashid, A. (2021). Beware suppliers bearing gifts!: Analysing coverage of supply chain cyber security in critical national infrastructure sectorial and cross-sectorial frameworks. *Computers & Security*, *108*, 102324. doi:10.1016/j.cose.2021.102324

Wang, E. K., Lin, C. W., Wu, T. Y., Chen, C. M., & Ye, Y. (2015, September). Privacy protection framework in social networked cars. In *International Conference on Multidisciplinary Social Networks Research* (pp. 553-561). Springer. 10.1007/978-3-662-48319-0_46

ADDITIONAL READING

Abrar, P. (2022, June 3). *Digital payments in India projected to reach $10 trn by 2026: Report*. Business Standard. Retrieved from https://www.business-standard.com/article/economy-policy/digital-payments-in-india-projected-to-reach-10-trn-by-2026-report-122060201089_1.html

Basu, O. (2022, April 29). *Two months of 2022 saw more cyber crimes than entire 2018: Why e-fraud is a ticking time bomb*. ZeeNews. Retrieved from https://zeenews.india.com/technology/two-months-of-2022-saw-more-cyber-crimes-than-entire-2018-why-e-fraud-is-a-ticking-time-bomb-2458733.html

Bhalero, S. (2022, April 12). *Cyber Crimes In India Witness 572% Increase In Last 3 Years! 14 Lakh Cases In 2021 Recorded By Govt*. Trak.in. Retrieved from https://trak.in/tags/business/2022/04/12/cyber-crimes-in-india-witness-572-increase-in-last-3-years-14-lakh-cases-in-2021-recorded-by-govt/

Bhalla, T. (2021, June 16). *Consumers more concerned about digital payment frauds: Survey*. Mint. Retrieved from https://www.livemint.com/news/india/consumers-more-concerned-about-digital-payment-frauds-survey-11623585064492.html

Buchholz, K. (2022, July 8). *China's Mobile Payment Adoption Beats All Others*. Statista. Retrieved from https://www.statista.com/chart/17909/pos-mobile-payment-user-penetration-rates/

Cybercrime Legislation Worldwide. (n.d.). UNCTAD. Retrieved from https://unctad.org/page/cybercrime-legislation-worldwide

Kelley, K. (2022, September 23). *What is Cybersecurity and Why It is Important?* SimpiLearn. Retrieved from https://www.simplilearn.com/tutorials/cyber-security-tutorial/what-is-cyber-security

Macknight, J. (2021, September 14). *Cyber security tips for the payments industry*. The Banker. Retrieved from https://www.thebanker.com/Comment-Profiles/Editor-s-Blog/Cyber-security-tips-for-the-payments-industry

Total number of digital payments across India from financial year 2018 to 2022. (2022, July 21). Statista Research Department. Retrieved from https://www.statista.com/statistics/1251321/india-total-volume-of-digital-payments/

ENDNOTES

1   https://www.simplilearn.com/tutorials/cyber-security-tutorial/what-is-cyber-security_

2   https://trak.in/tags/business/2022/04/12/cyber-crimes-in-india-witness-572-increase-in-last-3-years-14-lakh-cases-in-2021-recorded-by-govt/ (Accessed on 11 June 2022).

3   http://www.oxforddictionaries.com/definition/english/cybercrime (Accessed on 27 May 2022).

4   https://www.naavi.org/pati/pati_cybercrimes_dec03.htm (Accessed on 27 May 2022).

5   https://www.stealthlabs.com/blog/cyber-security-threats-all-you-need-to-know/

6   https://www.statista.com/statistics/1251321/india-total-volume-of-digital-payments/

7   https://www.business-standard.com/article/economy-policy/digital-payments-in-india-projected-to-reach-10-trn-by-2026-report-122060201089_1.html

8   https://www.statista.com/outlook/dmo/fintech/digital-payments/worldwide

9   https://www.statista.com/chart/17909/pos-mobile-payment-user-penetration-rates/

10   https://pib.gov.in/PressReleasePage.aspx?PRID=1808680

11   Economic times (date: 29 May 2022).

12   https://zeenews.india.com/technology/two-months-of-2022-saw-more-cyber-crimes-than-entire-2018-why-e-fraud-is-a-ticking-time-bomb-2458733.html (Accessed on 28 May, 2022).

13   https://www.meity.gov.in/content/icert (Accessed on 1 June 2022).

14   https://www.legalserviceindia.com/legal/article-1019-importance-of-cyber-law-in-india.html (Accessed on 15 June 2022).

Chapter 6
KYC Fraud:
A New Means to Conduct Financial Fraud – How to Tackle It?

Vijaya Geeta Dharmavaram

https://orcid.org/0000-0002-1052-1219

GITAM School of Business, India

Oly Mishra

Indian Institute of Foreign Trade, India

ABSTRACT

Know your customer (KYC) is a measure adopted by financial institutions like banks to render timely services to their legitimate customers. Cybercriminals are resorting to KYC fraud through Vishing and SMiShing attacks. Customers have been falling prey to such frauds in the name of KYC updation. The chapter proposes the application of the supervised machine learning model to detect KYC fraud related to SMS and prevent such frauds. A dataset of sample KYC fraud messages and non-fraud messages is taken to train the machine learning model. The model is trained to extract the relevant features that distinguish fraud messages from valid messages, thus detecting fraud messages. The model was tested with popular supervised machine learning algorithms. The proposed model may be made as part of a security patch in the messaging service. KYC fraud has become rampant in recent times, and the chance of an individual falling for such attacks are highest given that it is a mandatory process. Previous research studies provided generic solutions for such frauds.

INTRODUCTION

With the advent of the internet and mobile technology, online transactions and the virtual world has become a norm. From being an information resource and medium of communication, the internet has come a long way. The internet has paved the way for all financial transactions and business operations. With the emergence of smartphones, every individual has access to the power of the internet on their

DOI: 10.4018/978-1-6684-5827-3.ch006

handheld device. Almost all businesses want to cash in on this power by launching mobile apps that ensure interactions can be done anytime, anywhere in a more convenient fashion.

However, just as every coin has two sides, the internet and mobile technology have their adversity in the form of cybercriminals. This is evident in the number of cybercrimes that have been recorded. As per the FBI's report (FBI, 2021), 8,47,376 cybercrime complaints were reported in 2021, which is a 7% increase from 2020. The reported cybercrimes in the last five years (figure 1) show an increasing trend in all cybercrimes, including identity theft and fraud.

Figure 1. Number of cybercrimes reported from 2017-2021
Source: Federal Trade Commission, Consumer Sentinel Network

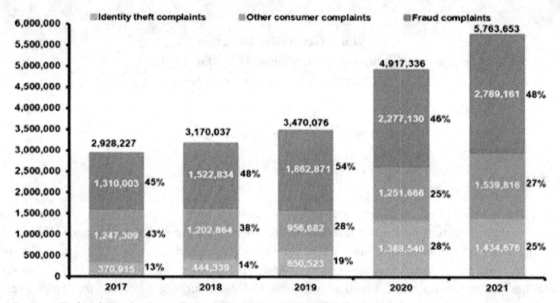

Source: Federal Trade Commission, Consumer Sentinel Network

The types of cybercrimes and the ingenuity with which they are carried out are becoming more and more difficult to detect and prevent. Cybercriminals often target human emotions of greed and fear to trap them. Fraud messages such as winning a lottery or inheriting property to lure the victim are used to target the victim's desire. In contrast, threats such as ransomware attack that holds victim's data for ransom or messages that threaten to block or steal a user's account or money target the victim's fear emotion. Fraudulent messages with a false promise of lottery or prize money are easier to detect if the victim is aware that they did not participate in such events to claim any winnings. However, a message from one's bank or financial services to divulge account/ personal information to ensure their accounts are not blocked is difficult to ignore or to be taken lightly.

One such attack that has recently become rampant is KYC fraud. KYC, which means "Know Your Customer / Client" is a process followed by several business firms, especially financial institutions such as banks, to know with whom they are conducting the financial transactions and to provide timely service. One primary reason for adopting the KYC process is to curb financial fraud. Financial frauds are common in different countries, irrespective of their economy. For instance, India reported 7,400 bank fraud cases in 2021 (Statista Research Department, 2021). UK registered a sum of £754M as stolen in the first half of 2021 (Peachey, 2021). The US witnessed a 109% increase in financial frauds in the early months of 2021 compared to the previous year (Leonhardt, 2021).

Financial firms adopt KYC as a mandated process to check such fraudulent activities. KYC process requires the customer to submit necessary documents that identify them to avail of the offered services. In this context, it is not unusual for people to receive messages from their banks asking them to complete the KYC process to avail of uninterrupted services. The fear of losing one's account leads the customer to take serious note of such messages and follow the required procedure. Cybercriminals are using this element of fear by sending fake messages to the victims and luring them in revealing their personal / account information.

Recently, several such cases of KYC frauds have been reported (The Times of India, 2022). The victims can be anyone irrespective of their occupation, education, or age. A few instances are shown below in figure 2.

Figure 2. Sample cases of reported KYC frauds
Source: Times of India

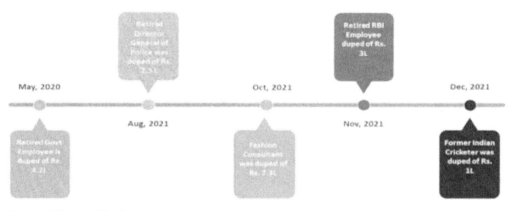

Source: Times of India

Understanding the scheme followed by the fraudster to trick their victims will give us insights on how to tackle it.

HOW KYC FRAUD IS CARRIED OUT

Vishing and smishing are two popular phishing techniques employed by fraudsters to carry out KYC fraud.

Vishing

In vishing, the fraudster reaches the victim over a phone, acting as a customer service representative. The victim may be asked to divulge their account credentials or install a remote viewing app. The fraudster convinces the victim that these are the necessary steps to carry out the KYC process. Once the fraudster gets access to either the account credentials or remote access, they would steal the amount from their bank or payment wallets. The victim may not even realize that amount is being stolen from their account till they hang up the phone. The fraudster would make sure that the victim is in the phone call till he finishes off the transaction (Despande, 2021).

Smishing

In case of smishing, the victim is sent messages with a fake link to update their KYC or a fake contact number to do the KYC process. The message is similar to the ones shown in figure 3.

Figure 3. Fake KYC Messages

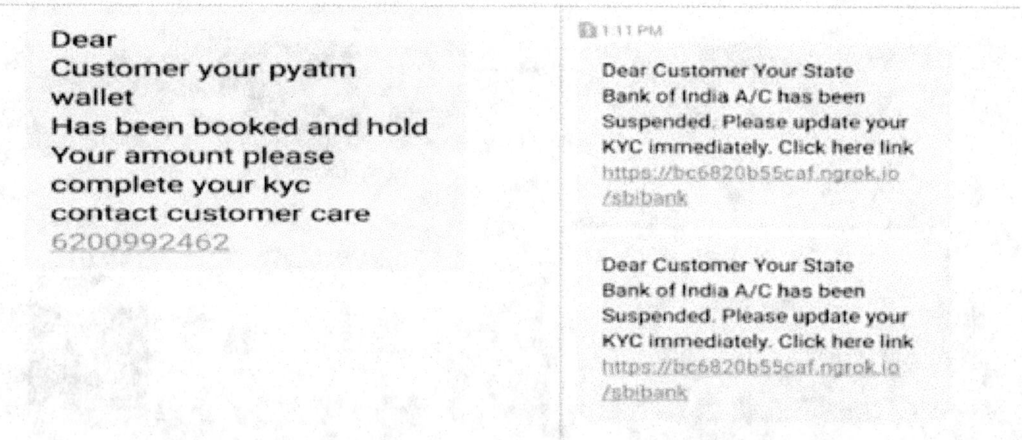

Dear
Customer your pyatm
wallet
Has been booked and hold
Your amount please
complete your kyc
contact customer care
6200992462

1:11 PM

Dear Customer Your State
Bank of India A/C has been
Suspended. Please update your
KYC immediately. Click here link
https://bc6820b55caf.ngrok.io
/sbibank

Dear Customer Your State
Bank of India A/C has been
Suspended. Please update your
KYC immediately. Click here link
https://bc6820b55caf.ngrok.io
/sbibank

KYC Fraud Caselets

Fraud SMS with a link usually takes the victim to a phishing website that looks similar to an authentic one. The victim's credentials are stolen when they try to log in, assuming it to be an actual website (Cert-In, 2021). In the case of SMS with a phone number, once the victim calls it, it takes the form of a vishing attack. One such real-case scenario that was published in the newspaper (Times of India) is illustrated below:

In June 2021, a 65-year-old accountant from Naranpura received a message asking him to update his KYC for a new mobile connection. The recipient was asked to call a particular phone number to complete the KYC process in that message. Once the accountant called the said phone number, a person identified as a service provider representative asked him to download an app and pay a small amount of Rs 20. When the accountant could not make the payment for some reason, he called back the spurious representative from his wife's phone. Based on the instructions received from the representative, he filled in his wife's bank details in the app and paid Rs. 20 online. Sometime later, he found that a total of Rs. 2.50 lakhs were debited from the bank account. Realizing he had been cheated, he got his bank accounts frozen and booked a complaint with the local police.

In the above case, the victim received a spurious SMS prompting a smishing attack but later took the shape of a vishing attack when the victim called the given phone number and fell prey to the fraud.

Similarly, a vishing attack may later take the form of a smishing attack, as illustrated in the following real-case scenario described below: (Times of India)

In July 2021, a 38-year-old fashion consultant from Pune received a phone call from a man claiming to be the representative of her mobile service provider. He asked her to update her KYC, failing which; her mobile services would be suspended. The suspect then sent her an SMS with a weblink. The victim clicked on the link and filled her bank and debit card details in the form, assuming it would be one step in updating the KYC process. A total of Rs.7.32Lakhs was transferred from her account using her debit card details. The victim complained to the local police, and an FIR was registered.

It is evident from the above two cases that fraudsters use different means to trap their victims, and it need not be a standalone vishing or smishing attack, but it can be a combination of vishing and smishing attacks.

HOW TO TACKLE IT?

Precautions by each individual are the most effective way to address this problem. SBI, in its press notice, has given 3-tips mantra to avoid KYC (Ojha, 2021):

1. Think before you click any link, 2. The bank never sends links to update the KYC, 3. Do not share your mobile number and confidential data with anyone.

Apart from that, SBI has been sending SMS (Figure 4) to its customer regarding the same.
In general, some of the safety precautions one can follow are:

1. Be wary of web links received over SMS. They could be phishing links.
2. Do not share password/OTP/credit/Debit card information with anyone, including bank staff.
3. Do not install remote access apps unless you are sure of the purpose and with whom you are dealing.
4. It is always a best practice to type the bank's website URL in the web browser rather than clicking on the link.
5. Know your customer care number on the official website rather than the one found in a web search or a third-party website.
6. Check all the permissions while installing apps on your smartphone.
7. The concerned authorities should be informed about fraud to minimize the damage and catch the culprit.

Figure 4. Alert SMS from SBI

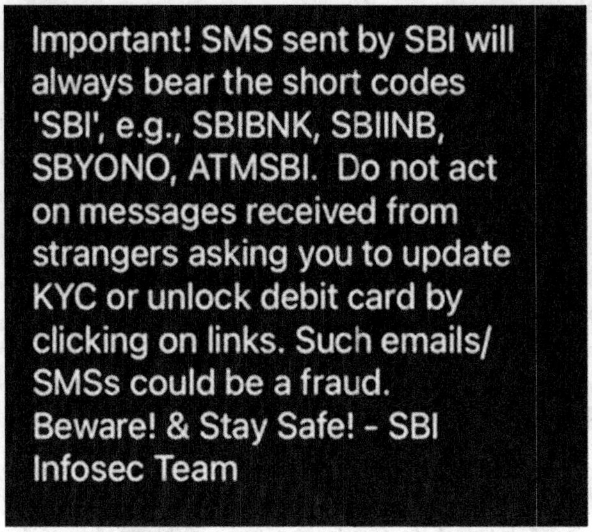

Important! SMS sent by SBI will always bear the short codes 'SBI', e.g., SBIBNK, SBIINB, SBYONO, ATMSBI. Do not act on messages received from strangers asking you to update KYC or unlock debit card by clicking on links. Such emails/SMSs could be a fraud. Beware! & Stay Safe! - SBI Infosec Team

These are a few safety measures an individual can take. However, not everyone is aware of these measures and unknowingly becomes a victim of KYC fraud, as evident with the number of KYC fraud cases that have been witnessed in recent times.

Since the KYC process requires storing customer's personal information, many models have been proposed in the past to ensure the safe upkeeping of KYC documents. A manual KYC process requires the customers to provide hard copies of their papers, and the service provider is supposed to safe keep these documents in some storage area. This does not offer any additional security and is prone to theft or physical damage (Rankhambe. & Khanuja, 2021). In the following section, we reflect on some of the studies that have been carried out in the past.

LITERATURE REVIEW

Blockchain technology is a prevalent choice among researchers for the safe storage of KYC documents and has been extensively used in the banking sector for secure transactions. Distributed ledger technology on the Ethereum platform (Parra Moyano & Ross, 2017) helps achieve effective cost distribution in the KYC process. Similarly, distributed ledger technology on R3 Corda was presented by (Kasturi and Pachaiyappan, 2018; Rutter, 2018). Storage of KYC details in off-chain and data hashes in the Ethereum blockchain has been proposed by several researchers (Norvill et al., 2019, Drăgan & Manulis, 2020, Patel et al., 2021, Steichen et al., 2018, Singhal et al., 2020). Such a method helps in addressing the storage limitation of the Ethereum platform. Some of the other techniques that were proposed for additional security are: storing encrypted data in the blockchain using the AES algorithm (Sundareswaran et al., 2020), public key encryption with QR code (Kumar & Nikhil, 2020), and re-hashing the key after every call (Alleman, 2019) are proposed (Rankhambe. & Khanuja, 2021) proposed the creation of a digital portfolio of online KYC documents. They suggested the usage of blockchains for the secure sharing of documents without the interference of intermediaries and smart contracts to enable the automatic execution of agreements.

Blockchain is a secure method for storing the data and ensuring that the documents do not fall into the wrong hands, which may lead to identity theft. This is useful in the service providers' actual KYC process. However, to mitigate the fraud KYC process in which the unsuspecting victims fall prey to spurious messages received on their mobile phone, some security measures in-built into the mobile phone would be more beneficial. Mobile software is periodically updated to give superior and secure services to their customer. With KYC fraud becoming rampant lately, a security patch in the mobile software that can detect spurious SMS significantly the one related to KYC fraud would help.

To differentiate fraud messages from valid messages, a learning model trained on how to distinguish these two types of messages can be built. Such automated models would help isolate suspicious messages from regular messages without user intervention. Creating a learning model comes into the purview of machine learning. Machine learning has been successfully used in cyber security (Murugesan, 2019) and especially in detecting smishing attacks (Balim & Gunal, 2019; Sonowal & Kuppusamy, 2018; Jain & Gupta, 2018). These methods are used to detect a Smishing attack which is general but not specific to KYC fraud. However, a machine learning model trained to detect KYC messages will go a long way to curb the menace of KYC fraud.

MACHINE LEARNING TECHNIQUES AND HOW TO INCORPORATE

Machine learning algorithms can be classified as supervised, unsupervised, semi-supervised, and reinforcement learning. A clear understanding of these techniques will help in understanding how they can be used to tackle KYC fraud.

Supervised Learning

What is it?

Supervised Learning finds input-output relationships based on a set of paired input-output training samples. It can also be called *"Learning with a Teacher"* (Haykin 1998), *"Learning from Labelled Data,"* or *"Inductive Machine Learning"* (Kotsiantis, 2007). Supervised learning algorithms can be divided into classification and regression based on the kind of output it predicts. The classification algorithm detects discrete output value, whereas regression is used to detect constant output value. Classification algorithms such as decision trees, SVM, naïve Bayes, and random forests are some of the popular algorithms. Prediction models are classification models and have their applications across domains. Supervised learning requires many labeled examples (known cases) to train the model.

How Can it be Used for the Detection of KYC Fraud?

In case of KYC fraud detection, a supervised learning model would be fed with different examples of fraud and legitimate messages and is trained to distinguish between these two messages. Such a model will help flag suspicious messages so that users are alert and cautious in responding to such messages.

Since such a model is built on the example messages clearly labeled as "fraud" and "not-fraud", the detection accuracy of such a model would be high.

Unsupervised Learning

What is it?

Unsupervised learning algorithms are often used to find natural groupings or clusters in the data. Unlabelled examples are fed into the algorithm, and the model finds the number of groups based on their similarities. Since these algorithms do not require labeled examples, they are often inexpensive to implement.

How Can it be Used for the Detection of KYC Fraud?

In the case of KYC fraud detection, an unsupervised learning algorithm would parse different text messages and differentiates them into other groups. The algorithm tries to form natural clusters based on similar message features. Based on the similarity, fraud messages are clustered in one group and valid messages in another. Once a message is delivered, an unsupervised model would parse the text message and put it in one of the groups. Since this algorithm does not have the support of labeled examples, the algorithm may not be as accurate as a supervised model in fraud detection.

Semi-supervised Learning

What is it?

Semi-supervised learning combines both supervised and unsupervised learning. A model is built using a small number of labelled examples (unlike supervised learning, which requires a large number of labelled examples) and many unlabelled examples. These algorithms are appropriate in cases labeled examples are scarce.

How Can it be Used for the Detection of KYC Fraud?

In the case of KYC fraud detection, a semi-supervised classifier can be built in the same way as a supervised model, where a model is trained with a limited number of labelled examples and will use many unlabelled examples with predicted output to detect fraud messages. The semi-supervised model may have better accuracy than unsupervised learning but may not be as accurate as supervised learning model.

Reinforcement Learning

What is it?

They are experiential learning algorithm which does not require any labeled examples to train. They learn through the reward system, which earns a reward for every correct response and punishment for every incorrect answer. The goal of the reinforcement learning model is to maximize its rewards. Reinforcement learning is often used in building games.

How Can it be Used for the Detection of KYC Fraud?

However, in detecting KYC fraud messages, a reinforcement learning model will act as an evolving model that can learn different variations in fraud messages over time. Not much work has been done in using reinforcement learning for detecting smishing attacks.

From the above discussion, a security program built using a supervised learning algorithm would help detect a fraud message from a valid message. A model that detects KYC-related fraud messages would give more accurate results. Such model incorporated in the mobile security software would ensure that the mobile users are cautioned against such messages. The following section reflects on how a supervised learning model can be built to detect KYC fraud messages.

BUILDING A SUPERVISED LEARNING MODEL

To build a supervised learning model to distinguish between fraud and legitimate messages, the model is trained with labeled examples of KYC fraud, KYC legitimate messages, and other legitimate messages. Sample examples of such examples are shown in Figures 5a, 5b and 5c.

Figure 5. (a) Fake KYC Messages. (b) Real KYC Messages. (c) Legitimate Non-KYC message

Fake KYC Messages   Real KYC Messages

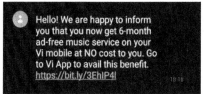

Legitimate Non-KYC message

The critical differences between fake and real KYC messages are:

1. Presence of phone number in fraud KYC message
2. Presence of web link in fraud KYC message
3. Misspelled service provider name in fraud KYC message
4. The presence of the KYC keyword in both fake and real message
5. Weblink may present in a valid non-KYC message but not in a real KYC message

A learning model would parse the text message and based on the above-said features; it would distinguish between a fake and valid message.

To validate and test this learning model, a sample dataset with 45 messages comprising of both KYC fraud and non-fraud messages is taken. From these messages, the above-discussed key five features were extracted. These messages were then labeled as "Fraud", "Not-Fraud," and "Check Message". The third category belongs to the messages that may not be a KYC fraud message but have suspicious elements.

The model was trained to differentiate between the three types of messages. The decision tree algorithm in the Weka platform, free software developed by the University of Waikato, New Zealand, was used to build the model. The screenshot of Weka's results is shown in Figure 6.

Figure 6. Weka results of decision tree model on the sample dataset

```
Size of the tree : 13

Time taken to build model: 0 seconds

=== Stratified cross-validation ===
=== Summary ===

Correctly Classified Instances          45              100      %
Incorrectly Classified Instances         0                0      %
Kappa statistic                          1
Mean absolute error                      0
Root mean squared error                  0
Relative absolute error                  0      %
Root relative squared error              0      %
Total Number of Instances               45
```

```
=== Detailed Accuracy By Class ===
```

	TP Rate	FP Rate	Precision	Recall	F-Measure	MCC	ROC Area	PRC Area	Class
	1.000	0.000	1.000	1.000	1.000	1.000	1.000	1.000	FRAUD
	1.000	0.000	1.000	1.000	1.000	1.000	1.000	1.000	CHECK_MSG
	1.000	0.000	1.000	1.000	1.000	1.000	1.000	1.000	NOT_FRAUD
Weighted Avg.	1.000	0.000	1.000	1.000	1.000	1.000	1.000	1.000	

```
=== Confusion Matrix ===

  a  b  c   <-- classified as
 15  0  0 |  a = FRAUD
  0 15  0 |  b = CHECK_MSG
  0  0 15 |  c = NOT_FRAUD
```

In the above screenshot, it is observed that a decision tree model, a supervised machine learning algorithm, was successfully able to differentiate the three different types of messages with 100 percent accuracy. The decision tree for the model built is shown in figure 7.

Figure 7. Decision Tree model for KYC fraud detection

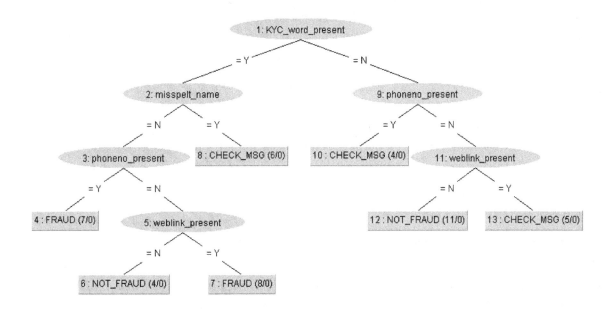

The above decision tree depicts how the model differentiates between the three classes of messages, i.e., "Fraud", "Not Fraud" and "Check Messages". Features such as phone number, weblink, and misspelled service provider name are the critical elements in detecting the fraud message. Based on these features, the model can detect whether a message is genuine or fraudulent. Detected fraud messages can be flagged as suspicious messages and placed in a quarantined folder. Incorporating such a model in mobile phone software as a security measure would ensure that an individual receives an alert on suspicious KYC fraud messages. Such a mechanism would ensure that non-suspecting user who is not much aware of these frauds is alerted and do not fall into the trap of the fraudsters.

CONCLUSION

As we are in the information age, using smartphones with internet capabilities is here to stay. Mobile banking and payment wallets are convenient ways of doing financial transactions these days. To facilitate hassle free and timely service, the KYC process was introduced. KYC helps the service provider know the customer or client to whom they offer their services. This would ensure that the customers are provided timely service and help prevent the financial assistance used for money laundering activities. Hence it is mandated that every customer/client has to go through the KYC process. With the KYC process becoming a mandated procedure, customers tend to respond to any messages from their service provider regarding updating KYC. However, one must be on one's guard since cyber criminals use smishing attacks to steal the credentials in the pretext of updating KYC. Such incidents are being witnessed nowadays, with many victims falling prey to such frauds. Even though one can be careful by following safety precautions of dos and don'ts in the online living, not many are aware of such. However, using machine learning techniques, a smartphone can be smarter by incorporating security measures such as a fraud detection system. Such model can detect fraudulent messages from the valid message and thus alert the individual to not to fall in the cyber criminal's trap. One such model idea is presented in the chapter to impress on the above. The proposed model was found effective on a sample dataset which shows that this can be adopted by mobile companies and creates a safer haven for their mobile users.

REFERENCES

Allemann, S. (2019). *Design and Prototypical Implementation of an Open Source and Smart Contract-based Know Your Customer (KYC) Platform* [Doctoral dissertation]. University of Zurich.

Balim, C., & Gunal, E. S. (2019). Automatic Detection of Smishing Attacks by Machine Learning Methods. In *2019 1st International Informatics and Software Engineering Conference (UBMYK)* (pp. 1-3). IEEE. 10.1109/UBMYK48245.2019.8965429

Cert-In. (2021). *Phishing websites hosted on NGROK platform, targeting Indian banking customers.* Available at: https://www.cert-in.org.in/

Deshpande, A. (2021, October 6). *'Update your KYC', a new trick adopted by cybercrooks to siphon off the money.* Available at:https://www.thehindu.com/news/national/telangana/update-your-kyc-a-new-fraud-trick-adopted-by-cybercrooks-to-siphon-off-the-money/article36856680.ece

Drăgan, C. C., & Manulis, M. (2020). KYChain: User-controlled KYC data sharing and certification. In *Proceedings of the 35th Annual ACM Symposium on Applied Computing* (pp. 301-307). 10.1145/3341105.3373895

FBI, (2021). *Federal Bureau of Investigation, Internet Crime Report 2021.* Internet Crime Complain Center (IC^3).

Haykin, S. (1998). Neural Networks: A Comprehensive Foundation (2nd ed.). Prentice Hall PTR.

Jain, A. K., & Gupta, B. B. (2018). Rule-based framework for detection of smishing messages in mobile environment. *Procedia Computer Science*, *125*, 617–623. doi:10.1016/j.procs.2017.12.079

Kasturi, R., & Pachaiyappan, V. (2018). Block Chain Technology (DLT Technique) for KYC in FinTech Domain: A Survey. *International Journal of Pure and Applied Mathematics*, *119*, 259–265.

Kotsiantis, S. (2007). Supervised Machine Learning: A Review of Classification Techniques. *Informatica Journal*, *31*, 249–268.

Kumar, M., & Nikhil, P. A. (2020). A blockchain based approach for an efficient secure KYC process with data sovereignty. *Int J Sci Technol Res*, 9, 3403–3407.

Leonhardt, M. (2021). *Online fraud attempt are up 25% in the US - here's why.* Available at: https://www.cnbc.com/2021/06/03/why-online-fraud-attempts-are-up-25percent-in-the-us.html

Murugesan, S. (2019), The cybersecurity renaissance: security threats, risks, and safeguards. *IEEE ICNL, 14*(1), 33-40. Available at: http://ieeecs-madras.managedbiz.com/icnl/19q1/p33-p40.pdf

Norvill, R., Steichen, M., Shbair, W. M., & State, R. (2019). Blockchain for the simplification and automation of KYC result sharing. In *2019 IEEE International Conference on Blockchain and Cryptocurrency (ICBC)* (pp. 9-10). IEEE. 10.1109/BLOC.2019.8751480

Ojha, S. (2021, June 7). *SBI warns of KYC fraud. 3 things you must do to you're your account safe.* Available at: https://www.livemint.com/money/personal-finance/sbi-warns-of-kyc-update-fraud-3-things-you-must-do-to-keep-your-account-safe-11623896065849.html

Parra Moyano, J., & Ross, O. (2017). KYC optimization using distributed ledger technology. *Business & Information Systems Engineering*, *59*(6), 411–423. doi:10.100712599-017-0504-2

Patel, D., Suslade, H., Rane, J., Prabhu, P., Saluja, S., & Busnel, Y. (2021). KYC as a Service (KASE)—A Blockchain Approach. In *Advances in Machine Learning and Computational Intelligence* (pp. 795–803). Springer. doi:10.1007/978-981-15-5243-4_76

Peachey, K. (2021). *Fraudsters steal £4m a day as crime surges.* BBC News. Available at: https://www.bbc.com/news/business-58649698

Rankhambe, B. P., & Khanuja, H. (2021). Hassle-Free and Secure e-KYC System Using Distributed Ledger Technology. *International Journal of Next-Generation Computing*, 74-90.

Rutter, K. (2018). If at First You Don't Succeed, Try a Decentralized KYC Platform: Will Blockchain Technology Give Corporate KYC a Second Chance? *R3 Reports, 3.*

Singhal, N., Sharma, M. K., Samant, S. S., Goswami, P., & Reddy, Y. A. (2020). Smart KYC using blockchain and IPFS. In *Advances in Cybernetics, Cognition, and Machine Learning for Communication Technologies* (pp. 77–84). Springer. doi:10.1007/978-981-15-3125-5_9

Sonowal, G., & Kuppusamy, K. S. (2018). Smidca: An anti-smishing model with machine learning approach. *The Computer Journal, 61*(8), 1143–1157. doi:10.1093/comjnl/bxy039

Statista Research Department. (2021). *Number of bank fraud cases across India between from financial year 2009 to 2021.* Available at: https://www.statista.com/statistics/1012729/india-number-of-bank-fraud-cases/

Steichen, M., Fiz, B., Norvill, R., Shbair, W., & State, R. (2018). Blockchain-based, decentralized access control for IPFS. In 2018 IEEE International Conference on Internet of Things (iThings) and IEEE Green Computing and Communications (GreenCom) and IEEE Cyber, Physical and Social Computing (CPSCom) and IEEE Smart Data (SmartData) (pp. 1499-1506). IEEE. doi:10.1109/Cybermatics_2018.2018.00253

Sundareswaran, N., Sasirekha, S., Paul, I. J. L., Balakrishnan, S., & Swaminathan, G. (2020). Optimised KYC Blockchain System. In *2020 International Conference on Innovative Trends in Information Technology (ICITIIT)* (pp. 1-6). IEEE.

The Times of India. (2022). *KYC Frauds*. Available at: https://timesofindia.indiatimes.com/topic/kyc-fraud(accessed on 16August, 2022)

Chapter 7
Governance of Digital Business in Industry 4.0:
Legal and Regulatory Aspects

Amit Kashyap
Nirma University, Ahmedabad, India

Pranav Saraswat
Nirma University, Ahmedabad, India

ABSTRACT

The importance of digital technologies for social and economic developments and a growing focus on data collection and privacy concerns have made the internet a salient and visible issue in global politics. The internet has transformed how we do business and created new opportunities for cross-border trade and investment, enabling small businesses worldwide to connect with customers and suppliers in the global market. In this chapter, the author conceptualizes the digital media business in India, which utilizes the internet to create the biggest platform for commerce worldwide. The author discusses regulations that are required in the cyber law and the safe harbour rule of cyber law, which is constantly harnessed by the digital media and e-commerce companies that act as intermediaries to protect them from the actions of the end-user on their platform.

INTRODUCTION

The development of the Internet has been nothing short of a technological revolution in today's fast-paced world. Every commercial transaction worldwide has been made simpler and has crossed national borders. India has grown into a sizable market for social media goliaths like Facebook, LinkedIn, Instagram, and Twitter (Mills & Plangger, 2015). Research shows how these digital intermediaries have become essential to online news distribution, giving publishers competition for attention and advertising and new opportunities to reach larger online audiences (Aneez et al., 2019). The new family of internet-based technologies are used in digital business, often known as e-business or e-commerce. Through these

DOI: 10.4018/978-1-6684-5827-3.ch007

technologies, individuals can interact in novel ways, new business models can be created, firms can run more effectively, and they can benefit from the emerging global network economy. Digital business companies are considered Intermediaries in cyber Space.

In the realm of IT, intermediaries come in several forms. Below are a few of them:

1. Telecom service provider (Tsp): This category includes all Indian businesses that provide telecom services.
    a. Vodafone, Aircel, Tata, Reliance, Airtel, and Idea are a few examples.
2. Internet service providers (ISPs) are the businesses that enable customers to connect to the Internet through a wireless connection, cable, or some other method.
    a. Gtpl and spigot are two examples.
3. Webhosting service provider: Organizations that provide hosting solutions.
    a. In plain English, we may explain that this website provides Space on server sites for storing files so users can access them from wherever.
    b. GoDaddy.com is one such.
4. Search Engines: A few good websites that assist people in finding particular information on the web. And give links to every webpage related to that specific search. Additionally, they provide a list of links in particular rank order.
    a. Among them are Google and Yahoo.
5. Online payment platforms: Paytm, Rupay, and Paypal are a few examples.
6. Online auction sites, such as eBay, provide one example.
7. Social media Websites: for instance, Instagram, Facebook, LinkedIn and Twitter
8. Blogging: Examples include wordpress.com and blogger.com.
9. Cyber café: This establishment offers internet access to customers. Cyber cafés are categorized as intermediaries under the IT Act of 2000.

COMPANY LAW AND DIGITAL BUSINESS

According to the relevant legislation, every company entity must register with the Ministry of Corporate Affairs. E-commerce startups are businesses formed under the Companies Act of 2013 and operate an online store or marketplace or be a foreign business or an out-of-country office, branch, or agency controlled or owned by an Indian citizen (Gupta, 2020). E-commerce refers to purchasing and selling services and products, including digital ones, through an electronic and digital network (Cockfield, 1999).

The company's integration procedure may be accessible at https://www.mca.gov.in/ and is online. The founder must approve his name and registered office address before a private limited company may be formed. It must have a minimum of two directors holding Director Status Codes (DSCs) and DINs (Digital Signature Certificates). The company's authorized share capital must be INR 1 lakh if registering as a one-person company. The incorporation process of a company in India also requires the Memorandum of Association (MOA) and Articles of Association (AOA) drafting as per Schedule I of Companies Act 2013 and uploading the stamped documents on the MCA Portal. Until these conditions are satisfied, the Registrar of Companies (ROC) provides a certificate of incorporation and CIN Number to the business at its registered office address.

IPR AND DIGITAL BUSINESS

Along with the increasing Internet use, various issues are coming up regarding the same. Out of all problems, one of the most significant issues is regarding an infringement of Intellectual property. Cyberspace intellectual property violations include many essential topics, such as any unauthorized or unlicensed use of trademarks, trade names, service marks, pictures, music, or other literary or artistic works. Different types of violations, such as deep hyperlinking, framing, metatags, spamming, and breaches of digital copyrights, have been caused by the distinctive structure of the Internet (Jain et al., 2021).

Copyright Issues

It has often been found that holding a service provider account is simpler than identifying the offender. Service providers are more likely to be held accountable than the initial offender for various reasons. The following is a list of some of the causes:

- There are occasions when it is pretty challenging to identify the actual infringement since there is a risk that they may have utilized an anonymous computer, making following them exceedingly tricky.
- When an infringement is from a foreign nation, issues are also raised about the jurisdiction.
- Several theories may be used to hold a service provider accountable. Here is an explanation of them: Direct, indirect, collateral, and contributing Liabilities
- **Direct:** When someone breaches an exclusive right of the copyright holder, this is known as a direct infringemeny.
- **Vicarious:** This kind of responsibility develops when a person acts to stop an infringement when they have the power to do so and stand to gain directly from the violation.
- **Contributory:** This principle applies when a person is personally involved in an infringement. The individual in this situation is already aware of how to carry out such an action. There has been a debate on which basis the service provider is liable. One extremist presents their view by holding service providers responsible under strict liability theory (direct and vicarious), while another picture holds them accountable under contributory theory; that is, a service provider can only be held liable if he infringes the copyright and has the knowledge for the same. Only knowledge about the infringement will make the service provider accountable, not by mere negligence.

Jain et al. (2021) also mentioned that, the service provider can only be held liable when he receives a complaint from a copyright holder but does not remove the illegal message.

This issue of the liability of service providers for the first time got attention in the WIPO copyright treaty in 1996 (Ali et al., 2021). However, Internet service providers' liability for copyright infringement was not directly addressed in the WIPO copyright treaty or the WIPO performances and phonograms treaty (Shalika, 2019). WIPO permits nations to adopt their rules for ISP's accountability under copyright law without prescribing any of its own (Shalika, 2019).

There is no covered provision defining the service provider's obligation under the Indian Copyright Act 1957 (Shushaanth and Prakash, 2018). Additionally, the courts have not yet had a chance to determine the liability threshold. Nevertheless, Section 51 of the Constitution addresses copyright infringement. The phrase "anywhere" is used in this section, and it may be inferred that it applies to internet service providers (Mohan and Mini, 2021). However, a specific clause doesn't outline a service provider's responsibility for copyright violations (Kundu, 2021).

To safeguard the innocent service providers, it has been expressly stated in sections 52(1) (b) and (c) that purpose and knowledge must be taken into consideration. Websites like YouTube and Yahoo, where other individuals upload or publish content that is genuinely not controlled by the service provider, have been kept while these rules have been included. Therefore, purpose and knowledge must be considered while holding service providers accountable.

The courts could not agree on a solution to this contentious standard of liability problem. The courts have established different rules to evaluate service providers' responsibility (Mills and Plangger, 2015).

United States District Court for the Middle District of Florida, in a case (Playboy Enterprise v. Frena, 1998) related to the service provider's responsibility examined the issue of trademark liability in cyber space. This case aimed to examine whether the Electronic Bulletin Board System was responsible for the actions taken by users who downloaded and uploaded copyrighted images. According to the defendants' claims, all the images were taken off as soon as they learned of the lawsuit. However, in this instance, the Court held the defendant accountable without considering their knowledge or purpose. This decision has drawn criticism since it placed an extremely risky burden on service providers, forcing them to keep an eye on their customers' private communications to catch suspected copyright infractions. The Court, in this instance, adopted the strict liability rule without considering intent or awareness.

The Court then utilized the vicarious and contributory theory of culpability in the case of Sega Enterprises Ltd. (Sega Enterprises Ltd. v. Maphia, 1996) decided by U.S. District Court Northern District of California rather than adhering to the precedent set in the earlier case. Instead of only blaming without intending to violate, the Internet and knowledge were searched in this instance.

A notice was then placed against Yahoo for unlicensed streaming of the work of Tseries in Super Cassettes Industries Ltd. Case (Super Cassettes Industries Ltd. V. Yahoo Inc. & Anr., 2008) Typically, Tseries uses multiple locations to licence their music and films. But Yahoo was operating without a permit. Despite Tseries sending a legal notice, the material was not taken off the website. In another case, Super Cassettes Industries Limited (Super Cassettes Industries Limited v. YouTube & Google, 2007) the claim was made by super cassettes industries where they stated that the business model of YouTube allows and encourages the profits that rise by using the copyrighted work uploaded on the website. As a result, an order was passed against yahoo where an injunction was passed restraining the use of music without a licence. Without paying the royalties, the same is carried out. In this instance, Google and YouTube were the targets of the decree.

According to the pattern of the earlier cases, strict liability was used to hold the service provider accountable at first, without taking into account their knowledge or intent. However, as time passed, the system changed, and now understanding and meaning are taken into account when holding service providers accountable.

The Copyright Act 1957 and the Information Technology Act 2000 provide legal protection for computer software in India (Raghav and Dewani, 2020). The Copyright Act protects computer programmes because they are recognized as protected works. The IT Act of 2000 stipulates that altering a computer program's "source code" is punishable (Suganya and Prema, 2021). On the other hand, this protection is limited to source codes "which are required to be retained or maintained under the law that is now in existence." Because of this, the "source code" of computer programmes that government organizations utilize is the only kind of code that the IT Act safeguards. The "source code" of private persons' programmes is not protected.

According to Section 13 (1) (a) of the Indian Copyright Act of 1957, which states that original literary, dramatic, musical, and creative works in India should be protected by copyright, "Databases" are protected as "literary works." (Suganya and Prema, 2021). As was previously established, computer programmes, tables, and compilations that comprise computer databases are considered literary works under the Copyright Act.

Patent Issues

A software patent is a sort of utility patent that covers any computer performance realized via the use of a computer programme. Because it grants the owner a monopoly over his creation and allows him to exploit it for some time at the expense of everyone else, a patent is a particularly desired kind of intellectual property. Of course, rules are in place to ensure the monopoly is not abused.

Whether or not software developments should be eligible for patent protection has been and will likely continue to be controversial. Computer programmes are not regarded as innovations in and of themselves, according to the European Patent Convention (EPC), to which the United Kingdom and another 30 countries are parties (Vindele, L., & Cane, R. (2022). This presents a unique challenge for intellectual property protection. In India, obtaining a patent requires submitting a patent application following the 1970 Patent Act, the controller of patents (Ramanna, 2002). The TRIPS agreement forbids the exclusion of software from patentability in general. In India, it is not possible to patent software or digital products. In many other countries throughout the globe, they may, however, be copyrighted (Adelman & Baldia, 1996). Computer programmes are excluded from patents, which is a global trend. However, it wasn't entirely apparent if copyrights protected computer programmes when the present UK Patent Act was passed in 1977 (Merges, 2007); copyright is now regarded as the ideal vehicle for protecting computer programmes. Computer programmes were not typically patented per se even before the 1977 Act (Merges, 2007). Despite this, there have been instances in both the United Kingdom (UK) and the United States of America (USA) in which patents have been granted for aspects of computer programming. These patents typically cover computer programming components of equipment or steps in an industrial process.

Trademark Issues

Trademark infringement and misleading use of marks or names that suggest a connection between the trademark owner or the business of that proprietor and the user of such a mark or name when such a connection does not exist are crimes that may be committed without fear of repercussion due to the nature of conducting business online, where a website may be shut down without warning and tracing the operators is difficult. Because of this, trademark infringement and misleading use of marks or names are crimes that may be committed without fear of repercussion. The exact grounds for objection, such as whether it includes actual trademark infringement, passing off, employing another person's name or mark as a domain name, or misappropriating well-known marks, vary from case to case depending on the particulars of the situation.

One of cyberspace's most important problems with intellectual property violations is trademark infringement. According to the ruling in the Yahoo case (Yahoo.com V. Akash Arora, 1999), a domain name serves the same purpose as a trademark and is not just an address. It is thus entitled to the same level of protection as a trademark. The Trade Mark Act of 1999's Section 28 gives trademark owners the right to use their marks and the ability to sue for violating that right and get an injunction, damages, and earnings accounting.

Domain names are the fundamental problem with trademarks on the Internet (Yahoo.com V. Akash Arora, 1999). The Court determined that domain names fulfil the role of a trademark in Mc Gees Case (Cardservice International Inc. v. Mc Gee, 1997). A domain name is a name that appears in the address of your website and is used to find the home page (Davis et al., 1996). A business or organization that employs a specific trademark is likely to include that trademark in its domain name. For instance, a reputable global firm that deals with computers uses the trademark Compaq. As a result, their internet address, "www.compaq.com," uses this name. Another organization may often utilize a well-known trademark on its website to capitalize on the brand. This kind of behaviour, called "cybersquatting," constitutes trademark infringement. In numerous nations, including the USA, UK, Canada, France, and Italy, cybersquatting has been recognized as illegal conduct (Wahdani, 2021). In reality, courts in Italy, where the legal discussion around trademarks and domain names is continuously evolving.

'Cyber squatters' cause the domain name dispute by registering a domain with a trademarked word on purpose phrases, a business name, a brand name, etc. There were several litigations over domain names, such as the "Marks & In Spencer's case (Marks & Spencer's V. One-in-A Million, 1998), sometimes known as the "Yahoo case (Yahoo.com V. Akash Arora, 1999)," any ill-faith trademark registration by online squatters to steal. The use of well-known trademarks for benefit has been rigorously prohibited, and the trademark owner now owns the mark. Domain names now have the same level of security as before given to Trademarks under Indian trademark law by ICANN Policy. Resolving disputes over domain names has been crucial in settling these domain name conflicts.

INFORMATION TECHNOLOGY LAW AND DIGITAL BUSINESS

Computers have evolved rapidly in the contemporary period because of the creation of neural networks, advancements in nanotechnology, and the ability of computers to carry out up to a billion operations in a single second. These days, computers are utilized for almost everything, and as a direct consequence, the number of crimes committed online has substantially increased.

The Information Technology Act of 2000 was passed in India after the United Nations General Assembly passed Resolution A/RES/51/162 on January 30, 1997. This resolution instructed the United Nations Commission on International Trade Law to draught a model law on electronic commerce, which India subsequently adopted (Kalia et al., 2016)

Corporate Liability

A firm is a distinct legal entity from its shareholders or members. The legal rule guides a company's responsibility if the Act's rules are broken by Section 85 of the Information Technology Act 2000 (Sumanjeet, 2010). Besides a business or other persons, a corporate body is considered a company under section 85. The word "director" in this section also includes a firm's partner. The Information Technology (Amendment) Act 2008 was passed to bring the current legislation into accordance with the United Nations Commission on International Trade Law's Model Law on Electronic Signatures (Asawat, 2010).

The only provision of the IT Act that dealt with data protection was section 43 (Wilson, 2010), which imposed civil penalties only in the event that certain acts were carried out without the permission of the computer's owner or the person in charge of the computer systems. This was the only provision that dealt with data protection. These acts included but were not limited to gaining access to a computer or computer system without permission; (ii) downloading or copying data that was stored in a computer or computer system; (iii) introducing computer viruses; (iv) causing damage to computers and data stored therein; (v) denying service to others, etc (Nappinai, 2010). This amendment act has made it mandatory for corporate entities to comply with these requirements by adding Section 43A, which requires corporate entities to handle sensitive personal information in a computer resource to ensure the employment of security practices and that secrecy is maintained. In addition, this section stipulates that corporate entities must maintain the confidentiality of the information (Seth, 2010).

Intermediary Liability

India is one of the economies with the quickest growth rates, and its e-commerce sector is expanding. The Indian e-commerce industry is anticipated to increase by $111.40 billion by 2025 (Ashalakshmi, 2022). By 2030, it's predicted to be $350 billion. (Kumar & Prasad 2022). This figure will rise even more when more residents sign up for internet access thanks to the "Digital India Programme."

E-commerce platforms benefit from safe harbour protection (also known as "intermediary protection") for effective operation and rapid company growth. By acting as an "intermediary" and facilitating the transaction between buyers and sellers, these marketplaces are protected from any responsibility that may result from their role as such. Consumers gain without a doubt from the expanding e-commerce business.

A "person who receives, stores, or transmits a message on behalf of another person or performs any service about such communication" is defined as an "intermediary"(IT Act 2008) under Section 2(1)(w) of the IT Act. This definition applies to any person who does any of these things. This includes network and internet suppliers, web hosting services, search engines, online marketplaces, online auction sites, and cyber cafés.

There is an explicit provision about the service provider's obligation in the event of a violation of the IT Act. Before the modification, section 79 exclusively discussed the service provider's release of the obligation under the current legislation (Bhattacharya & Roy, 2013). The 2008 modification is now relevant to all laws, including the Copyright Act. Section 79 of the IT Act outlines India's safe harbour protection strategy. The protection helps business owners develop and thrive in the market quickly with little spending on compliance or legal expenses. The framework exempts from responsibility a third party's information, data, or communication link made accessible or hosted by an intermediary (Prakash et al., 2021). The protection is subject to the requirement that the intermediary's role is restricted to granting access to a communication system used to transmit, temporarily store, or host information made accessible by third parties.

Additionally, the intermediate shouldn't start the broadcast or choose the recipient. Additionally, selecting or altering the transmission's information is not permitted. According to Section 79(2)(c), the intermediary must use reasonable diligence while performing his obligations under this Act and any further rules that the Central Government may establish (Prakash et al., 2021).

Additionally, if the intermediary assisted, encouraged, threatened, promised, or otherwise persuaded the conduct of the illicit Act, this protection will not be accessible. The exemption also does not apply if the intermediary fails to remove or disable access to any information, data, or communication link located in or connected to a computer resource controlled by the intermediary after becoming aware of actual knowledge or after being alerted by the appropriate Government or its agency that the information, data, or communication link is being used to commit the unlawful Activity.

E-COMMERCE PLATFORMS REGULATION

A marketplace model of e-commerce is an information technology platform that allows transactions between a buyer and a vendor. The e-commerce business controls the inventory of items and services in an inventory-based strategy and sells them directly to customers (direct selling model).

The Foreign Direct Investment in E-Commerce (or "the FDI Rules") 2016 and 2018 guidelines encompass marketplace and inventory-based e-commerce platforms (Soni, 2019). This categorization is under the Consumer Protection (E-Commerce) Rules, 2020 (Chawla & Kumar, 2021).

According to the RBI FDI Guidelines 2018, markets with inventory will be classified as inventory-based markets. E-commerce platforms could assist merchants with order fulfilment, shipping, warehousing, contact centre support, payment collection, and other services. They might also make it possible for purchases to be made in a manner that conforms with Reserve Bank of India rules. Under these guidelines, a marketplace company may continue to operate as a "passive participant" while offering additional services.

Recently, In the case of Amway India Enterprises (Amway India Enterprises (P) Ltd. v. IMG Technologies (P) Ltd., 2019), the Delhi High Court concluded that the Louboutin decision should be followed and that the FDI Guidelines should be considered after evaluating the "actual purpose" of the e-commerce platform. As a result, the marketplace-based approach will likewise be seen as an "active participant" in this parallel.

This was appealed in the case of Amazon Seller Services (Amazon Seller Services pvt. Ltd. v. Amway India Enterprises pvt. Ltd, 2019), The Delhi High Court Division Bench overturned its prior ruling because the Court misconstrued Section 79 of the IT Act. According to the Court, the statute did not distinguish between active and passive intermediaries for safe harbour protection, overturning Louboutin's maxim.

Although the e-commerce platform and its safe harbour status are still in question, this verdict has temporarily clarified the situation. The IT Act's framework, which deems e-commerce platforms (just like other platforms) to be an intermediary, is inconsistent with the assessment of intermediary protection at the trial stage. The trial cannot decide whether the platform is an intermediary, but it may conclude that it is not one and cannot make any claims of protection.

DIGITAL BUSINESS AND DATA PROTECTION

Currently, there is no explicit regulation protecting data protection or privacy in India (Burman, 2020). A variety of rules outlined in Section 43A of the Information Technology Act must be followed by any organization that gathers, maintains, or processes personally identifiable information. Under Section 43A, a body corporate is liable for compensating anybody who suffers injury due to the body corporate's negligence in upholding basic security precautions (Srinivas & Biswas, 2012). Any organization that collects, stores or processes personally identifiable information must comply with several requirements in Section 43A of the Information Technology Act (Verma, 2014). According to Section 43A, a body corporate is responsible for paying damages to any person who suffers harm due to the body corporate's carelessness in adhering to fundamental security measures (Kessler et al., 2014).

Section 72A of the IT Act makes it a crime to disclose information knowingly and willingly in violation of a legal contract. It states that anyone, including an intermediary, who reveals any material containing personal information about another person without that person's consent or in violation of a lawful contract while performing services under a legal agreement with the intent to cause or knowing that he is likely to cause wrongful loss or wrongful gain faces a year in prison.

Additionally, the terms "Privacy" are used in Sections 66E and 72 of the IT Act 2000. However, these two sections have nothing to do with data protection and deal with various offences that fall within the categories of "Obscenity" and "Responsibility of Police and Certifying Authorities."

According to Section 66E, violating someone's privacy by taking, sharing, or sending pictures of their private parts is punishable by up to three years in jail and a fine of up to 2,000,000.

DIGITAL BUSINESS GOVERNANCE AND COMPLIANCE

The Government published the Information Technology (Intermediaries Guidelines) Rules, 2021 in February 2021 to replace the Information Technology Rules, 2011 (hence referred to as "the IT Rules") (Shankar & Ahmad, 2021). Most regulations only apply to media organizations and social media intermediaries; however, Rule 3 outlines the due diligence that all intermediaries must do. The intermediary must make the terms and conditions, privacy statement, and user agreement available on its platform for anybody to access or utilize its computer resource. The users should be warned not to disclose any information violating these guidelines' patent, trademark, copyright, or other intellectual rights (Kumar & Jha, 2022). Data security measures, information retention, and knowledge transfer to authorized offices within 72 hours of receiving the order are other procedural compliances. Additionally, intermediaries must designate a grievance officer and provide a grievance redressal procedure (Kumar & Jha, 2022). Through this, the user or a victim may report a violation of this rule's requirements or any other issues involving the computer resources that are made accessible by it.

Although all companies that meet Section 2(1)(w) are "intermediaries," not all of them are eligible for the exemption under Section 79 of the IT Act.

There hasn't been a clear and consistent judicial view of e-commerce and safe harbour protection. The broad category of "e-commerce" includes a variety of players, from those that give a platform for sellers to submit their material without alteration to those who choose the sellers, shipping and packing services, etc. The Delhi High Court ruled in Christian Louboutin v. Nakul Bajaj (Christian Louboutin SAS v Nakul Bajaj, 2018) that a platform's ability to request an exemption under Section 79 depends on the operator's active or passive position. Regarding this, the Court explained 21 actions that might establish whether an e-commerce platform qualifies as an intermediary under Section 2(1)(w) of the IT Act. These activities include offering substantial discounts, ensuring product quality, registering members once they pay membership dues, providing members with specialized discounts, etc. When the platform's business involves many of the above elements, it will pass the threshold from being an "intermediary" to an "active participant." Using this justification, the Court determined that a platform cannot use Section 79 of the IT Act's intermediary protection after ceasing to serve as an intermediary.

As per Section 79, An intermediary is not responsible for any third-party content that is hosted or made available through such intermediary, as long as the following conditions are met:

- the violation is committed without the intermediary's knowledge;
- the intermediary exercises due care and complies with other regulations established by the Government.

Intermediary Guidelines

The diligence procedure intermediaries must follow to be eligible for the Section 79 exemption is set down in the 2011 Intermediary Rules, as amended in 2021 (Information Technology (Intermediary Guidelines and Digital Media Ethics Code) Rules, 2021). An intermediary must adhere to various regulations, including the duty to alert users of the computer resource not to submit any information that is, among other things, dangerous, obscene, or defamatory. Additionally, it cannot violate any trademark, copyright, patent, or other intellectual rights. The intermediary must "act" within 36 hours and, if necessary, cooperate with the owner or user of the information to remove it if it violates the rules against publishing the previously listed illegal material. The intermediary must adhere entirely to "the Act's" requirements and any other current legislation (Ashwini, 2022).

Reasonable Security Practices

Under Section 87(2)(ob) of the Information Technology Act, 2008, the Central Government has been given the authority to establish regulations governing appropriate security practices and procedures, as well as sensitive personal data or information that falls under the purview of Section 43A.

As a result, the Ministry of Communications and Information Technology came up with the Information Technology (Reasonable Security Practices and Procedures and Sensitive Personal Data or Information) (IT Rules) Rules10, which were put into force on April 11, 2011. (Department of Information Technology, 2011).

These laws established the "acceptable security policies and processes" that businesses must adhere to when working with customers' personal information.

A corporate body must follow the intermediaries' guidelines' acceptable security standards and procedures. As was already mentioned, it is essential to keep in mind that, under the explanation appended to Section 43 A, a body corporate receiving the information is only required to adhere to the IT Rules' standards in the absence of a written agreement between the parties or a current law that outlines security practises and procedures intended to protect such information from unauthorized access, damages, use, modification, and disclosure. One standard listed in this law that a business entity may follow is the International Standard IS/ISO/IEC 27001 on "Information Technology - Security Techniques - Information Security Management System - Requirements.".

CONSUMER PROTECTION

The Consumer Protection Act, 2019 (the "CPA") was enacted to expeditiously resolve consumer disputes and safeguard Indian consumers' rights against unlawful business activities and unfair trade practices. It repealed a three-decade-old antiquated statute and replaced it with one that covers current and modern business methods, such as selling products and services online or via e-commerce, direct selling, multi-level marketing, teleshopping, etc., in addition to the conventional techniques prevalent in the consumer market today (Parimala, S., & Ramachandran, M. 2022). On July 23, 2020, the Ministry of Consumer Affairs issued a statement announcing the Consumer Protection (E-Commerce) Rules, 2020, Food and Public Distribution to protect customers from deceptive or unethical business activities and respond to consumers' concerns (Saha & Khanna, 2021). The E-commerce Rules' primary objective is to regulate the Indian E-commerce sector and safeguard customers from corrupt business activities on these platforms. National governments, consumer advocacy organizations, and other parties have noticed how crucial consumer protection is in the service sector. These regulations primarily address the responsibilities and liabilities of eCommerce businesses that market and sell goods and services to clients online. All electronic merchants (e-tailers) registered in India or abroad who sell goods and services to Indian clients will be subject to the legislation. The new regulations allow the federal Government to step in and stop deceptive tactics in direct marketing and online commerce. They require online retailers to provide easy returns, deal with customer complaints, and forbid discrimination against firms on their platforms.

The following guidelines must be followed by any marketplace e-commerce business seeking to be free from liability for any information, data, or communication link made available or accelerated by it under paragraph (1) of section 79 of the Information Technology Act of 2001:

- a pledge by the vendors to keep the items and services they represent both online and when they are delivered to consumers accurate and of high quality;
- Marketplace e-commerce companies are required to keep records of information about vendors on their online platform, such as the name of the company, whether it is registered or not, the location of the business, a customer service number, any ratings or other aggregated comments about the vendor, and any other data required to help customers make well-informed pre-purchase decisions.
- The marketplace firm must also provide the seller's information, including the primary location of its headquarters and branches, upon the customer's request.
- Create a method for customers to track the status of their complaint submission.
- Marketplace e-commerce entities should provide critical terms and conditions governing their relationship with sellers on their platform and a description of any differentiated treatment it gives or may give between goods or services or sellers of the same category.
- Maintain information on the return, refund, exchange, and shipping, as well as payment methods and a system for resolving customer complaints.

CONCLUSION

Industry 4.0's digital business sector offers tremendous commercial potential. Legislators, judges, and legal counsel will need to address new legal issues that are brought about by these advancements. The legal debates around these issues are just getting started, and jurisdiction is still spotty at best. Industry 4.0 may have a significant impact on many legal areas, but it is unclear when and how much national and international legislators will take action—particularly in light of liability and regulatory concerns as well as data ownership difficulties.

With the expansion of digital business industry management of a companies must be accountable for data protection and IT security. The legal implications of the digital transformation of processes and the introduction of new business models must be considered from the beginning, in addition to the organisational and technological effects. Due to the fact that data analytics will establish a relationship with the individual, the protection of personal data will present new issues. Each entity need their consent before collecting data from their customers .The fact that data protection and IT security regulations vary from nation to nation further complicates matters.

REFERENCES

Adelman, M. J., & Baldia, S. (1996). Prospects and limits of the patent provision in the TRIPs Agreement: The case of India. *Vand. J. Transnat'l L.*, *29*, 507.

Ahmad, F. (2008). *Cyber Law in India*. Academic Press.

Ali, A. H. S., Saidin, O., Roisah, K., & Ediwarman, E. (2021). *Liability of Internet Intermediaries in Copyright Infringement: Comparison between the United States and India*. Academic Press.

Amazon Seller Services Pvt Ltd vs Modicare Ltd & Ors (2020) FAO(OS) 133/2019

Amway India Enterprises (P) Ltd v 1MG Technologies (P) Ltd, 2019 SCC OnLine Del 9061: (2019) 260 DLT 690 ¶ 308.

Aneez, Z. T., Neyazi, A., Kalogeropoulos, A., & Nielsen, R. K. (2019). *India digital news report*. Available at: https://ora.ox.ac.uk/catalog/uuid:9c884a81-204e-415c-a87c-6818ac88442e/download_file?file_format=application%2Fpdf&safe_filename=India_DNR_FINAL.pdf

Asawat, V. (2010). Information Technology (Amendment) Act, 2008: A New Vision through a New Change. *Available at SSRN 1680152*.

Ashalakshmi, R. K. (2022). *A Study on the growth of E-commerce during COVID-19 in India*. Available at: http://103.78.17.158:1443/jspui/handle/123456789/875

Ashwini, S. (2022) *Social Media Platform Regulation in India–A Special Reference to The Information Technology (Intermediary Guidelines and Digital Media Ethics Code) Rules, 2021*. Available at: https://www.nomos-elibrary.de/10.5771/9783748929789.pdf#page=215

Bhattacharya, D., & Roy, S. (2013). Contributory Liability Vis-a-Vis Strict Liability: Analyzing World Trends in ISP Liability Regime with Respect to the Indian Position. *GNLU L. Rev.*, *4*, 75.

Burman, A. (2020). *Will India's proposed data protection law protect privacy and promote growth?* Carnegie Endowment for International Peace. Available at: https://www.sciencedirect.com/science/article/pii/S0267364908001337?casa_token=9qC67i5bIVYAAAAA:NuikV0iS_E06kj7gn_Jzgs3G7Z0iu-YttxjeWkY_4HEwXwi0pda2mFnhDERcJ3FmAUdv2CeY

Cardservice Intern., Inc. v. McGee (1997), 950 F. Supp. 737 (E.D.Va. Jan. 16, 1997)

Chawla, N., & Kumar, B. (2021). E-commerce and consumer protection in India: The emerging trend. *Journal of Business Ethics*, 1–24. https://link.springer.com/article/10.1007/s10551-021-04884-3

Christian Louboutin SAS v Nakul Bajaj, (2018) SCC OnLine Del 12215: (2018) 76 PTC 508.

Cockfield, A. J. (1999). Balancing National Interests in the Taxation of Electronic Commerce Business Profits. *Tul. L. Rev.*, *74*, 133.

Companies Act 2013

Copyright Act 1957

CS (OS) No. 2192/2007, Available at https://ebtc.eu/index.php/services/184-ipr/ipr-landmark-cases/183-landmark-cases-copyright

CS(OS) 1124/2008, Available at http://courtnic.nic.in/dhcorder/dhcqrydisp_O.asp?pn=95892&yr=2008

Davis, C., Vixie, P., Goodwin, T., & Dickinson, I. (1996). *A means for expressing location information in the domain name system* (No. rfc1876). Academic Press.

Department of Industrial Policy and Promotion. (2016). *('DIPP'), Press Note No. 3*. Series.

Foreign Exchange Management Act, 1999

Gupta, D. (2020). Digital Platforms and E-Commerce in India–Challenges and Opportunities. *Available at SSRN 3577285.*

Information Technology Act 2000

Information Technology (Intermediary Guidelines and Digital Media Ethics Code) Rules 2021, Notification no. G.S.R. 139(E), Available at: https://mib.gov.in/sites/default/files/IT%28Intermediary%20Guidelines%20and%20Digital%20Media%20Ethics%20Code%29%20Rules%2C%202021%20English.pdf

Jain, A. K., Sahoo, S. R., & Kaubiyal, J. (2021). Online social networks security and privacy: Comprehensive review and analysis. *Complex & Intelligent Systems*, *7*(5), 2157–2177.

Kalia, P., Arora, R., & Law, P. (2016). Information Technology Act in India: e-Commerce value chain analysis. *NTUT Journal of Intellectual Property Law and Management*, *5*(2), 55–97.

Kessler, D. J., Ross, S., & Hickok, E. (2014). A Comparative Analysis of Indian Privacy Law and the Asia-Pacific Economic Cooperation Cross-Border Privacy Rules. *Nat'l L. Sch. India Rev.*, *26*, 31.

Kumar, A., & Jha, A. (2022). Information Technology Rules, 2021 of India in dock! A Critical evaluation of the Ã¢ Â Â Guidelines for Intermediaries and Digital Media Ethics Code. *Global Media Journal*, *20*(48), 1–9.

Kumar, V. V., & Prasad, N. C. (2022). E-Commerce: Problems and Prospects. *Specialusis Ugdymas*, *1*(43), 1621-1628. Available at: https://www.sumc.lt/index.php/se/article/view/183

Kundu, I. (2021). The Copyright System Is Unable to Effectively Respond to the Challenges Posed by Digitalization and the Internet. *Supremo Amicus*, *27*, 201. Available at: https://www.researchgate.net/profile/Irina-Atanasova-3/publication/339077032_COPYRIGHT_INFRINGEMENT_IN_DIGITAL_ENVIRONMENT/links/5e3c1f89458515072d838a02/COPYRIGHT-INFRINGEMENT-IN-DIGITAL-ENVIRONMENT.pdf

Marks & Spencer's V. One-in-A Million (1998) FSR 265

Merges, R. P. (2007). Software and patent scope: Report from the middle innings. *Texas Law Review*, *85*(7), 1627–1676.

Mills, A. J., & Plangger, K. (2015). Social media strategy for online service brands. *Service Industries Journal*, *35*(10), 521–536.

Mohan, G., & Mini, S. (2021). *The Various issues in Cyberspace that are not Addressed by the copyright Laws, from the Indian perspective.* Available at: http://14.139.185.167:8080/jspui/bit-stream/123456789/448/1/LLM_0220023_CAL.pdf

Nappinai, N. S. (2010). Cyber Crime Law in India: Has Law kept pace with emerging trends? An empirical study. *Journal of International Commercial Law and Technology, 5*(1). Available at: https://media.neliti.com/media/publications/28731-EN-cyber-crime-law-in-india-has-law-kept-pace-with-emerging-trends-an-empirical-stu.pdf

Parimala, S., & Ramachandran, M. (2022, May). A study on E-consumer awareness towards E-commerce Consumer Protection Act, 2019. In AIP Conference Proceedings: Vol. 2393. *No. 1* (p. 020110). AIP Publishing LLC.

Patent Act Trademark Act 1999

Playboy Enterprises, Inc. v. Frena (1993) 839 F. Supp. 1552 M.D. Fla.

Prakash, G. A., Sundaram, A., & Sreeya, B. (2021). Online exploitation of children and the role of intermediaries: An Indian legislative and policy perspective. *International Review of Law Computers & Technology*, 1–22.

Raghav, M., & Dewani, N. D. (2020). Intellectual Property Rights Protection in Cyberspace: An Indian Perspective. In *Impact of Digital Transformation on Security Policies and Standards* (pp. 169-182). IGI Global. Available at: https://www.igi-global.com/chapter/intellectual-property-rights-protection-in-cyberspace/251954

Ramanna, A. (2002). Policy Implications of India's Patent Reforms: Patent Applications in the Post-1995 Era. *Economic and Political Weekly*, 2065–2075.

Saha, A., & Khanna, S. R. (2021). Evolution of consumer courts in India: The Consumers Protection Act 2019 and emerging themes of consumer jurisprudence. *IJCLP*, *9*, 115.

Sega Enters. v MAPHIA (1996) 948 F.Supp. 923, 41 (1705) USPQ2d

Seth, K. (2010). IT Act 2000 vs 2008-Implementation, Challenges, and the Role of Adjudicating Officers. *National Seminar on Enforcement of Cyberlaw*. Available at: https://www.sethassociates.com/wp-content/uploads/2011/07/IT-Act-2000-vs-20083.pdf

Shalika, C. (2019). Online Copyright Infringement and the Liability of Internet Service Providers. *Available at SSRN 3464140*.

Shankar, R., & Ahmad, T. (2021). Information Technology Laws: Mapping the Evolution and Impact of Social Media Regulation in India. *DESIDOC Journal of Library and Information Technology*, *41*(4).

Shushaanth, S., & Prakash, G. A. (2018). A Study on Copyright Infringement in Cyberspace with Special Reference to the Liability of the Internet Service Provider for Infringement. *International Journal of Pure and Applied Mathematics*, *119*(17), 1503–1516. https://papers.ssrn.com/sol3/papers.cfm?abstract_id=3553588

Soni, S. (2019). Navigating E-Commerce Marketplace in India: A Study of Impact from Indian Regulations. *Available at SSRN 3435488.*

Srinivas, N., & Biswas, A. (2012). Protecting patient information in India: Data privacy law and its challenges. *NUJS L. Rev.*, *5*, 411.

Suganya, S., & Prema, E. (2021). Authorship of Copyrightable Works Created by Artificial Intelligence. *IUP Law Review, 11*(1). Available at: https://papers.ssrn.com/sol3/papers.cfm?abstract_id=3829579

Sumanjeet, D. (2010). The state of e-commerce laws in India: A review of Information Technology Act. *International Journal of Law and Management*, *52*(4), 265–282.

the Consumer Protection (E-Commerce) Rules, 2020

The Information Technology. (2011). *reasonable Security Practices And Procedures And Sensitive Personal Data Or Information*. Rules.

The Information Technology (Amendment) Act 2008.

Verma, A. (2014). Data protection law in India: A business perspective. *Journal of Commerce & Accounting Research*, *3*(1).

Vindele, L., & Cane, R. (2022). The role of intellectual property rights in the technological age. *Acta Prosperitatis*, 183. Available at: https://www.turiba.lv/storage/files/ap-13-makets-www_1.pdf#page=177

Wahdani, F. (2021). The legal character of domain names' cybersquatting. *Law, Society & Organisations*, *10*(1), 23-41. Available at: https://dea.lib.unideb.hu/dea/bitstream/handle/2437/326329/FILE_UP_5_LSO_10_2.pdf?sequence=1

Wilson, B. (2010). Data Privacy in India: The Information Technology Act. *Available at SSRN 3323479.*

Yahoo.com V. Akash Arora (1999) PTC (19) 201

ADDITIONAL READING

Brunel, A., & Liang, M. (1997). Trademark Troubles with Internet Domain Names and Commercial Online Service Screen Names: Roadrunning Right Into the Frying Pan. *International Journal of Law and Information Technology*, *5*(1), 1–27. doi:10.1093/ijlit/5.1.1

Rattan, J. (2011). *Cyber Law* (1st ed.). Bharat Law House.

Rohas, N. (2008). *Cyber Crime and Corporate Liability*. Wolter Kluwers India.

Chapter 8
Information Security Governance:
Need of the Hour

Sneha Verma
Banaras Hindu University, India

ABSTRACT

In today's IT-regulated era, data is nothing less than money. It is rightly said that a person who has data can become a millionaire. That is the power of data. For business organisations, information and business-related data is like blood. If there is any shortage or leakage, it could risk the life of the business. The business information has become a part of the valuable assets of the company. Thus, information security should be given high importance in the corporate governance system of the company. For this purpose, the role of the management of the company comes into focus. The management and the board of directors work towards the success of their company; thus, it is their sole responsibility to protect the valuable assets including the confidential business information. The board needs to make decisions regarding corporate governance by keeping the information security in consideration. Thus, information security governance is the need of the hour. The present chapter focuses on the importance of the information security governance in today's information-driven world.

INTRODUCTION

Information Security Governance is the new term that keeps popping up in the minds of the Boards and the management of the companies. Information security governance can be said as the system which involves the direction and control of IT security in an organisation. The growing vulnerability of cyber-risk has been the highlighted factor in almost all the surveys of information security. The data of the company has become one of the most critical assets and its protection is the sole responsibility of the company's management. Data, if leaked can prove to be detrimental for the survival of the company. Thus, there is a strong need to devise such a system which can protect and manage data as well as the business organisation.

DOI: 10.4018/978-1-6684-5827-3.ch008

Business organisations are bound to follow the principles of Corporate Governance as per the law of the nation. Corporate Governance sets out the ways and procedures by which business organisations are said to be directed and controlled. It defines those who are in power and those who are accountable in the organisation. Information security governance comes under the ambit of corporate governance. Governance is different from management. Management means taking those decisions which minimises risks; governance is concerned with as to who has the power to take those decisions. Information security governance is a part and parcel of Corporate Governance and can be viewed as the subset of it. Thus, information security governance is defined as the process as to how a company can meet the industry standards for cyber security. In other words, it refers to taking decisions for implementation of such rules and procedures that protects the information of the company. The term 'Information Security Governance' portrays how an organization's executive management deal with security (Posthumus & Solms, 2004). 'An information security programme is a risk mitigation method like other control and governance actions and should therefore clearly fit into overall enterprise governance.'

Information Security Governance: Guidance for Boards of Directors and Executive Management

The very main purpose of information security includes the protection of the confidential information of companies and to preserve the integrity of all the related stakeholders. It also includes preserving the authenticity of data and ensuring that it is in its most reliable form. The major general governance areas can be described as follows:

- Govern the operations of the business and preserve its critical assets
- Protect the market share of the organisation and also its stock price
- Supervise the conduct of the employees of the organisation
- Safeguard the reputation of the organization
- Make sure that compliance requirements as set out in the regulating laws are met and properly adhered to.

Objectives

1. To understand the meaning of information security governance.
2. To study the relationship between information security governance and long-term survival of companies.

Research Methodology

The present study is descriptive in nature. For that purpose, secondary data has been collected from different sources such as online newspapers, articles and journals.

LITERATURE REVIEW

Business organisations are increasingly becoming dependent on Information Technology for almost all of their activities. Solms and Strous (2003) in their chapter titled *INFORMATION SECURITY: A COR-PORATE GOVERNANCE ISSUE* highlighted the fact that information is indispensable for any business organisation. Therefore, it must be protected from all kinds of risks. This is the reason why security of information is the ultimate soul responsibility of the board of directors and management and thus, they must be held responsible and accountable for it. Also, there must be a sense of coordination between the internal and external specialists (in case of information security) working for the organisation. Identifying the role that information security plays, Von Solms and Von Solms (2005) in their paper titled *From information security to... business security?* found out that there is a need to properly understand how important information security is for the overall health of a business organisation. Companies have recently realised the business impact of information security and also the risks associated with not properly addressing it. Also, Von Solms (2006) in his research paper titled *Information Security- The Fourth Wave* concluded that Information security has become a part and parcel of a good Corporate Governance system. Various models have been developed keeping in mind the importance of information security governance. Von Solms and Von Solms (2006) in their paper titled *Information Security Governance: A model based on the Direct-Control Cycle* highlighted that all the levels of business activities in a company are related to Information Security Governance. The model as suggested by the author indicates a 3-level steps which includes planning of directives and principles as to what should be done in the context of information security governance; proper execution of those principles; and regular monitoring of whether the principles are properly executed or not. Again, Von Solms and Von Solms (2006) in their research papers titled *Information security governance: Due care* found out that it is the responsibility of the Board members to take due care of the most critical asset of the business organisation, i.e., information. They must ensure that all the critical assets are properly identified and protected as well so as to mitigate the negative effects that may arise out of the possible cyber-risk.

Aguilar (2014) in his paper titled *Boards of Directors, Corporate Governance and Cyber- Risks: Sharpening the Focus* concluded that good corporate governance is very significant for the survival of the organisation. The Board members perform this role very actively and work towards the interest of the stakeholders. Eugen and Petrut (2018) in their papers titled *Exploring the New Era of Cyber security Governance* highlighted the fact that ignorance of information security can adversely affect the business organisations. Fazlida and Said (2015) in their research paper titled "Information Security: Risk, Governance and Implementation Setback" found out that information security should be integrated with the business organisation's corporate governance framework keeping in mind the growing risk of information security. Also, good information security governance shows how much the business organisation (especially the banks and financial institutions) is serious towards protecting its critical assets. The Board of Directors ought to be more vigilant towards information security and must place more attention on it. Bahl and Wali (2014) in their research paper titled *Perceived significance of information security governance to predict the information security service quality in software service industry- An empirical analysis* concluded that if the objective of a business enterprise is to provide customer satisfaction and create trust and loyalty in the stakeholders then they must include information security governance in the corporate governance framework of the organisation. This will help in better understanding of customer needs and wants and thus providing better products/ or services as per customers' expectations.

This will also help in bridging any kind of gap between customers' expectations and actual delivery of products/ or services.

Role of Board of Directors in Information Security

Business corporations around the globe are managed and overlooked by the members of the Board and the top-level management team. The basic responsibility of a corporate director is to work towards the interests of the shareholders (i.e., owners of the company). Along with this basic responsibility, comes other responsibilities too such as the directors should be loyal towards the corporation and should carry out their responsibilities with care. In the case of *Indian States Bank Ltd. v Sardar Singh*, the court gave the judgement that the appointment of the Company Directors should be made in strict compliance with the Companies Act, 2013, and that the management of the company should be in responsible hands. Thus, the management is answerable and accountable to the true owners of the company, i.e., the shareholders/or stakeholders. The key functions of BODs in Corporate Governance can be listed as follows:

- Plan out the vision and mission of the company keeping in mind its current and future business operations.
- Determine the company goals and company policies.
- Decide and review the business strategies from time to time.
- Ensure proper delegation of authority and also monitor timely implementation of business plans and policies.
- Focus on the interests of the stakeholders and ensure that an effective communication bridge is maintained between management and stakeholders.
- Review the corporate governance practice of the company and make necessary amendments as and when required.

Apart from these duties, the top-level management people are also responsible for keeping the information asset of the company safely and securely. It is their sole responsibility to take decisions that serve the very purpose of the corporation and implement such decisions. There is a strong need for the Board members to understand and evaluate why information security needs to be governed. There are many reasons for that such as the risks and threats connected to information breach could have a significant impact on the organisation or the management has to develop a sense of trust among all the stakeholders and for that purpose also, information security has to be governed properly. Moreover, the reason that the top-level management is responsible for information security governance is that when any senior personnel of a company takes responsibility for something, all other employees working in the organisation will eventually follow them and act accordingly. In case of any breach of security, it is the Board of Directors who is ultimately held responsible. To avoid such circumstances, the Board has to act with due diligence and care in identifying the underlying risks, find out the best system of control and management, implement it accordingly and monitor it on a regular basis to find out the discrepancies, if any.

There have been many cases of cyber-attacks in recent times. Companies of different shapes and sizes fear a constant threat of cyber-attacks. India was among the top three nations that witnessed the most server access and ransom ware attacks in 2021. According to a report of CERT-In (*The Indian Computer Emergency Response Team*), a total number of 17,560; 24,768; 26,121 and 25,870 Indian websites were hacked during the years 2018, 2019, 2020 and 2021 respectively (as can be seen in Figure 1). The most recent case of cyber-attack/data breach is of Domino's India. In the month of May, 2021, there was a huge leak of customer data. It included full details of around 18 crores customers who had placed orders on their web portal either through mobiles or computer systems, including their names, addresses, delivery location, phone numbers and email IDs. The total number of orders was 18 crores. In such cases, cyber-attacks can be considered as a driving force that should put the Board of Directors and the management in active mode to address all kinds of risks associated with the cyber-crimes. Thus, it is the ultimate duty of the Board members and executive management to regularly ensure that there is a proper alignment of IT with the business strategies and that those business strategies make judicious use of IT.

Figure 1.
Source: Made by the author

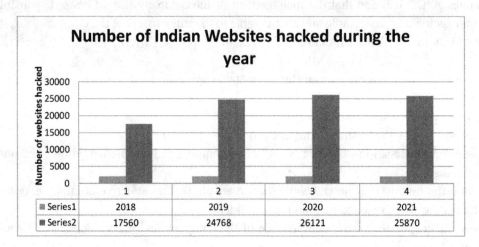

Importance of Information Security Governance

Businesses in today's era rely mostly on information technology for their operations to run smoothly. The main objective of every business organisation is to increase its revenue by increasing its sales. Business organisations have data that could be of immense value to competitors or to cyber criminals. Recent years have witnessed a large number of cases of data hacking and cyber-crimes. In the mid of July 2020, *Twitter* experienced a big spear-phishing attack. The cybercriminals put the admin panel of the site in jeopardy, got full control over famous Twitter users' accounts (both private and corporate) and offered a fake *Bitcoin* giveaway on their behalf. The hackers presented themselves as the company's IT department specialists and contacted many of the Twitter's remote workers and requested them for their work account testaments. The data received helped the cyber-attackers get direct access to Twitter's administrator tools, alter the accounts of various public figures, and post scam messages. Data loss can adversely affect companies for long years in the form of loss of reputation, loss of customer loyalty, decrease in revenue, etc. Thus, it has to take every step to mitigate the risk of information loss and embed a system of information security in every business strategy. This is where the importance of information security governance comes into picture. An information security governance framework aids business organisations to prepare for risks in advance, before they actually occur. This eventually helps businesses to re-evaluate the critical IT and business functions through:

- An integrated risk management system
- Bringing business strategy in line with IT strategy
- Thorough threat and vulnerability analysis
- Proper data governance and threat protection

A good information security governance framework is vital for the long-term survival of the company. It gives an assurance to the customers and employees that they are connected with a well secured company. Information security governance provides following benefits to a business organisation:

- Reduced uncertainty of business activities
- Strong base for risk management
- Optimum allocation of resources
- Protection from potential business risks
- Decisions based on accurate information
- Proper compliance of security policies
- Optimization of information security investment through value delivery

It is well known that all business-related activities are planned out in advance and executed accordingly. In the same way, information security must also be planned conscientiously and carefully, executed effectively and should be monitored regularly at the top-most level (Board of directors and the executive management) of the business organisation. Information security process goes from top to down in vertical order and it requires an exhaustive information security strategy that is clearly connected to the business processes and important objectives of the organisation. For information security to prove effective and adequate, it should cater to the needs of the whole organisational processes from one end to the other end, from physical to operational and to technical. Information security governance is pervasive in nature and has become an important organ of business organisations. Thus, it needs proper work and attention from time to time so that it connotes to the modern IT world.

Compliance Framework for Cyber Security in India

The increasing number of cyber- crimes in the country has left the nation in shock. To cope up with the situation, the Government of India is trying its best and is regularly devising mechanisms and refined regulations to create a shield for its citizens and business organisations and save them from the claws of web disasters. The business operations of all data centres, intermediaries and service providers come under the Jurisdiction of *Information Technology Rules, 2013.* The directive principles of this law has made it mandatory to report all the cyber-crime related incidents happening in the country in real-time to the Indian Computer Emergency Response Team.

Cyber space has become a common platform owing to the rapid technological advancements and it is being used by all the citizens, business organisations and the government as well. To address such an issue, the Indian Government has also come up with *National Cyber Security Policy- 2013.* The main objective of this policy is as follows:

- To create and maintain a safe cyber ecosystem in the country.

- To enhance adoption of IT in all the sectors by creating trust and confidence of everyone in the IT system.
- To establish a powerful regulatory framework for a secure cyberspace.
- To create a workforce of skilled professionals through continuous training and development.
- To create National and Sectoral level mechanism that functions 24X7 and actively responds to and resolves all kinds of cyber-attacks and cyber threats.
- To provide monetary benefits to business organisations for adopting prior approved security practices.
- To ensure full-fledged protection of the citizens' data who use cyberspace on day-to-day basis.
- To promote effective communication and promote responsible user behavior.

The cyber security policy works as an umbrella by protecting the interests of all the users of the cyber space. It also defines and works as a guidance in designing activities related to the security of information stored on cyber space. This helps business organisations, whether government or non- government, in devising business strategies that suits their needs and expectations. IT security frameworks abridge the industry-related standards and best practices into a set of guidelines which aids in proper design, implementation and maintenance of a secure IT environment. This ultimately helps businesses to overcome cyber- related complications and implement the right tools and processes to mitigate the cyber risk.

However, the cyber security policy needs an upgradation in all areas especially in manpower and technology. There are a lot of loopholes in the 2013 security policy. A review mechanism should be adopted to toughen the cyberspace related system and enhance the flexibility of the cyber infrastructure in the country, particularly critical infrastructure. For that purpose, the Government of India has planned to come up with a *New Cyber Security Strategy, 2020*. The main aim of this new strategy is to create cyber awareness through stricter audit procedures.

Information Technology Act (IT Act, 2000)

The Information Technology Act was passed in the year 2000. The section 69A of this particular act lays down provisions to block certain websites wherein the content is objectionable. Under section 69B, the Central Government is empowered to monitor, collect traffic data generated, transmitted, received or stored in any computer resource.

Cyber Regulations Appellate Tribunal (CRAT)

The Cyber Regulations Appellate Tribunal (CRAT) is coming under the Information Technology Act, 2000. It is established by the Central Government as the chief governing body which receives all the cyber security breaches as notified by the Central Government from time to time. The power of the Tribunal includes the following:

- Making sure that all the electronic records are made available.
- Regular examination of important documents by issuing commissions.
- Analysing the decisions based on the basics of the cyber security incident.
- Dismissal of the defaulter's application.

CERT-In (Indian Computer Emergency Response Team)

This national nodal agency started its operations in 2004. It is mainly responsible for providing instantaneous response to all the cyber- crime related incidents happening in the country. In the recent amendments in the Information Technology Amendment Act, the Indian Computer Emergency Response Team was officially assigned as the National Agency for Cyber Security Preservation. This National Agency acts as the leading task force which is responsible for-

- Advance forecasting of cyber security incidents and its prevention.
- Timely collection of data related to cyber- crimes, its critical analysis and proper diffusion.
- Chalking out the necessary measures to mitigate the risks associated with cyber security.
- Consistent coordination of cyber security related activities.
- Ensuing the necessary guidelines and precautions that work in the best interest of the public, thus managing the cyber- crimes.

CONCLUSION

Business organisations today rely more on digital/electronic media rather than pen and paper. On one hand, the usage of manual records including manual documentation of almost everything has reduced. This has proved to be good for the environment. On the other hand, all the records including financial records too are maintained and stored digitally. This has increased the risk of important information getting leaked and made available to cyber hackers. Good corporate governance framework plays a very significant role in shaping the future of a business organisation. It plays a key role in the long-term survival of companies. Business organisations have lately realised the importance of information security. Any compromise in adhering to it can prove fatal for the survival of the organisation. Even the boards may face charge of negligence if the information asset is misused or compromised. The non-adherence can lead to disclosure of confidential information, fraud and ultimately defacement of the credibility of the company. The number of cyber-attacks has seen an upsurge in the recent past. Thus, there is need for a proper coordination between organisational and global level to prevent the risk of cyber-crimes around the world. Information security governance has become the need of the hour. Apart from focusing on increasing sales and revenues, developing customer loyalty and achieving total satisfaction of all the stakeholders; organisations should also focus on how to prevent the breach of its most critical asset, i.e., data.

Suggestions

Thus, it is suggested to give more weightage to information security governance than what was needed before. It truly is the need of the hour. Especially after the pandemic, when everyone is dependent upon the cyber world. People, business organisations, government and society at large are more used to online working. So, the government agencies and organisations have to devise such a system that ensures smooth functioning of their work without hindering the security of their information asset.

REFERENCES

Aguilar, L. A. (2014, June). Boards of directors, corporate governance and cyber-risks: Sharpening the focus. In *Cyber Risks and the Boardroom conference*. New York Stock Exchange.

Eugen, P., & Petruţ, D. (2018). Exploring the new era of cybersecurity governance. *Ovidius University Annals. Economic Sciences Series*, *18*(1), 358–363.

Fazlida, M. R., & Said, J. (2015). Information security: Risk, governance and implementation setback. *Procedia Economics and Finance*, *28*, 243–248. doi:10.1016/S2212-5671(15)01106-5

Posthumus, S., & Von Solms, R. (2004). A framework for the governance of information security. *Computers & Security*, *23*(8), 638–646. doi:10.1016/j.cose.2004.10.006

Solms, E., & Strous, L. A. (2002, November). Information security: A corporate governance issue. In *Working Conference on Integrity and Internal Control in Information Systems* (pp. 115-133). Springer.

Von Solms, B. (2006). Information security–the fourth wave. *Computers & Security*, *25*(3), 165–168. doi:10.1016/j.cose.2006.03.004

Von Solms, B., & Von Solms, R. (2005). From information security to… business security? *Computers & Security*, *24*(4), 271–273. doi:10.1016/j.cose.2005.04.004

Von Solms, R., & von Solms, S. B. (2006). Information Security Governance: A model based on the direct–control cycle. *Computers & Security*, *25*(6), 408–412. doi:10.1016/j.cose.2006.07.005

Von Solms, R., & von Solms, S. B. (2006). Information security governance: Due care. *Computers & Security*, *25*(7), 494–497. doi:10.1016/j.cose.2006.08.013

ADDITIONAL READING

Cheney, M. (2022, February 1). *Information Security Governance: Guidance for IT Compliance Frameworks*. Linford & Co. Retrieved from https://linfordco.com/blog/information-security-governance-framework-it-compliance/

Rai, G. (2020, June 22). *India needs to review its 2013 cyber security policy*. Observer Research Foundation. Retrieved from https://www.orfonline.org/research/india-needs-to-review-its-2013-cyber-security-policy-68267/

Singh, V. (2015, July 15). *National Cyber Security Policy-2013*. SlideShare. Retrieved from https://www.slideshare.net/VidushiSingh5/national-cyber-security-policy2013

Special Correspondent. (2021, December 1). *Cyberattacks hit 26,000 Indian sites in 10 months*. The Hindu. Retrieved from https://www.thehindu.com/business/cyberattacks-hit-26000-indian-sites-in-10-months/article37796297.ece

Vachhatani, J. (2021, May 23). *Domino's India Faces Cyber Attack; Data Of 18 Cr Orders, Including Personal Info, Leaked*. RepublicWorld. Retrieved from https://www.republicworld.com/technology-news/other-tech-news/dominos-india-faces-cyber-attack-data-of-18-cr-orders-including-personal-info-leaked.html

Chapter 9
Cyber Security Policy in India:
Examining the Issues, Challenges, and Framework

Kush Kalra
University of Petroleum and Energy Studies, India

Bhanu Tanwar
University of Petroleum and Energy Studies, India

ABSTRACT

Cyber security policies can be defined as a formal set of rules that help regulate all the aspects of data and information exchange over the internet. These cyber policies are made with the goal to ensure the necessary regulations to protect people over cyber space and to allow a social freedom. It is necessary to maintain a balance between the two. Progress to expand the legislation to criminalize certain activities that pose as a threat to the society is rather a remarkable step for most countries. The first step is the introduction of a policy to the country. A policy is mostly used as a strategy to define different objectives and methods to address the issue of concern. Developing a policy helps the government to understand and define a required response to a problem. The battle against cybercrime cannot be solely won by introducing legislation. Certain strategies and measures that strengthen the fight against such crime and resolve conflicts are also needed.

INTRODUCTION

What are Cyber Security Policies?

The cyber security policies can be defined as a formal set of rules, which helps regulate all the aspects of data and information exchange over the internet. These cyber policies are made with the goal to only ensure the necessary regulations to protect people over cyber space but to allow a social freedom as well as it is necessary to maintain a balance between the two. As a progress to expand the legislation

DOI: 10.4018/978-1-6684-5827-3.ch009

to criminalize certain activities that poses as a threat to the society is rather a remarkable step for most of the countries.

The first and foremost step is the introduction of a policy to the country. A policy is mostly used as a strategy to define different objectives and methods to address the issue of concern. Developing a policy helps the government to understand and define a required response to a problem. The battle against cybercrime cannot be solely won by introducing legislations, but by introducing certain strategies and measures that strengthen the fight against such crime and resolving of conflicts.

In the continued fight against cybercrime there has been a constant unimportance given to injecting the legal framework into the existing policies. Such lack of crime prevention has only further escalated the issue in the country.

The Need of Cyber Security Policies

The cyber security is an essential step taken by the world governments to ensure the safety of each and every individual over the cyber space, these policies help lay down a procedure to act along with in case of any mishap. The need of cyber security policies is laid down briefly:

- **Efficiency:** The cyber policies enable the country to be efficient any case of the cyber security, these policies help by saving times and resources of the country. It lays down the duties of each individual official and tells them how to act in a particular situation.
- **Encourages an environment of discipline and accountability:** In case of human error which leads to a situation where the security is compromised and can lead to damages, then in such situations the policies will lay down the disciplinary actions to be followed. These policies are necessary to be established as they ensure the security of each and every person.
- **Helps educate people on security literacy:** Security policies not only lay down a wall against the threat to the confidentiality of the information and data of the organizations and people but also help people to fight against such threats by educating them, by increasing the awareness of norms and methods among the society regarding the policies. There are various cyber security policies that helps us in our day to day lives against such threats, few of such policies are mentioned as follows:
  - **Virus and spyware and protection provided by them:** Virus and spyware are an important peripheral essential for the computers, they help detect any kind of viruses in the computer that pose as a danger to the computer, and it not only detects but also repairs and removes such files that can cause a damage to the system's integrity. It also helps to detect suspicious behavior of such viruses and spyware that a user unknowingly allowed in their system and removes them by using advanced technologies such as SONAR heuristics and reputation data.
  - **Firewalls:** Firewall as the name suggests acts as a barrier between the computer and such threat, in other words it acts as a border to such suspicious and malicious threats and prevents them into entering the computer, and it also helps in detecting any kind of attacks instigated by cybercriminals and removes such kind of unwanted traffics over the network.
  - **Intrusion prevention:** Intrusion prevention policies are a type of policy that detects any kind of network threat and blocks them at their initial stage. It protects the computer's vulnerability by checking the ingredients of such package threats.

- ◦ **Application control and control over the device:** A threat is not necessarily be present over a network it can even come through any peripheral attached to the computer, this policy checks such peripherals and applications attached or installed in the system and removes such malicious files by blocking them or erasing them. The counterfeit products are the best example to this situation a mac desktop wouldn't recognize a device or even block any application that is not of an authentic nature, same situation is with the windows as well. It is due to these policies that such peripherals are blocked even before they can pose as a threat to the system.
  - ◦ **Live Update policies:** Such policies help the computer by defining the parameters of how often can a client or a person can contact the system for update. This policy can be categorised into two:
    1. LiveUpdate Content policy
    2. LiveUpdate Setting Policy

These contains settings which lays down the parameters to protect the system's integrity and its data.

- **Exception policy:** This policy helps in excluding application and processes by detecting them through the means of scans run by it (Duggal, 2016).
- **Host Integrity Policy:** This policy is used to enforce the system's security to keep the data secure against such threats. This policy has a requisite condition that the user's computer must have an antivirus installed on it.

Standards of Security

Written norms are an essential requisite to make cyber security measures efficient in order to tackle such crimes. Such written norms are referred to as cyber security standards, it helps in tackling the issue by laying down a prescribed manner for an ideal execution of the certain security measures (Ardhapurkar et al., 2010).

These standards involve a plethora of features such as, guidelines to tackles such issues, methods to be performed in order to maintain the integrity of the computer, and the reference framework given by the authorities. Security standards are provided as a general requirement for all the organizations irrespective of size, nature of industry and their work sector.

Following are the essential ingredients of any cyber security strategies.

ISO

ISO stands for International Organization for Standardization. International Standards make things to work. These standards provide a world-class specification for products, services and computers, to ensure quality, safety and efficiency. They are instrumental in facilitating international trade. ISO standard is officially established on 23 February 1947. It is an independent, non-governmental international organization. Today, it has a membership of 162 national standards bodies and 784 technical committees and subcommittees to take care of standards development (Hoffman, 2003, pp. 415-426). ISO has published over 22336 International Standards and its related documents which covers almost every industry, from information technology to food safety, to agriculture and healthcare.

Information Technology Act 2000 (Amended in 2008)

The Information Technology Act, 2000 was introduced on 17th of October, 2000. It was introduced with the aim to establish a framework that can provide a legal infrastructure to deal with the issue of cybercrime in the country. The IT Act is based on the United Nations Model Law on E-Commerce 1996 recommended by the General Assembly of United Nations. This act is also used to check misuse of cyber network and computer in India. It was officially passed in 2000 and amended in 2008. It has been designed to give the boost to electronic commerce, e-transactions and related activities associated with commerce and trade (Boulanin, 2013, pp. 218–226). It also facilitates electronic governance by means of reliable electronic records.

Copyright Act

The Copyright Act 1957 amended by the Copyright Amendment Act 2012 governs the subject of copyright law in India. This Act is applicable from 21 January 1958. Copyright is a legal term which describes the ownership of control of the rights to the authors of 'original works of authorship' that are fixed in a tangible form of expression. An original work of authorship is a distribution of certain works of creative expression including books, video, movies, music, and computer programs. The copyright law has been enacted to balance the use and reuse of creative works against the desire of the creators of art, literature, music and monetize their work by controlling who can make and sell copies of the work (Singer, 2014).

Patent Law

In order to deal with the new inventions that were constantly being introduced in the current developing advancements. In order to protect their authenticity and the hard work of the inventors, the patent law was introduced.

Under this law generally a patent was given to the inventor, which is the rights of the ownership of the invention and such rights were protected under this law.

Intellectual Property Rights

This act was introduced to protect the interest of the creators of the patents and the trademarks, and helped the creators benefit from their own creations and inventions. These IPR rights are outlined in the Article 27 of the Universal Declaration of Human Rights. It provides for the right to benefit from the protection of moral and material interests resulting from authorship of scientific, literary or artistic productions (Baron, 2002, pp. 263-278). These property rights allow the holder to exercise a monopoly on the use of the item for a specified period.

NATIONAL CYBER SECURITY POLICY 2013

The National Cyber Security Policy was implemented by the Department of Electronics and Information Technology, it was a policy framework which laid down the set of rules to be followed to help tackle the issue of cybercrime in the country (Beagle, 1999, pp. 82- 89). Prior to 2013 India lacked cyber policies (Banerjee, 2007, pp. 36-48).

In 2013, The Hindu newspaper, citing documents leaked by NSA whistle-blower Edward Snowden, has alleged that much of the <u>NSA</u> surveillance was focused on India's domestic politics and its strategic and commercial interests (Wikipedia, 2022).

The news caused an agitation among the people and thus the government came under pressure to implement a policy for India. Therefore, this public pressure led to the unveiling of the National Cyber Security Policy in 2013. This policy focused on the main point that how significant the information technology is in promoting the economic growth of the country.

Vision

This policy was implemented to safeguard the confidential and sensitive information including of information such as: - personal information, Banking and financial institution information, and the sovereign data. It laid down rules to secure the cyberspace for the Indian citizens, for the e-commerce businesses, and the government and helped any kind of unauthorized access that meddled with the privacy of the citizens. This policy had a requisite of a joint synergy between the public and private partnership via the medium of a technical and operational cooperation. As this joint venture was essential to tackle the cyber threat with aggressive measures and accustoming the practices to a secure future in the cyberspace.

Mission

The main objective of the National Cyber Security Policy was to safeguard the citizens present on the cyberspace and the privacy of the country's domestic matters. It laid down a set of rules and strategies that helped in tackling and answering any kind of cyber threat, reduce and prevent any kind of vulnerability that can pose as a threat to private and national security.

The policy document aims at encouraging all organizations whether public or private to designate a person to serve as Chief Information Security Officer (CISO) who will be responsible for cyber security initiatives. Organizations are required to develop their information security policies properly dovetailed into their business plans and implement such polices as per international best practices (Brecher, 1996, pp. 127 – 139). Provisions of fiscal schemes and incentives have been incorporated in the policy to encourage entities to install trustworthy ICT products and continuously upgrade information infrastructure with respect to cyber security (Tomar, 2013).

OBJECTIVES

- To ensure the security of the country over the cyberspace, and help creating an awareness among the people over the information technology system in India to achieve their trust and confidence, that will help the country in adopting the information technology in all the respective sectors of the economy (Kristensen, 2008, pp. 63–83).

- To build a framework that will assure the security of the policies being implemented and facilitating the actions for compliance to the global security standards.
- To enhance the regulatory framework of the country in order to have cyberspace system that free from any threat.
- To have a 24X7 mechanism to deal with any risk or issue regarding cyber threat which will help in gathering the required information that will help in tackling the issue. It will helps us by creating a required response for the situation under the crisis and how to manage it.
- A workforce of 500,000 professionals skilled in the coming 5 years to help deal with such threats by training them through a medium of capacity improving skill development.
- Fiscal benefits for the businesses who adopted security standards and practices.

Strategies

Secure Cyber Ecosystem

- National nodal agency was nominated to coordinate all the matters belonging to the cyber security issue of the country, and its roles and responsibilities were also defined under this policy
- All organization whether it be public or private of nature were required to nominate a senior officer as Chief Security Officer (CISO), who will be responsible for handling the cyber security initiatives.
- A security policy integrated with the respective business plans of organizations was required to be developed by the organization. Such policies should be implemented and created with the concept of smooth flow of information over the network and the proper mechanisms to secure this flow of information.
- A separate budget to be developed by organizations for introducing the cyber security policies for having a required response for any incident
- Fiscal schemes and initiatives were provided to promote the adoption of the new information structure to help strengthen the cyber security.
- Prevent the reoccurrence or any occurrence of such attacks by the technological development and proactive actions.
- Adoption of mechanism to help facilitate the information sharing and responding to cyber threats.

Creation of an Assurance Framework

- Global practices to be adopted in the cyber security and to be further comply with such practices to improve the cyber security position of the country.
- Developing an infrastructure that can examine and can approve that cyber security practices are being complied with.
- Adopting global practices to facilitate the risk assessment and risk management provisions in the country's cyber security policies and business organization (Geer, 2010, pp. 207-219).
- Secure applications and software development processes based upon global practices.
- Developing an Assessment framework to ensure conformity for a routine verification of complying with the cyber security practices, standards and guidelines.

- Inspiriting the organizations routinely check and assess the effectiveness and efficiency of the cyber security control measures of their IT departments, systems and networks.

Inspiring Open Standards

- Inspiriting the adoption of the open standards to help facilitate the data exchange and inter dependent operations for different products and services.
- Promotion of a consortium of both the public and private sectors to develop the possibility of tested and verified IT products.

Improving the Regulatory Framework

- Establishing a dynamic legal framework having a routine review to focus on the issue of cyber security of India due to the constant technological developments and its compatibility with the international standards of international security.
- A compulsory routine audit and assessment of the efficiency and effectiveness regarding the security of IT infrastructure with its affinity to the regulatory framework. (See also A Global Treaty on Cyber security and Cybercrime, available at: http://pircenter.org/media/content/files/9/13480907190.pdf (visited on April 20, 2022)
- To create an awareness and educate regarding the regulatory framework of the cyber security measures of India.

Developing Mechanisms to Cope up with the Cyber Security through Early Warning, Vulnerability Management and Response to Security Threats

- to develop National Level system, procedure, and mechanisms that can create the necessary scenarios to help in case of any future incidents by creating responsive and preventive measures by entities.
- To run an ever-running "National Level Computer Emergency Response Team (CERT-In) to act as a Nodal Agency for coordination of cyber security responsive measures in case of a crisis."
- To run the National Level Computer Emergency Response Team (CERT-In) in order to coordinate the communication process in between the sectors for efficient response to such crisis and its resolution.
- Adopting a cyber crisis management plan to handle with cybercrime related issues that can cause crisis for the national security of the country using a multi-disciplinary approach.
- Conducting cyber security drills and exercises at both national and sectoral level to help in assessing the security level of the preparedness in case of any incident.

Secure E-Governance Services

- Adopting global security practices, business continuity measures, and cyber crisis management implementing them in the e-governance initiatives to reduce the risks of cyber threats and improve cyber security.

- Emphasizing on the adoption of Public Key Infrastructure (PKI) in the government departments for trusted communications and secured transactions.
- Employing information security professionals to aid the e-governance initiatives and improve the security.

Protection and Flexibility of Critical Information Structure

- Constructing a protection plan for safeguarding the critical Information Structure and its assimilation within the business plans at an individual level. Such plan is comprised of mechanisms for protecting the flow of information, directories and standards, and crisis plans.
- To run an ever-running "National Critical Information Infrastructure Protection Centre (NCIIPC) to function as the nodal agency for critical information infrastructure protection in the country." (See also vikaspedia.in/ational-cyber-security-policy)
- To facilitate the protection of critical infrastructure, identification, examination, focusing, resolving and important resources established for the protection of critical information structure.
- A mandatory employment of security practices from the global levels, business continuity management and cyber crisis management plan by all individual sectors to reduce risk of any interruptions and improve the security of the country.
- Mandatory use of verified IT products which are certified by the authorities.
- A routine mandatory security audit of critical information structure.
- All security positions to be certified by CISO/CSO.
- A compulsory application and software development process based on global security practices.

Promoting Research and Development in Cyber Security

- Commencing the research and development initiatives to focus on each and every form of development intended at short-, medium- and long-term goals. Research and development programs are established for the advancement and development of systems in order to ensure their security throughout their life.
- To promote R&D to yield cost-effective, accurate primitive results in security solutions to address the varied range of cyber security challenges.
- To facilitate transition, diffusion and commercialization of the outputs of Research & Development into commercial products and services for use in public and private sectors.
- Establishing excellence centers in the field of strategic importance for security of cyberspace.
- Joint R&D programs and projects with the top agencies for research oriented on solutions (Kamath, 2013)

Abbreviating Supply Chain Risk

- To establish and retain infrastructure specialized in testing and facilities for the security of the IT product assessment and its requisite verification in accordance with the global standards and practices.
- Building trust relationships with product vendors and service providers for the betterment of end-to-end supply chain security.

- Developing awareness regarding the threats, vulnerabilities and emanation of such breach of security among individual sectors in the supply chain of IT products.

Development of the Human Resource

- Cultivating educational and training programs in formal as well as the informal sectors to back the cyber security requirements of the country.
- Establishing a nation-wide cyber training infrastructure through the private-public partnership.
- Security Concept labs for skill development and awareness in important aspects of the country.
- Institutional mechanisms for legislative agencies that can facilitate its capacity.

Cyber Security Awareness

- National awareness program on security of cyberspace would be introduced and promoted.
- Sustaining the security literacy and its awareness as well as campaigning through electronic media to aware the populace regarding the measures of cyber security.
- Conducting of cyber security workshops, seminars and supporting such workshops and seminars.

Effective Public-Private Partnerships

- Aiding alliance and teamwork of the individual sectors who are the stakeholders such as the private sectors in the field of cyber security and sheltering the critical information structure relating to any kind of cyber threats, liabilities and protective measures and establishing global practices.
- Developing models to aid in such alliance and teamwork of the sectors with the important stakeholders.
- A suggestion tank to store inputs regarding the improvement of cyber policies.

Sharing of Information and Cooperation

- Developing a system of mutual international relationships with other countries in the field of cyber security.
- Enhancing the global alliance among the cyber security agencies of the world.
- Creating mechanisms to facilitate the systems of information sharing.

Prioritized Approach for Implementation

- A specific approach prioritized to implement the policy to address the critical areas in its initial stance.

Shortcomings of the National Cyber Security Policy, 2013

The National Cyber Security helped the nation in adoption of security standard and practices that helped the country in securing a safe cyberspace system, however nothing can be perfect, and this policy had certain shortcomings, which are as follows: -

- The new technologies such as cloud computing were introduced in the country and therefore security provisions for adoption of such new technologies were not addressed.
- As each and every individual now present on the social media, and so are the criminals as well the problem that arose here as to how can we protect ourselves from such criminals. This situation was not addressed by the policy.
- There was also a need of system of tracking the cybercrime and constituting a platform where such information can be shared among both the public and private sectors (Mishra, 2002)
- It helped in creating a workforce, but it lacked consideration as to how the workforce will act i.e. will it only monitor the cyberspace or trained to achieve a defensive and offensive skills to tackle the issue of cyber threats.
- This policy enlisted safeguarding privacy of people as one of its aims, but there was no strategy to achieve this aim.

Why India Still Needs to Prioritize Cyber Security

The Cybersecurity Policy of 2013 is open and technology neutral. But it needs upgradation. The digital economy today comprises 14-15% of India's total economy and is targeted to reach 20% by 2024. India has more than 120 recognised 'data centres' and clouds. (ET Contributors, 2019)

A cyberattack was made on the Kudankulam nuclear power project in Tamil Nadu but was ignored by the government official even an audit confirmed the occurrence of the incident.

In the context of this incident the release of a new cyber security strategy is initiated and will be introduced in 2020.

The average data consumption of our country per person in a year is about in the ambit of 15-20 gigabits and with the adoption of new technological advancements such as- artificial intelligence, machine learning, and data analytics etc. our present cyberspace will become more complex and thus will give rise to new issues.

Sectors such as healthcare, retail trade, energy and media face advance persistent threats (APTs), as the latest reports of an Israeli spyware allegedly used to spy on Indian journalists and human rights activists attest. These incidents relating to data leakage, ransomware, ATM/credit cards denial of service, diversion of network traffic intrusion in IT systems and networks using malware are on rise. Attacks on embedded systems and IoT have also registered a sharp increase of late. Such incidents are being launched from cyberspace of different international jurisdictions (ET Contributors, 2019).

The private sector of the Indian economy has played an important role in administering the information infrastructure, especially in power, transportation and healthcare facilities. Therefore, it is necessary that a new direction toward the issue of cybersecurity is given, and policies should be refreshed.

India in the year 2019 had the most cyber-attacks and became the most cyber-targeted nation for three months (Dunlap, 2009, pp. 712-724). These cyber-attacks on India were of Ukraine, The Czech Republic, China and Mexico origin. These attacks targeted the critical sectors of the economy.

According to the data, 74,988 cyber-attacks targeting India originated in Slovenia. This was followed by Ukraine (55,772 attacks), Czech Republic (53,609 attacks), China (50,000 attacks), and Mexico (35, 201 attacks) (Mihindukulasuriya, 2020).

These attacks were executed by the botnets. Botnets are a technical device having the capabilities of a computer and network connectivity with each other. These botnets when used injects a malware in the device of the victim, and through the help of such malware botnets gain the control over the device.

Cyber-Attacks Recently Faced by India

India even after the establishment of our cyber security policy faced many cyber threats in the previous years, which affected the critical sectors of our economy. Some of those cyber-attacks faced by India are listed:

- **Cosmos bank, Pune**: In 2018 the Cosmos bank in Pune encountered a cyberattack, this attack jolted the entire banking sector of the Indian economy as the attackers were able bleed the Cosmos bank off Rs94.24 crores. This attack was executed by hacking the ATM server of the bank and stole the confidential information of the bank cardholders.
- **ATM systems became the main target:** In mid-2018 a cyberattack was faced by the Canara Bank where the bank's ATMs servers were hacked around Rs.20 lakh were stolen from the accounts of total 50 victims, and it was further noticed that the hackers had the confidential information of more than 200 users. Skimming devices helped the attackers in this cyberattack to steal from the accounts of the bank account holders.
- **UIDAI Aadhar Software:** Even the Aadhar software of India wasn't safe from these cyberattacks. In 2018 the personal records of around 1.1 billion Indian citizens were breached by a cyberattack, the UIDAI further stated that Indian websites have leaked the Aadhar detail of citizens of the country, this data comprised of PAN number, mobile numbers, biometrics of people, banks account details, and other sensitive personal details of the Indian citizens. This led to serious issue of national security in the country, it was further found that the anonymous sellers were selling personal Aadhar details of other people for Rs.500 over social media.
- **Healthcare websites**: US-based cybersecurity firms reported that hackers breached the Indian based healthcare websites by broking into them, where these hackers stole the patient records of around 68 lakh which also included the records of doctors as well.
- **SIM Swap Scams**: In August 2018, two cyber hackers were arrested by Mumbai police who were illegally transferring money from the bank accounts, these hackers were arrested from Navi Mumbai, they were transferred 4 crores from different bank accounts through fraudulently acquiring the SIM card data of the people. This attack was done through the online banking and even various companies accounts were also targeted by them.

Such attacks were the indication that India still needs to prioritise its cyber security policies in order to overcome the issue of cyber threat towards the nation.

UPCOMING CYBERSECURITY POLICIES AND INITIATIVES

Indian government in order to create a more cyber-secure nation for both at an individual and business level is going to disclose its new cybersecurity policies in the year 2020. The new policy aims at creating a more secure and trusted cyberspace environment which will be more flexible in nature and will emphasise on creating awareness regarding the cybersecurity among the young generations of India.

To create such a stringent framework, the country requires a huge budget. Ajeet Bajpai, the Director-General of the National Critical Information Infrastructure Protection Centre said, 'Considering the size and scale of our nation, we need approximately ₹25,000 crore budgets for the same. Also, there is a need to emphasise on the need to make cybersecurity a mandatory subject in the universities for high-decibel awareness (Das, 2019)

The following listed are the initiatives and the progress made by India towards implementing and creating its upcoming cybersecurity strategy:

- **CERT-In**: CERT-In (The Indian Computer Emergency Response Team), is the national agency which tackles the country's cybersecurity, and has helped in lowering the rate of cybercrime. Government employees all over India working in the Government agencies have participated in the cybersecurity awareness training to help fight against the issue of cybercrimes. CERT-In also issues advisories regarding the cyber vulnerabilities currently present in our society and the measures required to tackle such cybersecurity issues.
- **Cyber Surakshit Bharat**: The Ministry of Electronics and Information Technology (MeitY) in order to strengthen the cybersecurity system of India has launched the Cyber Surakshit Bharat initiative with the association of National e-Governance Division (Negd).

A proper governance is required because of the accelerated transformation of the governance system due to digitisation. This initiative will advance the awareness regarding cybercrime and capacity of the IT staff among all government departments.

In this venture of public-private partnership will offer series of workshop to make people aware about the practices of cybersecurity and help the government officials and business officials with tool kits to tackle cyber threats.

- **National Critical Information Infrastructure Protection Centre:** The National Critical Information Infrastructure Protection Centre (NCIIPC) is a central government establishment, constructed to safeguard country's sensitive information which if threatened can compromise the country's national security, economic growth and the public healthcare.

NCIIPC conducts cybersecurity exercises to keep the cybersecurity norms of our country in check and readiness of the government and the critical sectors, following are identified as 'critical sectors' by the NCIIPC:

1. Power and Energy
2. Banking, Financial Services and Insurance

3. Telecom
4. Transport
5. Government
6. Strategic and Public Enterprises

Appointment of Chief Information Security Officers

Due to the constant advancement of India and digitisation there came a need for adopting strict measures to prevent cyber threats. The national security is a very sensitive matter even the smallest of breach can cause a serious damage to our country's integrity and hamper our current situation, therefore a skilled leader is required that can protect such sensitivity of national security such leaders are called 'Chief Information Security Officers (CISOs)' that can ascertain the requirements to protect security during the period of constant technological advancements.

Website Audit

As the government websites are under a constant threat of hacking, phishing, data theft. The government has taken a step to conduct an audit of all the websites and applications of the government, this initiative is facilitated by 90 security auditing organisations.

Crisis Management Plan

The Indian government has developed and carried out a crisis management plan by all the sectors of government and the critical sectors as identified by the 'NCIIPC'.

These initiatives will not only strengthen the currently present cybersecurity strategies but will also prepare employees and leaders to prepare for any event of cyber threat. It further helps in managing cases of cyber interruption of the important functions in the listed critical sectors of the government.

Training and Mock Drills

Mock drills are an essential of any training as it helps in preparing the personnel in case of uncertainty, the Indian government has therefore started organising cybersecurity mock drills to compute the present cybersecurity attentiveness of the government sectors.

"According to (MeitY), 44 such drills have already been conducted by CERT-In this year. Also, reports have mentioned that around 265 organisations from varied states and sectors have participated in these drills."

Malware Protection

Cyber Swachhta Kendra is type of a cleaning bot launched by the central government for analysing and examining the malwares and detecting such programs, it includes certain tools that can be used to remove or erase such suspicious and malicious programs.

Personal Data Protection Bill

As on the individual level the government has introduced the bill of 'Personal Data Protection' which protect the Indian citizens from any global cyber threat.

This bill states that the confidential data of the Indian citizens will be stored locally, and only under certain conditions can be processed elsewhere. The bill further requires the social media companies to be more accountable and guides them to prevent circulation of any kind of offensive content.

CURRENT STATE OF CYBERSECURITY IN INDIA

India has grown in the area of its digital economy over the previous years, the Indian population has been observed to shift towards the digital platforms which helped India in achieving a breakthrough of 450 million mobile internet users.

In 2015 Reliance company introduced Jio to the Indian market, Jio's free voice calls and unlimited free internet in its initial stages helped the country to become more digital and a two-fold growth in terms of data usage was seen in a single year.

During her presentation of the Union Budget 2020 to parliament on February 2, Indian Minister of Finance Nirmala Sitharaman said: 'It is now a cliché – data is the new oil – and, indeed, analytics, artificial intelligence (AI), fintech and IoT are quickly transforming the way we deal with our lives. (Osbourne Clark, 2020).

Such facilities helped India to develop in the digital field and such development helped in acquiring the knowledge of the cyberspace among the youth as well as older generation of the country.

India has instilled its faith in Personal Data Protection Bill that it will help in addressing the growing issue of cyber threats with the aim to stricken the Indian security standards by implementing various safeguards and tough penalties for the criminals. Banking industry executive Shyam Sundar said that while banks' highest cybersecurity priority was protecting customer data, that job was growing ever more complicated. He said:

Banks deal with customers at every level – lending on the assets side through to opening accounts on the liability side. All customer data is considered personal data, but securing that data becomes more of a challenge as it is accessed across all levels of a digital ecosystem (Osborne Clark, 2020).

SUGGESTIONS

In regards with the constantly developing technologies, and computer-dimensions comes a need for adopting and establishing suitable methods to fight the issue of cybercrime, our existing framework need to be restructured to make it more effective in the current standard of technological advancement. Any kind of delay or negligence is enough to give the offender an opportunity to commit such attacks.

An active cooperation of citizens, institutions, and government is required to make a sound strategy against cybercrimes. Self-protection initiatives needs to be taken by people who are vulnerable to such crimes. Media plays an important role in creating awareness of such issues and warning people against such threats and dangers of cybercrimes. The legal preventive measure will become more effective in preventing cybercrimes when they will get the support of the entire Indian community (Duggal, 2016).

Strict Internet Security Measures

Internet has helped the commercial economy to boom. E-commerce has grown and become more popular day by day compared to when it was first introduced, for example when amazon came to India it was mostly used to sell books but now in the current time, we can purchase any thing from amazon. This increased use of computers and internet in the trade field also opened new ways for the criminals. The transactions are now mostly being carried out over the network which makes them vulnerable to unauthorized interceptions and frauds. Therefore, a strict mechanism is required to protect the e-commerce field against such attacks.

Encryption Technology

Encryption technology is an effective method to safeguard the sensitive information from cyber-attacks, it prevents cybercrimes by protecting such information present over the network. This technology should become mandatory in all government and semi-government agencies who are depended on the computerized transfer of information and data.

Firewalls

Firewalls is another device which protects the system against such unauthorized entries, firewalls act as a border between criminals and sensitive data and information.

Spam Accounts or False Accounts

These spam or fake fictitious accounts are becoming a prominent cause of menace in the society such fake accounts are used for phishing, cheating misrepresentation and frauds and due tot the anonymous nature of internet they are hard to track. The Information Technology Act lacks provisions against such fake accounts.

Self-Prevention by Computer Users

The computer and internet users should be aware of such threats and issues in the society and should spread the same for unaware people, self-regulation is the most effective way to prevent the growth of such crimes which can be further assisted by the internet service providers by giving out a certain ethic code to be followed by the users while giving them the internet facilities. A written agreement can be more useful in this scenario where if the service user indulge in any kind of illegal activity it would lead to breach of contract and the extended facilities would be terminated as soon as the breach is committed.

Use of Protection Software such as Biometric Protection or Voice Recognition

Use of protection software to prevent the systems from any kind of unauthorized access. This protection software is hard to get pass by as the biometrics or voice cannot be easily cracked. This technology can help the industries against such threats, these software helps in detecting any kind of interference in the system and prevent such interruption.

Discontinue the use of VPNs

VPN stands for 'A virtual private network', these VPNs masks the IP addresses of the internet users to prevent their identity from getting traced, which makes it harder for the government to track theses kind of illegal activities.

Improving the Cyber Forensics

The cyber forensics team of India need improvement so that it can provide the required assistance the investigation agencies in identifying the cases, locating them and preserving and extracting the digital information from the electronic devices in order to create and find the evidence in the courts.

Internet and Technology Awareness in India

As in the current period each and every sector of the economy is present on the cyber space and using internet to facilitate their business activities, but in the rural areas there is a lack of knowledge regarding the internet and even the basic knowledge of the computer. Measures need to be taken to eliminate this gap of divide of digitalization. Focus of the government on eliminating this gap is needed and access to the technology and knowledge should be provided to the rural society of India.

Blocking of Obscene and Suspicious Websites

The government of India has already taken measures to block the pornography websites as well as the torrent websites in India, but an advance screening system should also be implemented so that not only such obscene websites, but the websites who can pose as a threat towards the society and can hamper the national security should be blocked.

Regulating the Social Media

The social media platforms such as Instagram, Facebook, Snapchat should be regulated as to how to much information of someone can be accessed privacy measures need to establish to protect the privacy of the individuals.

REFERENCES

Ardhapurkar, S., Srivastava, T., Sharma, S., Chaurasiya, V., & Vaish, A. (2010). Privacy and data protection in cyberspace in Indian environment. *International Journal of Engineering Science and Technology*, *2*(5), 942–951.

Banerjee, J. (2007). Cyber Warfare and the Dilemmas of International Law. *Icfai Journal of International Relations*, *1*(3), 36–48.

Baron, R. M. F. (2002). Critique of the International Cybercrime Treaty, CommLaw Conspectus. *Journal of Communications Law and Policy*, *10*(2), 263–278.

Beagle, D. (1999). Conceptualizing an information commons. *Journal of Academic Librarianship*, *25*(2), 82–89. doi:10.1016/S0099-1333(99)80003-2

Boulanin, V. (2013). *Cybersecurity and the arms industry. SIPRI Yearbook 2013: Armaments, disarmament and international security*. Oxford University Press.

Brecher, M. (1996). Introduction: Crisis, conflict, war—State of the discipline. *International Political Science Review*, *17*(2), 127–139. doi:10.1177/019251296017002001

Contributors, E. T. (2019, November 1). *Why cybersecurity should be India's foremost priority.* Ciso. Retrieved from https://ciso.economictimes.indiatimes.com/news/why-cybersecurity-should-be-indias-foremost-priority/71847192?utm_source=Mailer&utm_medium=&utm_campaign=&dt=2019-11-01

Cybersecurity Asia - India's digital transformation drives cybersecurity re-evaluation. (2020, February 24). Osborne Clark. Retrieved from https://www.osborneclarke.com/insights/cybersecurity-asia-indias-digital-transformation-drives-cybersecurity

Das, S. (2019, December 18). Cybersecurity Policies & Initiatives By Indian Govt In 2019. *Analytics India Mag*. Retrieved from https://analyticsindiamag.com/9-cybersecurity-policies-initiatives-by-indian-govt-in-2019/

Duggal, P. (2016). International Conference on Cyberlaw, Cybercrime & Cybersecurity. *The International Review of Information Ethics, 25*.

Dunlap, C. J. Jr. (2008). Towards a Cyberspace Legal Regime in the Twenty-First Century: Considerations for American Cyber-Warriors. *Nebraska Law Review, 87,* 712.

Geer, D. E. Jr. (2010). Cybersecurity and national policy. *Harv. Nat'l Sec. J., 1,* i.

Hoffman, M. H. (2003). The Legal Status and Responsibilities of Private Internet Users Under the Law of Armed Conflict: A Primer for the Unwary on the Shape of Law to Come. *Wash. U. Global Stud. L. Rev., 2,* 415.

Kamath, N. (2013). Should The Law Beat A Retweet? Rationalising Liability Standards For Sharing Of Digital. *Indian Journal of Law and Technology, 9*(1), 4.

Kristensen, K. S. (2008). The absolute protection of our citizens: Critical infrastructure protection and the practice of security. In M. Dunn Cavelty & K. S. Kristensen (Eds.), *The politics of securing the homeland: Critical infrastructure, risk and securitisation* (pp. 63–83). Routledge.

Mihindukulasuriya, R. (2020, March 3). *India was the most cyber-attacked country in the world for three months in 2019.* The Print. Retrieved from https://theprint.in/tech/india-was-the-most-cyber-attacked-country-in-the-world-for-three-months-in-2019/374622/

Mishra, R. C. (2002). *Cyber crime: impact in the new millenium.* Authorspress.

Singer, J. B. (2014). User-generated visibility: Secondary gatekeeping in a shared media space. *New Media & Society, 16*(1), 55–73.

Tomar, S. (2013, August 26). *National Cyber Security Policy 2013: An Assessment.* IDSA. Retrieved from https://www.idsa.in/idsacomments/NationalCyberSecurityPolicy2013_stomar_260813

Wikipedia Contributors. (2022, January 26). National Cyber Security Policy 2013. In *Wikipedia, The Free Encyclopedia.* Retrieved 18:22, October 14, 2022, from https://en.wikipedia.org/w/index.php?title=National_Cyber_Security_Policy_2013&oldid=1068035612

ADDITIONAL READING

Barrett, N. (1997). *The State of the Cybernation: Cultural, Political and Economic Implications of the Internet.* Kogan Page.

Dunn Cavelty, M., & Kristensen, K. S. (2008). Introduction: Securing the homeland: Critical infrastructure, risk, and (in)security. In M. Dunn Cavelty & K. S. Kristensen (Eds.), *The politics of securing the homeland: Critical infrastructure, risk and securitization* (pp. 1–14). Routledge.

Iacono, S. C., & Freeman, P. A. (2006). Cyberinfrastructure-in-theMaking: Can We Get There from Here? In B. Kahin & D. Foray (Eds.), *Advancing Knowledge and the Knowledge Economy* (pp. 455–478). MIT Press.

Reidenberg, J. R. (1996). Governing networks and rule-making in cyberspace. *Emory Law Journal, 45,* 911.

Chapter 10
Security Issues and Solutions for Resource–Constrained IoT Applications Using Lightweight Cryptography

Kamalendu Pal

 https://orcid.org/0000-0001-7158-6481

University of London, UK

ABSTRACT

The internet of things (IoT) is ushering in a new dawn of technological innovations in recent decades for commercial applications. The technological innovation commercial applications manifested in two forms: (1) firstly, development of industrial products and services (e.g., procurement, manufacturing, transportation, and customer service) and, secondly, digitization of business activities. In this way, regular business operation-related data collection, preservation, and analysis using digital technologies (e.g., IoT) are shaping strategic value for companies. For example, the data exchange within and among affiliated devices company works is growing, and such systems' ubiquitous nature brings them into possession of business-sensitive data and information. Hence, industries are placing immense importance on the management of security and privacy of these data to maintain smooth business continuity. Moreover, IoT-based enterprise information systems often use cryptography to maintain data security.

INTRODUCTION

Over several decades business practices globally have been subject to three interesting trends – (i) the increasing access ability of information to enhance operational practice, (ii) the influence on digital data carrying networks for efficient information exchange, and (iii) the usefulness of wireless mobile communication technologies (e.g., fourth generation – 4G, fifth generation – 5G, and futuristic sixth generation – 6G). In order to capitalize on those opportunities, information and communication technologies (ICT) are ushering the ways of new applications with acceptable levels of security risk. In addition, these

DOI: 10.4018/978-1-6684-5827-3.ch010

applications create connectivity among real-world business objects to cyberspace. This way, cyberspace manifests a virtual world where people interact with smart objects, and distributed data communication networks interconnect the entire business operating environment.

In this business operating environment, smart objects' essential information (e.g., item of interest movement, temperature, airflow in an environment) are assessed with the help of various dedicated sensors connected to a wireless data communication network, which does not disturb the usual routine activities of the individual. In this way, a new world of technological evolution is shaping current industrial operating work practices, and IoT technology plays an essential role. The IoT is a technical term that refers to how things, such as sensors, smart meters, intelligent medical devices, radio frequency identification (RFID) tags, and other smart objects, are networked with the internet (or intranet) in real-time. The early concept of IoT starts in the late 1990s, with the initial introduction of RFID technology for industrial use. In addition, recent advancements in IoT technology and its applications in the industrial world are creating new challenges for the research and development community.

Based on network architecture, business models, or the application context, the world standardization organization, industry, and research and development communities have several definitions of the IoT. However, the two most essential components of its applications are – RFID technology and wireless sensor networks (WSNs). As a result, IoT technology has profound usage in several application areas, such as inventory management, transport traffic management, and industrial environment operation monitoring.

A simple RFID information system consists of RFID tags, readers, and data storage. A tag reader identifies the object, attached with a unique identification barcode, through radio signals. The system helps to identify, track, and monitor intelligent objects in an IoT network. WSN facilitates sensing and data communication services. In this way, a WSN consists of several intelligent sensors used in an industrial application (or bottom layer) environment, as shown in Figure 1, and these sensors help to sense and collect business process-related data. In addition, collected data are sent via one or multiple hops to a gateway station, as shown in the middle layer of the diagrammatic representation.

Figure 1. Simple layered architecture for IoT systems

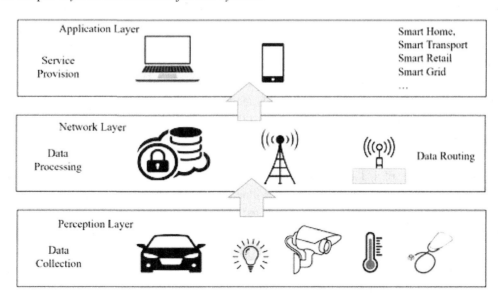

The WANs use various resource-constraint sensors for business application service monitoring. The service networks interlink different communication devices (e.g., sensors, gateways, routers) using wireless technologies (e.g., 4G, 5G, Long Term Evolution (LTE) – a standard for wireless broadband, Universal Mobile Telecommunications Service (UMTS) - a third generation broadband, Wi-Fi, satellite communication). The network layer provides the infrastructural facilities for the collected data from the perception layer and passes it to the application (or service) provision layer. It is an essential layer of the IoT-based information system architecture, and this layer integrates different communication technologies, which help the interconnectivity of smart IoT objects.

The top layer gathers the business process-related industrial data from the middle layer, process these data, and support the needed services to IoT-based system users. This way, it provides intelligent industrial applications (e.g., smart home, smart transport, intelligent healthcare) support. In a simple sense, IoT-based technology can create a dispersed vast area data communication network. Some specific IoT industrial applications are described below:

- *Smart Home Applications*: Smart home automation systems cover all possible aspects of the intelligent transformation of leaving space in residential areas. It helps control electronic items in an intelligent way, including remote monitoring. For example, from security to lighting and heating, intelligent home automation systems can cover any possible needs on demands from their household and differing daily routines. In addition, it also presents the facility of detecting emergency maintenance and triggering the alarm for the stakeholders.
- *Intelligent Transportation Management*: An intelligent transportation system (ITS) is a technology-guided management practice. It uses information technology applications that enhance the quality of transportation or achieve other outcomes based on applications that monitor, manage, or improve the transportation system's performance. ITS relies heavily on data collection, storage, analysis, and other activities. As a result, IoT-based applications play an essential role.
- *Disaster Management Systems*: The primary purpose of a disaster combating system is to use data gathering, storing, and analyzing the stored data to activate the alarm in case of emergencies. It consists of different applications (e.g., fire alarm, industrial application-specific alarm, natural disaster, hurricane, flood, and earthquake). In these applications, information technology often monitors environmental pollution – such as toxic gas emissions and toxic material content in water- are widespread examples.
- *Smart Healthcare Systems*: Healthcare service providers play a crucial role in every community, and these services depend on accurate and privacy-preserving information systems to improve patient-caring capabilities. Technological advancements usher rich healthcare-related data gathering, storing, and processing mechanisms using the sensor, the Internet of Things (IoT), intelligent techniques for data analysis, and service-oriented computing.

The central objective of IoT-based information systems is to create secure data communication networks that can gather, send, and process the collected data in data processing dedicated areas (Pal, 2021a). Many smartphone applications are integral to modern IoT networks, and security issues regarding the devices and transmitting data play an enormous role in industrial applications (Pal, 2022). Besides, the IoT technology security issues (e.g., privacy, access control, authorization) are also essential (Pal, 2020). Consequently, developing IoT-based information systems needs careful consideration during deployment and operation (Pal, 2021b).

This chapter's main objective briefly discusses IoT-based information systems security issues and lightweight cryptographic solutions. The chapter also describes some standard cryptography methods and reviews some lightweight cryptographic techniques. Finally, the chapter presents a concluding remark.

BACKGROUND AND IoT SYSTEM SECURITY LANDSCAPE

Any area where humans live or work needs a supporting infrastructure that connects all essential facilities and services, enabling the area to function correctly. A city's infrastructure, for example, includes components such as streets, electric power supply, telephone, water, and sewage lines but also schools, universities, retail stores, and law enforcement authority. Both the area's people and businesses depend on that infrastructure. In this way, cities with good infrastructure, for example, are considered more livable than cities with lousy infrastructure and are much more likely to attract businesses and residents. Likewise, valuable employees often choose firms with better facilities, management, and business processes. Automation of business processes and information systems plays an enormous role in modern society.

Organizational information systems automation has a long history, and it started in the 1960s in the United States of America, Europe, and other developed countries. Information technology (IT) plays a vital role from the very beginning in this automation process. In recent decades, the evolution of mobile communication technology has driven the importance of wireless communications usage as one of the ways to connect to the World Wide Web. However, the ability to communicate with people constantly on the go has emerged as one of the essential characteristics of modern information systems. As a result, modern wireless networks' research and development activities are gaining momentum to connect all aspects of organizational business activities through the network with much higher speed, exceptionally low latency, and ubiquitous connectivity.

Regardless of their application or operating environment, IoT devices are responsible for monitoring, controlling, and enhancing commercial information systems' connectivity and performance. Many diverse technologies, such as wide-area networks, data analytics, security platforms, and operating systems, are involved in the IoT spectrum for commercial applications.

There is no standardized architecture for IoT-based information system industrial applications. However, layered architectures are suggested by different vendors and research groups, such as three-layer (Borgia, 2014); five-layer (Bononi et al., 2014); service-oriented edge computing (Gubbi et al., 2013) (Pal & Yasar, 2020). Most of these multi-layered architectures reflect particular industrial applications. In addition, as a result of broad applicability, a plethora of the reported attacks targeting IoT devices are directed to such industrial applications. This chapter discusses security threats for industrial information systems using Figure 1 layered architecture that consists of three layers: (i) top layer (i.e., application layer), (ii) middle layer (i.e., networking layer), and (iii) bottom layer (i.e., perception layer) for specific operations. In addition, the individual layer must perform specific tasks for the interconnected smart object networks.

The network layer provides the infrastructural facilities for the collected data from the perception layer and passes it to the application (or service) provision layer. It is the essential layer of the IoT-based information system's architecture, and this layer integrates different communication technologies, which help the interconnectivity of smart IoT objects. The top layer gathers the business processes-related industrial data from the middle layer, processes these data, and supports the needed services for IoT-based system users.

The development of IoT technology has led to the universal connection of people, objects, sensors, and services. The central aim of IoT technology deployment is to provide network infrastructure with interconnection ability, interoperable communication methods and software-defined network connectivity, and incorporation of physical/virtual sensors, personal computers, intelligent devices, smart pharmaceutical items, anytime and on any network (Pal, 2022). The development of smartphone technology provides countless objects to be a part of the IoT network through different *mobile phone sensors*. For example, smartphone technologies are used in modern healthcare services; and a group of researchers (Hinch et al., 2020) presented an idea of a software-based solution for coronavirus *contact tracing*, highlighting the usability of smartphone devices' proximity sensors.

In this new era of digital connectivity, based on IoT technology, the possibility of data theft by hackers is a prevalent security problem. The tremendous growth in IoT-based information systems and their interconnections via networks has increased the dependence of businesses and individuals on the information stored and communicated using these systems. Hence, protecting sensitive data and other resources from disclosure, tampering, and systems from unauthorized data piracy attacks is urgent.

Figure 2 represents various types of security issues based on the above three-layer architecture. Tables 1 describes briefly the identified attacks in Figure 2.

Figure 2. Various categories of security attacks on IoT systems

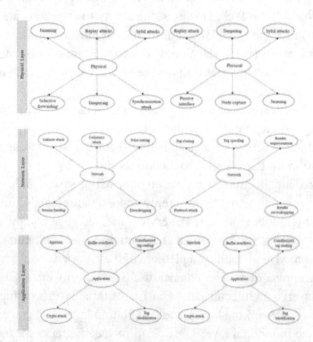

The processes of authentication, integrity, data confidentiality and data privacy are among the main elements of IoT-based information system security. Other significant concerns include identification, trust and access control, and data availability. The identification process is crucial for the network to decide whether or not the smart device can be trusted. Serious threats may arise from permitting an intruder to enter the secured network. In addition, IoT business applications must provide an operating environment that can detect these possible security threats and must be able to provide its device identity to other qualified devices. Therefore, devices interacting with their users must know their identity and can distinguish them too.

Table 1. Brief description of some known attacks

Category of Attack	Description
Jamming	This attack transmits undesirable signals to IoT devices, causing problems for users by keeping the network constantly busy.
Replay	The attacker first captures the authentication of a session. Then, the attacker replays authenticated sessions to gain access to the network without altering or interfering with the original session or sessions.
Sybil	They are mainly used to gain unauthorized access to IoT systems by targeting user identification.
Selective forwarding	Such attacks occur when a network node supposed to send the data packets along the right routing direction path discards some of the traffic that passes through it. Various types of selective forwarding attacks exist.
Tampering	The attacker physically modifies the device or the communication link.
Synchronization	This attack's primary function is disabling RFID tags.
Passive interface	The passive interface restricts outgoing advertisements.
Node capture	This is a physical attack in which the attacker captures a node and controls it physically. For example, the attacker might change or replace the capture node or manipulate the hardware components of the node or the IoT device.
Sinkhole	A sinkhole attack is a type of attack in which a compromised node tries to attract network traffic by advertising its fake routing update.
Unfairness	The attacker creates unfairness in resource utilization.
False routing	False Routing Attack: Disturbance caused by the attacker sending false route information to trouble a smooth communication.
Session flooding	The attacker exploits the known vulnerabilities of the victim's protocol to drain the available resources.
Eavesdropping	The attacker can obtain unencrypted information, such as a password supplied in response to a request.
Tag cloning	Clone valid RFID tag information.
Tag spoofing	In this attack, the process of unauthorized capturing of RFID tag information, including its unique tag ID (TID), and retransmitting this information to a reader, fooling it into believing that the data is coming from a legitimate transponder.
Reader impersonation	The concept of this attack is that the active adversary tries to run a new successful session with the target tag as a legitimate reader.
Protocol attack	The attacker manipulates protocol(s).
Reader eavesdropping	The concept of this attack is that the active adversary tries to run a new successful session with the target tag as a legitimate reader.
Injection	The attack exploits program errors to introduce malicious code into the system. For example, adversaries can use code injection attacks to steal sensitive data from users, get complete control of any system, or spread malware.
Buffer overflows	In this attack, a program or process tries to write extra data to a fixed memory block or buffer in a buffer overflow attack. This attack overflows the buffer boundaries to insert malicious codes.
Unauthorized tag reading	The attacker gets unauthorized Tag information.
Crypto attack	These attacks are focused on the ciphertext and try to break the encryption.
Tag modification	Most RFID tags use writable memory; as a consequence, modifying or deleting valuable information could be performed easily by an attacker.

In the case of IoT-based information systems, authentication is quite challenging as it usually requires appropriate authentication mechanisms, such as two-factor authentication. As in IoT, passive utilities are used, such as RFID tags or sensor nodes; the standard procedures commonly used in other IT sectors cannot be used, as these passive utilities cannot exchange too many messages with the authentication servers.

One of the essential aspects of an IoT-based information system is 'data integrity. The data transmission can be disrupted by plenty of factors that cannot be controlled by the nodes involved. For example, data changes during transmission, server outages, or electromagnetic interference. Hence, data integrity is preserved with the help of standard surveillance methods to protect the data transmitted from cyber-attacks and to avoid external interference in the communication itself. For this purpose, methods like checksums and cyclic redundancy checks (CRC) are used to guarantee data accuracy and reliability with the help of error detection mechanisms (Sicari et al., 2014).

Figure 2 presents a security attack analysis diagrammatic representation. In this representation, security attacks are classified around the application, network, and perception layers. Again, all attacks are differentiated into two groups: (i) RFID system attacks and (ii) WSN attacks.

The perception layer of an IoT network is very vulnerable to two distinct types of attacks: jamming (Shi & Perrig, 2004) and tampering (Modares et al., 2011). In addition, there exist several types of attacks on the network layer – for example – the Sybil attack (Karlof & Wagner, 2003) (Newsome et al., 2004), Sinkhole and Wormhole related issues (Karlof & Wagner, 2003) (Hu et al., 2003), Selective forwarding (Yu et al., 2006), and Hello flood attack (Newsome et al., 2004).

Intruder attacks in IoT generally span over the information system layers that encompass hardware, communication link and business services. Therefore, the solutions for IoT-based systems need to consider the security issues for three layers, as shown in Figure 2. Several challenges exist to securing IoT systems, for example, reliable communication, minimizing the operating environment's hostility, and providing adequate protection to data and privileges (Pal, 2022). Besides, there exist more security-related vulnerabilities at different layers.

Development of IoT Security Solutions

The central aim of using security solutions for IoT systems is to preserve privacy and confidentiality, ensuring the system's reliability to the end-users. Therefore, the solution and protection mechanisms are generally used, and cryptography plays an essential role in managing the security of IoT systems.

ENCRIPTION DESIGN OVERVIEW

Conventional cryptography refers to modern privacy protection is ciphers, and there are two types of such ciphers: stream ciphers and block ciphers. They differ in the way messages are processed. Messages are transformed into bit-strings, and then encryption/decryption work by bit map operations and manipulations involving a secret key that the sender and receiver share. The transformation of texts into bit-string does not form part of the security of the ciphers. Private key encryption is expected to produce *confusion* and *diffusion* on plaintext.

Stream Ciphers

Historically, stream ciphers came before block ciphers, and the earlier ones were natural successors of the classical ciphers. Stream ciphers are substitution ciphers that process texts one character at a time. Modern stream ciphers are used in applications where the amount of data is large and perhaps unavailable at the outset but needs to be encrypted online such as satellite TV signals and digital mobile phone traffic. In designing such cyphers, cryptographers tried to adhere to Auguste Kerckhoffs's Principles and concentrated on removing the need for statical analysis. Many stream ciphers have been developed, but they mainly differ in how the key is generated.

The one-time Pad: This is a stream cypher that generalizes the Vigenere cypher by taking the keyword to be a random string of characters that is as long as the plaintext, and hence repeated patterns in the ciphertext cannot aid in deducing the key.

Example:
>
> **P:** GIVEN C EVERY PLAINTEXT IS JUST AS LIKELY ...
> **Key:** SAJRN NFBSS BTYNOLIARH JLBFG YADLS GALB ...
> **C:** YIEQE PJWWJ ZIJNW YBEOA RDKZYRAVWAQEWZ ...

The one-time pad provides what is termed '*Perfect Security*' by Shannon's Theory of information security: "A cipher has perfect secrecy if and only if there are as many keys as possible plaintexts, and every key is equally likely".

Given any one-time pad ciphertext C and plaintext P of the same length, a key encrypts P to C. Hence, no amount of computation can help in decrypting an intercepted ciphertext since any plaintext of the same length is equally likely.

Spies have widely used the one-time pad – First, encode text as a series of 5-digits, then add key digit-by-digit without carrying. It is also used to encrypt some well-known political hotline (e.g., Washington to Moscow), where the pad is a tape of random bits combined with the plaintext by the exclusive or bit-operation. However, the one-time pad has a few problems. First, the longer the required one-time pad key is, the more impractical its transmission problem. The other major problem with the one-time pad is that it does not provide message integrity and is hence vulnerable to in-depth attacks, which results in falsification.

Example: Let us consider the following ten letters of a hypothetical wartime message:
>
> **P:** HEILHITLER
> **Key:** WCLNBTTDEFJ
> **C:** DGTYIBWPJA
> Intercepting C and slightly modifying it to DCYTIBWPJA would have adversely affected the sender.
> **C:** DCYTIBWPJA
> **Key:** WCLNBTTDEFJ
> **P:** HANGHITLER

Modern stream ciphers operate on bit-strings using a bit-string key randomly generated. In its simplest form, such a cipher XOR is the bits of the plaintext with those of the key. However, techniques have been developed to expand a relatively small secret key into a **keystream** of any length to overcome the problem that the one-time pad suffers from concerning lengthy keys.

Keystream Generators

This is a pseudorandom number generator which is initialized with a key and produces a long random bit-string. It is the main component in stream ciphers that combine the strength of the one-time pad with the simplicity of Vigenère in having a short key. The plaintext bits are XOR'd in their simplest model with the keystream bits; hence it should pass some tests of randomness, including:

- There should be the same number of ones and zeros.
- For each I, the probability that the i-th bit is equal to the bit in position i+ m is the same for any m ^{1} 0.

These and other statistical properties may be desirable but not be enough to make the corresponding cipher reasonably secure. Therefore, it is essential that knowing any number of consecutive keystream bits should not help in predicting the next bit. Therefore, the following methods are being incorporated into keystream generators for specific purposes.

- **Linear Feedback Shift Registers:** A key of n-bits is seeded randomly, and then every subsequent bit is the XOR of a specific pattern of bits in the previous block of k bits. The pattern is determined by a *primitive polynomial* of degree m < k, over Z_2 (i.e., coefficients are 0 or 1), and k is the order of the register. For a given primitive polynomial p(x), only those bits of the previous block whose position coincides with the non-zero terms of the polynomial are to be XOR'd.

For example, if the key is seeded by the 8-bit string 10011010, then the first 20-bit of an order 5 LFSR generated by the primitive polynomial: $X^4 + X + 1$, is:

Table 2.

The seed	The keystream
10011010	01110 10011 10100 11101 …

The use of primitive polynomials is essential for generating *random* effects. For example, if m is the degree of the polynomial, then all possible m-bit strings will appear in an order determined by the seed, and the list will be repeated in the same order. An LFSR is not useful for keystream generation because one needs to use polynomials of large degrees. However, many Keystreams generators are based on combing one or more LFSRs in some way.

- The Non-linear Filter Generator: An LFSR whose initial state is the secret key is used, and some of its state bits are then filtered through a non-linear function to provide the keystream.
- The Multiplexer Generator: Two LFSRs whose order has no common factor are used. Some of the first register bits are used as address lines to a multiplexer which selects the next bit of the keystream from the second register. This is used in a Satellite TV encryption stream cipher.

More than 2 LFSR's have been used in applications like mobile voice encryption. However, keystream Generators that are not based on Shift Registers have also been proposed.

Stream Ciphers suffer from two main problems: (i) replay attack – record old messages and re-send, and (ii) synchronization problem – the keystream generator at both ends must produce the exact key string. Block cyphers were designed to overcome these problems.

Block Ciphers

In industrial resource-constrained automated systems, smart objects' communication must overcome certain energy restrictions, efficiency, and performance restrictions. In these situations, standard stereotype cryptographic methods are not useable. For example, block cipher primitives constitute the most appropriate type of cryptographic algorithm. This category of ciphers transforms a binary text of a fixed length into a cipher text of the same length using a symmetric key to ensure communication security; lightweight block ciphers were introduced at the end of the 1990s (Smith, 1997).

Figure 3. Diagrammatic representation of substitution-permutation network

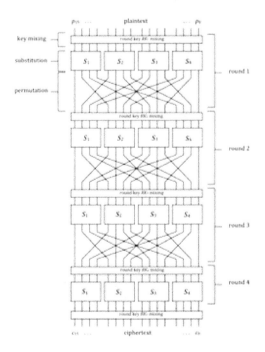

Substitution-Permutation-Networks

A substitution and permutation network (referred as an SP Network, or simply an SPN) is a well-known structure for realizing the characteristics of Shannon's product cipher. A SP network is shown in Figure 3.

Numerous cipher proposals over the years have used the concepts found in SPN. For example, the PRESENT cipher is an SPN and, most notably, AES has a structure that is very similar to an SPN. A simple example of an SP network is presented below. It has 16 inputs (and four rounds), fed into layers of 4-bit invertible S-boxes (i.e., substitution functions), each of which can be visualized as a lookup table containing a permutation of the numbers 0...15 (Note that 4-bits can represent these numbers).

SP-networks in the above arrangements are not secure. All the boxes can be reconstructed by a chosen plaintext attack. One way to strengthen SP-network ciphers is to add more rounds, but each round must be designed with care by adding "noise" and using secret keys.

Feistel Model of Block Ciphers

The Feistel Model of block cipher is a more complex block ciphers than the SP-networks model (Feistel Cipher, 2022). It provides a clear framework for reasoning about security. Most conventional block ciphers are based on this model. A Feistel based cipher has a ladder structure consisting of a few rounds. Messages are processed in blocks of fixed size (often 64-bits), and each block is split into two halves L and R. In each round, R is input into a "one-way" function that involves a secret key parameter. The output is XORed with L and then passed on to the next round as the new R while the old R is passed on as the new L.

Figure 4. Description of Feistel Network

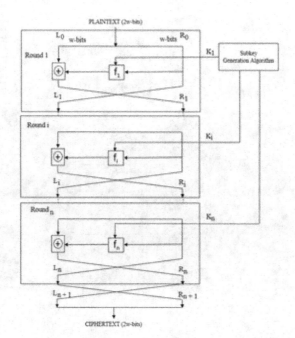

The round functions in a Feistel cipher must satisfy the property that makes decryption a mere application of the same round functions, on the ciphertext, but in the reverse order. Therefore, the round functions do not need to be invertible. Hence, these round functions do not have to have good diffusion and confusion characteristics. Figure 4 represents a Feistel model of block cipher's network.

DATA ENCRYPTION STANDARD (DES)

In the early 1970s a variety of encipherment devises were available in the market. With the rapid advances in computer and communication technology, the need for secure communication between different organizations started to grow faster. Moreover, encipherment is often introduced within the context of communication protocols. Except for military and governmental purposes, standing encryption systems does make commercial sense and provides good framework for quality control.

In 1973, the American National Bureau of Standards (NBS) initiated a program on standardizing encryption algorithms. It was agreed that the IBM response was the one that fits the published requirements. This was the DES encryption system, which is a development from the earlier scheme *Lucifer*. The DES, also known as the DEA, is a symmetric private key block-cipher. It was designed according to Shannon's Theory of Information security with the aim of achieving confusion and diffusion (Substitution is the mean of confusion, and Transposition as the mean of diffusion).

DES is a Feistel 64-bit block cipher, with 16 rounds. The round functions use standard arithmetic and logical operations on up to 64-bit numbers. It is suitable for implementation in software. A DES cipher has a private key of 56-bit length from which 16 48-bit parameters K_1, K_2, ..., K_{16} are derived using a complex but otherwise published iterative procedure. The procedure involves certain published permutations, splitting, and a certain bit operation. A data encryption standard is diagrammatically represented in Figure 5.

Figure 5. Description of DES cipher

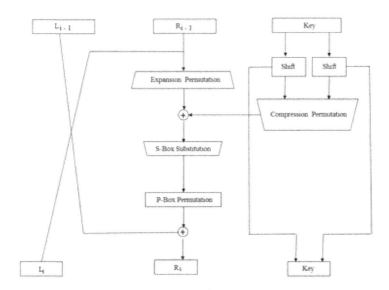

The i-th round function of a DES cipher consists of an expansion, followed by addition of K_i subkey, and then passed through a row of 8 S-boxes. Prior to the first Round the input is permuted in a certain way, and after the last round the inverse permutation is applied to get the cipher text.

An S-box is table of 4 rows (indexed by 00, 01, 10, 11) and 16 columns (indexed by 0000, 0001, 0010, …, 1111) containing the numbers 0 … 15. Note that, each these numbers can be expressed as a 4-bit string. An S-box is a substitution that compresses a 48-bit string into a 32-bits as follows: The rows are indexed by 00, 01, 10, and 11. The columns are indexed by 0000, 0001, 0010, …, 1111.

Example: S-Box 1 of the DES cipher

The j-th 6-bit t block of a 48-bit string is reduced to the 4-bit string in the j-th S-Box which is in the row determined by the numerical value of the first and last position of t, and in the column determined by the numerical value of the other 4 middle bits of t.

Example: If t = 110110 is the input to the S-box above, then it is replaced by the 4-bit in the row indexed by 10 and the column indexed by 1011. Hence, t is replaced by the 4-bit representation of 3, i.e., 0011 (please see the bolded entry in the above table).

As a Feistel cipher, DES decryption is achieved by the same encryption procedure but using the subkeys K_1, K_2, …, K_{16} in the reverse order (DES Cipher, 2022).

Figure 6. Diagrammatic representation of Triple DES (TDES)

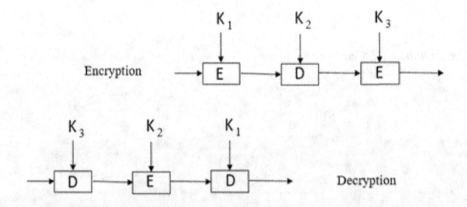

Triple DES: A diagrammatical representation of TDES is shown in Figure 6. There has been two criticisms of the DES at the preliminary stages. The first related to the wisdom of setting a standard for encryption, but it was also criticized for having too short a key. It is now widely accepted that a 56-bit key is not secure and has been broken using "**modest**" computer powers. Other than 56-bit key, have been considered. Longer keys result in more security, but efficiency may become a problem. Other than 16 iterations can be considered as way of improving efficiency, but less than 16 iterations weaken the system.

Triple DES is a block cipher that uses three different 56-bit keys and three executions of DES. Enciphering follows an **encrypt-decrypt-encrypt** (EDE) sequence, and deciphering follows a DED sequence, as shown above. TDEA cipher has the combined effects of taking a 168-bit key and 48 rounds, and yet it is as efficient as a single DES. The efficiency is a result of the fact that after the first two blocks, the three ciphers can work concurrently.

In lightweight block ciphers, design requires very generic bitwise operations (e.g., XOR, AND) and a specific Substitution box (S-box), which promotes an increased number of rounds. In addition, lightweight ciphers need unique cryptographic algorithms to implement information protection strategies.

Advanced Standard Encryption (AES)

AES received standardization in 2001 by the National Institute of Standards and Technology (NIST), and researchers have studied it since then. Different devices may require a different level of security at the security level, and each device will have a different power budget and throughput.

Figure 7. AES – Key Expansion

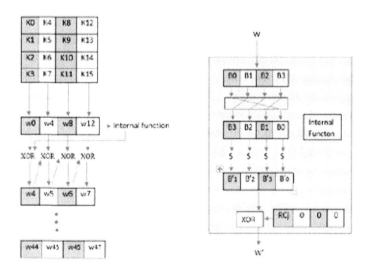

In the context of encryption design purpose (i.e., algorithm level), the security level will depend on the algorithm's construction and the key's length. AES has three different key sizes, which ensures different security levels. It has well-proven security and is widely used in data encryption for industrial applications. In addition, AES has low complexity and a higher security level (Agwa et al., 2017). AES core is divided into two paths: Data Encryption Path and Key Expansion Path. Overall, AES has four significant rounds.

1. Key Expansion: Round keys are derived from the cipher key. This step has three rounds itself, Rotate, S-Box, and Rcon – as shown in Figure 6.

2.   Initial Round: Add Round Key: Each byte of the state is combined with a block of the round key using bitwise XOR.
3.   Rounds:
     ◦   Sub Bytes: A non-linear substitution step where each byte is replaced with another according to a lookup table.
     ◦   Shift Rows: A transportation step where the last three rows of the state are shifted cyclically a certain number of steps.
     ◦   Mix Columns: A mixing operation which operates on the columns of the state, combining the four bytes in each column and Add Round Key.
4.   Final Round: All three rounds except Mix Columns.

A step-by-step key expansion of AES is shown in Figure 7. Block chippers have a fixed length of bits and different stages of transformation, determined by a symmetric key. Besides, this category of ciphers is very versatile and helpful for IoT-based information systems perspective. Another advantage is that this process has almost identical encryption and decryption methods. Hence, it is possible to be implemented with lesser resources. The following sections describe some of the well-known block chipper designs.

Design Trends in Lightweight Block Ciphers

Many new generation block ciphers use an additional input alongside the plaintext, and the key called a tweak manages the cypher's operation. This category of ciphers is known as tweakable block ciphers. In recent years, different trends are emerging in designing lightweight block ciphers. The design is often considering hardware and software levels, and different operational efficiency metrics are opening new types of block chippers. The main objectives of these efficiencies measure are to ensure a trade-off between cost, performance, and security. In this way, the best possible solutions that can be achieved are two-fold, and they are (i) a high-cost need to be paid to make a secure and fast chip, and (ii) a slow chip will be less costly and secure.

Development of IoT Security Solutions

The central aim of using security solutions for IoT systems is to preserve privacy and confidentiality, ensuring the system's reliability to the end-users. Therefore, the solution and protection mechanisms are generally used, and cryptography plays an essential role in managing the security of IoT systems.

LIGHTWEIGHT ENCRYPTION FOR IoT SECURITY

In order to get total end-to-end security, the IoT data communication network nodes need to be encrypted. Authentication provides an important method in identification of users and electro-mechanical machineries or devices. This way, authentication can combat attacks to the IoT-based information systems. There are different categories of authentication protocols developed for IoT technology: (i) asymmetric-cryptosystem based protocol, symmetric-cryptosystem based protocols (as shown in Figure 8), and hybrid protocols (Ferran et al., 2017).

Figure 8. Symmetric lightweight cryptography for IoT systems

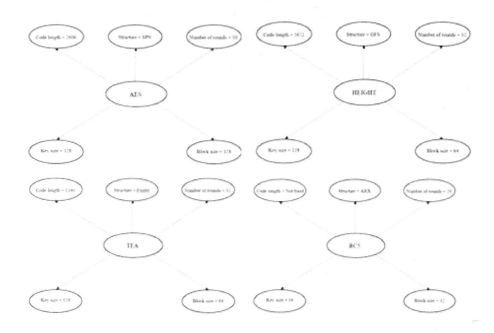

Since the IoT system users and devices communicate in two-ways, hence it needs authentication mechanisms security purpose. There are different types of authentication methods used and some of the recent research is described in the following section.

Related Research Work

Cryptographic techniques effectively guarantee IoT-based information systems' data confidentiality, integrity, and authentication mechanisms. In general, IoT-based systems devices suffer from usability-related issues, and they are (i) processing ability, (ii) memory capacity, and (iii) battery power. This way, standard cryptographic methods are unsuitable for resource deprived IoT elements (e.g., devices). However, lightweight cryptographic primitives are used for operational business processes, and these IoT devices are often resource constrained. For example, lightweight cryptographic methods are often segregated into four types: block ciphers, stream ciphers, hash functions, and elliptic curve cryptography (ECC) (Dhanda et al., 2020).

In a block cipher, plaintext block is encrypted simultaneously, while a stream cipher encrypts/decrypts a single bit or byte of plaintext/ciphertext. The hash function provides data integrity by creating a fixed-length message from an arbitrary-length message. ECC is a lightweight asymmetric cryptographic method that enacts the same security level as the Rivest-Shamir-Adleman (RSA) algorithm with a smaller key size. In addition, many research projects have been reported using lightweight cryptographic methods to produce essential security needs that encompass confidentiality, security, and individualistic identification.

Muhammad Usman and fellow researchers highlighted a security method (i.e., lightweight encryption) for an IoT-based application (Usman et al., 2017). The encryption method used in that research is a SP and Feistel network. The proposed system guarantees data confidentiality and integrity approaches.

Romana Shahada and colleagues reported on IoT-based remote healthcare monitoring systems' security-related issues (Shahzadi et al., 2019). In this report, the researchers discussed the shortfall of the Rivest Cipher (RC5) based block cipher method and presented an enhanced framework that uses a 2D chaotic map. The system also deployed a symmetric key schedule during the encryption and decryption methods.

In 2019 a research group proposed a wireless sensor networks encryption experimentation (Sharafi et al., 2019). The researchers used the SP network, and their presented framework is comparatively better secure than the other algorithms (e.g., RC5, Skipjack).

Hassan Noura and friends (Noura et al., 2019) presented a scheme for information systems. The scheme used a dynamic key-dependent data encryption technique, which is comparatively efficient in terms of encryption time than the Advanced Encryption System (AES) method because it needs only one iteration to create the ciphertext.

Liu and other researchers investigated secure real-time IoT-based information systems applications (Liu et al., 2020). The research group used two algorithms for data privacy protection in a minimum resource based IoT application.

Mohammad Wazid and other researchers proposed a lightweight user authentication method for hierarchical IoT applications (Wazid et al., 2017). In the presented scheme, the researchers used cryptographic hash function and symmetric cryptography techniques. Geeta Sharma and Sheetal Kalra proposed an IoT-based secure and efficient authentication framework for remote patient monitoring systems (Sharma & Kalra, 2019). The framework uses a lightweight hash function where the remote user and cloud service are mutually authenticated and share individual session key to secure future communications. This research paper presents a protected and effective user identification method for dispersed patient observation purpose.

Shen et al. (Shen et al., 2018) presented that their research was based on authentication protocols and used hash function and symmetric cryptography. Wu and other researchers proposed an efficient user authentication scheme for a wireless medical sensor network in an IoT-based information system (Wu et al., 2018). The scheme used multifactor authentication method. Ankur Gupta and fellow researchers presented a lightweight anonymous user authentication and key establishment scheme for wearable devices (Gupta et al., 2019).

Harbi and other researchers published a paper describing an enhanced ECC-based authentication and session key agreement scheme for wireless networks in IoT-based information systems (Harbi et al., 2019). The IoT interconnected network is organized into a cluster to reduce energy consumption. The security analysis justifies the data security of the presented system.

Deebak et al. (2019) presented a scheme for remote user authentication based on ECC, cryptographic hash function, and symmetric cryptography for competent healthcare IoT-based information systems. The proposed scheme involves the user's biometrics information to safeguard the user's impersonation attack.

Hakjun Lee and fellow researchers (Lee et al., 2020) described a multifactor user authentication method. Scheme for an IoT-based business operational environment. The proposed authentication framework uses lightweight and suitable for constrained IoT applications. Sadhukhan and other researchers (Sadhukhan et al., 2021) presented a multifactor user authentication method.

Many other groups of researchers presented their research findings on the implemented systems that use cryptography techniques for different industrial applications (Kaushik & Singh, 2018; Kaushik & Singh, 2020; Singh et al., 2020).

POTENTIAL ATTACKS AND SOME COUNTERMEASURES

IoT technology-based devices are being used in various consumer applications at home, offices, intelligent buildings, and smart cities are the few examples. Based on the application and the device type, data in these applications are private and confidential, but there is an increasing need to ensure that data sensed and sent by IoT devices are secured, both during transit and at rest. However, IoT devices, remarkably inexpensive and computationally limited, are not designed with any security mechanisms. These products, therefore, end up being attractive targets for adversaries. This chapter highlighted some of the IoT technology-associated security vulnerabilities. There is, therefore, a need to educate users about the potential risks of everyday consumer IoT devices, for example, by mapping them to the known security risks in the IoT perception layer. This is the focus of this section, where the findings can help consumer IoT device manufacturers strengthen their security design for other products. Finally, a few industrial examples guide remedies in the following case studies.

Case Study – Node Tampering Attack: It is a physical attack in which the attacker successfully captures the device hardware and manually tampers with its electronic circuit. A group of researchers considered one such case study on Itron Centron CL200 smart meter (Arias et al., 2017). The primary goal of the attack was to change the DeviceID of the smart meter. They replicated the ID of a different smart meter on its EEPROM, enabling the hacked smart meter to impersonate another one at the attacker's will.

This device's EEPROM chip is unprotected against illegitimate read or writes access. The chip can be made tamper-resistant by using anti-counterfeit hardware primitives like Physically Unclonable Functions (PUFs) as add-ons to the chip to secure the data in EEPROM. PUFs are cheaper alternatives to cryptographic software solutions and function as digital fingerprints allowing only authenticated devices to modify crucial data (Kumar et al., 2019).

Case Study – Eavesdropping Attack: In this attack, data traffic from the targeted IoT device is sniffed by an eavesdropping/man-in-the-middle (MITM) capable of extracting critical network information. A case study on a compromised smart scale, Fitbit Aria, is discussed in an exercise to explain this attack (PenTestPartner, 2019).

FUTURE WORK

The ubiquitous nature of IoT raises an essential set of issues about users' privacy and how to mitigate the diverseness of individual and commercial system needs regarding privacy services. It needs context-aware, adaptive, and user-centred privacy mitigating options. This way, the diversity of system privacy needs can be tackled using adaptive and context-awareness handling techniques of privacy profiles and governance regulations. It also includes the consideration of privacy in dynamic and heterogeneous operating environments. In addition, the number of connected smart devices has been increasing rapidly for different IoT-based commercial applications. Securing a vast number of connected devices in IoT applications is necessary to realize the full potential of IoT applications. Recently, researchers have proposed many security solutions for IoT. Machine learning has been proposed as one of the emerging solutions for IoT security, and reinforcement learning is gaining more popularity for Securing IoT systems. Unlike other machine learning techniques, reinforcement learning can learn the environment by having minimum information about the parameters to be learned. All these research issues will be considered in future work.

CONCLUSION

IoT technology-based pervasive computing uses devices to enhance various aspects of industrial and commercial applications. Such devices operate on limited resources; therefore, data processing, communication protocols and underlying technologies must be carefully chosen to meet strict operating requirements. Considering that the information they handle is, in many cases, private or safety-critical and must be appropriately protected from malicious attackers, the appliance of secure cryptographic components becomes imperative. In addition, lightweight cryptography uses the integration of cryptographic techniques and algorithmic steps that are used in resource-constrained devices.

Of the two critical categories of cryptographic algorithms, symmetric and asymmetric keys, the former performs well and is heavily deployed for confidentiality, preserving integrity and authentication mechanisms. The tested after-deployment robustness and experimental levels of security of well-known block ciphers (e.g., AES) make these ciphers good candidates for resource constraint applications. In this way, AES is the standard symmetric-key cipher used in cryptographic applications. Newer block ciphers are explicitly designed for resource constraints applications, opening new innovative ideas while providing novelties and enhancing the overall performance.

This chapter analyses the features of block ciphers, and presents a few critical constructs (e.g., SP-Network, Feistel Model, DES, and Triple DES). It also identifies suitable ciphers for various industrial and commercial application categories. In addition, this review briefly presented different architectural issues, attacks, and challenges to IoT security. Finally, the chapter presents recent cryptographic research works.

REFERENCES

Agwa, S., Yahya, E., & Ismail, Y. (2017). Power efficient AES core for IoT constrained devices implemented in 130 nm CMOS. In *Proceedings of the 2017 IEEE International Symposium on Circuits and Systems*, Baltimore, MD, USA, 28–31 May 2017,1–4.

Arias, O., Ly, K., & Jin, Y. (2017). Security and Privacy in IoT era. In *Smart Sensors at the IoT Frontier* (pp. 351–378). Springer.

Borgia, E. (2014). The Internet of Things vision: Key features, applications, and open issues. *Computer Communications*, *54*, 1–31.

Deebak, B. D., Al-Turjman, F., Aloqaily, M., & Alfandi, O. (2019). An authentic-based privacy preservation protocol for smart e-Healthcare systems in IoT. *IEEE Access: Practical Innovations, Open Solutions*, *7*, 135632–135649.

DES Cipher. (2022). https://en.wikipedia.org/wiki/Triple_DES

Dhanda, S. S., Singh, B., & Jindal, P. (2020). Lightweight Cryptography: A Solution to Secure IoT. *Wireless Person. Commun.*, 1–34.

ECC. (2022). https://en.wikipedia.org/wiki/Elliptic-curve_cryptography

Feistel Cipher. (2022). https://en.wikipedia.org/wiki/Feistel_cipher

Ferrag, M. A., Maglaras, L. A., Janicke, H., & Jiang, J. (2017). Authentication Protocols for Internet of Things: A Comprehensive Survey. *Security and Communication Networks*, 1–41.

Gubbi, J., Buyya, R., Murusic, S., & Palaniswami, M. (2013). Internet of Things (IoT): A vision, architectural elements, and future directions. *Future Generation Computer Systems*, *29*(7), 1645–1660.

Gupta, A., Tripathi, M., Shaikh, T. J., & Sharma, A. (2019, February). A lightweight anonymous user authentication and key establishment scheme for wearable devices. *Computer Networks*, *149*, 29–42.

Harbi, Y., Aliouat, Z., Harous, S., Bentaleb, A., & Refouf, A. (2019). A Review of Security in Internet of Things. *Wireless Personal Communications*, *108*, 325–344.

Harbi, Y., Aliouat, Z., Refoufi, A., Harous, S. A., & Bentaleb, A. (2019). Enhanced authentication and key management scheme for securing data transmission in the Internet of Things. *Ad Hoc Networks*, *94*(Nov), 101948.

Hinch, R., Probert, W., Nurtay, A., Kendall, M., Wymant, C., Hall, M., Fraser, C., Lythgoe, K., Cruz, A. B., Zhao, L., Stewart, A., Ferretti, L., Parker, M., Meroueh, A., Mathias, B., Stevenson, S., Montero, D., Warren, J., Mather, N. K., . . . Fraser, C. (2020). Effective configurations of a digital contact tracing app: A report to NHSX (NHSX Report). The Conversation Trust (UK). Available online: https://cdn. theconversation.com/static_files/files/1009/Report_-_Effectiv_App_Configurations.pdf

Hu, Y. C., Perrig, A., & Johnson, D. B. (2003). Packet leashes: A defense against wormhole attacks in wireless networks. In *Twenty-Second Annual Joint Conference of the IEEE Computer and Communications. INFOCOM 2003*. IEEE.

Karlof, C., & Wagner, D. (2003). Secure routing in wireless sensor networks: Attacks and countermeasures. *Ad Hoc Networks*, *1*(2), 293–315.

Kaushik, K., & Dahiya, S. (2018). Security and Privacy in IoT based EBusiness and Retail. *2018 International Conference on System Modeling & Advancement in Research Trends (SMART)*, 78–81. 10.1109/ SYSMART.2018.8746961

Kaushik, K., & Singh, K. (2020). Security and Trust in IoT Communications: Role and Impact. In S. Choudhury, R. Mishra, R. Mishra, & A. Kumar (Eds.), *Intelligent Communication, Control and Devices. Advances in Intelligent Systems and Computing, 989*. Springer. doi:10.1007/978-981-13-8618-3_81

Kumar, S., Satheesh, N., Mahapatra, A., Sahoo, S., & Mahapatra, K. (2019). Physical unclonable functions for on-chip instruction: Enhancing the security of the internal joint test action group network. *IEEE Consumer Electronics Magazine*, *8*(4), 62–66.

Lee, H., Kang, D., Ryu, J., Won, D., Kim, H., & Lee, Y. (2020, June). A three-factor anonymous user authentication scheme for Internet of Things environments. *Journal of Information Security Application.*, *52*, 102494.

Liu, T., Wang, Y., Li, Y., Tong, X., Qi, L., & Jiang, N. (2020, September). Privacy protection based on stream cipher for spatiotemporal data in IoT. *IEEE Internet Things J.*, *7*(9), 7928–7940.

Modares, H., Salleh, R., & Moravejosharieh, A. (2011). Overview of security issues in wireless sensor networks. *Third International Conference on Computational Intelligence, Modelling and Simulation (CIMSiM)*, 308–311.

Newsome, J., Shi, E., Song, D., & Perrig, A. (2004). The sybil attack in sensor networks: Analysis & defenses. *Proceedings of the 3rd International Symposium on Information Processing in Sensor Networks*, 259–268.

Noura, H., Couturier, R., Pham, C., & Chehab, A. (2019). Lightweight stream cipher scheme for resource-constrained IoT devices. *Proc. Int. Conf. Wireless Mobile Comput., Netw. Commun. (WiMob)*, 1–8.

Pal, K. (2019). Algorithmic Solutions for RFID Tag Anti-Collision Problem in Supply Chain Management. *Procedia Computer Science*, 929-934.

Pal, K. (2021a). Privacy, Security and Policies: A Review of Problems and Solutions with Blockchain-Based Internet of Things Applications in Industrial Industry. *Procedia Computer Science*.

Pal, K. (2021b). A Novel Frame-Slotted ALOHA Algorithm for Radio Frequency Identification System in Supply Chain Management. *Procedia Computer Science*, 871-876. 10.1016/j.procs.2021.03.110

Pal, K. (2022a). Application of Game Theory in Blockchain-Based Healthcare Information System. In Prospects of Blockchain Technology for Accelerating Scientific Advancement in Healthcare. IGI Global.

Pal, K. (2022b). Semantic Interoperability in Internet of Things: Architecture, Protocols, and Research Challenges. In Management Strategies for Sustainability, New Knowledge Innovation, and Personalized Products and Services. IGI Global.

Pal, K. (2022b). A Decentralized Privacy Preserving Healthcare Blockchain for IoT, Challenges and Solutions. In Prospects of Blockchain Technology for Accelerating Scientific Advancement in Healthcare. IGI Global.

Pal, K. (2022d). Cryptography and Blockchain Solutions for Security Protection of Internet of Things Applications. In Information Security Practices for the Internet of Things, 5G, and Next-Generation Wireless Networks. IGI Global.

Pal, K., & Yasar, A. (2020b). Semantic Approach to Data Integration for an Internet of Things Supporting Apparel Supply Chain Management. *Procedia Computer Science*, 197 - 204.

Pal, K., & Yasar, K. (2020a). Internet of Things and Blockchain Technology in Apparel Manufacturing Supply Chain Data Management. *Procedia Computer Science*, 450 - 457.

RSA. (2022). https://en.wikipedia.org/wiki/RSA

Sadhukhan, D., Ray, S., Biswas, G. P., Khan, M. K., & Dasgupta, M. (2021). A lightweight remote user authentication scheme for IoT communication using elliptic curve cryptography. *The Journal of Supercomputing*, 77(2), 1114–1151.

Shahzadi, R., Anwar, S. M., Qamar, F., Ali, M., & Rodrigues, J. P. C. (2019). Chaos based enhanced RC5 algorithm for security and integrity of clinical images in remote health monitoring. *IEEE Access: Practical Innovations, Open Solutions*, 7, 52858–52870.

Shannon, C. E. (1949). Communication Theory of Secrecy Systems. *The Bell System Technical Journal*, *28*(4), 656–715. doi:10.1002/j.1538-7305.1949.tb00928.x

Sharafi, M., Fotouhi-Ghazvini, F., Shirali, M., & Ghassemian, M. (2019). A low power cryptography solution based on chaos theory in wireless sensor nodes. *IEEE Access: Practical Innovations, Open Solutions*, *7*, 8737–8753.

Sharma, G., & Kalra, S. (2018, October). A lightweight multi-factor secure smart card based remote user authentication scheme for cloud-IoT applications. *Journal of Information Security Applications*, *42*, 95–106.

Shen, J., Chang, S., Shen, J., Liu, Q., & Sun, X. (2018, January). A lightweight multi-layer authentication protocol for wireless body area networks. *Future Generation Computer Systems*, *78*, 956–963.

Shi, E., & Perrig, A. (2004). Designing secure sensor networks. *IEEE Wireless Communications*, *11*(6), 38–43. doi:10.1109/MWC.2004.1368895

Sicari, S., Cappiello, C., Pellegrini, F. D., Miorandi, D., & Coen-Porisini, A. (2014). A security-and quality-aware system architecture for Internet of Things. *Information Systems Frontiers*.

Singh, K., Kaushik, K. A., & Shahare, V. (2020). Role and Impact of Wearables in IoT Healthcare. In *Proceedings of the Third International Conference on Computational Intelligence and Informatics*. Springer.

Smith, R. E. (1997). *Internet Cryptography*. Addison Wesley.

TinyOS. (2022). https://en.wikipedia.org/wiki/TinyOS

Usman, M., Ahmed, I., Aslam, M. I., Khan, S., & Shah, U. A. (2017). *SIT: A lightweight encryption algorithm for secure Internet of Things*. Available: https://arxiv.org/abs/1704.08688

Wazid, M., Das, A. K., Odelu, V., Kumar, N., Conti, M., & Jo, M. (2017, February). Design of secure user authenticated key management protocol for generic IoT networks. *IEEE Internet Things J.*, *5*(1), 269–282.

Wu, F., Li, X., Sangaiah, A. K., Xu, L., Kumari, S., Wu, L., & Shen, J. (2018, May). A lightweight and robust two-factor authentication scheme for personalized healthcare systems using wireless medical sensor networks. *Future Generation Computer Systems*, *82*, 727–737.

Yu, B., Yang, M., Wang, Z., & Gao, C. S. (2006). Identify Abnormal Packet Loss in Selective Forwarding Attacks. *Chinese Journal of Computers*, *9*, 1540–1550.

Zia, T., & Zomaya, A. (2006). Security issues in wireless sensor networks. In *International Conference on Systems and Networks Communications, ICSNC'06*. IEEE.

Chapter 11
Graphical Password Authentication System for Web and Mobile Applications in JavaScript

Anand Jha
Rustamji Institute of Technology, BSF Academy, Tekanpur, India

Kirti Raj Bhatele
Rustamji Institute of Technology, BSF Academy, Tekanpur, India

Prajeesh Philip
iD https://orcid.org/0000-0001-7356-872X
Rustamji Institute of Technology, India

Khushi Mishra
Rustamji Institute of Technology, BSF Academy, Tekanpur, India

ABSTRACT

RESTful API-based web and mobile applications are cross-platform and can be accessed from anyplace or anytime resulting in a smoother and easier user experience. This ecosystem creates a familiar environment for business applications, especially for small businesses. However, an increasing number of such applications creates opportunities to protect passwords from various attacks. Humans choose weak textual passwords due to easiness, which may lead to the most frangible connections in the chain of authentication. The graphical password offers a better approach of authentication for web and mobile applications in the emerging business world since it uses images as input instead of alphanumeric. It also makes it difficult for the attackers to crack. This study devises a system that allows the user or client application to authenticate by tapping the right cues over a series of images that the user selects while registering in the system. The system is implemented as a web service using JavaScript technology by ReactJS on client applications and NodeJS on server end.

DOI: 10.4018/978-1-6684-5827-3.ch011

INTRODUCTION

Stolen credentials can lead to devastating losses for businesses. Modern software applications function and live online in order to be easily accessible. Another reason for software to go online is the increasing use of mobile devices. Online applications include web and mobile applications that work around HTTP and REST API. Web and mobile applications can be the reasons for compromise of confidential company details, customer credit card numbers, personal details in the absence of robust authentication systems etc. So the big question is how technology can fuel businesses by going online while keeping the environment secure? Developing such a secure environment has numerous technological aspects, one of them is authentication. Authentication is the first and critical step of online software (Bhhogill, 2019). As businesses are leveraging technological advancement, secure authentication schemes are becoming obligatory to protect users, especially in the era of increasing online business applications. So the need for authentication is more crucial than ever before.

Authentication is the process to identify if the person is genuine and has been verified to have all the access to whatever services and resources are being provided. Using user password authentication is an important step which allows an application to approve the user's authenticity who is associated with the network assets (Abhijith, 2021). The most common type of user authentication is alphanumeric usernames and passwords. Web and mobile applications may lead to compromise of textual passwords using many techniques including dictionary attack, brute force attack, password divination, shoulder surfing etc. Although there are various types of user authentication systems, like smart cards and biometrics are also in use, they have their fallbacks too and might result to be more expensive than simple alphanumeric password authentication systems. One of the reasons that alphanumeric are very popular in today's world, can be because they are adaptable and easy to implement. Alphanumeric passwords must be able to fulfill two requirements, which can sometimes be conflicting to each other. The user must be able to remember it easily, plus it should be difficult enough for the attackers to predict them.

According to one study of fourteen thousand passwords, approximately 25% of the overall passwords were easily cracked by a 'dictionary' formed meticulously of only 3×10^6 words (Klein, 1990). This huge percent rate of success is not that rare, despite the fact that there are almost 2×10^{14} 8-character passwords made of numbers and upper and lowercase letters only. Psychological studies have shown that the human brain is much better at recalling images and recognizing them more easily than text (Nelson et al., 1976). It is known that humans choose passwords that are easy to predict by any imposter, targeted by dictionary and brute force attacks (Shnain et al., 2018). If we attempt to enforce a password policy which may be tough to break, it may lead to a rebellious outcome, such as users may store their strong password on a less protected or even an unprotected device. To help solve the limitations of alphanumeric passwords, a number of techniques have been proposed in the literature (Suo et al., 2005). Graphical passwords are a way to work on the fact that humans can retain images faster and more easily, in the hope that by reducing the burden on the client's memory, passwords with more security and ease for the users can be generated and hence, the user will not have to resort to bad practices. Further, textual or alphanumeric based passwords are at a big risk of many attacks like dictionary attacks, shoulder-surfing, password-guessing, spyware, keyloggers, etc.

Here, we discourse over a user authentication approach that enhances the security of the application authentication step beyond what is provided by the textual passwords. The designed system is HyperText Transfer Protocol (HTTP) based and analyzes graphical authentication of passwords, which the user can enter with a graphical user interface. Our study not only focuses on the memorability of the passwords, but also resolves the critical issue of password strength. In the proposed system, the password is made of one click-point per image for a number of images in a particular sequence. Such a graphical password scheme is called Cued Click Points (CCP). CPP can be thought of as a fusion of PassPoints (Wiedenbeck et al., 2005a, 2005b), Passfaces (http://www.realuser.com), and Story (Davis et al., 2004). The next image to be displayed will be based on the most recent clicked point, so the users can receive immediate feedback whether they have selected the right points or not, when being logging in. This offers both improved security and usability. This scheme appears to be helpful in increasing the workload for the attackers by supplementing the number of images in the application. Graphical passwords may not be the best choice in environments where there might be a serious threat of shoulder-surfing.

The idea of "graphical passwords" was introduced by Blonder (Blonder, 1996). It was his work that declared a scheme of password authentication, where the user gets to choose from a number of predetermined images on a display and has to select one or more already determined tap regions or positions on the presented image in an order that is particular to showcase their authorization to allow the user's access. However, no further work was done to explore the security and power of the proposed system.

Objective of this study is to develop a graphical authentication system based on Cued Click Point (CCP) technique as a web service (HTTP based) using JavaScript technology by ReactJS on client applications and NodeJS on server end.

WHAT IS AUTHENTICATION?

When we talk about security, a word that has been used around a lot is authentication. Authentication is basically a process of verifying whether the particular user is in fact who they claim to be. It is the first line of defense against any unauthorized access. When we log on to a device or a social media feed, the user has to follow a process to log them on to the server and allow them to use the provided service. The process of authentication helps the website visited to determine that the valid user has logged on and has gained the access. Attacks on the systems are always improving, and so is the need to have strong, secure systems. Secure authentication has become very necessary as the increased use of online services has multiplied, and hence the security of the user's data has to be protected from unauthorized access. Without following the process of authentication, nobody can enter the website and access any data. Cybercriminals can gain access to the user's data and steal their information if the authentication system is not secure enough.

HOW DOES AUTHENTICATION ACTUALLY WORK?

Authentication is a process by which an application or a system verifies that the user trying to gain access, is a legitimate user. Thus the authentication objective is to prevent any kind of illegal or unauthorized access to the system and its resources. The most common method of authentication is that the user is provided with a unique user ID and password during the registration phase. The system uses the provided data to verify and validate the incoming user whenever they might attempt to log-on in the future. These details will then be stored in the database of the system through an authentication server. Now, every time the user enters these credentials on the login page, he/she might only be granted access if the provided details match the ones that were stored in the database, otherwise the access is denied and the user cannot enter the website.

The mentioned process of authentication can be done using various methods. To authenticate a user, a system verifies them by one or more of three factors (layers) of authentication: (1) knowledge or something that the user knows, for example a password or unique pin (2) possession or something the user has, for example a key card and (3) inherence, something that is unique to the user, for example biometrics (fingerprint). (Mizrachi, 2021).

1.   Something that the user knows (Knowledge):

This is one of the cheapest and most common types of authentication used in online systems. This method involves questions that only the user can answer. For example, a username and password; or security questions like "What was your first pet's name?" or "What is your mother's maiden name?". The purpose of this is to verify the user's identity via these questions because only they might be able to answer these.

2.   Something that the user has (Possession):

This method uses a thing that you may have or possess, for example your mobile phone or a token, to log you in to the system. A verification link might be sent to your mobile screen, and only then will you be allowed access. OTP is also an example of this type of authentication.

3.   Something that the user is (Inheritance):

This method has to be the safest amongst the above-mentioned methods, but also a bit heavy on the company's pocket. A fingerprint or retinal scan can be commonly used to verify the user in this method. They might provide stronger security, but they have their own pitfalls like they are high cost and the process of identification is slow.

A strong authentication mechanism may include one or more layers of authentication, leading to two-factor authentication (2FA) or multifactor authentication (MFA) (Mizrachi, 2021):

1.   Single Factor Authentication
      a.   Token-based authentication
      b.   Biometric-based authentication
      c.   Certificate Based Authentication
2.   Two-Factor Authentication
3.   Multi-Factor Authentication (MFA)

Single Factor Authentication

Single-factor authentication uses only one type of credentials i.e. uses one factor (layer) to validate the identity of a user. This means that the user has to match a single credential to establish his/her identity during the authentication process. For example, Password-based authentication is a single factor authentication. Single factor authentication can be (a) password-based, (b) token based, (c) biometric based and (d) certificate based etc.

Password-Based Authentication

It is the most familiar kind of authentication. The password is a string of alphabets, special characters, numbers, which is known only to the concerned user (a user with a unique ID). During authentication, user ID and password combination is verified before granting access to services and resources.

Token-Based Authentication

Token-based authentication is a security method which uses a token to help the user to authenticate to the system. The users are provided a unique token upon being verified by the remote authentication servers. The user can then access the relevant service upon showing the provided token. The access is only allowed until the issued token expires. Some examples include key cards, bank cards, smart cards and JSON Web Token.

Biometric-Based Authentication

The biometric-based authentication is a security technique that manages both digital and physical resources. It became a favorable choice for authentication since it is easy to use. The user does not have any memory load and extortion risks are less in this type of authentication. Some examples include fingerprint sensors, iris scan and facial recognition. Although it has very high security, there are quite a few drawbacks: (1) it is more expensive to be implemented since it mandates an initial investment in endpoint hardware, (2) minimizing false-positives and minimizing friction-related churn while being user-friendly is a daunting task and (3) takes more time in the execution and identification process.

Certificate Based Authentication

Certificate based authentication uses digital certificates. Digital certificates can be used to verify the identity of a user or a service. Digital certificate contains information about the key, the certificate owner, and the digital signature of the organization that has issued the certificate. Certificates are issued by third-party organizations like VeriSign, GeoTrust, and DigiCert. Such organizations are known as Certificate Authorities (CA). If the certificate is valid, the certificate information can be used to validate the authenticity of the sender and to communicate securely. Digital certificates do not require any hardware; this makes them probably the first choice of administrators.

Two Factor Authentication

In two-factor authentication, the system asks the user to verify its identity twice using the same or different layers. For example, ATM withdrawal is an example of a two-factor authentication since it requires two items, card and pin.

Multi Factor Authentication

It uses any two or more authentication factors, out of which at least two must be of different categories. Combination of a bank card and a PIN for authentication is an example of multi-factor authentication since card and PIN belong to two different factors, something you have and something you know respectively. However, the combination of a password and a PIN does not qualify as multi-factor authentication since both items are from the same factor, something the user knows.

BACKGROUND AND RELATED WORK

Graphical authentication schemes are usually further divided into three main categories according to the type of obligatory cognitive ability to recall the password, (1) Recognition, (2) Recall and (3) Cued Recall. Recognition is based only on human memory, whereas, pure recall is the most difficult of them since the data or information has to be retrieved from the memory without any triggers. However, cued recall is almost in the middle of these two, as it offers a cue which will validate context and generate triggers to the stored memory. Amongst all the existing graphical authentication schemes, the one that most closely resembles all the aspects of Pass Points (Wiedenbeck et al., 2005a, 2005b), Story (Davis et al., 2004), and Pass faces (www.realuser.com) is Cued Click Point. It is theoretically an amalgamation of all these mentioned methods, and in implementation terms, it is mostly likely to be an upgraded version of Pass Points.

Pass faces (www.realuser.com) is a graphical authentication scheme that is based on the recognition of human faces. When registering, the client has to choose from a bigger set of images, and to log in, the client must be able to identify the images that they pre-selected in the registration phase from amongst the several false clones. (Davis et al., 2004) devised another version, where the results displayed how the users were able to accurately remember what images they pre-selected, but the image passwords selected by the users became predictable to the point of not being secure enough.

(Davis et al., 2004) later also proposed an alternative scheme, which is called Story, that uses images related to everyday life rather than using human faces as passwords and the users were required to select the images in a correct order. To help the users memorize the graphical passwords, and the sequence of images, the user was advised to create a small story using the selected images in their mind. Story was good for the user's to be able to remember them, and the choices made by the user were far less predictable. Then came the idea of using click-based graphical authentication systems, which originated with Blonder. (Blonder, 1996) proposed a scheme which used a sequence of clicks on predefined regions of an image to be used as the password. After that, another scheme was proposed by (Wiedenbeck et al., 2005a, 2005b). which is called PassPoints, where a password can be made up of several points anywhere on the selected image. (Birget et al., 2006) have devised a robust discretization scheme with three overlapping grids, allowing all the login attempts which were very closely correct to be accepted and converting the entered password into a cryptographic verification code. Wiedenbeck et al. (2005a, 2005b) studied PassPoints and its usability by a few separate in-lab studies, comparing alphanumeric passwords to PassPoints, and also tested whether the choice of image picked has any impact on the usability and determine the minimum tolerance square size. The conclusion of it was that PassPoints was a usable authentication scheme.

Even though there exists a number of graphical passwords, Cued Click Point (CCP) most nearly resembles the characteristics of Pass-Faces, Story and Pass-Points. CCP can also be, conceptually, a combination of the three, but in terms of its implementation, it mostly resembles Pass Points. It also avoids complex user training requirements that occur during certain types of password suggestions. This study develops a system that implements CCP graphical password scheme using JavaScript on both client as well as server end.

GRAPHICAL PASSWORD AUTHENTICATION

The graphical password uses the ability of the human brain to recall information from the past. Image passwords are used as an alternative to textual passwords, which are generally used for user's access. Graphical passwords are more accurate than text passwords. Several schemes have been proposed for graphical authentication. Graphical password authentication schemes can be categorized into two types (Sunil et al., 2014; Sharma S., 2017; Sri et al., 2020; Rao, 2019; Yang et al., 2021):

- Recognition based
- Recall based

Recognition-based

In recognition based techniques, the authentication process involves challenges, which either includes identification of images that are either random or that the user previously has chosen during the registration phase. It requires the users to have a number of images memorized during the password-user registration phase, and have them identify the images during the login phase. Human memory is amazing at remembering images or pictures that they have previously viewed, even for a short time period. In some schemes of graphical authentication, some details or information of the users are a shared secret of the system, i.e., user-specific data like the images that the user has selected during the registration process is saved in the system because they have to be displayed during the login phase.

One of the recognition-based schemes, which displays a number of image objects, selected by user previously along with a number of decoys and the user must click inside the area constrained by the pass objects, is *"Sobrado and Birgit"*. In Pass, people's faces are used for the authentication password. One of the other schemes, by Dhamija and Perrig, asks the user to pick several images out of many choices, and have to identify them later in the authentication login phase.

Recall-Based

In recall-based techniques, the user has to 'recall' the activities represented previously. In the authentication process, the user will recall the password that was selected or chosen at during registration stage. The user has to draw their password on a blank sheet or a grid like page. The user can secure the system using different techniques for password authentication.

There are three types of recall techniques, which are as follows:

- Free recall

- Cued recall
- Serial recall

Free Recall

The free call is where the user is given a list of items on each step, and they have to recall the list in any order. In graphical authentication where free recall technique is used, the user is responsible for the security of the system. The user has to create the password in such a way like they use the blank canvas or grid to draw a shape or object item during the registration, that is why it is called free recall.

Cued Recall

The cued recall is the method that uses cues for the user to retrieve image objects from their memory. This technique uses images that are then further cut up into grids and the user has to pick a particular cue point, and they will be represented using a pixel format.

Serial Recall

The serial recall uses a list of items or objects, and the user must remember them in a specific order or sequence only. This technique has an image that is divided into grids or a blank canvas, then the user must choose a few points on the same during the registration and memorize the order during the registration phase. The user has to click on the exact same points in the same order in an exact sequence when trying to log in. The points are to be in the same serial order, that is why it is called serial recall.

PROBLEM DEFINITION

Security practitioners and researchers have proposed many authentication schemes to provide security to systems in order to protect individual users and digital assets. The biggest limitations to strong, difficult to crack password authentication is the long-term memory of human beings. Commonly used passwords for authentication today are alphanumeric passwords. The user should be able to recall the password to log in, after the password has been chosen and memorized by them. Yet, the users forget the textual passwords regularly and it has been shown to be more prone to a number of attacks. Graphical password authentication can be useful here. As pictures and images are easier to memorize than texts, these graphical passwords are proven to be more secure and also, at the same time, images make it easier for the user to recall and to access their data.

PROPOSED SYSTEM

Considering the advantage of human's ability to easily recognize images and the memory triggers associated with viewing a new image, this study implements a cued click point scheme of graphical password in JavaScript. The cued click point (CCP) graphical authentication system helps the user to click on particular points on the image. The user uploads an image from their local storage, and then the clicked points are collected on the mouse clicks. After the user chooses the first image, the second image has to be chosen and their click point will be collected. The same process is repeated for 4 consecutive images during the registration phase. So, Cued Click Points (CCP) is a cued-recall graphical password technique where users click on any one point in an image for the sequence of images. (Ashok et al., 2017). If during the login process, the user clicks on a wrong point on the displayed image, then the next image displayed will be different from the one selected during the registration process. This shows an immediate response to the user that they have clicked on a wrong point. The user uses a client device (which displays the images) which will be used to get access to the online web server (which will authenticate the user).

SOLUTION

A graphical password authentication system is offered, which provides security to protect the users from any fatalities of attacks when entering passwords in public. In the introduced system, according to the correct location of the click-point, the next image is displayed to the user. The user will only be authenticated if they correctly click on the password images.

The proposed system consists of four core modules as depicted in figure 1. User module has two sub-modules.

Figure 1. Modules of proposed system

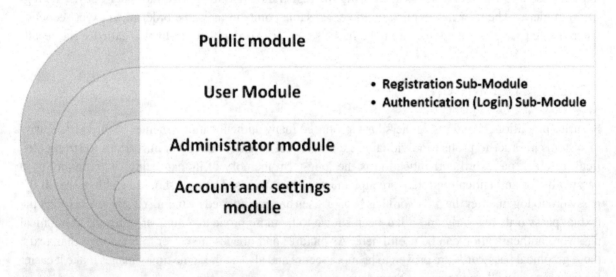

Public Module

It is the view end of the web application that anyone can access with the URL. It is public, but the information cannot be modified or deleted.

User Module

The user module has two sub-modules: (1) registration and (2) authentication (login) as portrayed in figure 2. During the registration phase, the web application asks the user to enter their details like username, name, email and graphical password. They all are then stored in the database in encrypted form. During the authentication (login) phase, the user has to use their username and the graphical password for accessing the home page of the application. It compares the values that the user entered with the information stored in the database. If the details entered are matched, then the user is logged onto the home page.

Figure 2. User module and its two sub modules

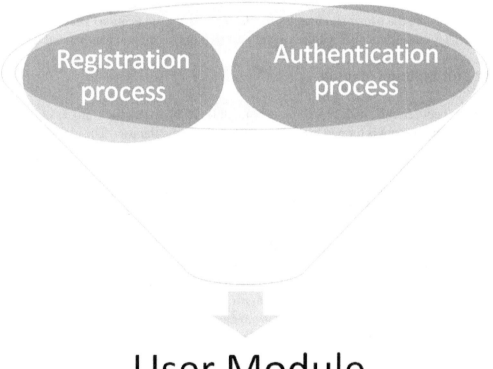

The steps for registration process is shown in figure 3 below.

Figure 3. Flow of registration process (registration sub-module) of user module

The steps for authentication process is shown in figure 4 below.

Figure 4. Flow of authentication process (authentication/login sub-module) of user module

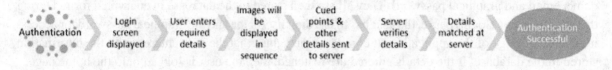

Administrator Module

The administrators are the owner and handles the database of the application. They have access to the user records. They can change their password and give or block access to unauthorized users.

Account and Settings Module

There is a link between this module and the user module. If the registration process of the user gets completed, then the account is formed in the database of that particular user. The users can modify their passwords and other settings using this module.

WHAT DOES THE PROPOSED SYSTEM PROVIDE?

Graphical password scheme acts as a possible alternative to textual passwords. Scientific research has shown that it is easier for humans to recognize and recall pictures that they've seen, even for a short amount of time, than it is easier to remember a textual password. It helps the user by removing the extra memory burden of trying to memorize different passwords. Even if they are able to remember the textual passwords, which often results in a weak and easy to guess password; research shows that these chosen textual passwords have been prone to a number of cyberattacks, like dictionary attacks or key loggers. Even though we have other authentication methods, like biometrics and multifactor authentication, they have their own drawbacks. The user might lose their phones or SIM cards and not be able to generate an authentication code. Biometrics provide a stronger security when compared to other methods, but it comes with a high cost, along with a slower identification process.

Graphical password authentication makes it possible to resist attacks like dictionary attacks, and hence, this resistance makes the system less vulnerable and more secure. The proposed system makes the experience very user-friendly and easy to navigate. Our scheme uses Cued-Click Point technique, which makes the system more secure and makes attacks based on hotspot analysis much more challenging for the attackers. CCP uses 4 consecutive images that the user chooses from their local storage during the registration phase, and they need to select one click point on each of them. This makes the recall and memorization much easier than when compared to picking 4 points on the same image. This is not only helpful to the user, as it lifts the burden of memorizing difficult alphanumeric passwords, but it makes it more difficult for the cyber attackers to break in the system. Hence, our proposed scheme has several advantages over the other already existing methods.

SYSTEM ARCHITECTURE

The architecture is responsible for how the proposed system should work. The proposed system uses Model View Controller (MVC) architecture. The MVC architecture is also suitable for developing web applications. MVC architecture has three interconnected layers: (1) Model layer, (2) View (display) layer and (3) Controller layer (Pop and Altar, 2014). This architecture makes web applications easier and faster. Figure 5 shows the MVC architecture.

Figure 5. Model View Controller Architecture

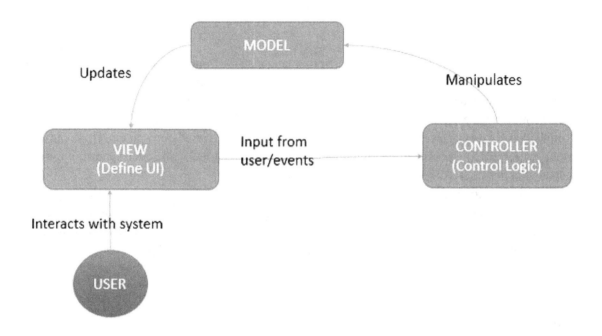

While developing applications, developers find it tough to separate User Interface (UI) from the application logic (Zhao et al., 2014). MVC architectural pattern is an effective way to develop efficient, stable, reusable and scalable applications (Ning et al., 2014) and helps developers focus on application features. MVC makes the application development process to become well-structured. This is the reason that MVC architecture has largely become a standard in modern software development. The MVC pattern is abstracted into three distinct parts: model, view, and controller (Huang et al., 2008).

1. **Model:** Model encapsulates core data, logical relationship, and business rules of the application. It responds to any request from the controller and or view. Model responsible for data manipulation i.e. insert, update, delete, search. But it cannot communicate directly with the view section, it does so via controller.
2. **View:** The view is the application interface visible to the user and clients. It is responsible for interaction with the clients. So it deals with presentation logic and is responsible for presenting data to the user/client. In HTTP based web and mobile applications, a view is usually an HTML

template file, which is set by the controller. A view will be loaded in the browser by the controller according to the client's request.

3. **Controller:** The controller is the processing part and contains application logic. The controller regulates the model and view. It requests the data from the model and loads the view accordingly (Chlipala, 2016).

IMPLEMENTATION

The proposed system is implemented using ReactJS, MongoDB, Express.js, and NodeJS.

ReactJS

Javascript is probably the most widely used scripting language for front-end development i.e. client side interactivity in web (HTTP) applications (Prokofyeva et al., 2017; Amanatidis A. & Chatzigeorgiou, A., 2016). ReactJS is a relatively new, flexible front-end JS library with extensive and diverse features to create robust, fast, effective and interactive front-end for mobile and web applications, especially applications that have extensive data visualization. It is a component based open source front end library (Fedosejev, A., 2015). RecatJS is the viewing layer in the Model View Controller pattern. So, ReactJS is responsible for the looks and feels of an app. (Pandit, 2021).

ReactJS is an extremely efficient performer. Its virtual DOM (Document Object Model) feature. Is the main reason for the efficiency of ReactJS. What happens is that ReactJS maintains a virtual document object model inside the memory. Whenever a change is made to the UI, virtual DOM is updated rather than instantly updating the browser DOM. Later with the help of an algorithm, only relevant and desired nodes of the browser DOM tree are updated, which results in lightning fast performance of the application.

MongoDB

Since the model stores data. Here we utilize MongoDB for storing all the user details. Various devices will be connected to the server with the help of the internet. The server will return the required data as a response whenever the user sends a request to the server. MongoDB is an open source, document-based, NoSQL (non-relational) database created by MongoDB Inc. MongoDB is a document database i.e. MongoDB uses documents and collections rather than the tables. A MongoDB document can also contain multiple embedded documents. JSON (JavaScript Object Notation) and BSON (Binary JSON) based documents or sub documents are the major components of the collections in MongoDB. Nonetheless, MongoDB also supports arrays and nested objects. MongoDB can mitigate capacity issues of traditional database systems i.e. it can manage massive volumes of unstructured data that can be amended by utilizing NoSQL systems like MongoDB. MongoDB is accommodating when the data needs to be accessed together, as they are stored together. Flexibility, robustness and scalability are the main attributes of MongoDB (Jose and Abraham, 2020).

Node.js

NodeJS is an open-source, cross-platform JavaScript runtime environment for server-side development. It is built on Chrome's V8 JavaScript engine. It helps to provide event-driven and non-blocking I/O. It removes the wait and continues to handle the next request. The availability of the vast number of open-source libraries are the reason for the capabilities of NodeJS. The proposed system uses NodeJS and supporting libraries, for instance (a) ExpressJS for http request and data handling, (b) pg for database connection handling, (c) body parser and cors for data conversions, (d) jsonwebtoken for session token creation, and Nodemon for continuous execution of the NodeJS server. (Sugandhi et al., 2021).

Express.js

Express.js is an open-source web-application server-side framework for Node.js. It was released in 2010 as a way to make it easier and quicker to develop web applications and APIs in Node.js. Express.js runs on Google's V8 JavaScript engine and thus it is a fast, un-opinionated, minimalist web framework. Node.js is a single threaded, event-driven execution environment for JavaScript. Multiple studies evaluating the usability of Express.js and Node.js have been done (Greiff, M., & Johansson, A., 2019) concluded that ExpressJS is very popular since it permits the use of JavaScript for both front-end and back-end development. (Karlsson, 2021).

RESULTS

In this section, we describe the proposed system through the screen shots of view layer of all modules as implemented using tools outlined in implementation section above.

Public Module (Home screen)

Public Module (home screen) is shown in figure 6.

User Module

User module comprises of two sub-modules: (1) Registration and (2) Authentication (login).

Registration

Registration process is shown in figure 7, 8 and 9. It begins when user click the *register* on home screen. User enter required details and insert 4 images along with click-points. Upon successful registration, the user is redirected to the home page and an alert message is displayed to the user.

Figure 6. Home screen (public module)

Figure 7. User clicks register on home screen to begin registration process

Authentication

Authentication process begins when user clicks *login* on the home screen. User enters the same credentials and the same click-points as used during the registration phase. The user is authorized if the credentials match and then welcome screen displayed in order to confirm that the user can now access the website. The authentication process is portrayed in figure 10, 11and 12.

Figure 8. User enter required details

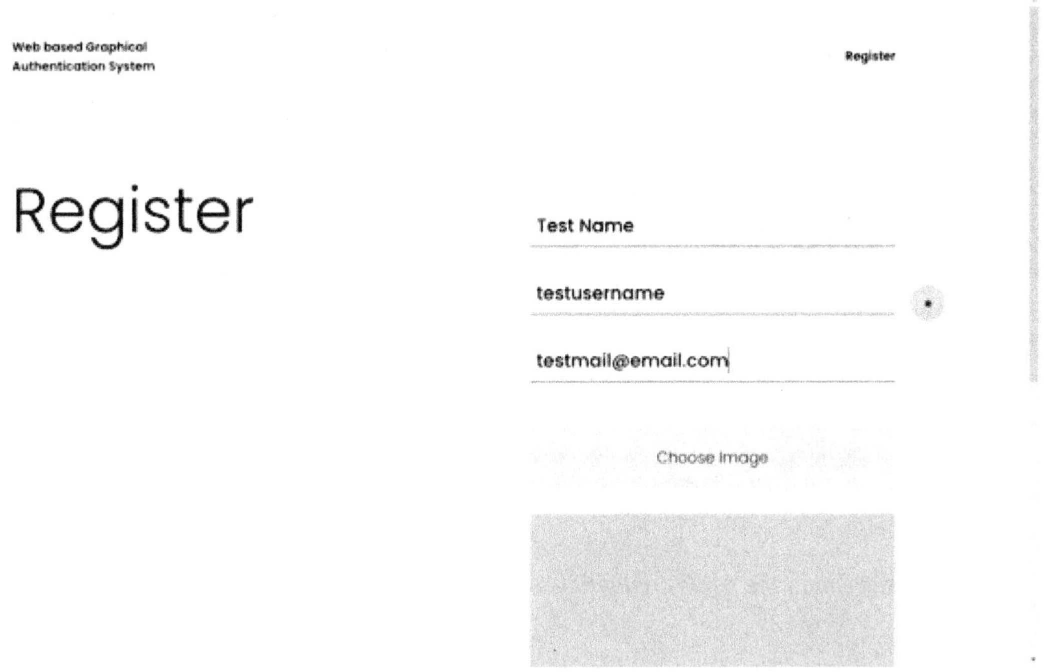

Web based Graphical
Authentication System

Register

Register

Test Name

testusername

testmail@email.com

Choose Image

Figure 9. User insert the images and choose their respective click-points (click-point is highlighted with a green dot)

testusername

testmail@email.com

Choose Image

Select upto 4 click-points as your
graphical password

Register

Already have an Account? Login

Figure 10. Authentication process begins when user clicks Login on home screen

Figure 11. User enters the same credentials and click-points as during the registration phase

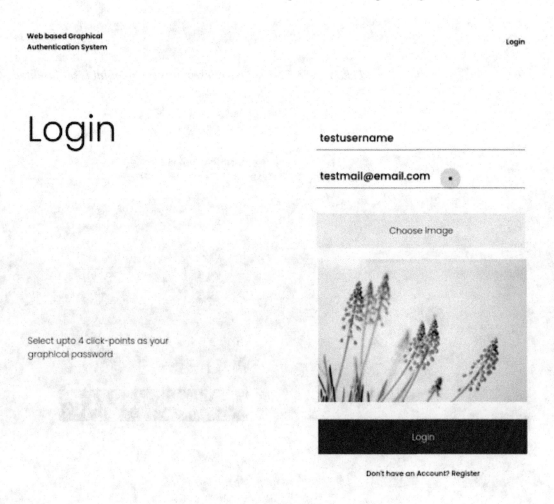

Figure 12. Welcome screen displayed upon successful authentication

Web based Graphical
Authentication System   Home

WELCOME

Login successful!

Administrator Module

Administrator module is shown in figure 13. This module can be used to edit details of and delete registered users.

Figure 13. Admin Panel

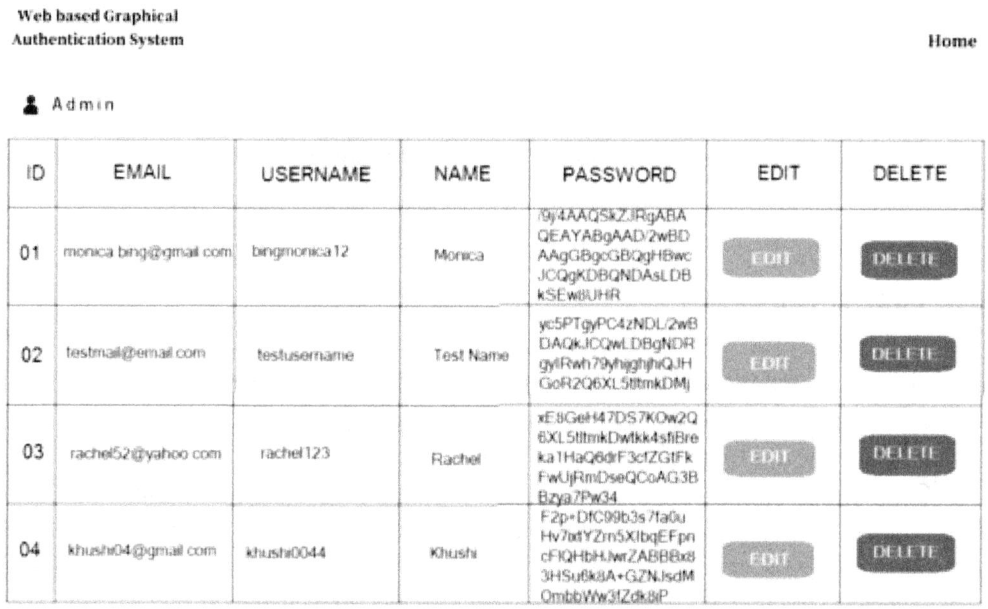

Web based Graphical
Authentication System   Home

  Admin

ID	EMAIL	USERNAME	NAME	PASSWORD	EDIT	DELETE
01	monica.bing@gmail.com	bingmonica12	Monica	79y4AAQSkZJRgABA QEAYABgAAD/2wBD AAgGBgcGBQgHBwc JCQgKDBQNDAsLDB kSEw8UHR	EDIT	DELETE
02	testmail@email.com	testusername	Test Name	yc5PTgyPC4zNDL/2wB DAQkJCQwLDBgNDR gyfRwh79yhgghjhiQJH GoR2Q6XL58tmkDMj	EDIT	DELETE
03	rachel52@yahoo.com	rachel123	Rachel	xE8GeH47DS7KOw2Q 6XL5tltmkDwtkk4sfiBre ka1HaQ6drF3cfZGtFk FwUjRmDseQCoAG3B Bzya7Pw34	EDIT	DELETE
04	khushir04@gmail.com	khushir0044	Khushi	F2p+DfC99b3s7fa0u Hv7xtYZrn5XIbqEFpn cFIQHbHJwrZABBBx8 3HSu6k8A+GZNJsdM OmbbVw3fZdk8iP	EDIT	DELETE

Account and Settings Module

This module can be used by the user to change its username, password, image files and click (touch) points. This module is portrayed in figure 14, 15, 16 and 17.

Figure 14. Updating username via account and settings module

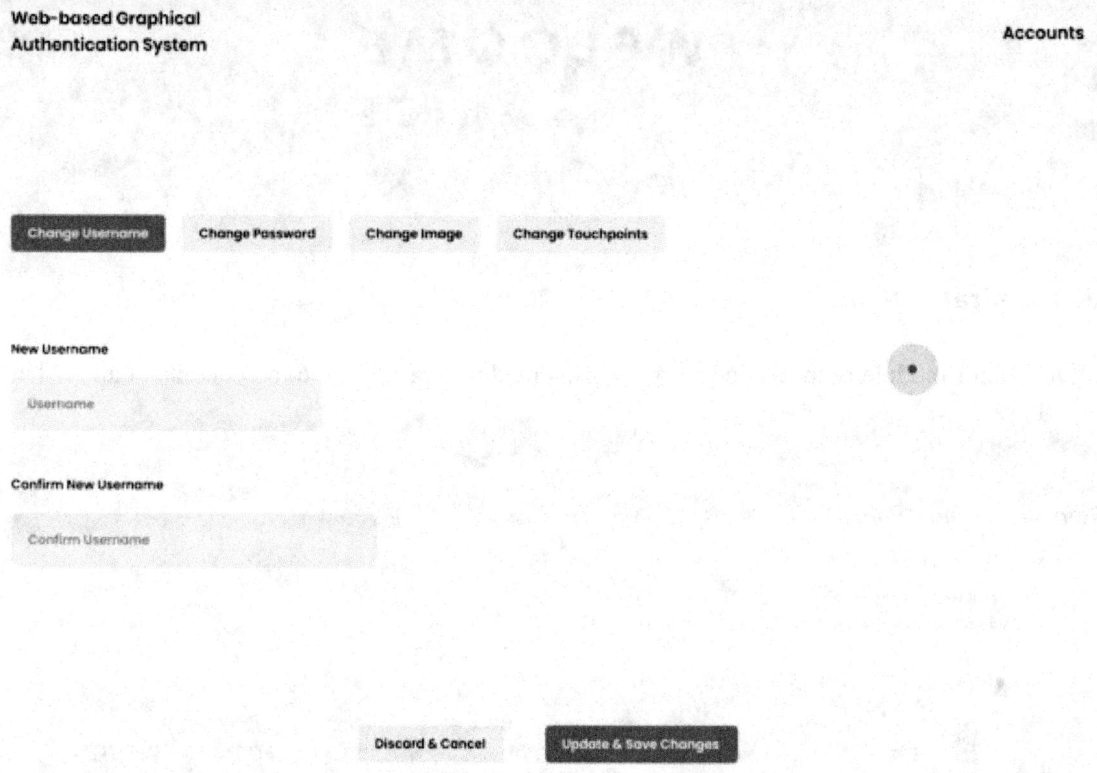

FURTHER DISCUSSION

Cued Click Point has been quite successful in security as well as for the user's experience. Studies have shown that this is much easier for the user to remember than other types of passwords. Users receive feedback at the same time if the user is on the wrong path. They can then narrow down where they caused an error. But Graphical passwords are not widely used in practice. Graphical authentication systems are not quite yet famous. They can yet be attacked in the following ways: (Ghiyamipour, 2020).

Figure 15. Updating password via account and settings module

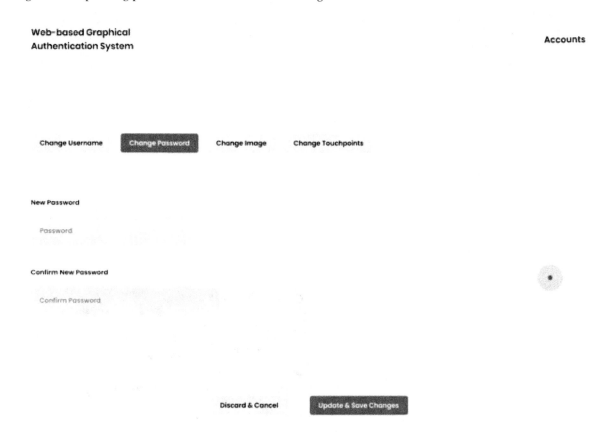

Figure 16. Updating images of graphical password via account and settings module

Figure 17. Updating click-points (touch-points) via account and settings module

Shoulder Surfing

When using a graphical password in an area with people around, the user can easily become a victim of shoulder surfing. The public place might not be the best place to use graphical authentication systems. One improvement that can be made to it is to use dual level security, which uses textual passwords along with a graphical authentication system.

For example, someone may watch over the user's shoulder while the user enters a password or records the user's input with an external device, like video cameras. (Papadopoulos et al., 2017)

Guessing

This is one of the most serious issues that is related with both textual and graphical passwords since users create short and short passwords to remember them easily, hence their passwords become predictable. Though, the new CCP technique has reduced the predictable behavior to some extent.

Brute Force Attack

Brute force attack is one of the methods used by hackers to find passwords. This is usually done by special software. In this attack, hackers do not take any action to decrypt the password. Instead, it uses software to try to guess the password and check all possible scenarios to find the correct password. This can be very time consuming if the password is complicated and lengthy. However graphical passwords are less susceptible to brute force search attacks than the normal text-based approach due to larger password space. Further, recall-based methods of authentication tend to possess bigger password spaces than the recognition-based technique. (Lashkari, 2014)

Spyware Attack

Spyware is a kind of malware installed on computers that collects information about users without their knowledge and permission. Adware, Trojan horse, keystroke-loggers, mouse-loggers, and screen-scrapers are examples of spyware. Spyware can steal almost any kind of data such as personal information, internet surfing habits, user logins, banking information, and is usually utilized by attackers to steal information. Key spyware cannot be used to break into graphical authentication systems. It is not yet clear whether the "mouse tracking" spyware will be an effective tool against image passwords or not. Graphical passwords are less vulnerable to spyware attacks than the traditional text-based approach. Since for inputting the graphical password users exploit the mouse, the mouse motion alone is not enough to break graphical passwords.

FUTURE ENHANCEMENTS

Increasing the Password Space

Maximizing the implied password space is one of the ways to make password based authentication more resilient to attacks. Some of the alternative to do so for cued click points (CCP) are

Increasing Number of Click-points

One way to increase the security of the password is to increase the number of click-points in the provided images. Though this may be a burden on the memory of the user.

Using More Images

More numbers of images can be used in the registration phase to reduce the overlap between password stages. This will also result in an increased effective password space.

Increasing the Image Size or Tolerance

An easy way to increase the effective password is to use larger images since reducing the tolerance is not possible past a threshold. However, increased image size may make it more vulnerable to shoulder-surfing attacks.

Adding a Challenge-response Scenario

To reduce chance of shoulder surfing, a challenge-response scenario can be added. In the challenge-response scenario, the user will be presented with a challenge from the server side, and the user has to give the response according to the condition of the challenge. If the given response is correct, then the access will be granted.

CONCLUSION

The goal of a graphical password authentication system is to improve the security and the usability of the system. Also, the user's ability to recognize and remember images faster and more easily is the reason why graphical passwords should be made more common in today's world. Cued Click Point (CCP) has more security and advantages than Pass Point. Pass Point uses one image and multiple click-points on that same image, but CCP uses one click-point per image and hence, the user can easily recognize the point they clicked during the registration phase. It also increases the amount of work that the attackers have to do by forcing them to first collect all the images of the particular user and then run hotspot analysis on every single image. The advantages of the graphical authentication system outweigh the disadvantages. For example, the login time is very fast as when compared with the login time of textual passwords. A drawback can be that we need a much larger storage space for graphical passwords than alphanumeric passwords. Graphical passwords are more resilient to various attacks like dictionary attacks, brute force attacks, spyware attacks and guessing. ReactJS is selected for implementing CCP since (1) it is probably the most popular framework, (2) it can be used for both web and mobile applications using HTTP and REST API.

REFERENCES

Abhijith, S., Soja, S., Sreelekshmi, K. U., & Samjeevan, T. T. (2021). 'Web based Graphical Password Authentication System', eMangalam College of Engineering, Kottayam, India. *International Journal of Engineering Research & Technology, 9*(7).

Amanatidis, T., & Chatzigeorgiou, A. (2016). Studying the evolution of PHP web applications. *Information and Software Technology*, *72*, 48–67. doi:10.1016/j.infsof.2015.11.009

Ashok, P., Prianka, R. R., Lavanya, R., & Gokila, R. G. (2017). Dynamic Cued Click Point Algorithm to Provide Cryptographic Password Authentication. *International Journal of Pure and Applied Mathematics*, *117*(21), 961–965.

Baruffa, G., Femminella, M., Pergolesi, M., & Reali, G. (2020, March). Comparison of MongoDB and Cassandra Databases for Spectrum Monitoring As-a-Service. *IEEE eTransactions on Network and Service Management*, *17*(1), 346–360. doi:10.1109/TNSM.2019.2942475

Bhogill P., (2019). *5 Ways to Secure Your Business in A Multi-Cloud World*. Academic Press.

Birget, J. C., Hong, D., & Memon, N. (2006). Graphical passwords based on robust discretization. *IEEE Transactions on Information Forensics and Security*, *1*(3), 395–399. doi:10.1109/TIFS.2006.879305

Blonder, G. (1996). Graphical password. *United States Patent 5559961*.

Chlipala, A. (2016). Ur/Web: A Simple Model for Programming the Web. *Communications of the ACMVolume*, *59*(August), 93–100. doi:10.1145/2958736

Davis, D., Monrose, F., & Reiter, M. K. (2004). On user choice in graphical password schemes. In USENIX security symposium (Vol. 13, No. 2004, pp. 11-11). Academic Press.

Fedosejev, A. (2015). *React.js essentials*. Packt Publishing Ltd.

Ghiyamipour, F. (2020). Secure graphical password based on cued click points using fuzzy logic. *Security and Privacy*, *4*(2). Advance online publication. doi:10.1002py2.140

Greiff, M., & Johansson, A. (2019). *Symfony vs Express: A Server-Side Framework Comparison*. Academic Press.

Huang, S. Q., & Zhang, H. M. (2008). Research on Improved MVC Design pattern based on Struts and XSL. In *2008 International Symposium on Information Science and Engineering* (Vol. 1, pp. 451-455). IEEE. 10.1109/ISISE.2008.252

Jose, B., & Abraham, S. (2020). Performance analysis of NoSQL and relational databases with MongoDB and MySQL. *Materials Today: Proceedings*, *24*, 2036–2043. doi:10.1016/j.matpr.2020.03.634

Karlsson, O. (2021). *A Performance Comparison Between ASP.NET Core and Express.js for creating Web APIs* (Dissertation). Retrieved from http://urn.kb.se/resolve?urn=urn:nbn:se:hj:diva-54286

Klein, D. V. (1990, August). Foiling the cracker: A survey of, and improvements to, password security. *Proceedings of the 2nd USENIX Security Workshop*, 5-14.

Lashkari, A. H. (2014). GPIP: a new graphical password based on image portions. *18th International Conference on Circuits Systems Communications and Computers (CSCC 2014)*.

MizrachiA. (2021). https://frontegg.com/author/aviadmizrachi

Nelson, D. L., Reed, V. S., & Walling, J. R. (1976). Pictorial superiority effect. *Journal of Experimental Psychology. Human Learning and Memory*, *2*(5), 523–528. doi:10.1037/0278-7393.2.5.523 PMID:1003125

Ning, W., Liming, L., Yanzhang, W., Yi-bing, W., & Jing, W. (2008). Research on the web information system development platform based on MVC design pattern. In *2008 IEEE/WIC/ACM International Conference on Web Intelligence and Intelligent Agent Technology* (Vol. 3, pp. 203-206). IEEE. 10.1109/WIIAT.2008.64

PanditN. (2021). https://www.c-sharpcorner.com/article/what-and-why-reactjs

Papadopoulos, T. N., Durmus, E., & Memon, N. (2017). Illusion (2017). PIN: Shoulder-surfing resistant authentication using hybrid images. *IEEE Transactions on Information Forensics and Security*, *12*(12), 2875–2889. doi:10.1109/TIFS.2017.2725199

Pop, D. P., & Altar, A. (2014). Designing an MVC Model for Rapid Web Application Development 24th DAAAM International Symposium on Intelligent Manufacturing and Automation, 2013. *Procedia Engineering*, *69*, 1172–1179. doi:10.1016/j.proeng.2014.03.106

Prokofyeva, N., & Boltunova, V. (2017). Analysis and practical application of PHP frameworks in development of web information systems. *Procedia Computer Science*, *104*, 51–56. doi:10.1016/j.procs.2017.01.059

Rao, A. (2019). *Cyber Security-a New Secured Password Generation Algorithm with Graphical Authentication, and Alphanumeric Passwords Along with Encryption* [Doctoral dissertation]. Old Dominion University.

Sarker, I. H., & Apu, K. (2014). Mvc architecture driven design and implementation of java framework for developing desktop applications. *International Journal of Hybrid Information Technology*, *7*(5), 317–322. doi:10.14257/ijhit.2014.7.5.29

Sharma, S., Mate, G. S., Pawar, M., Patil, S., & Gole, S. (2017). *Cued Click Point (CCP) Algorithm For Graphical Password To Authenticate Shoulder Surfing Resistance*. Savitribai Phule Pune University Tathawade.

Shnain, A. H., & Shaheed, S. H. (2018). The use of graphical password to improve authentication problems in e-commerce. In. AIP Conference Proceedings: Vol. 2016. *No. 1* (p. 020133). AIP Publishing LLC. doi:10.1063/1.5055535

Sri, K. H., Vardhan, M. V., Nikitha, K., Kiran, K. M., & Saritha, A. K. (2020). Graphical Password Authentication. *Journal of Xi'an University of Architecture & Technology*, *12*(4), 1006–7930.

Sugandhi, R., Soumya, V., Jha, M., Sanyasi, A. K., Adhikari, A., & Awasthi, L. M. (2021). Development of electronic record-keeping software for remote participation in Large Volume Plasma Device upgrade using Angular 2 and NodeJS web technologies. *The Review of Scientific Instruments*, *92*(7), 075102. doi:10.1063/5.0049037 PMID:34340411

Sunil, S. S., Prakash, D., & Shivaji, Y. R. (2014). Cued click points: Graphical password authentication technique for security. *International Journal of Computer Science and Information Technologies*, *5*(2).

Suo, X., Zhu, Y., & Owen, G. S. (2005). Graphical passwords: A survey. In *21st Annual Computer Security Applications Conference*. IEEE.

Wiedenbeck, S., Waters, J., Birget, J. C., Brodskiy, A., & Memon, N. (2005). Authentication using graphical passwords: Effects of tolerance and image choice. In *Proceedings of the 2005 symposium on Usable privacy and security* (pp. 1-12). 10.1145/1073001.1073002

Wiedenbeck, S., Waters, J., Birget, J. C., Brodskiy, A., & Memon, N. (2005). PassPoints: Design and longitudinal evaluation of a graphical password system. *International Journal of Human-Computer Studies*, *63*(1-2), 102–127. doi:10.1016/j.ijhcs.2005.04.010

Yang, T. Y., Shamala, P., Chinniah, M., & Foozy, C. F. M. (2021, February). Graphical Password Authentication For Child Personal Storage Application. *Journal of Physics: Conference Series*, *1793*(1), 012065. doi:10.1088/1742-6596/1793/1/012065

Zhao, H., Zhang, H., & Chen, Q. (2014). The research of dynamic statistics chart based on MVC design pattern. In *2014 IEEE International Conference on System Science and Engineering (ICSSE)* (pp. 56-59). IEEE. 10.1109/ICSSE.2014.6887904

Chapter 12
Security Issues in Blockchain–Based Businesses

Rajesh Yadav
GITAM University, India

Digvijay Singh
BML Munjal University, India

ABSTRACT

A few years back, it was arduous to identify cyber-security in the day-to-day activities of an organization. Writing extra code-lines was considered insignificant, and the term was considered more advanced than the current times. Most businesses were doubtful about changing their plans so that they could combat this danger as the notion of "it won't occur to me" was famous. Cyber-security is now no longer a "forbidden silo." It is considered a necessity and is no longer selective. The organization must have its security planning in such a manner that it plays an important role in its business as well as the decision-forming in the significant matters of the company. In today's scenario, organizations must have a check on their defense system to ensure security in operations. They use updated solutions and have proper information on vulnerabilities and security issues that persist at the moment. This chapter throws light on security issues in blockchain-based businesses.

INTRODUCTION

Blockchain and its Components

Blockchain technology is basically the simplest form of a digital ledger. It is like a personal ledger in terms of recording different transactions. But technically it is different from the conventional methods of centralizing things. It is completely based upon a decentralized approach where the blockchain is shared and a distributed ledger is used to record the transactions.

DOI: 10.4018/978-1-6684-5827-3.ch012

Figure 1.

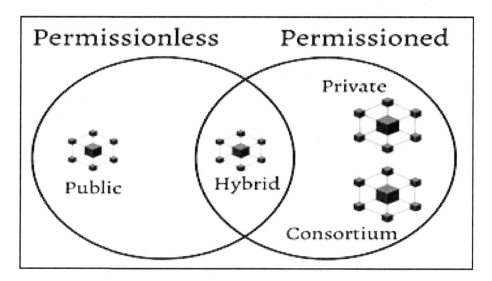

This ledger is immutable and is responsible for facilitating transactions in a business network. It is ideal state of delivering information as it is transparent. Key factors of this technology comprise of 3 things- Smart Contracts, Immutable records, and distributed ledger. The main benefits of using a blockchain technology over the conventional methods is mainly because of the greater trust and more efficiencies which are offered by the distributed ledger. There are mainly 4 types of blockchains. Each type has a special purpose and is highlighted below.

- **Public blockchain-** This type of blockchain is open to all for the participation. Bitcoin is one of the biggest public blockchain where multiple users can join it. Public blockchains carry a drawback of consisting weak security.
- **Private blockchain-** This type of blockchain is not open for public participations, however, it is similar in terms of decentralization like the public blockchain. In a private blockchain, one organization is responsible for governing the network and the participants for executing the consensus protocols.
- **Permissioned blockchain-** Most of the business organizations relying on the blockchain based solutions use a private block chain but set up a permissioned network. This type of blockchain is called as permissioned blockchain. It sets a restriction in the network participation. Only invited participants can be permitted to join the blockchain network.
- **Consortium blockchain-** The Hyperledger is considered as a consortium blockchain. It is not open to all and is applicable in the cases of smaller groups which takes advantages in terms of throughput, privacy, speed, and less energy consumption.

Elements of Blockchain

Decentralization

The concept of decentralization was introduced for dispersing functions from a system rather than relying on central authority. In blockchain, there is no single authority due to which users have extended access which is not being controlled by any government organization. To ensure decentral working, a peer-to-peer network was incorporated where operations are carried by different authorities and no authority can hold the complete access. It helps with the validation of miners who is basically a user of blockchain.

Consensus

Consensus model is an agreement between different entities. It helps in the unanimous working of the complete blockchain. The entire blockchain cannot be controlled by single authority however for governance, it is tracked by a single authority. To work on a new block, a consensus is required to prove the existence of the true block. This model is basically used to maintain the consistency were nodes are required to produce the output, it also maintains a check on the aliveness of all the participating nodes by checking their results. It helps to manage the failure caused by any node by using a fault tolerance mechanism to recover it.

Transparency

Blockchain technology offers transparency and removes the slightest chances of corruption. Each node user is associated with a strong cipher id which makes it difficult to make it public. All the transactions and interactions are organized to eliminate the risks associated with individual profits. Since nodes are required to reach the consensus, it brings transparency to the complete working and constant audit trails which are performed by the blockchain technology ensures the correct processing of data and transactions.

Anonymization

It is one of the key elements of the blockchain. Anonymity ensures the privacy of transactions and nodes. Sometimes it becomes difficult for maintaining this anonymity in a public blockchain ledger. To maintain the anonymization, a cipher key is generated for each miner which keeps the identity of the miner hidden from others. The address generated for user lacks the mechanism of keeping it private due to which the most of crypto currencies are considered as pseudo-anonymous.

Blockchain Applications in Business World

With the passage of time, business owners are getting verse with the importance of incorporating blockchain technology as part of their business to be prepared for the future. Looking at the great benefits which this emergent technology provides, multiple sectors are working to streamline their business with the optimal usage of blockchain based applications.

Figure 2.

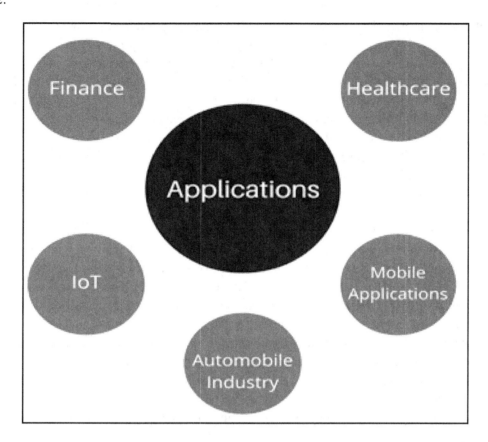

Finance

The blockchain technology has a great potential in the finance sector. It brings transparency to its customers. Initially the technology was implemented to develop the most popular cryptocurrency Bitcoin. Other cryptocurrencies which came into existence use a standard structure of blockchain but somehow use different algorithms to achieve the consensus. The blockchain based finance is purely based on the smart contracts. A simple explanation of the practical implementation consists of 2 nodes- buyer and a seller, 2 parameters- data and payment. A smart contract ensures the validation and can possess information related to data transfer, payment done and received by a buyer and seller respectively. While using the blockchain based financial service, some security challenges are faced. Any organization who is running a finance business needs to ensure an authorized transaction. Similarly, a blockchain based finance requires to maintain authentic transactions but a common security concern is always linked to ensure authorized and correct access to the data. To gain an access to the blockchain based network and data, there arises a need to implement a synchronous control for authentication and authorization.

Healthcare

Healthcare sector requires a public blockchain which is secure, scalable and maintains privacy of data. It can be optimized to maintain blocks containing mainly 3 types of data- health records, images, and relevant documents. Healthcare data, when stored and accessed via blockchain, faces storage and throughput limitations. Usually, a bitcoin power blockchain is not recommended for healthcare as it will result in the users getting access to the copy of every other individual present in the specific network. This is not the ideal way of storing data and is bandwidth intensive. This leads to wastage of resources in the network and have concerns regarding data throughput. For the blockchain implementation in the healthcare sector, there is a need of devising an access control manager for the storage and management of data. The blockchain comprises only the list or index of the data of the users. It acts as a metadata catalog with reference to location and patient information and the information can only be accessed by the legitimate user. For the improvement in efficiency of accessing data, the information is timestamped, encrypted, and retrieved by some unique identifier.

The data related to healthcare is stored in data lakes which are data repositories of blockchain. They can store data in any form hence, they are valuable for research and analysis purposes. Data lakes help in providing support for technologies like mining, querying, machine learning and analysing texts. The information present in them is encrypted and digitally signed to get rid of privacy issues and make it restricted to legitimate users. Every new record in a data lake is also encrypted and signed digitally. The owner of the data has complete control over the sharing of data as well as its access. For accessing and updating every record, a pointer must be maintained which uses the unique identifier of the user. The individual can give access rights to other people as well as authorize people to update the information in the blockchain. Blockchain provides various advantages for the sector of health care as it has features like commodity hardware, open-source, and open application programming interface. They help in fast and easy synergy between the systems and are scalable to large volumes of user data. Blockchain helps individuals in accessing the data source to attain precise data in time. The blockchain commodity hardware gives low-cost computation and helps in addressing the synergy challenges within the healthcare sector. An added advantage of the blockchain architecture is its disaster recovery attribute and fault tolerance. Due to data being distributed among various servers, there is not a single failure point that exists in the network.

IoT

IoT devices are usually provided with a unique identifier which can then communicate over a network without depending on human interaction. Many business organizations dealing in blockchain based IoT use it for the purpose of storing and accessing data in IoT. It enables a user working remotely to privately access the data in a network. When a user is registered, a random id is generated, and the user is required to send the data using the generated id. Once the data is transferred to the storage, validation of the transaction is done to confirm the storage availability. Since IoT devices are added in bulk globally, resulting in many business organizations have identified the urgent requirement of such devices and have observed a potential business associated with these devices which can help to accelerate their growth. Some applications of IoT in blockchain are stated below:

- **Goods transportation:** Transportation of commodities is not an easy task as there are different parties having their own priorities. If it is replaced by an IoT- enabled blockchain, it can be useful to store information like- shipping status, arrival time, positions linked with their movement. It helps the parties to trust by having a look at the records and these immutable blockchains enable quick movement of goods.

- **Tracking of Components:** Looking at the safety and regulatory compliance, tracking of different components play an essential role. Blockchain based ledgers enable to store data generated from the IoT devices which can be further reviewed by parties. This information can be shared with the concerned authorities.
- **Logging of operational maintenance information**: Critical machines can be tracked safely and maintained efficiently with the help of IoT. Blockchain gives a tamper free ledger of the operational information as well as its maintenance for any device, from an engine to an elevator. The third-party repair partner can keep an account on the blockchain for the maintenance work and putting its record on the ledger. These records can be used by the government organizations for verification purposes.

Mobile Applications

Blockchain based applications rely on p2p service for transfer of data and using decentralized payments. A simple explanation can be given by introducing 2 nodes- customer and mobile application. A customer can always access this mobile app for purchasing and in return get the receipt for the payment done. A smart contract can manage the data by uploading it to a database. A blockchain will allow the mobile applications to access the digital wallets for payment purpose and make successful transactions. Using a blockchain based mobile application becomes portable and is more acceptable.

Automobile Industry

Modern day vehicles are connected to different sort of network applications. With this flexibility of getting connected to a network a base for the usage of blockchain technology has high potential in the domain. Smart vehicles are using automotive architectures to address the common challenges and bring a revolutionary change in the domain. The automobile industry has adopted the usage of blockchain technology mainly because of 2 reasons-

- **Incorporating payment facility in vehicles:** The users can always pay the car gas fee or any electric charges depending upon the type of vehicle. It works by triggering any event or action via the smart contract which can be used to send money from the wallet to the gas/charging station. A similar advantage of doing the payment can be incorporated for doing the payments for parking's and any other financial transaction.
- **Autonomous data:** The blockchain plays an important role for storing necessary data in case of a self-driving car. As the vehicles move, the data can be generated and simultaneously data can be fetched for trip purpose. This localization can include data like maps, roads, traffic signals and traffic patterns. The vehicle being processed through a blockchain technology can also maintain a complete information of the vehicle maintenance.

BACKGROUND

Security issues associated with blockchain based businesses

Potential Attacks

Liveness Attack

A Liveness attack is responsible to delay the acknowledgement time of a particular transaction. It delays the time required for confirmation. Liveness attack is possible on two of the biggest and most demandable cryptocurrencies- Bitcoin and Ethereum as well. It works in three stages- preparation, denial and delay caused in the overall blockchain. In delay phase, an attacker usually takes an advantage against the parties and build their own private chain and further make a delay in a block to cause denial in the transaction. At last, the attacker tries of decreasing the transaction chain rate (Lin, 2017).

Double Spending Attack

In case of a duplicate transaction involving equivalent transferred fund is known to cause a problem which is generally regarded as the Double-spending attack. There is a potential flaw represented in the digital cash because when the attack occurs, this token can be spent twice. If the token is spent, it is not possible to avoid this double-spending problem. The situation cannot avoid it even if the consensus mechanism of each blockchain validates the transaction. "If a miner controls more than half of computational capacity amongst all miners, in theory, loses their power to control double spending incentives" (Joshi, 2018).

51% Vulnerability Attack

The blockchain technology make use of a distributed consensus mechanism. These mechanisms are used to maintain and establish a trust. Blockchains carry a 51% vulnerability on the distributed consensus mechanism resulting in a potential exploitation which can be caused by an attacker. In Proof of Work blockchains, if a minor hash can occupy more than 50% hash of the entire blockchain, there is a possibility of 51% vulnerability being exploited and initiated as an 51% attack. Once this attack is started, an attacker can make manipulations by changing information relevant to the blockchain (Gomathi, 2021).

Private Key Security Attack

All Blockchain based businesses possess a private key which is mandatorily created for the usage of blockchain. This key can allow a user to access data. Suppose an attacker gets the access to a private key of blockchain finance organization, then the key possessor can actually go through the details related to the funds and can verify any sort of transaction which has happened. The key should be saved and kept secret as once lost cannot be recovered in any case. Many malicious software's are constantly running just to steal these cryptographic keys in order to gain access to a target blockchain. Only if the digital signature algorithm is vulnerable then, an attacker can exploit that vulnerability to recover or steal the private key for malicious purposes. One major drawback is the difficulty of tracking the attacker possessing the private key (Morabito, 2018).

Transaction Privacy Leakage

Business organizations which use blockchain based systems should take some measures for protecting transaction privacy. Confidential information of users can be leaked which can promote crime. Bitcoin uses the approach of a one-time account for receiving cryptograms where each user is assigned with a secret key. By implementing this approach, it becomes hard for an attacker to identify if the transaction has been involved in which password violation. Moreover, the actual consumption of the coin during the transaction is also not inferred because of the "mixins" which can be included by a user. Sometimes, a wallet privacy leakage is also evident where the user information is revealed. A similar type of leakage has been exploited in the past (Sengupta, 2020).

Selfish Mining Attack

Some miners engage in selfish mining assaults to squander legal miners' processing power or acquire undeserved profits. Self-employed miners strive to establish a long private chain rather than digging a public chain. It allows them to discover fresh blocks, but the honest miners continue to dig the public chain but when the honest miners get aware with these exposed blocks, they are at a situation where their time, money and resources are wasted. It results in preventing the honest miners from earning but the selfish miners who don't deserve any earning try to manage the situation and take an unfair advantage of it (Kumar, 2018).

DAO Attack

Dao are the decentralized autonomous organizations which are used as funds for crypto and distributed spaces. These organizations are used for the funds due to the lack of central authority. It allows the investors to have a complete control and access to the money. An open-source platform Slock.it was deployed to build smart locks and it was distributed to the community managing Ethereum. It was able to raise US$120 million but after 20 days of deployment, an attacker was able to steal 50% of the raised amount. It was regarded as one of the major attacks on the consensus model of Ethereum. Due to the presence of a vulnerability in the DAO, the attacker was able to exploit it and further perform the malicious part of stealing (Sengupta, 2020).

BGP Hijacking Attack

BGP is Border Gateway Protocol which is used for on the networks. It allows to share the information related to the network routing. An attacker can manage to intercept this blockchain based network by doing some manipulation with the protocol due to which the data can be rerouted and modified as per the attacker. This attack is commonly known as BGP hijacking which carries a major vulnerability due to the increasing concentration of mining pools. An attacker can exploit this vulnerability by dividing the blockchain network of bitcoin and slower down the propagation speed of each block (Kumar, 2018).

Balance Attack

This type of attack is used by the attackers to make a simple delay in the mining process. The idea is to make necessary changes in the validated groups and subgroups using same power for mining process. Further the attacker ensures that more mining is done in other subgroups to make it more important than the group responsible for transaction. In case the transaction was not shown, the attacker can still create a fake block which has a higher probability than the subtree containing information related to the transaction (Kumar, 2018).

Sybil Attack

An attacker uses this attack to destroy the reputation system. The attacker tries to take the entire control of the network by creating different accounts and nodes. It is focused towards influencing the network decisions. Threat actor tends to manipulate this security system by forging identity in p2p network. But if the nodes are required to show a proof for the identities like the private blockchain then they will require a permission and not be able to forge any identity further (Kumar, 2018).

CONCLUSION

Blockchain technology is highly appraised and recognized because of its peer-to-peer mechanism as well as decentralized structure. Due to these highly important features, it can be used widely in numerous areas and can be applied in all domains. The blockchain has been effective in transforming the IT field. It has the power to bring together countries, governments, and companies globally. This review paper has been written keeping in mind the wide usage of blockchain in various real-life examples. Firstly, the structure of blockchain has been discussed along with its components and characteristics. Then the applications of blockchain have been discussed in various domains. The issues related to privacy, security as well as the vulnerabilities of blockchain have also been explained in the paper. The analysis of various attacks which can be performed on the blockchain-based systems have been elaborated in the given review.

Thus, the chapter summarizes the components, applications, abundant opportunities, challenges, and attacks that come as a result of blockchain applied business. The attacks have been explored to make the people aware of these aspects and they can efficiently combat them. Blockchain can be considered as the Internet that was present a few decades back. As blockchain offers security and support, it is gradually being implemented in every technology to obtain better efficiency and usability. It is expected that soon blockchain techniques will become a well-known phenomenon. There are surely many limitations and boundation that one can feel while using blockchain-based storage systems, but the use of cyber-security will surely ease the process of coping with these vulnerabilities and attacks in a more refined way.

REFERENCES

Gomathi, S., Soni, M., Dhiman, G., Govindaraj, R., & Kumar, P. (2021). A survey on applications and security issues of blockchain technology in business sectors. *Materials Today: Proceedings*.

Joshi, A. P., Han, M., & Wang, Y. (2018). A survey on security and privacy issues of blockchain technology. *Mathematical Foundations of Computing, 1*(2), 121.

Kumar, N. M., & Mallick, P. K. (2018). Blockchain technology for security issues and challenges in IoT. *Procedia Computer Science, 132*, 1815–1823.

Lin, I. C., & Liao, T. C. (2017). A survey of blockchain security issues and challenges. *International Journal of Network Security, 19*(5), 653–659.

Morabito, V. (2017). *Business innovation through blockchain.* Springer International Publishing.

Sengupta, J., Ruj, S., & Bit, S. D. (2020). A comprehensive survey on attacks, security issues and blockchain solutions for IoT and IIoT. *Journal of Network and Computer Applications, 149*, 102481.

Chapter 13
Cybersecurity Management in South African Universities

Nkholedzeni Sidney Netshakhuma
iD https://orcid.org/0000-0003-0673-7137
University of Mpumalanga, South Africa

ABSTRACT

The study aimed to assess cyber security at South African universities. The researcher will use literature to assess the state of cybersecurity at South African universities. The results from the literature review revealed poor implementation and adherence of cyber security strategy and standards by employees and students; poor cyber security awareness relative to information communication technology (ICT) infrastructures and assets; and lack of strategy and framework to implement cyber security management. The study recommends continuous monitoring and evaluation of information management systems at various South African universities with the view to assess the state. A replica of the study may be studied in other part of the world.

INTRODUCTION

The study assessed the cyber security threats such as security of information faced by South African universities from 1994 until present. The security breach was caused by ineffectice cybersecurity policies, lack of cybersecurity management training and awareness, lack of information communication technology and ineffective infrastructure. The significance of cybersecurity in modern societies is undisputed. Numerous studies in diverse fields such as information communication technology, finance management, risk management, records, and archives management, and security management add value to cybersecurity management. This shows a relationship between cybersecurity and other disciplines. In this chapter, the term South Africa university was used interchangeably with the Higher Education Institution of South Africa.

DOI: 10.4018/978-1-6684-5827-3.ch013

The researcher used the case study of the South African universities to assessed the state of cybersecurity. The results from the literature review revealed ineffective development of cyber security policy by staff. Furthermore, students were not aware of the risk posed by a hacker in their internet environment. This study recommends organizations develop a cyber security management system. The study recommends universities develop a framework in compliance with national legislation.

BACKGROUND

Cybersecurity occurs as a form of hackers attacking business information in an electronic environment (Borgman, 2018; Moskai, 2015, p. 97; Villegas-Ch, Garges, Viteri 2021). Hackers accessed the organization's remote server to damage electronic contents management systems which store data in the networked and the physical infrastructure (Kundy & Lyimo, 2019). To prevent hacking, the security breaches requires organizations to enhance security systems by ensuring that a governance structure or committee was established to execute the oversight role over security management compliance. Executive management of the institutions were responsible to establish such committee. An organization developed systems and processes to ensure that measures were in place to control access to networked systems and the information contained. Cybersecurity threats required to be protected by various organizations all over the world.

Security of information was identified as one of the risks in the strategic or operational risk registers of universities (Abdulrauf & Fombad, 2017, p. 106). As a preventive measurement, universities developed an action plan to counter the threat posed by hackers. The effective way to implement an action plan was to facilitate cybersecurity workshops, and develop processes and procedures to comply with Legislation such as *the Protection of Personal Information Act no. 4 of 2013 (POPIA)* and *the Promotion of Access to Information of 2002 (PAIA)*.These legislations advocate for the protection of personal information. This implied that organisations should regularly clear content that was no longer active, such as data relating to a university program, and develop a data privacy breach management process, Universities should develop a cyber security policy to protect its data from attack. The policy should be developed in compliance with the above mentioned legislations. Process and procedure were to aligned with the organization's requirements. The retention schedule should be embedded in the university system, develop backup and restoration policies and procedures., provide user access management policies and procedures, and provide IT security policy. Protection of information applies to all employees and university stakeholders.

Higher education institutions in South Africa adopted content management systems to aid in teaching, learning, and research. Hackers used the internet to tackle their systems. Universities are not supposed to work in isolation with other universities on system sharing (Olatunbosun, Edwards, and Martineau, 2018, p. 07).

PROBLEM STATEMENT

In compliance with the PAIA and POPIA, universities were to balance access and protection of information lawfully. Furthermore, they were to champion the protection of personal information of data subjects. This so because South African universities were confronted with security threats to their information resources which may impede access to their strategic and operational activities and negatively affect access to information. The explosion of cyber-attacks and threats and the integration of sophisticated devices on organization networks had created security challenges which lead to the loss of information (Opara & Dieli, 2021). It seems that there was no industry best practice existed that provides the right state-of-the-art security protection for university systems across the world (Ceross, 2018, p. 99). Universities experienced network leaks, unauthorized access, and access attacks on their information management system. Hence it was the responsibility of the Information Communication Technology department to monitor the security of information. Some of the systems attacked by hackers were not described by the Information Communication Division which makes it a challenge to identify a list of content management systems purchased by the university. Some universities' divisions purchased electronic content management systems without consultation with the ICT division. This demonstrate lack coordination in the content management system of various universities. University should have a list of information systems procured. (Botha, Globlerr, & Eloff 2017). Information Communication Technology should handle all the queries posed by various divisions. The complaint handling process should be developed and guided by documented policies and procedures for receiving and responding to complaints or enquires concerning the security of information. (Ceross, 2018, p. 100). Data breaches included human elements and uncertainties as well as organizational understandings and operations. The literature review found that though not adequate, personnel in universities adopted some strategies and measures to secure university information. However, the advance in information communication technology affected how the university manages its information and records. It appears the South African universities were not effectively utilizing information communication technology to ensure the smooth running of the information management. Preliminary findings indicate poor security management practices at some South African universities have been a source of risks to the institutions leading to inefficiency in their business.

THE OBJECTIVE OF THE STUDY

To assess the cyber security threats such as security of information faced by South African universities from 1994 until present. This is an assessment of the cyber security threat faced by the South African Institution of Higher learning form 1994 until present.

The following research questions guided the book chapter.

- What are the challenges faced by universities on security information?
- What are the strategies for protecting universities information against cyberattacks?
- What preventative measures are to be in place at the South African universities to prevent cybersecurity?

The researcher embarked on this research because of limited research conducted on cybersecurity in South African universities. However, in other countries, extensive research was conducted. South African higher Institutions of learning, like other African universities, are affected by the data bridge of information.

The COVID – 19 contributed to higher education institutions of learning in South Africa to develop an information management system for teaching and learning. This demonstrates that COVID – 19 is a game-changer for universities to strengthen information security.

It appeared South African Institution of higher Learning switching to hybrid teaching and learning models had exposed level of skills to provide online educations. A lack of access to online learning and digital skills puts students at risk of falling behind their peers. This deepens access to information. Most students used a password to access universities' information communication technology which had an impact on the security of information. This chapter assessed the security of universities' storage as to whether they were effective to manage data. This was so because information storage was significant in the management of university records. Universities' information systems were managed on different platforms. This implies that there were approaches to data management.

The research was limited to South African public universities. South African public universities were targeted by a hacker. Cybersecurity management systems was the most important building block in the security of information. However, previous researchers conducted little research on cyber security. Therefore, South African universities need to protect university information to live up to their mission of teaching, learning, and research. Highlighting the challenges of cybersecurity might enable universities to work towards finding solutions to any attack on university systems.

RESEARCH METHODOLOGY

Researcher relied on qualitative research method. The case study of universities was chosen to conduct this study to allow in depth, multi-faceted exploration of cybersecurity . The aim of using case study was to provide insights into cyber security issues. The research applied the literature as the overall strategy utilized to carry out research that defines logical plan to handle research questions. A literature review is significant because it allows the researcher to assess and analyze literature. The literature reviewed utilized in this chapter included cloud computing, privacy, records management, and security management. The research articles, reports, and physical records on cybersecurity were retrieved. The literature review indicated the fact that cloud computing contributed to the protection of privacy and personal information.

Qualitative data, in the form of literature review, were analysed thematically using the following themes: Research department, internationalization, admissions, registrations, graduations and management of information, organizational diversity, Committee management decision making, collaboration culture, POPIA compliance, Cloud storage and governance, data governance, information communication technology, IoT Technology and cybersecurity training and awareness

RESEARCH DEPARTMENT

Various academic departments and academics created records for the advancement of universities. The mandate of the research department is to promote sustainable access to digital research data. The research department is responsible for coordinating research activities with faculties. This implies South African higher education institutions develop applications and system tools that assist in the monitoring and tracking of research activities. (Borgman, 2018, p. 368). This demonstrates that universities coordinate the collection of data from various academic departments. Document analysis shows that research universities drive the knowledge economy worldwide (Chirikov, 2013. p. 456). Research outputs are useful for policy development and decisions making. South African universities found themselves contending with vast quantities of data related to research.

The research departments develop database management systems to manage research outputs. Departments develop processes and procedures for identifying data subject access requests (Borgman, 2018, p. 378). There should be evidence of the collection of data within the universities. This is so because researchers, lecturers, and students are responsible to collect data from sources.

Data were protected against any form of threat. This was because universities established institutional repositories to preserve institutional records. Furthermore, universities develop a Back-Up system and restoration policy to restore information (Chisita and Chiparausha, 2021, p. 137). These backup and restoration policies were monitored regularly to check for information breaches. The Information Communication Division should be responsible for the management of cybersecurity within institutions. This was because information Communication divisions, departments, and units oversight the security of information. This department is significant to the management of information. This provides opportunities for universities to migrate their information to reliable electronic content management systems. This contributes to building the culture of keeping information about the organization.

INTERNATIONALIZATION

The cyber security issue is international and multinational issues. It intertwined with national security, competitiveness, and various national legislations. Because of its complexity, cybersecurity requires a holistic approach management of information. This implies universities to promote cooperation with various stakeholders through signed agreements on the exchange of students, and teaching and learning exchange programs. Internationalization programs in South Africa are guided by national laws. (Abdulrauf and Fombard, 2016, p. 67). This was especially significant, especially in data protection which requires a harmonization for effective implementation. University become a leader in the privacy of information by increasing cooperation and internationalization (Chirikov, 2013, p461). It seems that most International organizations requested information from various South African universities that may compromise the privacy of individuals.

Sharing of information can benefit organizations to gain business partners. This requires universities to develop information governance framework is shared on a global platform. University governance framework is to comply with the United States of America Patriotic Act of 2021 (Ghorbel, Ghorbel, and Jmaiel, 2017, p. 2774). In terms, of the United States of America Patriotic Act, the American government accessed any databases stored in their countries with suspicious information.

Various legislation in South Africa prohibited the storage and transfer of data in other countries. Department of Higher Education in South Africa assessed countries with privacy legislation, to allow universities to enter into agreements on the international exchange of students and staff exchange program

Internationalization promote universities to share information with various stakeholders. This implies universities develop effective institutional repositories to store data. Information stored must be accurate, and complete manner to enhance sharing of information Such sharing processes led other South African universities to compromise privacy. International organizations access university data to rank universities. Universities with effective content management systems provided data for the ranking universities. Information provided by universities enables them to be ranked world-class.

Universities need to collaborate with other organizations to combat cyberattacks on the electronic environment. Universities also collaborate with local partners such as municipalities, government departments, and non-profit organizations for cyber security advocacy.

ADMISSIONS, REGISTRATIONS, GRADUATIONS, AND MANAGEMENT OF INFORMATION

University administration functions includes admissions, registration, graduation, and management of information. Universities administrators are responsible for students' admissions, registrations, graduations, and management of information annually. During registration, personal data such as personal identity documents, passports, and academic records are administered. The registration functions create data useful for planning and decision-making by universities. This implies that personal information should be managed in a secure environment.

Administrative departments were aware of security because of personal information generated by university information management systems. Registrars are responsible for the administrative sections of universities and coordinating information security. They are the chief administrative and compliance officer of the university. He/she oversee and ensure effective and timeous academic administrative support in the maintenance of academic structures and standards. The office of the registrar collaborate with the Information and Security management division to ensure the management of security. However, it seems that universities operated in silence to ensure information security. It seems that some universities were hesitant to undertake risk assessment initiatives including security awareness because of concerns relating to lack of expertise, and administrative staff awareness. It seems that some universities have the pieces of a successful communicative initiative. Universities may benefit through security awareness and initiatives on information management awareness.

ORGANIZATIONAL DIVERSITY

Diversity literature relates to universities is abounding with methods to provide universal guidelines on teaching and learning. South African universities' functions differ from government departments because their functions are a combination of public and private affairs. Universities have various stakeholders.

Each university in South Africa has established organizational culture and tradition to handle security issues. Cyber security responses are determined by the organizational culture and behavior of the university. The diversity is reflected in the extent of the resources, in the mandate allocated to various institutions, and in the defined balance between university security of information. Within the university, information security officers experience limited budget and record keeping space. Most South African universities define their priorities in terms of, first, service of teaching and learning programs. University management needs to prioritize the management of information. While there were long–term security awareness benefits of the security of university management. Most universities may not provide security to their staff. Despite diverse of various universities, some universities share several concerns and experience similar pressures within the university setting.

Some factors may affect the management of information (Gangire, Da Veiga & Herselman, 2020, p. 627). Human factors were influenced by circumstances which caused certain behavior. Both employees and staff taught information security standards. The training and awareness program on cyber security management may be promoted to various universities. Employees must be aware of security management compliance. Another factor that influences the security of information is culture. Information culture security is cultivated through employee interaction (Nel and Drevin 2019, p. 149). This is when employees share information to execute their duties in their work environment. Information culture to be aware of the type of information created by the institution and consider the issue of ethics during the handling of information. The importance of using passwords to access information.

COMMITTEE MANAGEMENT DECISION MAKING

Unlike organizational setup where there is a hierarchic management structure, South African university structures are decentralized and flatter. Governance structure of university include council which play a role of oversight. Most data control is created in these committees. Universities' strategic decisions are taken by committees. The decision made by universities is mainly done at the Committee Management level.

COLLABORATION CULTURE

One of the university's functions is engagement and partnership. South African universities have a culture of collaboration. Universities' functions require the collaboration of divisions, departments, divisions, or units. Data sharing in the process of collaboration. This implies any ICT is an enabler to enhance a culture of sharing information.

"Archivists and records managers were often not included as a list of stakeholders who collaborated on cloud computing and security management" (Ferguson-Boucher and Convey, 2011, p.226). Hence, professionally staffed and recognized records managers are also a relatively recent phenomenon to assist cyber security. It is the view of the researcher that information professionals were included in cloud computing to ensure preservation of institutional memory. The industries were interested in the university in research and other activities. Collaboration is necessary because it increased cyber security in public and industrial domains and enforces research and development (Kharchenko et al., 2016). Collaboration should be based on organizational cyber security models. The strategic goal of university-industry cooperation is to develop an integrated infrastructure in computer, software, and network technologies security. Training and awareness of cybersecurity is to be based on this model. This will ensure that users limit to providing people with university information. The challenge of external stakeholders is that users are influenced by external stakeholders. This led external stakeholders to access information. Furthermore, universities relied on external stakeholders to design and develop cyber security systems which posed a challenge to the privacy of information. This is so because external stakeholders university challenge. External access to university information management systems. It seems that systems designers focused on enriching themselves or making a profit when designing cyber security management systems.

POPIA COMPLIANCE

The legislation promote privacy of information in any organization (Khatoun and Zeadally, 2017, p. 8). The high law of South Africa enacted in 2013 makes privacy provisions. Legislature to enact acts to comply with the legislature. There was a concern about the bridge of privacy in many organizations all over the world (Kudo et al., 2007). Privacy is a human right that needs to be protected against any violations (Ghorbel, Ghorbel & Jmaiel, 2017, p. 2768). The right to privacy has been universally accepted. Countries enacted privacy legislation to ensure compliance with international norms to protct human rights.

South public and non-public organizations including South African universities must comply with POPIA and other related legislation governing information security. The POPIA has been signed into law on November 26ᵗ 2013. Therefore, South African organizations and individuals are to comply with the national legislation' and regulations. POPIA is a step towards full compliance with international privacy. Organizations are required to develop privacy policies (Ghorbel, Ghorbel, & Jmaiel, 2017, p. 2775). It is important to ensure that staff complies with the privacy policy. This is so because most data users are not aware of how their privacy can be compromised due to the bridge of privacy. The South African government established an independent entity, known as the Information Regulator. The Information Regulator is responsible to issues enforcement notices to the responsible party such as the university when there was compliance with the violation of the privacy of information. They are also responsible to monitor compliance with the legislation. The enforcement process of privacy should consider aspects such as privacy and confidentiality of information.

Several laws emphases on providing people right to access information. For example, the PAIA makes provision for access to information. PAIA was passed in parliament to ensure that people do have rights to information. Certain information is not supposed to be made public. An organization should consider privacy, and confidentiality when providing access to various stakeholders.

The Electronic Communication and Transaction Act (ECTA) (No. 25 of 2002) responsibly promotes the use of a content system (Marutha 2019). The information generated on the content management system is controlled effectively and efficiently. University ensure that content management systems must be built to prevent access by unauthorized users.

In 1996, the South African public sector stated that Minimum Information Security Standards (MISS) were established to ensure that the privacy of information is protected and defended. No university is immune from records forgery, records theft, and deliberate records destruction. Any valuable records such as tender contracts, payment vouchers, and student files are susceptible to all the above and common records criminal.

University is required to develop a records and archives management system. A registry system is a basis for records security and is almost non -existence in most South African universities. A personal office, a preferred records storage space for most officials in the university, cannot guarantee security for records. The potential risk to records is exacerbated by the practice with the university of sharing office space. In an officer-sharing environment, records security is compromised as it is a challenge to hold staff accountable for the loss or destruction of records. However, it should also be emphasized that a registry system without adequate control measures such as vetting of officials, as it is prevalent within the university, cannot serve as an effective system zone for the safekeeping of records. The underlying assumption is that all public sector organizations such as universities possess at their disposal, records that need to be protected from unauthorized users. Universities are to determine security measures to protect the use of information.

MISS is a policy document that has profound implications on how records are managed in universities. Universities offices are obliged to give particular attention to the following elements of records management:

- Establishment of registries
- Development, implementation, and maintenance of records classification systems and
- Document security.

CLOUD STORAGE AND GOVERNANCE

A computing system may be used to access information. Storing of information using the cloud is gaining popularity in universities. It seems that universities adopted cloud storage to store information. However, cloud computing provides a challenge for university program professionals (Ferguson -Boucher & Convery, 2011, p. 221). The challenges faced by professionals are the lack of knowledge of information systems management and database management. Despite these challenges, most organizations adopted cloud-based services to store data for long-term preservation. (Bushey, Demoulin & McLelland, 2015, p. 125). For advanced universities, Cloud storage is a digital management strategy. Universities adopted cloud storage to enhance security management and protection of information and to improve compliance with relevant legislation.

Cloud computing was a threat to an organization that does not have well-prepared information plan (Ghorbel, Ghorbel, & Jmaiel, 2017, p. 2763). All projects and initiatives that entail processing information are assessed against the impact on compliance at the planning stage. The development of cloud storage led the organization to store data in clouds. Clouds' environments require the security of information. South African universities develop a strategy to move data into cloud storage.

Review of literature shows that most South African universities outsource services of cloud computing because they lack internal experts on cloud computing. Service providers are outsourced to provide service to universities. Despite their lack of expertise, universities see advantages of cloud computing to control records on electronic records management systems (Stuart and Bromage, 2010, p. 219). Most organizations ensure that they share information on an electronic platform. This means that universities share the costs of the management of information. Organizations reduce some of the challenges they face. Despite these benefits, most organizations are not adopted the SharePoint platform because of a lack of trust (Ferguson-Boucher and Convery, 2011, p. 225). Baloyi and Kotse (2017, p. 1) agreed that lack of trust in public and private institutions should be a worry to universities. All people should be confident in the system of the university.

The challenge associated with the management of information on the cloud is the fact that the third party controls the cloud computing system. Some third parties violated service agreements and privacy by sharing organization information. The researcher recommended universities train their internal experts to ensure effective management of data and information. Universities are to hire information professionals to design cloud computing systems. This will limit the threat to personal information.

A document analysis indicated that cloud computing system was not done consistently because of limited resources. Universities are to ensure that enough budget was allocated to cloud computing and overloaded Information Technology system.

Most organizations lack control of data stored on a cloud (Stuart & Bromage, 2010, p. 220). This may be because the organization purchased the system without conducting an impact assessment. Organization did not conduct a risk assessment. The value of storing data on a cloud system is not yet determined. There is a challenge to control records once they are stored on a cloud system (Stuart & Bromage, 2010, p. 220). It seems organizations lack a formal periodic process to verify completeness and accuracy of the information collected and disseminated in an electronic system. The cloud system needs to be reviewed and updated regularly. It seems that universities lack a system to monitor and review cloud computing systems regularly. Because most of information is stored on an online database is not easy to monitor breaches of privacy. Some of these data stored online have business value to an organization.

DATA GOVERNANCE

Cyber security is a concept of information governance (Masmali & Miah, 2021). This concept involved the roles of the university management, and the development of policies, processes, and procedures. Despite these mechanisms in place, a threat to cyber security is poor implementation and adherence to cyber security strategy. Furthermore, security management is not part of the executive management. Most universities have not yet developed policies and procedures on cyber security which posed risk to information management.

Most government institutions were not yet fully transformed to embrace information communication technologies strategy (Klett, 2019, p. 86). The lack of a system delays the provision of information to communities. The need for governance arises because of the need to promote accountability and transparency. Furthermore, there was a need to safeguard information against loss. Loss of information at universities mitigate cybersecurity management through the protection derived from good corporate governance. Research conducted by (Mullon & Ngoepe, 2019, p. 105) stressed organizations develop governance frameworks in compliance with applicable legislation. This implies South African universities develop a governance framework to manage data.

A positive correlation between governance and records management was demonstrated at a higher institution of education in South Africa (Phiri and Tough, 2018). Governance and records management is a baseline for information security management. (Khumalo & Baloyi, 2017, p. 01). Organizations were to manage their data following their policies. (Stuart & Bromage, 2010, p. 220). Organizations create, share, store, and used records. Records support universities program. Therefore records created by organizations were to be reliable, accessible, authentic, and accurate. Governance was necessary to improve the records management system. However, this does not imply universities with good records management will have good governance. Universities develop an internal system to manage records effectively. Records management internal systems include records management policy records management procedure manuals, and records management forms.

Organizations were to monitor information systems to ensure the security of information regularly (Ghorbel, Ghorbel, & Jmaiel, 2017, p. 2775). The ineffective monitoring of privacy affects the management of privacy within an organization. Organizations were to develop policies and procedures to address the cyber security issues. The knowledge and understanding of cyber security assist universities to manage information governance. At the present of writing this book chapter, universities are to invest in governance issues to ensure the preservation of institutional information. (Klareld, 2015).

INFORMATION COMMUNICATION TECHNOLOGY

Information Communication Technology is an enabler for any organization. It is an enabler of teaching and learning (Krishnaveni & Meenakumari, 2010, p. 289). The Information Communication Technology program is an enabler to registration, admission processes, communication services, records management processes, finance, library, and research functions. Universities take advantage of ICT in performing academic services as the strategic function of the university (Maria & Haryani, 2011, p. 13). Most university process management systems require effective records management systems.

Most organizations has poor information communication technologies infrastructure such as un-updated systems patches. Because of poor information communication technology structures, disgruntled users launch retaliatory attacks to sabotage systems. User misuse of university systems compromised management of systems. The increased use of ICT in the infrastructure of universities promoted interest in universities (Khartoum & Zeadally, 2017, p. 2). Incorporating Information Communication technology opens various security and privacy issues in universities.

Management of information is dependent on Information Communication Technology (ICT) as a critical component. The risk was introducing Information Communication technology in university systems while the staff was not aware of the system. University communities increased to use of un-safe wifi networks to access their emails and so on, thereby exposing to various types of cybersecurity (Khatoun & Zeadally 2017). The implementation of university functions was dependent on aspects such as digital security, infrastructure safety, and personal safety. Therefore, this requires the university to develop content management systems. The security attack was based on how universities managed their information and infrastructure. Attacked universities should consider how universities are protected against any form of attack.

Document analysis shows that the information communication technology of most South African universities is integrated with business functions. This shows information communication technology supports the business program to achieve its objectives.

IoT TECHNOLOGY

IoT is defined as a relationship of information systems to provide information to organizations (Tawalbeh et al., 2020, p.1). IoT is used for educational purposes to share information. The remote locations can be used to communicate with various users through the system. The Internet of things (IoT) has a significant impact to improve university security and safety. Wi-fi enables the likes of networked CCTV (McLoughlin, 2022). Universities adopted Geogencing to use for GPS. The IoT improves the lifestyle of individuals through automated services. The automation of systems promoted privacy and security challenges.

Smart campuses are significant to ensure affordable and sustainable ways of achieving smart-building conversations. Systems must be available to all parts of university infrastructure to prevent hackers to access the university system (Tawalbeh et al., 2020).

CYBERSECURITY TRAINING AND AWARENESS

Organisations raised awareness of cyber security (Grobler et al., 2012, p. 215; Moskal, 2015, p. 101). Organisation have been obliged to fulfill the interest of the university community by ensuring that education on cyber security was conducted. In general, cyber security education was underdeveloped in South Africa. The South African universities could support skills and knowledge development amongst educators.

Students and staff were most users of an information management system. The review of the literature indicated that cybersecurity increased because of a lack of user awareness (Potgieter, 2019). This implies that universities were to conduct training and awareness on cyber security. The purpose of awareness and training was to educate the users about the significance of information. Users of systems can be stimulated to protect the university from a link or be used by other users. Most organizations applied security education to promote awareness and training. The education system should integrate the security of information. All stakeholders could contribute to the security of information within an organization. To implement the cybersecurity management process, each university stakeholder raised awareness of cybersecurity management. It was therefore necessary for organisations to conduct training and awareness on cybersecurity management. Awareness may entail distribution of regular emails to staff to share their information with various stakeholders. This implies higher education to develop a course on Cyber security management. The syllabus of this course should include the following: protection of personal information, and cybersecurity management. Soft skills awareness such as communication and marketing was used as a form of awareness (Potgieter, 2019, p. 273).

It appears that university communities were not aware of user awareness training on cyber security. Therefore, cybersecurity awareness raised in the form of Security Education, Training, and Awareness (SETA) for students. Moskal (2015, p. 101) stated that the establishment of cybersecurity section at universities provides opportunities for students to learn, collaborate, conduct research, and have hands-on training on technology. This implies that students access all records. Higher Institutions of learning were required to develop a security checklist to ensure that all role-players such as students, staff, and service providers were aware of the security and privacy of university information. Hence the research proposed a role-based security awareness model to promote the dissemination of information.

It seems the staff were not trained in Information Communication Technology infrastructure and technology. The lack of monitoring and understanding of the policies were threats for South African universities to manage the cyber security issues and improve security. This shows that a security audit was not initiated.

The researcher was of the view that cybersecurity training and awareness may lead to the advancement of university security of information. Cybersecurity training should be compulsory in an institution. Well, training and awareness are significant for the information management security of institutions. Training and awareness on cybersecurity should include aspects of information communication technology and records management.

CONCLUSION

Despite the available of PAIA, POPIA and universities policies on cybersecurity in South Africa universities, most organization experience cybersecuirty threat. The literature review shows that universities staff and students were not fully trained on cybersecurity management or security awareness were not conducted on the risk of cybersecurity management in universities. Management of security reguires knowledge of information communication technology.

Recommendations

Continuous monitoring and evaluation of inbound network traffic load on firewalls and system resources.

Universities should embark on cyber risk assessment of their assets.

There is also a need to ensure that universities conduct cyber security information security audits on regular basis. Universities should invest in the establishment of the cyber security infrastructure to support their business operations. Cyber security infrastructure means hardware, software, data management, and appointing the right people for cyber security management.

- Develop a backup and recovery plan
- Management of passwords.
- Continuous training and development of staff on cyber security.

Contributions and Implications

This study evaluates whether South African universities place a system to ensure the protection of university information against cyber attacks. In turn, investigating that question allowed the researcher to discuss whether businesses can leverage university information. This research may offer new insight into cybersecurity management. This research assisted tertiary institutions in South Africa to raise awareness of cybersecurity management. Universities division, departments, divisions, and units are to play a meaningful role during collaboration to ensure that various organizations are to ensure that cybersecurity is in place. The results may suggest that South African universities should ensure that cybersecurity is part of the university strategy.

Areas for Further Studies

Further research needs to be conducted to address issues of cyber security. This can be done by trying to answer the following questions. First, what is the real effect of cybersecurity in an organization? There is evidence from a university that the security of information is not considered the strategic function.

Second, what are the most steps in preventing security threats at South African universities?. Organizations are to develop cyber security in line with their organization's mission.

Thirdly, How can organizations ensure effective security management of the university?

All these questions are necessary for the further development of cybersecurity management in universities.

REFERENCES

Abddulrauf, A. L., & Fombad, M. C. (2017). Personal Data Protection in Nigeria: Reflections on Opportunities, Options, and Challenges to Legal Reforms. *The Liverpool Law Review*, *38*(2), 105–134. doi:10.100710991-016-9189-8

Abdulrauf, A. L., & Fombad, M. C. (2016) The African Union's data protection Convention 2014: a possible cause for celebration of human rights in Africa? *Journal of Media Law*, (1), 67 – 97.

Baloyi, N., & Kotze, P. (2017). Are Organisations in South Africa Ready to Comply with Personal Data Protection or Privacy Legislation and Regulations? *ISTOfrica 2017 Conference Proceedings*. www.IST-Afric.org/conference2017

Borgman, C. L. (2018). Open data, grey data, and stewardship: Universities at the privacy frontier. *Berkeley Technology Law Journal*, *33*(2), 365–412.

Botha, J., Globler, M.M., Hann, J., & Eloff, M.M. (2017). *A High-Level Comparison between the South African Protection of Personal Information Act and International Data Protection Laws*. Academic Press.

Bushney, J., Demoulin, M., & McLelland, R. (2015). Cloud Service Contracts: An Issue of Trust. *Canadian Journal of Information and Library Science*, *39*(2), 128–158. doi:10.1353/ils.2015.0009

Chirikov, I. (2013). Research universities as knowledge networks: The role of institutional research. *Studies in Higher Education*, *38*(3), 456–469. doi:10.1080/03075079.2013.773778

Chisita, T. C., & Chiparusha, B. (2021). An Institutional Repository in a Developing Country: Security and Ethical Encounters at the Bindura University of Science Education, Zimbabwe. *New Review of Academic Librarianship*, *27*(1), 130–143. doi:10.1080/13614533.2020.1824925

Ferguson-Boucher, K., & Convery, N. (2011). Storing information in the cloud–A research project. *Journal of the Society of Archivists*, *32*(2), 221–239. doi:10.1080/00379816.2011.619693

Gangire, Y., Da Veiga, A., & Herselman, M. (2021). Assessing Information Security Behaviour: A self – determination theory perspective. *Information & Computer Security*, *29*(4), 625–646. doi:10.1108/ICS-11-2020-0179

Grobler, M., Van Vuuren, J., & Leenen, L. (2012). Implementation of a cyber Security Policy in South Africa: Reflection on Progress and the Way Forward. *International Federation for Information Processing*, *386*, 215–225. doi:10.1007/978-3-642-33332-3_20

Kharchenko, V., Sklyar, V., Brezhnev, E., Boyarchuk, A., Starov, O., & Phillips, C. (2016, June). University-Industry Cooperation in Cyber Security Domain: Multi-Model Approach, Tools and Cases. In *Proceedings of the University-Industry Interaction Conference: Challenges and Solutions for Fostering Entrepreneurial Universities and Collaborative Innovation* (pp. 265-283). Academic Press.

Khatoun, R and Zeadally, S (2017) Cybersecurity and Privacy Solutions in Smart Cities Enabling Mobile and Wireless Technologies for Smart Cities: Part 2. *IEEE Communications Magazines*.

Khumalo, B. N., & Baloyi, C. (2017). The possible benefits of freedom of information laws to the records management landscape in the ESARBICA region. *Information Development*, 1–5.

Klared, A. S. (2015). 'Isn't it information assets we're really talking about?' A discourse analysis of a panel discussion on digital archives. *Architectural Record*, *36*(2), 167–178. doi:10.1080/23257962.2015.1058245

Klett, E. (2018). Theory, regulation and practice in Swedish digital records appraisal. *Records Management Journal*, *29*(1/2), 86 – 102.

Krishnaveni, R., & Meenakumari, J. (2010). Usage of ICT for Information Administration in Higher Education Institutions – A study. *International Journal of Environmental Sciences and Development*, *1*(3), 282–286. doi:10.7763/IJESD.2010.V1.55

Kudo, M., Araki, Y., Nomiyama, H., Saito, S., & Sohda, Y. (2007). Best practices and tools for personal information compliance management. *IBM Systems Journal*, *46*(2), 235–252. doi:10.1147j.462.0235

Kundy, E. D., & Lyimo, B. J. (2019). Cyber security threats in higher learning Institutions in Tanzania, A case of University of Ausha and Tumaini University Makumira. Olva Academy – School of Researchers, 2(3).

Maria, E., & Haryani, E. (2011). Audit Model Development of Academic Information System: Case Study on Academic Information System of Satya Wacaa. *Journal of Arts, Science & Commerce*, *11*, 12–24.

Marutha, N. (2019). The application of legislative framework for the management of medical records in Limpopo Province, South Africa. *Information Development*, *35*(4), 1–13. doi:10.1177/0266666918772006

Masmali, H., & Miah, J. S. (2021). Emergent Insgith of the Cyber Security Management for Saudi Arabia Universities: A Content Analysis. *Pacific. Journal of the Association for Information Systems*, *13*(3), 1–18.

McLoughlin, M. (2022). *Development of 'smart' university campus is within reach*. University World News. https://www.universityworldnews.com/page.php?page=UW_Mai

Moskai, J. E. (2015). A model for Establishing a Cybersecurity Centre of Excellence. *Information Systems Education Journal*, *13*(6), 97–103.

Mullon, A. P., & Ngoepe, M. (2019). An integrated framework to elevate information governance to a national level in South Africa. *Records Management Journal*, *29*(1/2), 103–116. doi:10.1108/RMJ-09-2018-0030

Nel, F., & Drevin, L. (2019). Key Elements of an information security culture in organizations. *Information & Computer Security*, *27*(2), 146–164. doi:10.1108/ICS-12-2016-0095

Olatunbosun, B. S., Edwards, J. N., & Martineau, D. C. (2018). Capturing The Existential Cyber Security Threats from the Sub- Saharan Africa Zone through Literature Database. KSU *Proceedings on CyberSecurity Education, Research and Practice, 3*. https://digitalcommons.kennesaw.edu/ccerp/2018/research/3

Opara, U. E., & Dieli, J.O. (2021). Enterprise Cyber Security Challenges to Medium and Large Firms: An analysis. *I.J of Electroncis and Information Engineering*, *13*(2), 77 – 85.

Phiri, J. M., & Tough, G. A. (2018). Managing university records in the World of Governance. *Records Management Journal*, *28*(1), 47–61. doi:10.1108/RMJ-11-2016-0042

Potgieter, P. (2019). The Awareness Behaviour of Students On Cyber Security Awareness by Using Social Media Platforms; A Case Study at Central University of Technology. *Kalpa Publications in Computing*, *12*, 272–280. doi:10.29007/gprf

Stuart, K., & Bromage, D. (2010). Current State of Play: Records management and the Cloud. *Records Management Journal*, *20*(2), 217–225. doi:10.1108/09565691011064340

Villegas-Ch, W., Ortiz-Garces, I., & Sanchez-Viteri, S. (2021). Proposal for an Implementation Guide for a Computer Security Incident Response Team on a University Campus. *Computers*.

ADDITIONAL READING

Chandarman, R., & Van Niekerk, B. (2017). Students cybersecurity awareness at a private tertiary educational institution. *The African Journal of Information and Communication*, *20*(20), 133–155. doi:10.23962/10539/23572

Gcaza, N., & Von Solms, R. (2017). A strategy for a cybersecurity culture: A South African perspective. *The Electronic Journal on Information Systems in Developing Countries*, *80*(1), 1–17. doi:10.1002/j.1681-4835.2017.tb00590.x

Kshetri, N. (2015). Cybercrime and cybersecurity issues in the BRICS economies. *Journal of Global Information Technology Management*, *18*(4), 245–249. doi:10.1080/1097198X.2015.1108093

Sutherland, E. (2017). Governance of cybersecurity – the case of South Africa. *The African Journal of Information and Communication*, *20*(20), 83–112. doi:10.23962/10539/23574

KEY TERMS AND DEFINITIONS

Cloud Computing: This is a process of using an internet system to store, manage and process data.

Cyber Security: It is the process of ensuring that networks that constitute cyberspace are protected against privacy.

Data Protection: It is the protection of privacy in an electronic environment.

Governance: The system introduced by universities to ensure compliance with appropriate legislation and framework.

Information Privacy: This is the relationship between the collection and dissemination of data, technology within an organization.

Internationalization: This is a process of ensuring that the university engaged with other institutions nationally and internationally to promote and market the university.

South African Universities: These are 26 public South African universities established in South Africa.

Chapter 14
Africa and Council of Europe Strategic Partnership on Cybersecurity

Oluchukwu Ignatus Onianwa
University of Ibadan, Nigeria

ABSTRACT

This chapter examines Africa's strategic partnership with the Council of Europe in the development and advancement of cybersecurity on the continent. Africa is one of the continents in the world with a strong presence of information and communication technology users. Unfortunately, both government institutions and private sectors in Africa are experiencing an increase in cyber-related attacks. Different initiatives through CoE are being developed to combat the menace of cyber-attacks in Africa.

INTRODUCTION

The 21st Century development is tied to information and communication technology mainly in business sector. The growing influence of ICT in public and private business organisations via the internet has enhanced citizen connections virtually and unlock new frontier of contact for citizens and government of nations (Gyem, 2022, p.2). More importantly, businesses in Africa and Europe are getting digitally compliance and integrated for optimal performance and seamless service delivery (Africa-Europe Alliance, 2019, p.7).

While it is necessary to nurture businesses digitally ensuring information security in business ventures have become a common trend among big corporations (Nweze-Iloekwe, 2022, p. 1), because while commerce are getting technologically conformed (Audit Analytics, 2022, p.3), there is Cybersecurity risks jeopardizing the growth and development of digital economy (Kshetri, 2016, p.2). Frequent news abounds in Africa and even in Europe about cyber attacks or computer-related crimes against companies and business institutions (World Bank and United Nations, 2017, p.6).

DOI: 10.4018/978-1-6684-5827-3.ch014

This chapter examines Africa's strategic partnership with the Council of Europe (CoE) in the development and advancement of Cybersecurity. While the study adopts a case study approach for data analysis, it utilizes secondary sources such as books, journal articles, newspapers and internet sources for data collection. Since it became a dominant discourse in the field of information technology scholarly analysis of Cybersecurity from multilateral and diplomatic perspectives has been limited. Thus, this study contributes to the ongoing conversation on Africa's place in the global debates on cyber diplomacy.

This paper argued that no business enterprise is immune from cyber threats. That Africa is the hotbed of cybercrime is not in doubt. Thus, continuous partnership with multilateral organizations is cardinal towards ameliorating the menace. While Africa is not CoE's major region of operation, the European organization find it necessary to partner with African governments to reduce cybercrime emanating from African countries through collaboration on building strong institutions, legislative reforms, capacity-building, electronic evidence, awareness creation and borderless intelligences sharing with law enforcement agencies in Africa. The first section of the paper is conceptual clarifications while the second section looks at the Cybersecurity situation in Africa. The third section examines European and African relations on Cybersecurity and the fourth section deals with the African partnerships with CoE on Cybersecurity.

Research Questions

The following research questions serves as a guide to this study.

1. What is the condition of cyber security in Europe and Africa?
2. What factors leads to cybercrime in Europe and Africa?
3. Why do Europe and Africa collaborate on cyber security?
4. What prompted the Council of Europe to form partnership with Africa on Cybersecurity?

Conceptual Clarifications

No single definition of Cybersecurity exists. However, it means a set of issues associated with information and national security (Van der Meulen et al., 2015, p.13). Cybersecurity is delineated to digital technologies and their existence is confined within a given nation's influence. Customarily, it has been elevated as very relevant for national security. This usually comprises debates on the military applications of computers and telecommunications, security of intelligence data, and critical infrastructures (Cole, 2008, p.9).

Similarly, Yokohama (2017, p.13) conceptualized Cybersecurity as a measure guaranteeing safe and secure usage of the internet. Concretely, Cybersecurity is simply part of overall corporate security management. Businesses must take Cybersecurity measures as they address other security management issues (Chikelue, 2020, p.246). Nweze-Iloekwe (2022, p. 1) argues that Cyber security guarantees data protection for a better-secured information society.

Apart from scholarly definitions, credible international organisations have also conceptualized Cybersecurity from different perspectives. For instance, according to the International Telecommunication Union (2012) Cybersecurity as the collection of tools, policies, security concepts, security safeguards, guidelines, risk management approaches, actions, training, best practices, assurance and technologies that can be used to protect the cyber environment and organization and user's assets (ITU, 2012, p.7). That no single acceptable definition of Cybersecurity exists shows that the industry is consistently evolving side by side with digital advancement and change in cyber user's behaviors.

CYBERSECURITY, EMERGING TRENDS, AND CHALLENGES

The greatest gift of mankind in the twentieth century is the ability to access information via the internet from anywhere around the world. People from different nationalities, race, ethnicity, tribe, and communities are now able to find any information they seek via the internet technology. With ease of getting information via the internet the proposition that digital technology is now part and parcel of everyday life in human society is a reality.

Singer and Allan (2014) states that, a decade ago cyberspace was just a term from science fiction used to describe the nascent network of computers linking a few university laboratories, today, the entire modern life, from communication to commerce to conflict, fundamentally depends on the Internet (Singer and Allan, 2014, p.1).

The International Telecommunication Union report cited in World Economic Forum Global Cybersecurity Outlook 2022 revealed that fixed broadband access has increased significantly on all continents as a direct result of teleworking, distance learning, remote entertainment and telemedicine. Thus, digital transformation is the main driver of increasing cyber resilience (ITU, 2012, p.3).

Innovations in digital technology have paved the way for the development of cyberspace security. Data privacy and security is now top security measures of organizations (Nikhita and Ugander, 2014, p.2). The rising financial growth and inclusiveness is facilitated through digital innovations which would not have been possible many years ago. Nations are creating different means of making financial transactions more flexible and affordable for businesses and services by anchoring on digitization processes.

The compromisation of digital business interests aroused the consciousness of safeguarding the cyberspace from unauthorized sources. For the protection of cyber economy is dependent on digital codes configuration and intelligence safety measures Brooks et al. (2018) argued that, an effective Cybersecurity defense consists of securing the infrastructure, mobile phone devices, local networks and computer perimeters (Charles, 2018, p.1).

With the threats that affecting computer systems, phone or other device connected to the internet, security has become a responsibility not just for law enforcement authorities or business leaders, but for every individual (Donaldson, 2018, p.1). Daniel (2018, p.2) maintained that while the use of technology increasing every day, so also the growth of Cybersecurity experts.

Corporate organizations and government institutions have come to terms on the importance of Cybersecurity in the navigation of digital cyberspaces and information structural designs. At the root of Cybersecurity are systems, processes, people, private institutions and government agencies, being, the nucleus for data generation hosted on the cyberspace for public consumption and building of a resilience society (Best Cybersecurity Practices Report, 2022, p.1).

Without Cybersecurity measures information confidentiality would be at a great risk, resulting into chaos and conflicts. Through technological innovations Cybersecurity architectures are built to protect the information spaces from being overtaken by cyber predators. Since these technologies hold important information regarding a person their security has become a must thing (Nikhita and Ugander, 2014, p.1).

The safety and stability of the cyberspace is achieved with emerging technologies. Cyber threats increase side by side with massive rush for the development of digital methods of combating it. Law enforcement agencies gain valuable knowledge from the available data to detect, identify and efficiently classify the most prevalent cyber incidents and predict future threats (Onyinye et al., 2021, p.1).

Cloud remains the prominent emerging technology in the Cybersecurity sector. Many big companies including government institutions have a significant portion of their IT infrastructure in the cloud. However, because users who store their data in the cloud are not able to check the cloud systems themselves, they need some other way to get protected against information leaks due to people accessing their data without authorization (Satoshi et al., 2014, p.57).

Data analytics is the second emerging technology in the field of Cybersecurity. Since financial and educational institutions have access to sensitive personal information, data breaches could have significant reputational implications. Protecting data is paramount to satisfying client data security and privacy expectations as well as meeting regulatory requirements. Meanwhile, regulators take note of large amounts of personal data captured and stored by companies, as well as their resiliency and data integrity (Satoshi et al., 2014, p.57).

Another emerging Cybersecurity related technology is artificial intelligence and cognitive technology. These advanced automation and machine learning technologies present a new set of solutions that can assist financial and business institutions transform operations and achieve cost reductions. In an increasingly cloud-native connected world, access control is once again a priority since these technologies expands identity and device proliferation, which creates additional identity types and new authentication requirements (The Financial Services Information Sharing and Analysis Center, pp.10-11).

A firewall is a software program or piece of hardware that helps screen out hackers, viruses, and worms that try to reach personal computer over the Internet. All messages entering or leaving the internet pass through the firewall which examines each message and blocks those that do not meet the specified security criteria. Hence firewalls play an important role in detecting the malware (Nikhita and Ugander, p.5).

While the emerging new technologies are very important in navigating the cyber security landscape the goal of protecting the cyberspace has remained elusive due to challenges facing the sector. The underinvestment in research and incentives is affecting the efficient use of the emerging technologies to fight Cybersecurity risks. Security is not being considered an integral component of technology innovations. This means that technologies are developed with little or no consideration for malicious threats, as has happened in the past. Without the right incentives to prevent this, there is a risk of insufficient security functionality and later costly retrofit (World Economic Forum Future Series Report, 2020, pp.15-16).

Skill gaps have further contributed to these challenges and the loophole for Cybersecurity threats across the global cyberspace. According to Andrew (2022) ransomware is the most prevalent emerging business risk threatening business continuity and operations (Andrew, 2022, p.2). Ransomware affiliate programs enable a larger group of criminals to attack big corporations and public institutions by threatening them with multilayered extortion methods and distributed-denial-of-service (Schwartz, 2021, p.3).

Malware are viruses, Trojans, worms and other software that gets onto the computer without your knowledge. When such software is downloaded, it infects the computer system and destroys valuable information. Spam and phishing spam is the use of electronic messaging systems to send unsolicited bulk messages and emails indiscriminately (Maitanmi et al., 2013, pp.21-22). Phishing emails encourage computer users to visit bogus websites. The email instructs the victim to follow a link to enter crucial information such as login details, personal information, bank account details or anything else that can be used to defraud their victims (Premium Times, 2018, p.3).

Espionage or hacking into adversarial systems to extract sensitive or protected information is the most pervasive use of state-sponsored cyber capabilities. The rapid diffusion of cyber capabilities and surveillance technology gives a wide range of actors the ability to conduct cyber espionage. For example, Pegasus malware, among the most sophisticated pieces of espionage software ever invented was discovered to have infected systems in eleven African countries (Jacqueline, 2009, p.13).

Business Email Compromise Scams BEC targets thousands of victims around the world. As part of the BEC scams, emails are sent to employees of various companies directing that funds be transferred to specified bank accounts. The emails, however, are not legitimate. Rather, they are either from email accounts with a domain name that was very similar to a legitimate domain name. After victims complied with the fraudulent wiring instructions, the transferred funds were quickly withdrawn or moved into different bank accounts (Kunle, 2022, p.2).

Digital extortion is another form of cybercrime which comprises of blackmailing and sextortion. These harmful actors persuade persons with either fake claims or proof of wrong personal data or records, for which the dupe is instructed to pay in substitute for retrieving the data or not exposing it online (Interpol's Cybercrime Directorate, 2021. p.14).

Cybercrime Situation in Europe and Africa

Europe and Africa are important continents with high rates of cybercrime. Cybercrime have sophisticated past traditional crimes and now posed a threat to businesses and the national security of every country, including technologically advanced nations (Gyem, 2022, p.4). Australia is one of the countries in Europe plagued with cybercrime. The Australia's National Plan to Combat Cybercrime 2022 revealed that online fraud and scams are cybercrime that is highly prevalent in Australia. In 2021, the Australian Competition and Consumer Commission's (ACCC) scam watch received an average 700 scam reports with $870,000 lost each day. Further research by the ACCC in 2021 highlighted that 68% of people who encountered a scam did not report the scam (Australia's National Plan to Combat Cybercrime, 2022, p.5).

The riskiest country for cybercrime in Europe is the United Kingdom. The UK loses over £27 billion per annum due to Cybercrime, with the predominant victims being the UK businesses (Harrison, 2021, p.3). Nord VPN Cybersecurity report (2022) revealed that the UK is rank first in terms of cyber security risk in side by side with the United States with 0.931 percent on the Global Cybersecurity Index which is calculated based on legal, technical, organizational and capacity building factors on a country level. And it is at the epidemic proportions with an average of 330 Britons suffering from cyber-attack per minute. Unfortunately, most people do not even realize that they have experienced a hack at all (Finch, 2022, p.1).

Behind the UK is France, which has the second-highest cybercrime rate in Europe. French people experience social media account hacking because they tend to very simple, utilize easy-to-guess passwords for many different accounts. This let hackers to easily get into more than one account. This suggests why French people believe the risk of becoming a victim of cybercrime is increasing (Harrison, 2021, p.3).

Skeldon (2021) argued that Germany comes third on the list of European nations with increased cybercrime. In 2021, German Federal Police estimated 8 percent increase in cybercrime in 2020. The Head of the Germany's Federal Criminal Police Office BKA's cybercrimes division, Carsten Meywirth, said some 108,474 cybercrimes had been reported in 2020, a 7.9 percent increase over 2019 and more than twice as many as in 2015. Among the primary threats to German businesses and public institutions in 2020 is ransomware attacks (DW, 2021, pp.1-4). Despite this, many Germans are not informed about the risks of cybercrime with huge number of citizens lacking knowledge about the dangers which have made them easily prone to cybercrime.

African continent is highly attractive to cybercriminals owing to high degree of digitization. According to Serianu, cybercrime cost African economies $3.5 billion in 2021 (Kshetri, 2019, p.2). Cybercrime on the continent has moved far beyond email scams with data breaches, government surveillance, and online scams encroaching on personal privacy whether it is personal photos, login credentials or medical histories (Symantec, 2016, p.12).

South Africa suffers more cybercrime attacks than any other country in Africa (Skye, 2016, p.3). According to Trend Micro cited in the Interpol Africa Cybersecurity Assessment October 2021 report, from January 2020 to February 2021, South Africa had 230 million cyber threat detections. 219 million detections were related to email threats. Ransomware and BEC are the highest threats in the country (Interpol, 2021, p.9).

Nigeria's cybercrime rate is unprecedented. Nigeria is ranked third most targeted country for cybercrime in Africa. Between the first and second quarters of 2021, there was a 32 percent jump in malware in trojan horse attacks in Nigeria (Guardian, 2022, p.2). The 2022 Check Point Research Threat Intelligence Report for Nigeria shows that the number of attacks that per business experienced each week in Nigeria is 2,308 across all sectors being a figure that is still higher for firms in the finance and banking sectors (Emma, 2022, p.3).

According to Kaspersky (2022) Security Network Data for corporate users, revealed that in the second quarter of 2022 Kenyans experienced different types of cyber-attacks with 5, 098, 534 phishing attacks detected, a growth of 438 percent when compared to the first quarter. Backdoor detections in Kenya increased in the second quarter to 10,300 being 53 percent increase and the share of users affected by backdoor increased by 11 percent. Backdoor enable a series of long unnoticed cyber espionage campaigns which result in significant financial or reputational losses and may disrupt the victim organization's operations.

In early October 2020, Uganda's telecom and banking sectors were plunged into crisis due to a major hack that compromised the country's mobile money network, usage of which has significantly increased during the COVID-19 pandemic. At least $3.2 million was estimated to have been stolen in that incident. Hackers used around 2,000 mobile SIM cards to gain access to the mobile money payment system to steal huge sum of money belonging to banks in Uganda (Signé and Kevin, 2021, p.3).

Malawi is another African country exposed to cyber-attacks and activities. It lacked appropriate legal framework and Cybersecurity initiatives to deal with digital fraud in the country. Manda (2018) argued that presently, there is no cyber legislation in Malawi and strongly authorizes strategies to combat cybercrime (Jideani, 2018, p.26).

Ghana has the highest presence of online transactions. Due to the prevalence of cybercrime in Ghana, foreign merchants get discouraged from trading in their financial institutions or doing business through a digital platform for the fear of being defrauded (Nir, 2016, p.4). According to Ghana Cyber Security Authority (2022) as at June 2022 online impersonation is the most critical cyber threat in Ghana for online businesses. The threat took a significant proportion of online scam operations ever committed in the country. The unrestricted nature of online activities has prompted an increase in online impersonation with numerous social media accounts registrations (Joy Business, 2022, p.3).

Purpose for Cybercrime

A number of factors contribute to rising cybercrimes in Europe and Africa. According to Interpol (2021), the first is the high rate of internet connectivity with more individuals online with low levels of digital security awareness. Poor awareness of cyber security and cyber hygiene particularly amongst vulnerable users such as the elderly leads to dramatic increase in cybercrime (Interpol, 2021, p.2). Having no knowledge of how cyber criminals operate makes it difficult to discover how to avoid them even they use different methods unknown to victims to gain access to vital data for financial gains.

Second factor is the mobility of online businesses with staff working remotely on less secured networks. Greater mobility and wider network access have led to a sharp boost in the number of employees working remotely, including from home. As a direct result, more commercial and official communication and transactions are being conducted over less secure domestic or public computer systems and networks, and people working from coffee shops (Interpol, 2021, p.1)

Thirdly, relative anonymity which decreases the chance of being caught on the act enhances cybercrime (Interpol, 2021, p.4). Such anonymity can be provided through legitimate online tools such as Bitcoin and other crypto currencies (Sheelagh and Caitriona, 2020, p.26). Cybercrime are carried out based on numerous motives. But it is done due to unemployment, poverty, peer pressure and financial gains.

High population utilization of smart phones or computer creates a fertile ground for flourishing of cybercrime. Cyber threats degenerate into cyber terrorism, espionage and cyber warfare (World Bank and United Nations, 2017, pp.10-11). As McLoughlin (2018) reveals fraudsters dispatch emails that appear to originate from confidential sources akin to corporate officials or merchant ordering staff to transfer funds to account number owned by them. Real visibility provides insights into actual behavior (McLoughlin, 2018, p.3).

In Africa low public knowledge about the real risks of cybercrimes and ignorance has further fueled cyber-attacks and online swindlers, coupled with the fact that, cyber users in Africa do not have up-to-date technical security measures like anti-virus packages, and many of the operating systems used are not regularly patched (Kritzinger and Solms, 2012, p.3) in addition with shortage of ICT skills needed to checkmate cybercrime in Africa (Sutherland, E. 2017, p.99).

Underreporting of cybercrime is the grounds for its increase in African and European societies. The cybercrime victims are often reluctant to report the incidents to appropriate authorities for further actions that would lead to arrest and prosecution of the culprits. The affected persons lack the financial capacity to pursue their cases at the law court for they believed that justice won't be served coupled with acts of sluggishness by the security agencies in launching an extensive investigation into the matter.

Euro-Africa Relations on Cybersecurity

Europe and Africa are deeply connected through their history and people via trade, investment, aid and culture. They have mutual interests in these areas especially digitization and technological advancement (Van Raemdonck, 2021, p.2). However, cybercrime is heavily threatening Euro-Africa economic relationships as businesses in the two continents are constantly targeted by networks of cybercriminals.

Cyber security is at the forefront of diplomatic and political spheres of European and African nations (Amazouz, 2019, p.12). A Digital Economy Task Force was established by European Union to coordinate Euro-Africa actions on cybercrime and ensure a stress-free business landscape and the progress of financial business (Africa-Europe Alliance, 2019, p.16), to discuss the challenges facing the African and European cyber diplomatic efforts (EU Cyber Direct, 2020, p.1).

The Euro-Africa relation is designed to strengthen cyber security legislation of both continents. No country can succeed alone in developing cyber legislation. They have to learn from each other's experiences and the operations of the judiciary in the process of delivering equitable legislation to the masses.

Legislation and regulation are crucial to enable the rights of citizens on the Internet and protect them from cybercrime and the unauthorized use of personal data (Turianskyi, 2020, p.3).

African countries namely Ghana, Kenya, Madagascar, Mauritius, Nigeria, Rwanda, South Africa, Togo, Uganda and Zimbabwe have been implementing new measures to protect and secure the personal information of their citizens. This legislative exercise can be more effective with active cooperation with sovereign nations and civil society organizations in Europe (McKenzie, 2022, p.1).

Euro-Africa strategic partnership was established to strengthen good working relationships between the European and African security agencies in detecting cybercrime on the two continents. That cybercrime is deeply entrenched internationally with strong networks across continents of Africa and Europe makes it pertinent for the adoption of a pro-active approach for timely global cooperation for traditional law enforcement tools and methodologies are ineffectual in tackling cybercrime. Instead, there has to be symbiotic relationships and collaborative efforts at the global level to thicken anti-cybercrime operations (Jacquline, 2009, p.1).

Addressing the issue of cyber diplomacy and resilience is at the core of Euro-Africa relations. Discussions on cybercrime, cyber security and how future digital technology is developed, diffused and deployed cannot be the sole preserve of richer nations alone. Africa's more digitally advanced states needs cooperation with European nations to articulate the continent's digital priorities coherently and convert this into organizational strength (Karen, 2022, p.3).

Technological upgrade in Africa is another important component of the Euro-African cooperation, in the wake of China and the United States' resolve to become a key partner on the continent, both in terms of stringing democracy and human rights and accelerating opportunities to trade in Africa's marketplaces. Africa's relations with Europe serve as the avenue to be catapulted into the global supply chain of high technologies and increased presence in the global digital space (Ricart, 2020, p.4).

Euro-Africa cooperation is geared towards strengthening cyber-norms, values and stability. Preserving cyber stability is a collaborative effort. And state actors in Africa devise cooperative mechanisms to observe and implement norms and include them in their national cyber policy or strategies. Through a collaborative approach to norms implementation, the technical community, with its expertise and experience of day-to-day cyber operations, can help expedite the observation of norms in cyberspace (Calandro, 2020, p.3).

Capacity building is at core of Euro-Africa relations on cyber security. International cooperation, in addition to focusing on building institutional capacity, is built on trust through the creation of fair and just partnerships between European and African stakeholders. In this digital ecosystem based on cooperation, local knowledge and expertise are key resources to fight cybercrime and build a firewall of cyber security (Calandro, 2020, p.4).

Euro-Africa relation is device to promote public-private partnerships on Cybersecurity. Curtailing cybercrime is highly effective through public-private partnerships especially among the security agencies. The vital function of information technology in enhancing the work of the law enforcements from public and private sectors cannot be underestimated. Through inter agency connections they share information on specific targets and mould a functional strategy in tracking down cybercrime syndicates anywhere around the world (Jacqueline, 2009, p.21). Thus, Euro-Africa diplomatic relations on Cybersecurity promotes public-private partnerships for it is an effective way of easy detection of cyber-related crime in urban and down to rural areas in Europe and Africa.

Cybersecurity Organizations in Europe and Africa

The drive towards combating cybercrime in Africa won't be effective without the existing collaborative efforts between the states and international organizations working in the field of cyber security (World Economic Forum, 2022, p.1). In Europe and Africa, there are many supranational and private organizations working tirelessly for a better secured cyberspace.

Europol is the law enforcement agency of the European Union specializes on anti-cybercrime operations. It set up the European Cybercrime Centre (EC3) to strengthen the law enforcement response to cybercrime in the EU and to help protect European citizens, businesses and government from online crime. The EC3 takes a three-pronged approach to fight against cybercrime; forensics, strategy and operations in Europe and Africa (Europol Cyber Security Intelligence, 2022, p.2).

The European Union Agency for Cybersecurity, ENISA, is the Union's agency dedicated to achieving a high common level of cyber security across Europe. Established in 2004 and strengthened by the EU Cybersecurity Act, the European Union Agency for Cybersecurity contributes to EU cyber policy, enhances the trustworthiness of ICT products, services and processes with cyber security certification schemes, cooperates with Member States and EU bodies, and helps Europe prepare for the cyber challenges of tomorrow. Through knowledge sharing, capacity-building and awareness rising, the agency works together with key stakeholders to strengthen trust in the connected economy (Enisa, 2022, p.1). ENISA is a master in intelligence gathering. Its vision it in tandem with the quest for better security of the entire Europe only that its operations has been restricted to fight against cybercrime which is cardinal in achieving European financial security, building trusts and confidence in the European cyberspace.

United Nations Organization for Drug and Crime draws upon its specialized expertise on criminal justice systems response to provide technical assistance in capacity building, prevention and awareness raising, international cooperation, and data collection, research and analysis on cybercrime. It is saddled with the responsibility of conducting a comprehensive study of the problem of cybercrime and responses to it by UN Member-states including Africa (UNODC, 2013, p.5).

International Telecommunication Union is another prominent organization involve in the formulation and implementation of global strategy for cyber security. The World Summit on the Information Society (WSIS) recognized the real and significant risks posed by inadequate cyber security and the proliferation of cybercrime. At WSIS, world leaders and governments designated ITU to facilitate the implementation of WSIS Action Line C5, dedicated to building confidence and security in the use of ICTs. In this regard, the ITU launched the Global Cybersecurity Agenda (GCA) on 17 May 2007, alongside partners from governments, industry, regional and international organizations, academic and research institutions (Gercke, 2012, p.2).

Interpol is a high-profile security institution in the United States that helps member countries to identify, triage and coordinate the response to cyber threats. Its strategy comprises of threat assessment and analysis, trends monitoring detection and positive identification of cybercrime, cybercriminals and cybercrime groups through threat assessments, analysis and trends monitoring of Cybersecurity threats in different regions across the world including Africa (Interpol, 2017, p.4).

The Global Forum on Cyber Expertise (GFCE) is a multi-stakeholder community of more than 120 members and partners from all regions of the world, aiming to strengthen cyber capacity and expertise globally. The GFCE has extensive expertise and experience on Cybersecurity in the African region. Various GFCE members and partners are involved in large cyber capacity programs in Africa. The

GFCE seeks to strengthen cyber resilience in the African region in close collaboration with all relevant stakeholders (The Global Forum on Cyber Expertise, 2021, p.2).

The African Union Cyber Security Expert Group (AUCSEG) was established On September 20, 2018, when the African Union Commission (AUC), Department of Infrastructure and Energy through its Information Society Division called for a team of experts and professionals on cyber security across Africa to join its African Union Cyber Security Expert Group (AUCSEG). This was based on a resolution reached by its Executive Council earlier in January of the same year to create an Africa Cyber Security collaboration and coordination committee to advise the AUC and policy makers on Cyber strategies. The responsibilities of the AUCSEG are to advise the AUC and African Heads of State, on technical, policy, legal and other related Cyber security matters at the national, regional, and continental levels (Council of Europe, 2021, p.2). While the AUCSEG is continentally focused it partners with other sister cyber security organizations across the world to achieve its goals and objectives on Cybersecurity.

CYBERSECURITY: CoE-AFRICA'S STRATEGIC PARTNERSHIP AND COLLABORATIVE EFFORTS

While cybercrime is a global problem which affects everybody how to ameliorate the problem has become a contentious issue. A strategy of cooperation both at national and international levels has become more vital towards addressing cybercrime.

The Heads of State and Government of the Council of Europe had on 10 and 11 October 1997 at the occasion of their second summit adopted an Action Plan based on the common responses to the development of new information technologies based on the standards and values of the Council of Europe. A Resolution No. 3 was adopted at 23rd Conference of the European Ministers of Justice held in London 8 and 9 June 2000, which encouraged the negotiating parties to invite the largest number of states to become parties to the proposed CoE convention. The CoE Convention on Cybercrime known famously as the Budapest Convention was opened for signature on 23 November 2001 (UNODC, 2017, p.1). The Convention provides a legal framework for international cooperation on cybercrime and electronic evidence (Council of Europe, 2017, p.2).

Budapest convention is viewed by European countries and their partners as the only authentic framework for collaboration between states to deal with cybercrime (Panagiotis, 2017, p.21). It was signed on 23 November 2001 at Budapest. While it was elaborated by the CoE with the active contribution of Canada, Japan, South Africa and the USA, any state can accent to implement it. About 49 countries signed the document and ratified by 42 member-states, including countries that are not part of the CoE (Thomas, 2014, p.3). The signatories of the convention are legally bind by common standards and procedures, and it facilitates cooperation between them (Thomas, 2014, p.6).

The Convention is the major connector to CoE-Africa's strategic relationship on Cybersecurity. Mauritius became Africa's first nation to sign the Budapest Convention, being part of its vision to become a smart island with a safe and more secure digital environment. As part of the joint initiatives of the EU and the CoE on Global Action on Cybercrime Extended (GLACY+), Mauritius became grown to be Africa's hub for regional capacity building on cybercrime (Council of Europe, 2017, pp.10-12).

Ghana is another African country that took advantage of the CoE-Africa partnership in the formulation of its Cybersecurity policies (Andoh, 2019, p.2). Ghana consented to the Budapest Convention in December 2018 making it the 62nd state to have signed the treaty and the fifth country in Africa to consent to the convention, after Mauritius, Senegal, Cape Verde and Morocco. Additionally, Ghana had ratified the AU Malabo Convention. While digitization brings opportunities to attain future goals, crimes committed through the use of computer systems need to be taken seriously (Andoh, 2019, p.2).

On 29 June 2022, Nigeria joined other 66 countries that signed and ratified the Budapest Convention. The instrument was signed by President Muhammadu Buhari and was transmitted to the Council of Europe on 6 July 2022. According to Head of Strategic Communication, Office of the Nigeria's National Security Adviser, Zakari Usman Nigeria's ascension to the league of countries that signed the Budapest instrument is a great boost to international cooperation with strong benefits such as provision of common standards and procedural legal tools for efficient investigations of cybercrimes, as well as the preservation and transfer of electronic evidence (Ayitogo, 2022, p.3).

The rationale for collaboration between the CoE and Africa on Cybersecurity is to pursue cybercrime and cyber security policies or strategies with the objective of ensuring an effective dispensation of criminal justice to cyber offences by means of computers as well as to any offence involving electronic evidence (Global Action on Cybercrime, 2016, pp.5-11).

The second is to collaborate in reformation of cyber security laws. Adequate legislation is the basis for criminal justice measures on cybercrime and the use of electronic evidence in criminal proceedings. The continuous review of legislation that meets human rights and rule of law requirements are a strategic priority. Strengthen data protection legislation in line with international and European standards (Global Action on Cybercrime, 2016, pp.5-11).

Africa collaborates with the CoE to boost implementation of domestic law enforcement training strategy to ensure that law enforcement agencies have the skills and competencies necessary to investigate cybercrime, secure electronic evidence, carry out computer forensic analysis for criminal proceedings, assist other agencies and contribute to network security (Global Action on Cybercrime, 2016, pp.5-11).

Effective investigations of cybercrime and other offences involving electronic evidence are often not possible without the cooperation of service providers. However, such cooperation needs to take into account the different roles of law enforcement and of service providers as well as the privacy rights of users (Global Action on Cybercrime, 2016, pp.5-11).

Differences and Modalities of CoE-Africa collaboration on Cybersecurity

The differences of approaches of Europe and Africa on the issue of cyber security are based on laws formulated at the respective institutional levels. There are different institutional laws on Cybersecurity in Europe and Africa. The AU Convention is, on the one hand, broader than the Budapest Convention in that it covers electronic transactions; personal data protection and cyber security and cybercrime. Hence, on its own the AU Convention cannot assist its member states achieve their stated objective of harmonizing cybercrime domestic law and enabling cooperation against cybercrime between parties (Jamil, 2016, p.5).

Meanwhile, the approach of the CoE on cybercrime consists of three interrelated elements. Namely, setting common standards, follow up and assessment of implementation, and technical cooperation for capacity building. The Cybercrime Convention Committee (T-CY) carries out assessments of the implementation of the Budapest Convention by the parties, adopts guidance notes and maintains working groups to identify responses to emerging challenges. Capacity-building on cybercrime has been an essential element of the approach of the Council of Europe from 2006 onwards (The Council of Europe,

2018, p.5). These policy documents clearly states the CoE's acceptable standards adopted in dealing with issues of Cybersecurity in Europe and Africa.

The CoE modality on cyber security is capacity-building. Capacity building responds to needs such as knowledge acquisition, advice on legislation and enabling criminal justice practitioners to apply new laws in the execution of cybercrime (Global Project on Cybercrime 2013, p.5). The next modality is legislation. Legislation on cybercrime and electronic evidence is a suitable starting point to enter into dialogue with national government. Supporting law reforms is levelheaded since criminal justice is based on law (Global Project on Cybercrime, 2013, p.5).

The African Union's Internet Security Infrastructure Guidelines for Africa signed on 30 May 2017 adopted multi stakeholder and collaborative security modalities in dealing with the issue of cyberspace security on the continent with four cardinal principles, namely, awareness, responsibility, cooperation and adherence to fundamental rights and internet properties (Tomas and Minarik, 2022, p.1). All Cybersecurity operations in Africa are guided accordingly by these fundamental principles.

CoE and Africa Relations on Cybersecurity: A Geopolitical Dimension

Europe-Africa relations on cyber security are made possible because of the new trends of global competition on digital technology. Africa has always been the focus of the great powers as they source for digital markets to sell their technological products given the huge population of Africans that are using digital assets such as computer and smart phones.

The CoE chose to form an alliance with Africa on Cybersecurity because of the European's readiness to upgrade and transfer technology to Africa, at a time when China, Russia and the United States are competing with one another to become a major player in the region, both for influence and access into new markets. African states relies on European nations for increasing transfer of technology in detecting cyber fraud and tracking down global cartel of cyber criminals operating in between the two continents (Carbone, 2021, p.6).

Meanwhile, the United States tries to offset Chinese and Russian influence, seeks to maintain its cutting-edge advantage on military artificial intelligence and other technologies, and backs and protects the interests of its major technology companies in Africa. While European nations are engaged in building privacy standards and data protection, they use the attractiveness of its digital market to promote digital partnerships with Africa solely to cut excessive competition from China, Russia, and the US (Ringhoff and Torreblanca, 2022, p.4).

The CoE is mindful of the fact that if the West did not accelerate its cooperation with Africa on Cybersecurity Russia and China would take over such an important digital diplomatic relation. African is now a new theatre for cyber diplomacy and influence in terms of accepting standards and procedures required to fight technological breaches.

Europe needs African countries for a better secured cyberspace and total elimination of cybercrime. Africa, on the other hand, needs Europe as its most relevant trade partner, investor and donor, as well as maintaining stability and security efforts across the continent (Carbone, 2021, p.7). The two continents cannot do without each other in the fight against cybercrime amid the ongoing integration of security technologies across the globe.

CONCLUSION

In Africa, the fight against cybercrime is a daunting task. This precarious situation informed CoE-African collaborations in dealing with the overwhelming cyber criminality on the continent. CoE-Africa's strategic partnership on Cybersecurity is another avenue for deepening human rights and guaranteeing the security of technology in Africa. While digitalization promises equal stakes in innovation and policy formulation in the Cybersecurity sector, the consciousness of latent risks in the sector is not doubted. Because Europe is the major destination of cybercrime CoE-Africa relations ensure that new digital policies and programmes are developed. Given the high penetration of the internet in Africa Europe had a strong desire to protect her interests amid the Russo-Chinese actions in Africa including technological and Cybersecurity activities. Cooperation with the CoE is a good omen that needs to be supported by African states for it would lead to a reduction of cybercrime, internet fraud, cyber terrorism, cyber trafficking, espionage and hacking of computer systems of national governments and private companies and curtail financial corruption, human trafficking, terrorism and email hacking in Africa.

Recommendations

- Europe-Africa relations should be strengthened based on equity and fairness. Both continents should recognize that cybercrime is not peculiar to any region, and that no country is immune from the menace; thus, cease the opportunity to continuously develop joint initiatives towards combating cybercrime.
- The fight against cybercrime should be anchored on mutual importance and not primordial interests.
- There should be effective synergy and good working relationship between European and African security institutions on the frontline of the fight against cybercrime through exchange of vital information and latest technologies on Cybersecurity.
- Africa and European governments should continuously share ideas on Cybersecurity legislation and reforms. This is necessary in the development of international standards and practices on Cybersecurity in line with the Budapest and Malabo Convention.
- There is the need to bridge the skill gap in Cybersecurity through investment in knowledge acquisition of skills to operate latest Cybersecurity technologies. An enabling environment should be created for cyber security and information and communication technology professionals in Europe and Africa to work together towards developing new technologies and methods of fighting cybercrime.

REFERENCES

Africa-Europe Alliance. (2019). *New Africa-Europe Digital Economy Partnership Report of the EU-AU Digital Economy Task Force: Accelerating the Achievement of the Sustainable Development Goals*. European Union.

African Academic Network on Internet Policy. (2022). *Cyberspace Security In Africa: Where Do We Stand?* https://aanoip.org/cyberspace-security-in-africa-where-do-we-stand/

African countries call on Ghana's Cyber security Authority for collaboration and support. (2022, April 25). *Joy Business.* https://www.myjoyonline.com/african-countries-call-on-ghanas-cyber-security-authority-for-collaboration-and-support/

African Union Commission. (2018). *GLACY+: Cybersecurity and Cybercrime Policies for African Diplomats Held in Addis Ababa Ethiopia 11-13 April 2018.* Council of Europe.

African Union Commission (2018). *AUC and Council of Europe Join Forces on Cybersecurity.* Addis Ababa: Directorate of Information and Communication African Union Commission.

African Union Commission. (2018). *African Forum on Cyber Crime: Policies and Legislation, International Cooperation and Capacity Building Conference Programme Draft, Addis Ababa* 16-18 October, 2018. Addis Ababa: African Union Commission and Council of Europe.

Africanews, R. (2021). *Africa: Can a strong cyber security strategy be an engine for growth?* https://www.africanews.com/2022/05/16/africa-can-a-strong-cybersecurity-strategy-be-an-engine-for-growth/

Amazouz, M. S. (2019). *International Cyber Security Diplomatic Negotiations: Role of Africa in Inter-Regional Cooperation for a Global Approach on the Security and Stability of Cyberspace.* Academic Press.

Andoh, D. (2019). *Communications Ministry commits to tackle cyber crime.* https://www.graphic.com.gh/news/general-news/ghananews-communications-ministry-commits-to-tackle-cyber-crime.html

AU-EU Digital Economy Task Force. (2021). *New Africa-Europe Digital Economy Partnership: Accelerating the Achievement of the Sustainable Development Goals.* European Commission.

Australian Government. (2022). *National Plan to Combat Cybercrime 2022.* Australian Government Press.

Ayitogo, N. (2022, August 22). Nigeria signs Budapest Convention on Cybercrime. *Premium Times*, 3.

Calandro, E. (2020, July 1). *Africa, Capacity building, Cyber diplomacy, Digital policy. Directions.* https://directionsblog.eu/partnering-with-africa-on-cyber-diplomacy/

Carbone, G. (2021). *The EU in Africa: Will Member-States follow the Lead?* https://www.euractiv.com/section/africa/opinion/the-eu-in-africa-will-member-states-follow-the-lead/https://www.euractiv.com/section/africa/opinion/the-eu-in-africa-will-member-states-follow-the-lead/

Charles, J. B., Christopher, G., Philip, C., & Donald, S. (2018). *Cybersecurity essentials.* Sybex.

Chikelue, Onodugo, Arachie, & Ugonna. (2020). Blockchain Technology For Cyber Security: Performance Implications On Emerging Markets Multinational Corporations, Overview Of Nigerian Internationalized Banks. *International Journal of Scientific and Technology Research, 9*(8), 246.

Cole, K., Chetty, M., LaRosa, C., Rietta, F., Schmitt, D. K., Goodman, S. E., & Atlanta, G. A. (2008). *Cybersecurity in africa: An assessment.* Sam Nunn School of International Affairs, Georgia Institute of Technology.

Council of Europe. (2013). *Strategic Priorities in the Cooperation against Cybercrime Adopted by the Meeting of Ministers and Senior Officials of Ministries of Interior and Security, of Ministries of Justice and of Prosecution Services of countries and areas participating in the CyberCrime@IPA project Dubrovnik, Croatia, 15 February 2013.* www.coe.int/cybercrime

Council of Europe. (2017). *Acceding to the Budapest Convention on Cybercrime: Benefits The Budapest Convention on Cybercrime.* Cybercrime Division of Council of Europe.

Council of Europe. (2017). *East African countries meet in Mauritius to address the growing threat of cybercrime in the region, 10-12 July 2017.* Council of Europe and European Union.

Council of Europe. (2018). *C-PROC activity report for the period October 2017 September 2018 Information Documents SG/Inf(2018)32.* Council of Europe.

Council of Europe. (2021). *Second African Forum on Cybercrime Policies and Legislation, investigation and International Cooperation: Conference Programme Online 28-29 June, 2021.* Council of Europe.

Council of Europe and Project Cybercrime@Octopus, (2015). *The state of cybercrime legislation in Africa: An overview.* Council of Europe.

Council of Europe Global Action on Cybercrime. (2016). *Strategic priorities for cooperation on cybercrime and electronic evidence in GLACY countries Adopted at the closing conference of the GLACY project on Global Action on Cybercrime Bucharest, 26-28 October 2016.* Author.

Cybercrime: Britain Losing The War, Say MPs. Sky News. (2013, July 30). *Sky News.* https://news.sky.com/story/amp/cybercrime-britain-losing-the-war-say-mps-10438834

Cybercrime Programme Office of the Council of Europe. (2019). The global state of cybercrime legislation 2013 – 2019: A cursory overview. Council of Europe.

Cybercrime Programme Office of the Council of Europe. (2021). *Cybercrime and the rule of law, including benefits of the Budapest Convention for Mauritius Keynote Address of Hon. Attorney General of the Republic of Mauritius.* Council of Europe.

Cybercrime: Two Nigerians, six others arrested for allegedly stealing $15 million from U.S. firms. (2018, June 26). *Premium Times.* https://www.premiumtimesng.com/news/headlines/273879-cybercrime-two-nigerians-six-others-arrested-for-allegedly-stealing-15-million-from-u-s-firms.html

Direction Blog. (2020). *Africa, Capacity building, Cyber diplomacy, Digital policy.* https://directionsblog.eu/partnering-with-africa-on-cyber-diplomacy/

EFCC and Fraud suspects. (2021, December 6). *Premium Times.* https://www.premiumtimesng.com/opinion/499424-from-taking-it-with-consent-to-hacking-it-with-contempt-by-alex-otti.html

European Union: Africa the Journey. (2020). *Cyber Security: Challenges.* https://www.euafricathejourney.com/challenge/cyber-security/#toggle-id-1

European Union and Council of Europe Partnership Facility. (2015). *Cybercrime and cyber security strategies in the Eastern Partnership region Results of a regional workshop Chisinau, Republic of Moldova, 12 – 14 November 2014.* www.coe.int/cybercrime

European Union Cyber Direct. (2020). *EU-Africa Cyber Consultations*. https://eucyberdirect.eu/events/eu-africa-cyber-consultations

Europol Cyber Security Intelligence. (2022). *European Cybercrime Centre (EC3)*. Europol.

Finch, W. (2022, 30 June). Exclusive: Cyber-criminals are hacking an average of 330 Britons A Minute: shock new research has suggested as experts warn it has reached 'epidemic proportions. *Daily Mail*. https://www.dailymail.co.uk/news/article-10970571/amp/Cyber-criminals-hacking-average-330-

Gercke, M. (2016). *Understanding cybercrime: a guide for developing countries*. Academic Press.

Gyem, F. (2022, August 10). Cyber Security Initiatives for Protecting a Country. *Premium Times*. Retrieved from https://www.premiumtimesng.com/opinion/547973-cyber-security-initaitves-for-protecting-a-country-by-fom-gyem.html

Gyem, F. (2022 September 10). ICT as a colossal symbol of Nigeria's digital economy. *Premium Times*. https://www.premiumtimesng.com/opinion/552586-ict-as-acolossal-symbol-of-nigerias-digital-economy-by-fom-gyem.html

Hacker in front of computer. (2020, October 26). *Forbes Africa*. https://www.forbesafrica.com/technology/2020/10/26/cybersecurity-covid-19-or-not-cybercrime-is-here-to-stay/

Harrison, J. (2021, November 30) The UK is The Most Dangerous Country in Europe for Cybercrime. *The Fintech Times*. https://thefintechtimes.com/the-uk-is-the-most-dangerous-country-in-europe-for-cybercrime/?utm_source=dlvr.it&utm_medium=twitter

Insider-related Cybersecurity Incidents in East Africa Increase by 55% in 3 Months. (2020, June 29). *News Security Technology*. https://pctechmag.com/2020/06/insider-related-cybersecurity-incidents-in-east-africa/

Interpol's Cybercrime Directorate. (2021). *African Cyber Threat Assessment Report: Interpol's Key Insight into Cybercrime in Africa*. Interpol Publications.

Interpol's Cybercrime Directorate. (2021). *National Cybercrime Strategy: Guide Book*. Author.

Jacqueline, F. (2009). *Cybercrime in South Africa: Investigating and Prosecuting Cyber Crime the Benefits of Public-Private Partnerships*. Price Water House Coopers.

Jamil, Z. (2016). Comparative analysis of the Malabo Convention of the African Union and the Budapest Convention on Cybercrime. Bucharest: Council of Europe.

Jideani, P. C. (2018). *Towards A Cybersecurity Framework For South African E-Retail Organisations* [Master's thesis]. Faculty of Informatics and Design at the Cape Peninsula University of Technology, South Africa.

Kaspersky. (2022, August 17). *Backdoor Computer Malware in Africa skyrocketed in the second quarter of 2022*. https://kaspersky.africa-newsroom.com/press/backdoor-computer-malware-in-africa-skyrocketed-in-the-second-quarter-of-2022?lange=en

Kaspersky. (2022). *What is cybercrime?* https://www.kaspersky.com/resource-center/threats/what-is-cybercrime

Kritzinger, E., & Solms, S. (2012). A Framework for Cyber Security in Africa. *Journal of Information Assurance and Cybersecurity*. http://www.ibimapublishing.com/journals/JIACS/jiacs.html

Kshetri, N. (2016). Cybersecurity and Development, Markets, *Globalization &. Developmental Review*, *1*(2). https://digitalcommons.uri.edu/mgdr/vol1/iss2/3

Kshetri, N. (2019). Cybercrime and Cybersecurity in Africa. *Journal of Global Information Technology Management*. Advance online publication. doi:10.1080/1097198X.2019.1603527

Manda, T. D. (2018). *Manda Maturity of Cybersecurity initiatives in Malawi: A comparison with the drive for fast and ubiquitous Internet connectivity*. DiploFoundation. www.diplomacy.edu

McLoughlin, J. (2018). *J2 Software supports global reports of alarming increase in numbers of e-mail attacks: South Africa is no exception*. https://www.j2.co.za/j2-software-news/294-j2-software-supports-global-reports-of-alarming-increase-in-numbers-of-e-mail-attacks-south-africa-is-no-exception

Ngila, F. (2021, December 16). Why firms must invest more in cyber security. *Business Daily*. https://www.businessdailyafrica.com/bd/corporate/technology/firms-must-invest-more-cyber-security-3654090?view=htmlamp

Nigeria is experiencing unprecedented cyber attacks. (2021, September 7). *Business Day*. https://businessday.ng/amp/news/article/nigeria-is-experiencing-unprecedented-cyber-attacks

Nikhita, G. R., & Ugander, G. J. R. (2014). *A Study of Cyber Security Challenges and Its Emerging Trends On Latest Technologies*. https://www.researchgate.net/publication/260126665

Nord V. P. N. (2021). *Cybersecurity Risk Index*. nordvpn.com/cri/

Nweze-Iloekwe, N. (2022). *The Legal and Regulatory Aspect of International Cybercrime and Cybersecurity: Limits and Challenges* [Dissertation]. The Golden Gate University School Of Law, Department Of International Legal Studies, In Fulfillment Of The Requirement For The Conferment Of The Degree Of Scientiae Juridicae Golden Gate University School of Law.

Okonji, E. (2022, June 8). Rising Trends of Cyber attacks in Nigeria. *Thisdaylive*. https://www.com/amp/s/www.thisdaylive.com/index.php/2022/06/08/rising-trends-of-cyberattacks-in-nigeria-2/amp

Online impersonation becoming a major threat to businesses on social media-Cyber Security Authority. (2022, July 21). *Joy Business*. https://www.myjoyonline.com/online-impersonation-becoming-a-major-threat-to-businesses-on-social-media-cyber-security-authority/

Onyekpeze, O., Olumide Owolabi, O., & Bisalla, H. I. (2021). Classification of Cybersecurity Incidents in Nigeria Using Machine Learning Methods *Covenant Journal of Informatics & Tongxin Jishu*, *9*(2).

Panagiotis, T., Georgios, C., Silvia, P., Prokopios, D., Lauri, P., Dimitra, L., & Andrea, D. (2017). *Cybersecurity in the EU Common Security and Defence Policy (CSDP) Challenges and risks for the EU: Study EPRS/STOA/SER/16/214N*. European Union.

PC Technology. (2020). *News insider-related Cybersecurity Incidents in East Africa Increase by 55% in 3 Months*. https://pctechmag.com/2020/06/insider-related-cybersecurity-incidents-in-east-africa/

Pipikaite, A., Gretchen, B., Akshay, J., & Jurgens, J. (2022). *Global Cybersecurity Outlook 2022: Insight Report*. World Economic Forum.

Symantec Report. (2016). *Cyber Crime and Cyber Security Trends in Africa*. Author.

Serianu Report. (2017). *Demystifying Africa's Cyber Security Poverty Line*. Africa Cyber Security Report.

Report, S. (2018). *Africa Cybersecurity Report and Cybersecurity Skill Gaps*. Bostwana.

Ricart, R. J. (2020). *European Union's foreign policy and technology in Africa*. Real Instituto Elcano Global Presence. https://www.realinstitutoelcano.org/en/european-unions-foreign-policy-and-technology-in-africa/

Ringhoff, J., & Torreblanca, J. I. (2022). *Policy Brief: European Power: The geopolitics of technology: How the EU can become a global player*. https://ecfr.eu/publication/the-geopolitics-of-technology-how-the-eu-can-become-a-global-player/?amp

Russian hacker group Killnet claimed responsibility for the attacks. (2022, August 18). *Aljazeera*. https://www.aljazeera.com/amp/news/2022/8/18/estonia-says-it-repelled-cyber-attacks-claimed-by-russian-group

Saeed, M., & Osakwe, S. (2021). *Are African Countries doing enough to ensure Cybersecurity and Internet Safety*. The International Telecommunication Union. https://www.itu.int/hub/2021/09/are-african-countries-doing-enough-to-ensure-cybersecurity-and-internet-safety/

Satoshi, T., Makoto, K., Kunihiko, M., & Yasuko, F. (2014). Trends in Cybersecurity and Latest Countermeasures. *Hitachi Review*, *63*(5), 264–269.

Schwartz, M. (2021, November 12). *Pace of Cybercrime Evolution Is Accelerating, Europol Warns*. Bank Info Security. Retrieved from https://www.bankinfosecurity.com/pace-cybercrime-evolution-accelerating-europol-warns-a-17902?utm_source=Twitter&utm_medium=CollateralSM&utm_campaign=editorial_post

Scott, E. D., Chris, K. W., & Stanley, G. S. (2018). *Understanding Security Issues*. Walter de Gruyter Incorporated.

Seger, A. (2017). *Enhancing regional and international cooperation to improve the rule of law in cyberspace Being a paper delivered Regional Conference On Cybercrime 27 – 29 June 2017 Cebu City, Philippines organized by the Philippine Department of Justice in cooperation with the Council of Europe under the GLACY+ project*. Academic Press.

Sharma, S. (2022). Cybersecurity as a service: A freedom movement to defeat cybercrime August 15, 2022. *Times of India*. https://timesofindia.indiatimes.com/blogs/voices/cybersecurity-as-a-service-a-freedom-movement-to-defeat-cybercrime/?source=app&frmapp=yes

Sharma, S. (2022). Cybersecurity as a service: A freedom movement to defeat cybercrime August 15, 2022. *Times of India* https://timesofindia.indiatimes.com/blogs/voices/cybersecurity-as-a-service-a-freedom-movement-to-defeat-cybercrime/?source=app&frmapp=yes

Sheelagh, B., & Caitriona, H. (2020). Cybercrime: Current Threats and Responses. *A Review of the Research Literature.*

Signé, L., & Signé, K. (2021). *How African states can improve their cyber security*. https://www.brookings.edu/techstream/how-african-states-can-improve-their-cybersecurity/

Singer, P. W., & Allan, F. (2014). *Cybersecurity and Cyber war: What you Need to Know*. Oxford University Press.

Skeldon, P. (2021, December 10). Analysis: What is the reality of real-world and cybercrime in Europe? *Telemedia*. https://www.telemediaonline.co.uk/analysis-what-is-the-reality-of-real-world-and-cybercrime-in-europe/

Sutherland, E. (2017). Governance of Cybersecurity: the case of South Africa. *The African Journal of Information and Communication,* (20), 83-112. doi:10.23962/10539/23574

Świątkowska, J. (2020). Tackling cybercrime to unleash developing countries' digital potential. Pathways for Prosperity Commission Background Paper Series no. 33.

Taha, M. (2016, March 10). *Cybercriminals target millions of bank app users*. https://www.abc.net.au/news/2016-03-10/cybercriminals-target-millions-of-bank-app-users/7237220

Tal, G., & Nayia, B. (2020). *Insight Report: Partnership against Cybercrime Shaping the Future of Cybersecurity and Digital Trust*. World Economic Forum.

Terebey, S. (2016, September 22). *African Union Cybersecurity Profile: Seeking a Common Continental Policy*. https://jsis.washington.edu/news/african-union-cybersecurity-profile-seeking- common-continental-policy/

Terebey, S. (2016). *African Union Cybersecurity Profile: Seeking a Common Continental Policy*. The Henry M. Jackson School of International Studies, University of Washington.

The European Union Agency for Cybersecurity. (2022). *Towards a Trusted and Cyber Secure Europe.* https://www.enisa.europa.eu/about-enisa

The European Union Institute for Security Studies. (2021). *Regionalized multilateralism? EU-Africa cooperation in cyberspace*. https://www.iss.europa.eu/content/regionalised-multilateralism-eu-africa-cooperation-cyberspace

The European Union Institute for Security Studies. (2021). *Cyber Conflict Prevention on the EU-Africa Security Agenda*. https://www.iss.europa.eu/content/cyber-conflict-prevention-eu-africa-security-agenda

The Global Forum on Cyber Expertise. (2021). *AUC-GFCE Collaboration: Enabling African countries to identify and address their cyber capacity needs*. https://thegfce.org/auc-gfce-collaboration-enabling-african-countries-to-identify-and-address-their-cyber-capacity-needs/

Thomas, R. (2014). *The rise of cyber-diplomacy: the EU, its strategic partners and Cybersecurity*. Working Paper No. 7. Madrid: European Strategic Partnership Observatory and Fride.

Tomas, M., & Audrey, G. (2022). *Internet Infrastructure Security Guidelines for Africa Unveiled by the African Union.* https://ccdcoe.org/incyder-articles/internet-infrastructure-security-guidelines-for-africa-unviled-by-african-union/

Toyin, F. (2022, August 18). Cut soap for me. *Premium Times.* https://www.premiumtimesng.com

Turianskyi, Y. (2020). *Africa and Europe: Cyber Governance Lessons. African Perspectives Global Insights.* South African Institute of International Affairs.

United Nations Office on Drugs And Crime. (2013). *Draft: Comprehensive Study on Cybercrime.* United Nations.

United Nations Office on Drugs and Crime. (2017). *Capacity-building on cybercrime and E-evidence: the Experience of EU/Council of Europe Joint Projects, 2013-2017 Non-Paper Submitted by European Union.* Council of Europe. Document No. CCPCJ/EG.4/2017/CRP.2/6.

U.S. Embassy Ghana. (2021). *Remarks by Chargé d'Affaires Nicole Chulick on Protection of Critical Information Infrastructure Directive held on October 1, 2021 during the Cybersecurity Awareness Month Launch.* United State Government.

Van der Meulen, N., Jo, E. A., & Soesanto, S. (2015). *Cybersecurity in the European Union and beyond: exploring the threats and policy responses.* Academic Press.

Van Raemdonck, N. (2021). *Africa as a Cyber Player.* https://eucyberdirect.eu/research/africa-as-a-cyber-player

World, E. F. F. S. R. (2020). *Cybersecurity, emerging technology and systemic risk.* University of Oxford.

World Bank and United Nations. (2017). Combating Cybercrime: Tools and Capacity Building for Emerging Economies. Washington, DC: World Bank License.

Yokohama, S. (2017). Business Management and Cyber Security. *NTT Corporation Journal, 1*(1), 123.

ADDITIONAL READING

Abdul-Hakeem, A. (2021). *AhA notes: Setting the scene and goals of the event 2nd African Forum on Cybercrime and CoE hub: Cybercrime investigations in practice.* Addis Ababa: African Union Cybersecurity Experts Group (AUCSEG).

Abdul-Hakeem, A., & Allen, N. D. F. (2021, March 8). *African Lessons in Cyber Strategy.* Africa Center for Strategic Studies. Retrieved from https://africacenter.org/spotlight/african-lessons-in-cyber-strategy/

Adamu, A. G., & Aliyu, M. B. (2021). The Current State of Cybersecurity Readiness in Nigeria Organisations. *International Journal of Multidisciplinary and Current Educational Research, 3*(1), 154–162.

Alhassan, T. (2017). Cybersecurity In Africa: The Threats And Challenges. *Cyberpolitik Journal, 3*(5). https://www.Cyberpolitikjournal.org

Allen, N. (2021). *Africa's Evolving Cyber Threats*. Spotlight. https://africacenter.org/spotlight/africa-evolving-cyber-threats/

Amzath, F., & Claude, C. F. (2007, July 16). *Cybercrime in Africa: Facts and figures*. https://www.scidev.net/sub-saharan-africa/features/cybercrime-africa-facts-figures/

Amzath, F., & Claude, F. A. (2016). *Cyber facts and figures*. https://www.scidev.net/sub-saharan-africa/features/cybercrime-africa-facts-figures/

Anaesoronye, M. (2022, January 18). *Cyber Risks, Biggest Concern for Companies in Nigeria, Africa and Middle East in 2022 says Allianz Risk Barometer*. https://businessday.ng/amp/news/article/cyber-risks-biggest-concern-for-companies-in-nigeria-africa-middle-east-in-2022/

Andrews, A. (2009). Understanding the West African cyber crime process. *African Security Review*, *18*(4), 107. doi:10.1080/10246029.2009.9627562

Antonio, N. G. S. (2010). *Africa: A necessary continent in European and African Response to Security Problems in Africa*. Spanish Institute for Strategic Studies Casa Africa Working Group No. 4/09.

Auguste, Y. (2012). *The AU Draft Convention on Cybersecurity and E-transactions Being a Paper presented at the AU Convention on Cooperation against Cybercrime held on 6-8 June 2012*. Strasburg: Council of Europe.

Beckford, M. (2015, August 30). Police chiefs: We can't cope with cybercrime: Stunning admission in secret briefing shows toll of criminals exploiting the dark web. *Daily Mail*. https://www.dailymail.co.uk/news/article-3215699/amp/Police-chiefs-t-cope cybercrime-Stunning-admission-secret-briefing-shows-toll-criminals-exploiting-dark-web.html

Borrello, E. (2015, July 29). *Security agencies reveal 11,000 cyber security incidents targeting businesses, critical infrastructure*. https://www.abc.net.au/news/2015-07-29/security-agencies-reveal-11,000-cyber-security-incidents-in-2014/6656660

Carbone, G. (2021). *The EU in Africa: will Member States follow the lead?* Euractiv. https://www.euractiv.com/section/africa/opinion/the-eu-in-africa-will-member-states-follow-the-lead/

Cheri, M. (2016). *Cybercrime and Cybersecurity Trends in Africa*. The Hague, The Netherlands: Global Government Affairs and Cybersecurity Policy at Symantec. https://thegfce.org/cybercrime-and-cyber-security-trends-in-africa/

Chike, O. (2019, December 27). Low prosecution of cyber-crime worries stakeholders. *Guardian*. https://guardian.ng/technology/low-prosecution-of-cyber-crime-worries-stakeholders/

Du Toit, R., Hadebe, P. N., & Mphatheni, M. (2018). Public perceptions of Cybersecurity: A South African context. *Acta Criminologica: African Journal of Criminology & Victimology*, *31*(3), 111–131.

Faustine, N. (2021). *Why firms must invest more in cyber security*. https://www.businessdailyafrica.com/bd/corporate/technology/firms-must-invest-more-cyber-security-3654090?view=htmlamp

Hamzat, L. (2019). *Cybersecurity in Africa – The Way to Go*. https://cybersecfill.com/cybersecurity-in-africa/

Hood, M. (2019). Cybersecurity in Africa: The Boring Technology Story that Matters. *Article in Crossroads, 2-3*. Advance online publication. doi:10.1145/3368077

Iginio, G., & Nanjira, S. (2015). *Cyber Security and Cyber Resilience in East Africa: Global Commission on Internet Governance. Paper Series No. 15*. London: Chatham House The Royal Institute of International Affairs. https://www.ourinternet.org

Kertysova, K., Frinking, E., Dool, K. V. D., Maričić, A., & Bhattacharyya, K. (2018). *Cybersecurity: Ensuring awareness and resilience of the private sector across Europe in face of mounting cyber risks. Study of The Hague Centre for Strategic Studies for The European Economic and Social Committee*. EESC.

Kwasi, A., Nabeel, M., Aminata, A. G., & Martin, S. (2018). Assessing Cybersecurity Policy Effectiveness in Africa via a Cybersecurity Liability Index. *TPRC 46: The 46th Research Conference on Communication, Information and Internet Policy*.

Lusthaus, J. (2019 November 19). *The Criminal Silicon Valley Is Thriving: Eastern Europe's cybercriminals are highly sophisticated. Can they be coaxed into more honest work?* https://www.nytimes.com/2019/11/29/opinion/the-criminal-silicon-valley-is-thriving.html

Macmillan, K., Seharish, G., Ahmed, D., & Jeremiah, G. (2022). *The role of Cybersecurity and data security in the digital economy*. UNCDF Policy Accelerator.

Malatji, M., Marnewick, A. L., & von Solms, S. (2020). Cybersecurity Policy and the Legislative Context of the Water and Wastewater Sector in South Africa. *Sustainability, 13*(1), 291.

Mitchell, J. (2022, June 16). *Africa faces huge cybercrime threat as the pace of digitalization increases*. Investment Monitor. Retrieved from https://www.investmentmonitor.ai/analysis/africa-cyber-crime-threat-digitalisation

Mustapha, A. (2022). *Africa needs effective policies to tackle cybercrime: Deputy Communications Minister*. https://www.google.com/amp/s/www.modernghana.com

Nemr, M. (2022). *Mind about Cyber Threats to Your Business*. https://www.businessdailyafrica.com/bd/lifestyle/personal-finance/mind-about-cyber-threats-to-your-business-3716634?view=htmlamp

Newman, U. R., & Eboibi, F. E. (2021). *African governments and the influence of corruption on the proliferation of cybercrime in Africa: wherein lies the rule of law?* doi:10.1080/13600869.2021.1885105

Orji, U. (2015). Multilateral Legal Responses to Cyber Security in Africa: Any Hope for Effective International Cooperation? *7th International Conference on Cyber Conflict: Architectures in Cyberspace,* 110-111.

Pavlova, P. (2020). Human-rights based approach to Cybersecurity: Addressing the security risks of targeted groups. *Peace Human Rights Governance, 4*(3), 391–418.

Spence, N. (2021). *Digital skills shortage sees cybercrime in Africa increase*. https://securityafricamagazine.com/digital-skills-shortage-sees-cybercrime-in-africa-increase/

Veerasamy, N., Thulani, M., & Kiru, P. (2019). Contextualizing Cybersecurity Readiness in South Africa. Pretoria: Council for Scientific and Industrial Research (CSIR) and South Africa Link Centre, South Africa.

Chapter 15
Synthesis of Evidence on Existing and Emerging Social Engineering Ransomware Attack Vectors

Abubakar Bello
Western Sydney University, Australia

Alana Maurushat
Western Sydney University, Australia

ABSTRACT

As the threat landscape continues to evolve, users are becoming less aware, ignorant, or negligent, putting their confidential data at risk. Users easily fall prey to socially engineered ransomware attacks that encrypt and lock a computer or mobile device, holding it hostage unless a ransom is paid. The cryptoware encrypts data securely, making it almost impossible for anyone except the hacker to unlock the device. This research conducts a systematic review to identify methods for executing socially engineered ransomware attacks. Using a CRI framework, 122 studies were synthesized from 3209 research articles highlighting gaps in identifying and analyzing attack vectors, as well as the need for a holistic approach to ransomware with behavioural control as part of the solution. Human vulnerability was found to be a critical point of entry for miscreants seeking to spread ransomware. This review will be useful in developing control models that will educate organisations and security professionals to focus on adopting human-centered solutions to effectively counter ransomware attacks.

INTRODUCTION

The internet, various technology and cyber-enabled devices, systems and application have become interwoven in the daily lives of people. Majority of people spend hours on various devices accessing the internet for work, to seek information, communicate, transact business, study, socialize, including

DOI: 10.4018/978-1-6684-5827-3.ch015

entertainment (Larose et al., 2001). This has created tremendous benefits, effects and opportunities for individuals, businesses, and governments. However, various security threats exist and continue to emerge, with many users not aware, ignorant or negligent of these security risks (Madan, Sofat, & Bansal, 2022; Kostopoulos, 2017). Since the inception of COVID-19 pandemic and the risk of contamination in social settings, people have resorted to access and communication within the cyber space more than ever. Thus, technology users, including employees working from home, are at risk of encountering a cyberattack such as ransomware, and having their confidential information compromised by criminals.

The United State Department of Justice has described ransomware extortion as a new business model for cyberattack. Ransomware, as the name suggests, is a form of extortion using malware or malicious codes, where data and confidential information is held ransom until a sum of money is paid for its release. In 2018, the internet crime complaint center (IC3) in the U.S report 1,493 cases of ransomware extortion valued at about $3.6 million not including loss of business, time, document or files (FBI, 2018). Ransomware victims still pay the ransom to cybercriminals despite warnings and advice not to pay (Moore, 2016). The rapid rise and spread of ransomware suggest that it is profitable for cybercriminals as a significant number of technology users lack appropriate cybersecurity awareness and education against socially engineered ransomware attacks (Alqahtani & Sheldon, 2022). A socially engineered ransomware attack refers to the psychological manipulation, influence or deceiving of individuals to install a malware that infect and encrypts data on their device for digital extortion.

Cybersecurity is now a matter of both international and national concern; the security stakes are increasing for the public and private sector regarding ransomware attacks. Recent ransomware attacks target all user categories, businesses and government departments and critical infrastructures. Therefore, mechanisms for security empowerment, awareness and education against socially engineered ransomware attacks is crucial. To this end, this study aims to identify, systematically, the current and potential methods that can be used to launch socially engineered ransomware attack against technology users. The study begins by providing an overview of ransomware, followed by the research method used to investigate and analyze ransomware attack vectors.

BACKGROUND

Ransomware made its first appearance in 1989; it was deployed as a Trojan called PC CYBORG, victims were socially engineered to install the infected floppy disk they received by mail (Wilding, 1990). The encryption process was triggered when the victim's system reboots counts get up to 90, allowing the malware to spread during the dormancy period. The victims were required to post ransom cheque to recover the lost files and directories. Although rudimentary, it paved the way for the sophisticated socially engineered ransomware attacks reported today. The 1989 ransomware encryption functionality was weak and easy to decrypt as the decryption keys could be extracted from the code of the Trojan (O'Kane et al., 2018).

Traditionally, cryptography provided protection, privacy and security to users; however, the birth of Cryptovirology allowed cryptography to be used offensively (Young & Yung, 2017). In a security symposium, Young & Yung (1996) highlighted that cryptovirology would allow criminals to install viruses and malicious codes that can mount extortion-based attacks when deployed on a host system. Cryptovirology has proven to be a formidable threat 20 years later. Ransomware strains today are more sophisticated and operate within an ecosystem with the ability to adapt and evolve when deployed within an environment (Zimba & Chishimba, 2019). Figure 1 below shows the explosive growth of crypto-ransomware types since the period of 2013.

Figure 1. Timeline showing the increasing number of ransomware strain and threats from 2013-2020 adapted from F-Secure (2017)

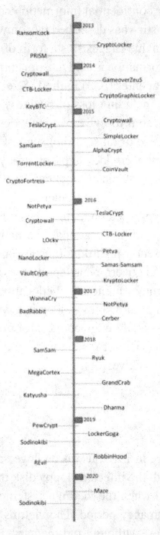

Ransomware attacks are evolving as technology advances; research shows that cryptography is an essential tool for securing the cyberspace and used to perpetuate criminal activities (Wood & Eze, 2020; Yan, 2019; A. L. Young & Yung, 2017). Research shows that ransomware strains are becoming more sophisticated and resilient, enabling easy propagation across any platforms, devices and via a range of vectors (Sharma et al., 2020). Humayun et al. (2020) study suggests that it is critical to securely manage and maintain the emerging applications and technologies that user's adopt as they may are prone to security threats especially ransomware.

In the past, attackers used a wide range of malware software and applications such as worms, viruses, and Trojans, to disrupt computer networks and systems. Today, ransomware attacks use psychological manipulations and strong encryption technologies to gain access to a victim's system or device, completely encrypting the data files and/or lock the device until a ransom is paid, usually through an anonymous channel (Grillenmeier, 2022). These new variants of ransomware employ sophisticated business models of encryption and extortion leveraging on technological advances to achieve a profitable goal (Zimba, 2017). Therefore, it is vital to understand the emerging attack vectors that could be socially engineered by attackers to propagate ransomware threats.

RESEARCH METHOD

A systematic literature review requires a means to search, select, identify, evaluate and interpret relevant literature on a particular subject or phenomenon of interest (Kitchenham & Charters, 2007; Tranfield et al., 2003). This review process followed the guidelines of Kitchenham (Kitchenham & Charters, 2007). A review protocol was developed as part of the review process, including research question(s), data collection, guide and method to be followed.

To shed light on the current knowledge and potential methods of ransomware attacks against people, this work investigates the following research questions:

(1)   What are the existing socially engineered ransomware attack vectors that have been addressed?
(2)   What are the emerging methods of socially engineered ransomware?
(3)   What are the knowledge gaps in socially engineered ransomware research?
(4)   What methods are available to manage socially engineered ransomware attacks?

Search Scope and Strategy

Search scope

Before proceeding with the literature search, a clarification of the scope of this review was defined out. The research on socially engineered ransomware spans to other areas such as phishing, human behavior, cryptology and others. Although the study draws on the phishing and human behavior literature in the context of this review, it is largely examined in relation to attack vectors. The term phishing is used in a narrow sense to investigate the attack vector that could be potentially used to launch socially engineered ransomware attacks. The goal of this review is not to provide an exhaustive list of attack vector but rather to identify those closely linked to socially engineered ransomware attacks.

Search Strategy and Terms for Automated Searches

The search strategy used to construct the search phrases used in the review process are as follows:

*   Identify major terms from the research questions;
*   Identify alternative synonyms for major terms;
*   The use of Boolean OR to incorporate alternative spellings and synonyms and;

- The use of Boolean AND to link the major terms in the search phase.

("Ransomware" OR "Crypto-ransomware" OR "Locker-ransomware" OR "Cryptoware" AND "social engineering" OR "human factors")

The initial literature search sorted and looked over articles published from 1960 to 2019, however no suitable evidence was found between 1960 and 1999. Therefore, the search was restricted to articles published between 2000 and January 2021 corresponding to the period this review. The literature search included articles that used the word 'ransomware' in the title, abstract or keywords.

The initial search of Google Scholar yielded 2410 articles. The first 100 results were included in the paper selection. The reason for this limitation is that Google Scholar ranks articles the way researchers do and the most relevant result will always appear on the first page (von Krogh et al., 2012).

Search Resources

The search was limited to peer-reviewed journals and some conference proceedings. The search was conducted using digital libraries, which search for a combination of different resources. The digital libraries selected were IEEE Xplore, Google Scholar, ACM digital library, Science Direct and Scopus – the most prominent digital libraries for published cybersecurity research. In the final paper selection, the forward-backward search process was conducted to include other relevant references.

Study Selection Criteria Procedures

The list of ransomware studies identified by the search was evaluated against a set of inclusion and exclusion criteria discussed below.

Inclusion Criteria

First, all studies had to be peer reviewed and written in English to be included in the review. The paper must contain information related to ransomware as a type of malware that encrypts and locks system files and data until the payment of a ransom is made. Conference proceedings on ransomware were included.

Exclusion Criteria

Studies were excluded from the review if they were solely on malware, virus, and cryptography analysis, grey literature such as commentaries, dissertation, book chapters, blogs and news reports. Also, non-English language publications, articles focusing on the economics or legal aspects of ransomware were excluded. Conference posters, PowerPoint presentation and articles with only an abstract were further excluded.

Study Quality Assessment

An assessment of relevance to determine the quality of studies was made according to the guidance set by Kitchenham and Charters (2007). This allowed for an assessment of the papers relevant to the research questions. The assessment was based on three criteria:

Figure 2. Literature search and select process

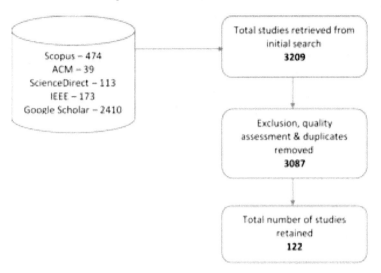

- A clear statement of the inclusion and exclusion criteria described
- The literature search covered all likely relevant studies
- A clear context and detail of ransomware in relation to the research objectives

After the selection phase, 164 articles were transferred to the EndNote reference manager, and the abstracts were examined in detail by two reviewers. Where both reviewers could not agree on an article, a third reviewer was invited to examine the article and decide. The quality assessment was applied to the selected 164 studies, 42 more studies were removed as not relevant based on the inclusion and exclusion criteria.

LITERATURE ANALYSIS

Data analysis was conducted on the 122 articles retained after the selection process. Analysis began with the descriptive analysis of the studies and analysis of the result using Crime, prevention Review and Investigation approach.

Descriptive analysis: The majority of the 122 selected papers were published within the last five years, with 2016 marking the initial spike in publications before the WannaCry ransomware attack in 2017. After 2017, more conference and journal articles on ransomware were published often focused on the WannaCry ransomware case studies

In terms of content, most articles carried out an analysis of the different strains or variants of ransomware to develop applications and design systems to detect ransomware attacks and take steps to remove the deployed ransomware. Figure 3 shows that there is an upward trend on studies examining ransomware; following this trend, in the future, there will be a significant number of studies relating to ransomware as ransomware attacks increases.

Figure 3. Number of scholarly publications over time

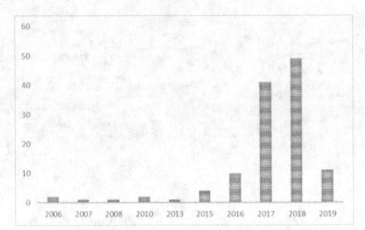

Table 1. Keyword frequency analysis

Research theme	Count
Detection	53
Analysis	43
Classification	43
Prevention	24
Vectors	18
Recovery	9
Defence	9
Android	8
Mitigation	8
Future trends	7
Crime	6
Cloud	6
Investigation	6
Machine Learning	6
Health	5
Windows	4
Payload	3
Deploy	3
IoT	3
Awareness	2
Forensics	2
Life cycle	2
Resilience	2
Gamification	2
Risk Management	1
Data mining	1

Significant keywords: An analysis of keywords to convey the primary focus of the 122 studies selected showed that ransomware detection, analysis and behavior classification was prevalent. Table 1 above shows the research theme across the 122 studies, excluding the literature search phrases. The majority of ransomware literature investigates methods of ransomware detection, prevention, classification and analysis of ransomware families. This is important because it shows that the majority of the studies are focused on technical measures around the subject of ransomware.

RESULTS

The results of the systematic analysis are discussed in light of the Shaikh et al. (2016) crime, prevention review and investigation approach. First, an overview of ransomware crime, prevention review and investigation are examined, followed by a detailed discussion of ransomware prevention research gaps.

Crime, Prevention Review and Investigation of Ransomware

Ransomware is a prominent security threat not only to organizations but to private individuals who access and conduct transactions using the internet. This review shows that the majority of ransomware research is focused on methods to detect ransomware when suspicious activities are noticed within network traffic. One aspect often overlooked in ransomware studies is the crime, that is the extortion from victims (Li & Liao 2022). The literature usually examines and proffer solutions to detect, mitigate and prevent ransomware threats and attacks. Therefore, in order to present a comprehensive understanding of ransomware, the result of this systematic review is analyzed using the Crime, prevention Review and Investigation (CRI) approach suggested by Shaikh, Shabut, & Hossain (2016), adapted for socially engineered ransomware as illustrated in Figure 4.

Figure 4. CRI approach (Shaikh, Shabut, & Hossain, 2016) adapted for socially engineered ransomware

A crime prevention, review and investigation approach to ransomware proposes to examine the crime factor in ransomware attacks, review techniques on prevention and investigate research gaps. The CRI approach presents a holistic understanding of ransomware to address the study's research questions of identifying current and potential attack vectors, understanding the evolving and uncharted socially engineered ransomware attack territory, and highlighting the critical gaps for future research.

Crime: Ransomware Extortion

According to the FBI's Internet Crime Complaint Center (IC3), losses of about $5.52 billion due to ransomware attacks have been reported between 2013 and 2017 (FBI, 2017). Ransomware is now a profitable crime venture used by cybercriminals to extort money from the victims of a ransomware attack (Salvi & Kerkar, 2016; Tandon & Nayyar, 2019). Despite the advice not to pay the ransom when an attack occurs (Moore, 2016), often, payment is the only way to recover the encrypted files, but in many cases, decryption of system files is not guaranteed (O'Kane et al., 2018).

A few studies in this review discussed the ransomware extortion process but as an overview of ransomware analysis rather than as an avenue that propagates cybercrime (Hampton & Baig, 2015; Bhardwaj et al., 2016; Salvi & Kerkar, 2016; O'Kane et al., 2018). This review emphasizes socially engineered ransomware as a significant avenue for cybercrime that currently affect all categories of technology users.

Ransomware Attack Framework

Although ransomware first appeared in 1989, the research field is very recent with the majority of studies published from 2016. Ransomware attacks are usually successful and profitable for cybercriminals due to the following core technologies:

- a secure reversible encryption to lock the victim's files (Young & Yung, 2017)
- an anonymous communication system for decryption tools and keys, and
- a concealed method of payment (Hampton & Baig, 2015; Craciun et al., 2018).

The trend observed in this review shows that numerous studies analyze and classify ransomware in the experimental environment to develop solutions that could detect, mitigate, prevent and possibly delete ransomware variants. However, as most ransomware are often socially engineered, technical solutions developed are not enough to mitigate and combat the ransomware threats. There are two major approaches to ransomware attacks; socially engineered attacks and spoofing.

Social engineering: Social engineering is one of the primary techniques used to propagate ransomware malware. Social engineering is the science of employing psychological manipulation on a human being to lead them to reveal confidential information or to perform actions that allow unauthorized access into a network (Gallegos-Segovia et al., 2017). Phishing attack techniques are widespread and closely linked to social engineering. Phishing refers to a scalable act of deception whereby impersonation is used to obtain information from a target often through a digital channel such as an email (Lastdrager, 2014). In a socially engineered ransomware attack, a victim is manipulated to install a malicious application that encrypts data or locks the victim's device and demands payment for decryption or restoration of the data and device. The internet has contributed to the success and scalability of socially engineered ransomware attacks. As highlighted previously, ransomware encrypts a victim's file and demands payment in exchange for locked files; this feature is what distinguishes ransomware from traditional malware (Al-rimy, Maarof, & Shaid, 2018). Research suggests that socially engineered attacks via malicious emails appears to be more popular in the propagation of ransomware codes (Shaikh et al., 2016). Socially engineered ransomware is now more pervasive, persistent, complex, sophisticated, and aggressive (Abraham & Chengalur-Smith, 2010; Ribeiro, 2022).

Spoofing: Spoofing refers to an attack where a victim is made to communicate with an attacker through a hoax copy of an original email, website or phone call or can be more technical such as creating a shadow copy of domain name system or internet protocol address (Felten et al., 1997; Rugo et al., 2022). In a few cases, cybercriminals create and host a fake website, where the victims are directed to the fake site to give their confidential information in exchange for a supposed genuine service (Shaikh et al., 2016). Criminals use social engineering, phishing, and spoofing techniques to convince their victims to access malicious applications, links or download updates from a shadow copied website to aid ransomware propagation to the victim's device or across a network.

Ransomware Lifecycle

The lifecycle of ransomware begins from the moment a malicious code or application is dispersed and ends when the attacker makes financial demands. Several actions between the victim's device and the attacker's Command-and-Control (C2C) server take place during this lifecycle for the hijack to be successful (Hampton et al., 2018; Tandon & Nayyar, 2019). The entire ransomware process involves the four stages illustrated in Figure 5 and discussed below:

Figure 5. Ransomware lifecycle

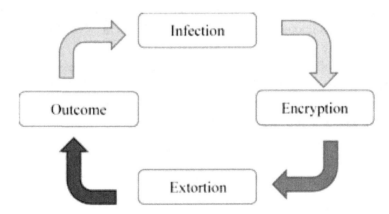

Infection: There are over 4 billion internet users worldwide and about 7 billion internet-connected devices, with additional 100 billion devices or more expected to be connected to the internet due to the Internet of Things (Bello & Mahadevan, 2019; Lueth, 2018; O'Kane et al., 2018). A cybercriminal may employ social engineering technique to lure a victim into clicking a malicious phishing email attachment, redirect the victim to a spoofed site or a drive-by download to disseminate the ransomware into the victim's device. Security researchers often obtain samples of an infection code for analysis and development of possible detection solutions (Hull et al., 2019). This review analysis shows that the majority of studies often focus on the technicalities of ransomware infection.

Encryption: Once the ransomware infection is successful, the cybercriminal employs the cryptographic process to search and encrypt the victim's files or lock down their device. The ransomware code usually targets and encrypt the victim's files and documents, critical system files, backup files, attached devices and shared network drives (Hampton et al., 2018; O'Kane et al., 2018). This review does not include cryptovirology or ransomware cryptography. However, encryption is a core process necessary for the ransomware crime to proceed to the next stage in the lifecycle (Bajpai et al., 2018; Zimba & Mulenga, 2018).

Extortion: In this stage, the victim is made aware of the infection by the cybercriminal. The ransomware software displays a prompt to the victim that files have been encrypted, and timely remittance of the ransom will ensure the decryption of files or release of locked devices, otherwise, files will be deleted permanently. As previously mentioned, ransomware is profitable for cybercriminals as a result of electronic payments and anonymous payment channels such as MoneyPak, DarkCoin or BitCoin (Salvi & Kerkar, 2016).

Outcome: The ransomware lifecycle is completed in this final stage based on the actions of the victim. There are three possible outcomes in this stage: a) the victim's is able to eliminate the ransomware code from their devices and restore all encrypted files, b) the victim succumb to the extortion crime and remit the ransom via the anonymous channels for restoration of files and devices, or c) no payment is made, the ransomware is not eliminated and the victim's files are lost or destroyed.

Ransomware Vectors

Ransomware vectors are the attack transmission channel that enables the propagation of malicious ransomware code (Zimba et al., 2017). The most common vector that criminals use to deliver a ransomware payload is through email attachments employing social engineering tactics to convince a victim to open an email that activates the malicious code in an email or attachments (Salvi & Kerkar, 2016; Zimba et al., 2017; O'Kane et al., 2018).

Attack vectors vary and differ in their degree of stealthiness, effectiveness and complexity. Examples of ransomware attack vectors are malicious email, malvertisement, use of online advertising to propagate ransomware codes and exploit kits that utilize the vulnerabilities on a device to launch a ransomware attack. Some common and evolving attack vectors also used in socially engineered ransomware attacks are explored below.

Email: the previous section 3.2 presented social engineering as an easy and fast technique used in the propagation of ransomware. Phishing is a persisting issue, and the majority of socially engineered ransomware utilize various forms of phishing, especially emails (Gallegos-Segovia et al., 2017). Email remains popular as it affords cybercriminals a cheap and easy avenue to reach millions of unsuspecting users (Al-rimy, Maarof, & Shaid, 2018; Ferreira, 2018; O'Kane et al., 2018). A cybercriminal only needs to send out a malicious email that contains the ransomware payload. When a victim opens the mail, the payload is triggered and begins the ransomware lifecycle process. An analysis of ransomware email showed that victims fall prey to phishing emails because of social engineering techniques used in framing the subject lines, employing a persuasive characteristic and urgency (Ferreira, 2018).

Man-in-the middle (MITM): MITM attack occurs when an attacker or malicious third party covertly takes control of a seemingly protected and encrypted channel of communication (Conti et al., 2016). The cybercriminal within the compromised network can intercept sensitive data, but also direct the victim to the spoofed website where the ransomware payload will be deployed. MITM is usually executed using various communication channels such as Near Field Communication (NFC), Bluetooth, Long-Term Evolution (LTE) and Wi-Fi.

Remote desktop protocol (RDP): RDP is a service that allows users to connect to a server and access applications from another location. Ransomware attacks via RDP have been on the rise since 2016 due to the administrative privilege it may give cybercriminals if they successfully gain access to the system. RDP as an attack vector could be used to propagate ransomware on a large scale, by installing malicious files on all devices within the network (Wang et al., 2018).

Internet of Things (IoT): IoT ransomware attacks is a growing trend and likely to increase as more device are incorporated into an IoT environment. IoT devices span from Fitbit wearables to smart home and cars, and they are constantly accessing the internet gathering and distribution data (Al-rimy, Maarof, & Shaid, 2018). A malicious IoT device as a ransomware vector could cause severe disruptions to networks, surveillance systems, critical infrastructures and manufacturing in the future (Bello & Mahadevan, 2019; Sharma & Arya; 2022). For example, the Android.Lockdroid.E ransomware that accessed IoT devices and locked smart TVs (Symantec, 2015).

Application Programming Interfaces (APIs): An API is a set of procedures and functions that allows two or more software applications to communicate with each other. As an attack vector, a cybercriminal could obfuscate an API call and stealthily deploy a ransomware code within the network to infect the connected devices (Chen et al., 2017). The articles analyzed in this review focused on methods of detecting ransomware by monitoring and extracting API calls to create a pattern that identifies malicious API calls (Chen et al., 2017; Hampton et al., 2018; Sheen & Yadav, 2018).

Review: Ransomware Prevention

The trend observed in this review shows that security professionals usually obtain samples of ransomware infection code, analyze and classify them based on attack attributes to provide possible solutions. There is an abundant of ransomware research focused on the development of detection, defense, prevention, prediction and possible recovery solutions. However, these solutions do not present a silver bullet for ransomware attacks. For example, security analysts are still seeking solutions to disable the NotPetya ransomware after it gains access to a victim's device, no fixed solution has been found (Lika et al., 2018). Ransomware prevention solution requires a holistic approach. Unfortunately, studies often focus on preventive solutions for ransomware codes and social engineering techniques as silo events. This review section makes a case for research to focus on a holistic preventive solution for socially engineered ransomware. The ransomware prevention techniques presented in this section are categorized into user and system/network levels.

User Level

One solution to ensure the prevention of ransomware attacks is to incorporate users as part of the ransomware solution. Luo and Liao (2007) are among the first academics to study and propose a ransomware prevention framework. The ransomware framework focused on policy regulation, access control and management, exposure analysis and report, awareness training and education (Luo & Liao, 2007). More than a decade after Luo and Liao (2007) proposed this framework, academic literature is less focused on the human aspect in ransomware prevention. More recently, Ferreira (2018) highlighted the dearth of ransomware research focused on user-related solutions. Security researchers often develop conceptual models and proposed solutions to a ransomware attack. For example, Dion et al. (2017) developed a prototype to gamify the procedure of a ransomware attack. Lika et al. (2018) developed a conceptual preventive solution intended to educate users on NotPeyta attack through a gamification process. These studies propose highly conceptual solutions that have not been empirically tested despite the increasing rate of ransomware attacks. Socially engineered ransomware preventive solutions require more human-focused approach as human are the primary vectors used in socially engineered ransomware attacks.

System/Network Level

The studies that examine ransomware prevention and detection usually propose solutions from a network or system perspective. Some studies propose platform-based detection solutions to deal with ransomware (Alzahrani et al., 2017; Hampton et al., 2018; Maiorca et al., 2017), while others focus on specific ransomware such as crypt-ransomware (Moore, 2016; Scaife et al., 2016; Al-rimy, Maarof, Prasetyo, et al., 2018). This section presents several researched techniques used in ransomware prevention.

Neural network detection approach: Homayoun et al. (2019) proposed a Deep Ransomware threat Hunting and Intelligence System (DRTHIS) by combining Long Short-Term Memory (LSTM) and Convolutional Neural Network (CNN) to detect ransomware and their families within seconds. The research model analyzed large samples of crypto-ransomware families and achieved a precision and recall (F-measure) value of 0.996 in detecting ransomware with a true positive rate of 0.972 and a false positive of 0.027 (Homayoun et al., 2019). Azmoodeh et al. (2018) on the other hand studied ransomware detection based on energy consumption within IoT networks to halt the effect of a ransomware attack within a network. They analyzed four classifiers: k-Nearest Neighbor (KNN), Neural Network (NN), Support Vector Machine (SVM) and Random Forest (RF) on power usage. The results from their experiment showed that KNN using Dynamic Time Wrapping (DTW) achieved an optimal performance and achieved a detection rate of 95.5% and precision rate of 89.19% within an IoT network (Azmoodeh et al., 2018). Neural network, from a technical perspective, presents a brilliant solution in detecting ransomware and their families.

Machine learning-based detection approach: Machine learning (ML) techniques enables a defined set of algorithms to continually monitor, search and analyze computer networks, systems and devices for abnormal processes that might initiate suspicious alteration activities (Torres & Yoo, 2017). In recent studies, ML is proposed as an effective technique in detecting ransomware resulting from an intelligent algorithm that learns and classify ransomware variants and families. For example, Sgandurra et al. (2016) proposed EldeRan, a dynamically based approach used to test, analyze and classify 582ransomware belonging to 11 families. The result from the study showed that EldeRan achieved a detection rate of 96.3%. Similarly, Zhang et al. (2019) collected 1787 ransomware samples from eight families, using N-gram sequence and Term Frequency-Inverse Document Frequency (TF-IDF), their result achieved an accuracy rate of 91.43%. ML detection techniques have proved effective for malicious programs; however, some ransomware families may not be adequately analyzed and classified. Additional, new ransomware strains may incorporate logic bomb (Datta & Acton, 2022) techniques (waiting for a user action before carrying out an attack) or require a shorter encryption time which may allow the ransomware to escape detection via ML techniques.

Data-centric detection approach: Data-centric approach monitors user's resources that are subject to attack rather than the malicious process that carries out the ransomware attack. Azmoodeh et al. (2018) proposed a detection approach that monitors ransomware energy consumption to distinguish ransomware from non-malicious applications. The detection technique creates energy consumption log files of the most popular Android applications, and ransomware. Analysis of the log files are retrieved and labelled according to the application type (goodware or ransomware) (Azmoodeh et al., 2018). Scaife et al. (2016) proposed a technique focused on monitoring the real-time change of user data, over time the accumulated observations allows an analyst to examine multiple suspicious indicators rather than relying on one isolated indicator to detect ransomware activities. Data-centric ransomware detection techniques are not sufficient as they often require the user to make a final decision on whether a specific activity is not malicious, thereby sacrificing a part of data before the ransomware is detected.

Investigation of Research Gaps

Socially engineered ransomware is a growing menace and currently affect individuals, businesses and the government. Cybercriminals psychologically manipulate human weaknesses using social engineering techniques to trick victims into installing ransomware on their device. The ransomware accesses the victim's data and files on the infected device, encrypts, locks the device and demand ransom payment for decryption and restoration of data. The review conducted in this study shows that ransomware research is very recent, and academic publications have increased in the last three years, increasing the general knowledge on ransomware. However, there are a couple of areas that ransomware research often covers such as detection and preventive measures that involve mainly technical aspects of ransomware attacks. This section highlights the gaps and potential opportunities available for future research on ransomware.

Ransomware ecosystem: Current ransomware research usually dissect, analyze and categorize ransomware strains in programmed virtual environment. Ransomware today exist in an ecosystem that adopts several aspects of Darwin's theory of evolution: inherited variations, ability to adapt and survive, and humans now play a part in the propagation of ransomware. In the last two decades, ransomware strain has evolved with technology, giving rise to several variations modified from previous malicious codes. Ransomware attacks could be socially engineered enabling the attacks to be more deceptive, sophisticated and mostly irreversible. Future research could benefit from the evaluation of a human-centric ransomware ecosystem that analyze new breeds of ransomware for effective solutions to counteract future attacks.

Holistic ransomware detection and prevention: Currently, ransomware detection and prevention solutions are somewhat generic and technically focused. Most studies focus on the Windows operating system for PC and Android for mobile devices. There are only a handful of articles that explored other operating systems and platforms. Sufficient understanding of ransomware analysis in multiple OS environments is needed to ensure that ransomware detection and prevention solutions are efficient (Chayal, Saxena, & Khan, 2022). Technology users access the internet and web applications using different devices and platforms susceptible to ransomware attacks. Scaife et al. (2016) analysis of ransomware variants in the same environment substantiate this fact: ransomware behaves differently in different environments when they infect a victim's device. Ransomware detection and prevention research could benefit from examining ransomware in the context of the multiple platforms that users operate from when accessing the internet.

IoT attack trajectories: Ransomware research on IoT devices is another area that future research should investigate. By 2020, research forecasts that there will be over 20 billion IoT devices (Bello & Mahadevan, 2019). Recently, cybercriminals have successfully propagated IoT-based ransomware infecting smart TVs; more research needs to focus on more IoT devices and network. Ransomware could be propagated through smart devices and sensors that access the internet; research is required to explore these interconnected technologies as possible ransomware attack vectors.

Quantum cryptography: Cryptographic technology was initially conceived as a purely protective technology until cryptovirology was born. Cryptovirology facilitated ransomware and internet extortion creating a new business model for cyber criminals. Quantum computing is predicted to render current encryption methods as unsafe; quantum cryptography is expected to advance data security. Research needs to get ahead of cybercriminals in investigating the offensive side of quantum cryptography (Ahmad et al., 2022), that is, socially engineered ransomware employing quantum cryptovirology technology.

Human aspects of ransomware: Ransomware research is currently very technical focused. Ransomware testing and experiment are conducted in virtual environments void of the human elements who are often the victim in a ransomware attack (Tasnim & Sarker, 2022). Ransomware research needs a more holistic approach that incorporates the human and technical aspects to counter cybercriminals. Over a decade after Luo and Liao (2007) proposed a ransomware prevention framework, academia is yet to provide an update that addresses ransomware regarding the current technology trends. Technology has evolved, increase in computing power has led to mobile, wearable technologies, IoT devices and networks that are intertwined with individual's daily lives (Bello, Murray, & Armarego, 2017) and these individuals are less aware of the threats that socially engineered ransomware poses.

DISCUSSION

This study presents a systematic review of existing research on ransomware dominated by the following research questions: What are the existing socially engineered ransomware vectors? What are the emerging attack methods? What are the knowledge gaps? What are the available methods used to managed socially engineered ransomware? In this section, discussion of the results of the systematic review and trends is done within the context of the research questions.

Firstly, the existing socially engineered ransomware attack vectors in response to the first research question is emphasized. It is essential to highlight that emails remains one of the easiest and fastest attack vectors used in ransomware attacks. Also, emails present an avenue for cybercriminals to employ social engineering tactics and engage with their victim to deploy a ransomware payload. The Internet of Things (IoT) is the next attack vector that could speed up the propagation of socially engineered ransomware as they are easily vulnerable to threats. In the cause of this review, it can be observed that researchers take a generic approach to ransomware research on IoT and focused on detection and mitigation strategies rather than user awareness and education.

As discussed above, IoT-based ransomware is an emerging attack vector that is yet to be fully exploited by cybercriminals. IoT devices regularly interact within vast networks, exchanging data between devices, sensors, servers and humans (Bello & Mahadevan, 2019; Humayun et al., 2020). A man-in-the-middle attack could allow an attacker to access a compromised IoT device, gain entry into a network and deploy a ransomware payload. Most IoT and smart devices do not have or require security applications such as anti-virus preinstalled, leaving them vulnerable to security risks. The result of the analysis shows that IoT has not received enough recognition as a potential trigger point for the next big socially engineered ransomware attack.

The main knowledge gap observed from the analysis is the dearth of the human aspects in ransomware research. Humans are highly susceptible to socially engineered ransomware attacks (Gallegos-Segovia et al., 2017), and ransomware research is yet to incorporate the human side as the one step in developing socio-technical ransomware prevention, detection and mitigation solutions. Additionally, there is less focus on ransomware research on IoT devices as an attack vector for socially engineered ransomware.

The results show that the majority of the academic literature is geared towards ransomware detection, analysis of ransomware families, classification of ransomware strains and development of ransomware detection solutions. Socially engineered ransomware is currently managed using a very generic and technical approach focused on detection solutions rather than incorporating a holistic approach that acknowledges every aspect especially the socio-technical of the ransomware lifecycle (Ferreira, 2018).

Overall, the findings of this study contribute to the body of knowledge and literature regarding ransomware by providing insight into the traits of technology users that make them more vulnerable to social engineering ransomware attack techniques, as well as insight into effective methods needed for disrupting the progression of such attacks. The study findings can also help refine and expand on theories that predict cybersecurity behavior to seed further qualitative and quantitative research.

LIMITATIONS

In the last decade, there has been an increase in ransomware attack; the result of this study's analysis shows that current ransomware variants research and analysis of attack vectors need further investigation despite the increasing number of ransomware related publications. Future research could explore other literatures and grey areas excluded in the scope of this study to investigate and understand the technicalities of novel ransomware variants and their methods of propagation. Additionally, this study investigated ransomware using a crime, prevention review and investigation approach to understand socially engineered ransomware attacks. Future studies could explore additional variables that employ psychological game theoretic models to investigate the relationship between social engineering malicious insider intentions and methods of deterrence given the increasing use of ransomware applications.

CONCLUSION

This study examined socially engineered ransomware as an extortion crime; a review of ransomware prevention techniques; and an investigation of ransomware research gaps. Ransomware attacks are becoming more sophisticated, employing social engineering to psychologically manipulate victims to install ransomware payloads. Socially engineered ransomware is a challenge, and with more devices and systems connecting to the Internet of Things, ransomware attack prevention will be the responsibility of government bodies and departments. In light of the on-going COVID-19 pandemic and stay home orders, there is a significant spike in ransomware attacks using social engineering tactics, targeting the majority of internet users (including school children). COVID-19 themed lures for ransomware is claiming several victims using phishing-based attack vectors to exploit individuals concerned over the coronavirus pandemic and the safety of their family and friends. There is also evidence of remote working increasing the risks of a successful ransomware attack due to weaker home network controls. More creative ways of extorting ransoms have also been emerging with threat concepts of 'double and triple extortion', where ransomware encrypts data and forces individuals to pay ransom, and then sends the data to several threat actors that threaten to release the data unless additional ransom is paid. Moreover, new variants of ransomware that can by-pass antivirus software are rapidly emerging and offered as Ransomware-as-a-Service (RaaS) providing cybercriminals easy access to exploit internet users.

The review carried in this study highlights the need for a holistic approach to ransomware research that includes human aspects as a part of the solution in the development of ransomware detection, prevention, and mitigation strategies. Hence, the focus of the second part of this study will comprise of high-level documentary analysis contrasted with reported ransomware incidents and would be inward-facing, looking only at the procedures, if any, in organizations as well as cyber security agencies that have been developed and spread to the public for awareness and education on dealing with socially-engineered ransomware attacks. Data collection would be based on a sample of several cyber security experts comprising of junior, middle and senior level management, as well as home technology users to capture key insights on increasing ransomware risks and deployed controls.

REFERENCES

Abraham, S., & Chengalur-Smith, I. (2010). An overview of social engineering malware: Trends, tactics, and implications. *Technology in Society*, *32*(3), 183–196. doi:10.1016/j.techsoc.2010.07.001

Ahmad, S., Mehfuz, S., & Beg, J. (2022). Empirical Analysis of Security Enabled Quantum Computing for Cloud Environment. In *Quantum and Blockchain for Modern Computing Systems: Vision and Advancements* (pp. 103–125). Springer. doi:10.1007/978-3-031-04613-1_3

Alqahtani, A., & Sheldon, F. T. (2022). A Survey of Crypto Ransomware Attack Detection Methodologies: An Evolving Outlook. *Sensors (Basel)*, *22*(5), 1837. doi:10.339022051837 PMID:35270983

Al-rimy, B. A. S., Maarof, M. A., Prasetyo, Y. A., Shaid, Z. M., & Ariffin, A. F. M. (2018). Zero-day aware decision fusion-based model for crypto-ransomware early detection. *International Journal of Integrated Engineering*, *10*(6), 82–88. doi:10.30880/ijie.2018.10.06.011

Al-rimy, B. A. S., Maarof, M. A., & Shaid, S. Z. M. (2018). Ransomware threat success factors, taxonomy, and countermeasures: A survey and research directions. *Computers & Security*, *74*, 144–166. doi:10.1016/j.cose.2018.01.001

Alzahrani, A., Alshehri, A., Alharthi, R., Alshahrani, H., & Fu, H. (2017). An Overview of Ransomware in the Windows Platform. *2017 International Conference on Computational Science and Computational Intelligence (CSCI)*, 612–617. 10.1109/CSCI.2017.106

Azmoodeh, A., Dehghantanha, A., Conti, M., & Choo, K.-K. R. (2018). *Detecting crypto-ransomware in IoT networks based on energy consumption footprint*. Academic Press.

Bajpai, P., Sood, A. K., & Enbody, R. (2018). A key-management-based taxonomy for ransomware. *2018 APWG Symposium on Electronic Crime Research (ECrime)*, 1–12.

Bello, A. G., Murray, D., & Armarego, J. (2017). A systematic approach to investigating how information security and privacy can be achieved in BYOD environments. *Information and Computer Security*, *25*(4), 475–492. doi:10.1108/ICS-03-2016-0025

Bello, A., & Mahadevan, V. (2019). A Cloud Based Conceptual Identity Management Model for Secured Internet of Things Operation. *Journal of Cyber Security and Mobility*, *8*(1), 53–74. doi:10.13052/jcsm2245-1439.813

Bhardwaj, A., Avasthi, V., Sastry, H., & Subrahmanyam, G. V. B. (2016). Ransomware digital extortion: A rising new age threat. *Indian Journal of Science and Technology*, *9*(14), 1–5. doi:10.17485/ijst/2016/v9i14/82936

Chayal, N. M., Saxena, A., & Khan, R. (2022). A review on spreading and Forensics Analysis of Windows-Based ransomware. *Annals of Data Science*, 1-22.

Chen, Z.-G., Kang, H.-S., Yin, S.-N., & Kim, S.-R. (2017). Automatic Ransomware Detection and Analysis Based on Dynamic API Calls Flow Graph. *RACS*, 196-201.

Conti, M., Dragoni, N., & Lesyk, V. (2016). A Survey of Man In The Middle Attacks. *IEEE Communications Surveys and Tutorials*, *18*(3), 2027–2051. doi:10.1109/COMST.2016.2548426

Craciun, V. C., Mogage, A., & Simion, E. (2018). *Trends in design of ransomware viruses*. Academic Press.

Datta, P. M., & Acton, T. (2022). From disruption to ransomware: Lessons From hackers. *Journal of Information Technology Teaching Cases*.

Dion, Y. L., Joshua, A. A., & Brohi, S. N. (2017). *Negation of Ransomware via Gamification and Enforcement of Standards*. Academic Press.

FBI. (2017). *2017 Internet Crime Report*. Federal Bureau of Investigation.

FBI. (2018). *2018 Internet Crime Report*. Federal Bureau of Investigation. https://www.ic3.gov/media/annualreport/2018_IC3Report.pdf

Felten, E. W., Balfanz, D., Dean, D., & Wallach, D. S. (1997). *Web Spoofing: An Internet Con Game* (Technical report 540-96; p. 9). Princeton University.

Ferreira, A. (2018). Why Ransomware Needs A Human Touch. *2018 International Carnahan Conference on Security Technology (ICCST)*, 1–5.

F-Secure. (2017). *F-Secure State of Cyber Security 2017*. F-Secure Corporation.

Gallegos-Segovia, P. L., Bravo-Torres, J. F., Larios-Rosillo, V. M., Vintimilla-Tapia, P. E., Yuquilima-Albarado, I. F., & Jara-Saltos, J. D. (2017). Social engineering as an attack vector for ransomware. *2017 CHILEAN Conference on Electrical, Electronics Engineering, Information and Communication Technologies (CHILECON)*, 1–6. 10.1109/CHILECON.2017.8229528

Grillenmeier, G. (2022). Ransomware–one of the biggest threats facing enterprises today. *Network Security*, *2022*(3). doi:10.12968/S1353-4858(22)70029-3

Hampton, N., & Baig, Z. A. (2015). *Ransomware: Emergence of the cyber-extortion menace*. Academic Press.

Hampton, N., Baig, Z. A., & Zeadally, S. (2018). Ransomware behavioural analysis on windows platforms. *Journal of Information Security and Applications*, *40*, 44–51. doi:10.1016/j.jisa.2018.02.008

Homayoun, S., Dehghantanha, A., Ahmadzadeh, M., Hashemi, S., Khayami, R., Choo, K.-K. R., & Newton, D. E. (2019). DRTHIS: Deep ransomware threat hunting and intelligence system at the fog layer. *Future Generation Computer Systems*, *90*, 94–104. doi:10.1016/j.future.2018.07.045

Hull, G., John, H., & Arief, B. (2019). Ransomware deployment methods and analysis: Views from a predictive model and human responses. *Crime Science*, *8*(1), 2. doi:10.118640163-019-0097-9

Humayun, M., Jhanjhi, N., Alsayat, A., & Ponnusamy, V. (2020). *Internet of things and ransomware: Evolution, mitigation and prevention. Egyptian Informatics Journal.* doi:10.1016/j.eij.2020.05.003

Kitchenham, B., & Charters, S. (2007). *Guidelines for performing Systematic Literature Reviews in Software Engineering.* Technical Report EBSE 2007-001. https://www.elsevier.com/__data/promis_misc/525444systematicreviewsguide.pdf

Kostopoulos, G. K. (2017). Cyberspace and Cybersecurity (2nd ed.). Taylor & Francis.

Larose, R., Mastro, D., & Eastin, M. S. (2001). Understanding Internet Usage: A Social-Cognitive Approach to Uses and Gratifications. *Social Science Computer Review*, *19*(4), 395–413. doi:10.1177/089443930101900401

Lastdrager, E. E. (2014). Achieving a consensual definition of phishing based on a systematic review of the literature. *Crime Science*, *3*(1), 9. Advance online publication. doi:10.118640163-014-0009-y

Li, Z., & Liao, Q. (2022). Preventive portfolio against data-selling ransomware—A game theory of encryption and deception. *Computers & Security*, *116*, 102644. doi:10.1016/j.cose.2022.102644

Lika, R. A., Murugiah, D., Brohi, S. N., & Ramasamy, D. (2018). NotPetya: Cyber Attack Prevention through Awareness via Gamification. *2018 International Conference on Smart Computing and Electronic Enterprise (ICSCEE)*, 1–6. 10.1109/ICSCEE.2018.8538431

Lueth, K. L. (2018, August). *State of the IoT 2018: Number of IoT devices now at 7B - Market accelerating.* IOT Analytics. https://iot-analytics.com/product/state-of-the-iot-02-2017/

Luo, X., & Liao, Q. (2007). Awareness Education as the Key to Ransomware Prevention. *Information Systems Security*, *16*(4), 195–202. doi:10.1080/10658980701576412

Madan, S., Sofat, S., & Bansal, D. (2022). Tools and Techniques for Collection and Analysis of Internet-of-Things malware: A systematic state-of-art review. *Journal of King Saud University-Computer and Information Sciences.*

Maiorca, D., Mercaldo, F., Giacinto, G., Visaggio, C. A., & Martinelli, F. (2017). R-PackDroid: API Package-based Characterization and Detection of Mobile Ransomware. *SAC*, 1718-1723.

Moore, C. (2016). Detecting ransomware with honeypot techniques. *2016 Cybersecurity and Cyberforensics Conference (CCC)*, 77–81. 10.1109/CCC.2016.14

O'Kane, P., Sezer, S., & Carlin, D. (2018). Evolution of Ransomware. *IET Networks*, *7*(5), 321–327. doi:10.1049/iet-net.2017.0207

Ribeiro, J. V. A. (2022). A brief overview of ransomware behavior analysis challenges. *Brazilian Journal of Development*, *8*(5), 38275–38280. doi:10.34117/bjdv8n5-365

Rugo, A., Ardagna, C. A., & Ioini, N. E. (2022). A Security Review in the UAVNet Era: Threats, Countermeasures, and Gap Analysis. *ACM Computing Surveys*, *55*(1), 1–35. doi:10.1145/3485272

Salvi, M. H. U., & Kerkar, M. R. V. (2016). Ransomware: A cyber extortion. *Asian Journal for Convergence in Technology, 2.*

Scaife, N., Carter, H., Traynor, P., & Butler, K. R. B. (2016). CryptoLock (and Drop It): Stopping Ransomware Attacks on User Data. *2016 IEEE 36th International Conference on Distributed Computing Systems (ICDCS)*, 303–312.

Sgandurra, D., Muñoz-González, L., Mohsen, R., & Lupu, E. C. (2016). *Automated Dynamic Analysis of Ransomware: Benefits, Limitations and use for Detection.* https://arxiv.org/abs/1609.03020

Shaikh, A. N., Shabut, A. M., & Hossain, M. A. (2016). A literature review on phishing crime, prevention review and investigation of gaps. *2016 10th International Conference on Software, Knowledge, Information Management & Applications*, 9–15. 10.1109/SKIMA.2016.7916190

Sharma, R., & Arya, R. (2022). Security threats and measures in the Internet of Things for smart city infrastructure: A state of art. *Transactions on Emerging Telecommunications Technologies*, 4571. doi:10.1002/ett.4571

Sharma, S., Kumar, R., & Krishna, C. R. (2020). RansomAnalysis: The Evolution and Investigation of Android Ransomware. In M. Dutta, C. R. Krishna, R. Kumar, & M. Kalra (Eds.), *Proceedings of International Conference on IoT Inclusive Life (ICIIL 2019), NITTTR Chandigarh, India* (*Vol. 116*, pp. 33–41). Springer Singapore. 10.1007/978-981-15-3020-3_4

Sheen, S., & Yadav, A. (2018). Ransomware detection by mining API call usage. *2018 International Conference on Advances in Computing, Communications and Informatics (ICACCI)*, 983–987. 10.1109/ICACCI.2018.8554938

Symantec. (2015). *Android.Lockdroid.E.* https://www.symantec.com/security-center/write-up/2014-103005-2209-99

Tandon, A., & Nayyar, A. (2019). A Comprehensive Survey on Ransomware Attack: A Growing Havoc Cyberthreat. In V. E. Balas, N. Sharma, & A. Chakrabarti (Eds.), *Data Management, Analytics and Innovation* (Vol. 839, pp. 403–420). Springer Singapore. doi:10.1007/978-981-13-1274-8_31

Torres, P. E. P., & Yoo, S. G. (2017). Detecting and neutralizing encrypting Ransomware attacks by using machine-learning techniques: A literature review. *International Journal of Applied Engineering Research: IJAER*, *12*(18), 7902–7911.

Tranfield, D., Denyer, D., & Smart, P. (2003). Towards a Methodology for Developing Evidence-Informed Management Knowledge by Means of Systematic Review. *British Journal of Management*, *14*(3), 207–222. doi:10.1111/1467-8551.00375

Tasnim, N., & Sarker, I. H. (2022). Ransomware family classification with ensemble model based on behavior analysis. Preprints. () doi:10.20944/preprints202201.0454.v1

von Krogh, H., Haefliger, Spaeth, & Wallin. (2012). Carrots and Rainbows: Motivation and Social Practice in Open Source Software Development. *Management Information Systems Quarterly*, *36*(2), 649. doi:10.2307/41703471

Wang, Z., Wu, X., Liu, C., Liu, Q., & Zhang, J. (2018). RansomTracer: Exploiting cyber deception for ransomware tracing. *2018 IEEE Third International Conference on Data Science in Cyberspace (DSC)*, 227–234. 10.1109/DSC.2018.00040

Wilding, E. (Ed.). (1990). *Virus Bulletin*, 20.

Wood, A., & Eze, T. (2020). The Evolution of Ransomware Variants. *9th European Conference on Cyber Warfare and Security*. https://chesterrep.openrepository.com/handle/10034/623242

Yan, S. Y. (2019). Offensive Cryptography. In *Cybercryptography: Applicable Cryptography for Cyberspace Security*. Springer. doi:10.1007/978-3-319-72536-9_9

Young, A. L., & Yung, M. (2017). Cryptovirology: The birth, neglect, and explosion of ransomware: Recent attacks exploiting a known vulnerability continue a downward spiral of ransomware-related incidents. *Communications of the Association for Information Systems*, *60*(7), 24–26.

Young, A., & Yung, M. (1996). Cryptovirology: Extortion-based security threats and countermeasures. *Proceedings 1996 IEEE Symposium on Security and Privacy*, 129–140. 10.1109/SECPRI.1996.502676

Zhang, H., Xiao, X., Mercaldo, F., Ni, S., Martinelli, F., & Sangaiah, A. K. (2019). Classification of ransomware families with machine learning based on N-gram of opcodes. *Future Generation Computer Systems*, *90*, 211–221. doi:10.1016/j.future.2018.07.052

Zimba, A. (2017). *Malware-Free Intrusion: A Novel Approach to Ransomware Infection Vectors*. Academic Press.

Zimba, A., & Chishimba, M. (2019). Understanding the Evolution of Ransomware: Paradigm Shifts in Attack Structures. *International Journal of Computer Network and Information Security*, *11*(1), 26–39. doi:10.5815/ijcnis.2019.01.03

Zimba, A., & Mulenga, M. (2018). A dive into the deep: Demystifying WannaCry crypto ransomware network attacks via digital forensics. *International Journal on Information Technologies & Security*, *4*(2).

Zimba, A., Wang, Z., & Chen, H. (2017). Reasoning crypto ransomware infection vectors with Bayesian networks. *2017 IEEE International Conference on Intelligence and Security Informatics (ISI)*, 149–151. 10.1109/ISI.2017.8004894

Compilation of References

Abddulrauf, A. L., & Fombad, M. C. (2017). Personal Data Protection in Nigeria: Reflections on Opportunities, Options, and Challenges to Legal Reforms. *The Liverpool Law Review*, *38*(2), 105–134. doi:10.100710991-016-9189-8

Abdulrauf, A. L., & Fombad, M. C. (2016) The African Union's data protection Convention 2014: a possible cause for celebration of human rights in Africa? *Journal of Media Law*, (1), 67 – 97.

Abhijith, S., Soja, S., Sreelekshmi, K. U., & Samjeevan, T. T. (2021). 'Web based Graphical Password Authentication System', eMangalam College of Engineering, Kottayam, India. *International Journal of Engineering Research & Technology, 9*(7).

Abraham, S., & Chengalur-Smith, I. (2010). An overview of social engineering malware: Trends, tactics, and implications. *Technology in Society*, *32*(3), 183–196. doi:10.1016/j.techsoc.2010.07.001

Adelman, M. J., & Baldia, S. (1996). Prospects and limits of the patent provision in the TRIPs Agreement: The case of India. *Vand. J. Transnat'l L.*, *29*, 507.

Africa-Europe Alliance. (2019). *New Africa-Europe Digital Economy Partnership Report of the EU-AU Digital Economy Task Force: Accelerating the Achievement of the Sustainable Development Goals*. European Union.

African Academic Network on Internet Policy. (2022). *Cyberspace Security In Africa: Where Do We Stand?* https://aanoip.org/cyberspace-security-in-africa-where-do-we-stand/

African countries call on Ghana's Cyber security Authority for collaboration and support. (2022, April 25). *Joy Business*. https://www.myjoyonline.com/african-countries-call-on-ghanas-cyber-security-authority-for-collaboration-and-support/

African Union Commission (2018). *AUC and Council of Europe Join Forces on Cybersecurity*. Addis Ababa: Directorate of Information and Communication African Union Commission.

African Union Commission. (2018). *African Forum on Cyber Crime: Policies and Legislation, International Cooperation and Capacity Building Conference Programme Draft, Addis Ababa* 16-18 October, 2018. Addis Ababa: African Union Commission and Council of Europe.

African Union Commission. (2018). *GLACY+: Cybersecurity and Cybercrime Policies for African Diplomats Held in Addis Ababa Ethiopia 11-13 April 2018*. Council of Europe.

Africanews, R. (2021). *Africa: Can a strong cyber security strategy be an engine for growth?* https://www.africanews.com/2022/05/16/africa-can-a-strong-cybersecurity-strategy-be-an-engine-for-growth/

Aguilar, L. A. (2014, June). Boards of directors, corporate governance and cyber-risks: Sharpening the focus. In *Cyber Risks and the Boardroom conference*. New York Stock Exchange.

Agwa, S., Yahya, E., & Ismail, Y. (2017). Power efficient AES core for IoT constrained devices implemented in 130 nm CMOS. In *Proceedings of the 2017 IEEE International Symposium on Circuits and Systems*, Baltimore, MD, USA, 28–31 May 2017,1–4.

Ahmad, F. (2008). *Cyber Law in India*. Academic Press.

Ahmad, S., Mehfuz, S., & Beg, J. (2022). Empirical Analysis of Security Enabled Quantum Computing for Cloud Environment. In *Quantum and Blockchain for Modern Computing Systems: Vision and Advancements* (pp. 103–125). Springer. doi:10.1007/978-3-031-04613-1_3

Ali, A. H. S., Saidin, O., Roisah, K., & Ediwarman, E. (2021). *Liability of Internet Intermediaries in Copyright Infringement: Comparison between the United States and India*. Academic Press.

Allemann, S. (2019). *Design and Prototypical Implementation of an Open Source and Smart Contract-based Know Your Customer (KYC) Platform* [Doctoral dissertation]. University of Zurich.

Allen, F., McAndrews, J., & Strahan, P. (2002). E-finance: An introduction. *Journal of Financial Services Research*, 22(1), 5–27. doi:10.1023/A:1016007126394

Alqahtani, A., & Sheldon, F. T. (2022). A Survey of Crypto Ransomware Attack Detection Methodologies: An Evolving Outlook. *Sensors (Basel)*, 22(5), 1837. doi:10.339022051837 PMID:35270983

Al-rimy, B. A. S., Maarof, M. A., Prasetyo, Y. A., Shaid, Z. M., & Ariffin, A. F. M. (2018). Zero-day aware decision fusion-based model for crypto-ransomware early detection. *International Journal of Integrated Engineering*, 10(6), 82–88. doi:10.30880/ijie.2018.10.06.011

Al-rimy, B. A. S., Maarof, M. A., & Shaid, S. Z. M. (2018). Ransomware threat success factors, taxonomy, and countermeasures: A survey and research directions. *Computers & Security*, 74, 144–166. doi:10.1016/j.cose.2018.01.001

Al-Zahrani, A. (2022). Assessing and Proposing Countermeasures for Cyber-Security Attacks. *International Journal of Advanced Computer Science and Applications*, 13(1). Advance online publication. doi:10.14569/IJACSA.2022.01301102

Alzahrani, A., Alshehri, A., Alharthi, R., Alshahrani, H., & Fu, H. (2017). An Overview of Ransomware in the Windows Platform. *2017 International Conference on Computational Science and Computational Intelligence (CSCI)*, 612–617. 10.1109/CSCI.2017.106

Amanatidis, T., & Chatzigeorgiou, A. (2016). Studying the evolution of PHP web applications. *Information and Software Technology*, 72, 48–67. doi:10.1016/j.infsof.2015.11.009

Amazon Seller Services Pvt Ltd vs Modicare Ltd & Ors (2020) FAO(OS) 133/2019

Amazouz, M. S. (2019). *International Cyber Security Diplomatic Negotiations: Role of Africa in Inter-Regional Cooperation for a Global Approach on the Security and Stability of Cyberspace*. Academic Press.

Amway India Enterprises (P) Ltd v 1MG Technologies (P) Ltd, 2019 SCC OnLine Del 9061: (2019) 260 DLT 690 ¶ 308.

Andoh, D. (2019). *Communications Ministry commits to tackle cyber crime*. https://www.graphic.com.gh/news/general-news/ghananews-communications-ministry-commits-to-tackle-cyber-crime.html

Aneez, Z. T., Neyazi, A., Kalogeropoulos, A., & Nielsen, R. K. (2019). *India digital news report*. Available at: https://ora.ox.ac.uk/catalog/uuid:9c884a81-204e-415c-a87c-6818ac88442e/download_file?file_format=application%2Fpdf&safe_filename=India_DNR_FINAL.pdf

Ardhapurkar, S., Srivastava, T., Sharma, S., Chaurasiya, V., & Vaish, A. (2010). Privacy and data protection in cyberspace in Indian environment. *International Journal of Engineering Science and Technology*, 2(5), 942–951.

Arias, O., Ly, K., & Jin, Y. (2017). Security and Privacy in IoT era. In *Smart Sensors at the IoT Frontier* (pp. 351–378). Springer.

Arnaboldi, F., & Rossignoli, B. (2015). Financial innovation in banking. In *Bank risk, governance and regulation* (pp. 127–162). Palgrave Macmillan. doi:10.1057/9781137530943_5

Asawat, V. (2010). Information Technology (Amendment) Act, 2008: A New Vision through a New Change. *Available at SSRN 1680152.*

Ashalakshmi, R. K. (2022). *A Study on the growth of E-commerce during COVID-19 in India.* Available at: http://103.78.17.158:1443/jspui/handle/123456789/875

Ashok, P., Prianka, R. R., Lavanya, R., & Gokila, R. G. (2017). Dynamic Cued Click Point Algorithm to Provide Cryptographic Password Authentication. *International Journal of Pure and Applied Mathematics, 117*(21), 961–965.

Ashwini, S. (2022) *Social Media Platform Regulation in India–A Special Reference to The Information Technology (Intermediary Guidelines and Digital Media Ethics Code) Rules, 2021.* Available at: https://www.nomos-elibrary. de/10.5771/9783748929789.pdf#page=215

AU-EU Digital Economy Task Force. (2021). *New Africa-Europe Digital Economy Partnership: Accelerating the Achievement of the Sustainable Development Goals.* European Commission.

Australian Government. (2022). *National Plan to Combat Cybercrime 2022.* Australian Government Press.

Avizienis, A., Laprie, J. C., Randell, B., & Landwehr, C. (2004). Basic concepts and taxonomy of dependable and secure computing. *IEEE Transactions on Dependable and Secure Computing, 1*(1), 11–33. doi:10.1109/TDSC.2004.2

Ayitogo, N. (2022, August 22). Nigeria signs Budapest Convention on Cybercrime. *Premium Times*, 3.

Ayyagari, R. (2012). An exploratory analysis of trends of data breaches from 2005-2011: Trends and insights. *Journal of Information Privacy and Security, 8*(2), 33–56. doi:10.1080/15536548.2012.10845654

Azmoodeh, A., Dehghantanha, A., Conti, M., & Choo, K.-K. R. (2018). *Detecting crypto-ransomware in IoT networks based on energy consumption footprint.* Academic Press.

Bailey, D., & Wright, E. (2003). *Practical SCADA for industry.* Elsevier.

Bajpai, P., Sood, A. K., & Enbody, R. (2018). A key-management-based taxonomy for ransomware. *2018 APWG Symposium on Electronic Crime Research (ECrime)*, 1–12.

Balim, C., & Gunal, E. S. (2019). Automatic Detection of Smishing Attacks by Machine Learning Methods. In *2019 1st International Informatics and Software Engineering Conference (UBMYK)* (pp. 1-3). IEEE. 10.1109/UBMYK48245.2019.8965429

Baloyi, N., & Kotze, P. (2017). Are Organisations in South Africa Ready to Comply with Personal Data Protection or Privacy Legislation and Regulations? *ISTOfrica 2017 Conference Proceedings.* www.IST-Afric.org/conference2017

Banerjee, J. (2007). Cyber Warfare and the Dilemmas of International Law. *Icfai Journal of International Relations, 1*(3), 36–48.

Bara, A., & Mudzingiri, C. (2016). Financial innovation and economic growth: Evidence from Zimbabwe. *Investment Management and Financial Innovations, 13*(2), 65–75. doi:10.21511/imfi.13(2).2016.07

Baron, R. M. F. (2002). Critique of the International Cybercrime Treaty, CommLaw Conspectus. *Journal of Communications Law and Policy, 10*(2), 263–278.

Baruffa, G., Femminella, M., Pergolesi, M., & Reali, G. (2020, March). Comparison of MongoDB and Cassandra Databases for Spectrum Monitoring As-a-Service. *IEEE eTransactions on Network and Service Management, 17*(1), 346–360. doi:10.1109/TNSM.2019.2942475

Bayl-Smith, P., Taib, R., Yu, K., & Wiggins, M. (2022). Response to a phishing attack: Persuasion and protection motivation in an organizational context. *Information and Computer Security, 30*(1), 63–78. doi:10.1108/ICS-02-2021-0021

Beagle, D. (1999). Conceptualizing an information commons. *Journal of Academic Librarianship, 25*(2), 82–89. doi:10.1016/S0099-1333(99)80003-2

Bello, A. G., Murray, D., & Armarego, J. (2017). A systematic approach to investigating how information security and privacy can be achieved in BYOD environments. *Information and Computer Security, 25*(4), 475–492. doi:10.1108/ICS-03-2016-0025

Bello, A., & Mahadevan, V. (2019). A Cloud Based Conceptual Identity Management Model for Secured Internet of Things Operation. *Journal of Cyber Security and Mobility, 8*(1), 53–74. doi:10.13052/jcsm2245-1439.813

Bhardwaj, A., Avasthi, V., Sastry, H., & Subrahmanyam, G. V. B. (2016). Ransomware digital extortion: A rising new age threat. *Indian Journal of Science and Technology, 9*(14), 1–5. doi:10.17485/ijst/2016/v9i14/82936

Bhattacharya, D., & Roy, S. (2013). Contributory Liability Vis-a-Vis Strict Liability: Analyzing World Trends in ISP Liability Regime with Respect to the Indian Position. *GNLU L. Rev., 4*, 75.

Bhogill P., (2019). *5 Ways to Secure Your Business in A Multi-Cloud World*. Academic Press.

Birget, J. C., Hong, D., & Memon, N. (2006). Graphical passwords based on robust discretization. *IEEE Transactions on Information Forensics and Security, 1*(3), 395–399. doi:10.1109/TIFS.2006.879305

Blonder, G. (1996). Graphical password. *United States Patent 5559961.*

Borgia, E. (2014). The Internet of Things vision: Key features, applications, and open issues. *Computer Communications, 54*, 1–31.

Borgman, C. L. (2018). Open data, grey data, and stewardship: Universities at the privacy frontier. *Berkeley Technology Law Journal, 33*(2), 365–412.

Botha, J., Globler, M.M., Hann, J., & Eloff, M.M. (2017). *A High-Level Comparison between the South African Protection of Personal Information Act and International Data Protection Laws*. Academic Press.

Boulanin, V. (2013). *Cybersecurity and the arms industry. SIPRI Yearbook 2013: Armaments, disarmament and international security*. Oxford University Press.

Brecher, M. (1996). Introduction: Crisis, conflict, war—State of the discipline. *International Political Science Review, 17*(2), 127–139. doi:10.1177/019251296017002001

Burman, A. (2020). *Will India's proposed data protection law protect privacy and promote growth?* Carnegie Endowment for International Peace. Available at: https://www.sciencedirect.com/science/article/pii/S0267364908001337?casa_token=9qC67i5bIVYAAAAA:NuikV0iS_E06kj7gn_Jzgs3G7Z0iu-YttxjeWkY_4HEwXwi0pda2mFnhDERcJ3FmAUdv2CeY

Bushney, J., Demoulin, M., & McLelland, R. (2015). Cloud Service Contracts: An Issue of Trust. *Canadian Journal of Information and Library Science, 39*(2), 128–158. doi:10.1353/ils.2015.0009

Calandro, E. (2020, July 1). *Africa, Capacity building, Cyber diplomacy, Digital policy. Directions*. https://directionsblog.eu/partnering-with-africa-on-cyber-diplomacy/

Carbone, G. (2021). *The EU in Africa: Will Member-States follow the Lead?* https://www.euractiv.com/section/africa/opinion/the-eu-in-africa-will-member-states-follow-the-lead/https://www.euractiv.com/section/africa/opinion/the-eu-in-africa-will-member-states-follow-the-lead/

Cardservice Intern., Inc. v. McGee (1997), 950 F. Supp. 737 (E.D.Va. Jan. 16, 1997)

Cert-In. (2021). *Phishing websites hosted on NGROK platform, targeting Indian banking customers.* Available at: https://www.cert-in.org.in/

Charles, J. B., Christopher, G., Philip, C., & Donald, S. (2018). *Cybersecurity essentials.* Sybex.

Chawla, N., & Kumar, B. (2021). E-commerce and consumer protection in India: The emerging trend. *Journal of Business Ethics*, 1–24. https://link.springer.com/article/10.1007/s10551-021-04884-3

Chayal, N. M., Saxena, A., & Khan, R. (2022). A review on spreading and Forensics Analysis of Windows-Based ransomware. *Annals of Data Science*, 1-22.

Chen, Z.-G., Kang, H.-S., Yin, S.-N., & Kim, S.-R. (2017). Automatic Ransomware Detection and Analysis Based on Dynamic API Calls Flow Graph. *RACS*, 196-201.

Chikelue, Onodugo, Arachie, & Ugonna. (2020). Blockchain Technology For Cyber Security: Performance Implications On Emerging Markets Multinational Corporations, Overview Of Nigerian Internationalized Banks. *International Journal of Scientific and Technology Research*, 9(8), 246.

Chirikov, I. (2013). Research universities as knowledge networks: The role of institutional research. *Studies in Higher Education*, 38(3), 456–469. doi:10.1080/03075079.2013.773778

Chisita, T. C., & Chiparusha, B. (2021). An Institutional Repository in a Developing Country: Security and Ethical Encounters at the Bindura University of Science Education, Zimbabwe. *New Review of Academic Librarianship*, 27(1), 130–143. doi:10.1080/13614533.2020.1824925

Chlipala, A. (2016). Ur/Web: A Simple Model for Programming the Web. *Communications of the ACM Volume*, 59(August), 93–100. doi:10.1145/2958736

Christian Louboutin SAS v Nakul Bajaj, (2018) SCC OnLine Del 12215: (2018) 76 PTC 508.

Chua, J. A. (2021). Cybersecurity in the healthcare industry-A collaborative approach. *Physician Leadership Journal*, 8(1), 23–25.

Ciampa, M. (2012). *Security+ guide to network security fundamentals.* Cengage Learning.

Cisco. (2022, August 17). *What is a ddos attack? distributed denial of service.* Cisco. Retrieved from https://www.cisco.com/c/en/us/products/security/what-is-a-ddos-attack.html#~ddos-explained

Cockfield, A. J. (1999). Balancing National Interests in the Taxation of Electronic Commerce Business Profits. *Tul. L. Rev.*, 74, 133.

Cole, K., Chetty, M., LaRosa, C., Rietta, F., Schmitt, D. K., Goodman, S. E., & Atlanta, G. A. (2008). *Cybersecurity in africa: An assessment.* Sam Nunn School of International Affairs, Georgia Institute of Technology.

Companies Act 2013

Conti, M., Dragoni, N., & Lesyk, V. (2016). A Survey of Man In The Middle Attacks. *IEEE Communications Surveys and Tutorials*, 18(3), 2027–2051. doi:10.1109/COMST.2016.2548426

Contributors, E. T. (2019, November 1). *Why cybersecurity should be India's foremost priority.* Ciso. Retrieved from https://ciso.economictimes.indiatimes.com/news/why-cybersecurity-should-be-indias-foremost-priority/71847192?utm_source=Mailer&utm_medium=&utm_campaign=&dt=2019-11-01

Copyright Act 1957

Cost of Data Breach Report 2021. (2021). IBM. Retrieved from https://www.ibm.com/downloads/cas/J01XNXRO/name/05477c943ab64485.pdf

Council of Europe and Project Cybercrime@Octopus, (2015). *The state of cybercrime legislation in Africa: An overview.* Council of Europe.

Council of Europe Global Action on Cybercrime. (2016). *Strategic priorities for cooperation on cybercrime and electronic evidence in GLACY countries Adopted at the closing conference of the GLACY project on Global Action on Cybercrime Bucharest, 26-28 October 2016.* Author.

Council of Europe. (2013). *Strategic Priorities in the Cooperation against Cybercrime Adopted by the Meeting of Ministers and Senior Officials of Ministries of Interior and Security, of Ministries of Justice and of Prosecution Services of countries and areas participating in the CyberCrime@IPA project Dubrovnik, Croatia, 15 February 2013.* www.coe.int/cybercrime

Council of Europe. (2017). *Acceding to the Budapest Convention on Cybercrime: Benefits The Budapest Convention on Cybercrime.* Cybercrime Division of Council of Europe.

Council of Europe. (2017). *East African countries meet in Mauritius to address the growing threat of cybercrime in the region, 10-12 July 2017.* Council of Europe and European Union.

Council of Europe. (2018). *C-PROC activity report for the period October 2017 September 2018 Information Documents SG/Inf(2018)32.* Council of Europe.

Council of Europe. (2021). *Second African Forum on Cybercrime Policies and Legislation, investigation and International Cooperation: Conference Programme Online 28-29 June, 2021.* Council of Europe.

Craciun, V. C., Mogage, A., & Simion, E. (2018). *Trends in design of ransomware viruses.* Academic Press.

CS (OS) No. 2192/2007, Available at https://ebtc.eu/index.php/services/184-ipr/ipr-landmark-cases/183-landmark-cases-copyright

CS(OS) 1124/2008, Available at http://courtnic.nic.in/dhcorder/dhcqrydisp_O.asp?pn=95892&yr=2008

Culnan, M. J., & Williams, C. C. (2009). How ethics can enhance organizational privacy: Lessons from the ChoicePoint and TJX data breaches. *Management Information Systems Quarterly*, *33*(4), 673–689. doi:10.2307/20650322

Cybercrime Programme Office of the Council of Europe. (2019). The global state of cybercrime legislation 2013 – 2019: A cursory overview. Council of Europe.

Cybercrime Programme Office of the Council of Europe. (2021). *Cybercrime and the rule of law, including benefits of the Budapest Convention for Mauritius Keynote Address of Hon. Attorney General of the Republic of Mauritius.* Council of Europe.

Cybercrime: Britain Losing The War, Say MPs. Sky News. (2013, July 30). *Sky News.* https://news.sky.com/story/amp/cybercrime-britain-losing-the-war-say-mps-10438834

Cybercrime: Two Nigerians, six others arrested for allegedly stealing $15 million from U.S. firms. (2018, June 26). *Premium Times*. https://www.premiumtimesng.com/news/headlines/273879-cybercrime-two-nigerians-six-others-arrested-for-allegedly-stealing-15-million-from-u-s-firms.html

Cybersecurity Asia - India's digital transformation drives cybersecurity re-evaluation . (2020, February 24). Osborne Clark. Retrieved from https://www.osborneclarke.com/insights/cybersecurity-asia-indias-digital-transformation-drives-cybersecurity

Daki, H., El Hannani, A., Aqqal, A., Haidine, A., & Dahbi, A. (2017). Big Data management in smart grid: Concepts, requirements and implementation. *Journal of Big Data*, *4*(1), 1–19. doi:10.118640537-017-0070-y

Das, S. (2019, December 18). Cybersecurity Policies & Initiatives By Indian Govt In 2019. *Analytics India Mag*. Retrieved from https://analyticsindiamag.com/9-cybersecurity-policies-initiatives-by-indian-govt-in-2019/

Das, S., Nippert-Eng, C., & Camp, L. J. (2022). Evaluating user susceptibility to phishing attacks. *Information and Computer Security*, *30*(1), 1–18. doi:10.1108/ICS-12-2020-0204

Datta, P. M., & Acton, T. (2022). From disruption to ransomware: Lessons From hackers. *Journal of Information Technology Teaching Cases*.

Davis, C., Vixie, P., Goodwin, T., & Dickinson, I. (1996). *A means for expressing location information in the domain name system* (No. rfc1876). Academic Press.

Davis, D., Monrose, F., & Reiter, M. K. (2004). On user choice in graphical password schemes. In USENIX security symposium (Vol. 13, No. 2004, pp. 11-11). Academic Press.

Deebak, B. D., Al-Turjman, F., Aloqaily, M., & Alfandi, O. (2019). An authentic-based privacy preservation protocol for smart e-Healthcare systems in IoT. *IEEE Access: Practical Innovations, Open Solutions*, *7*, 135632–135649.

Demertzis, K., Tsiknas, K., Taketzis, D., Skoutas, D. N., Skianis, C., Iliadis, L., & Zoiros, K. E. (2021). Communication Network Standards for Smart Grid Infrastructures. *Network (Bristol, England)*, *1*(2), 132–145.

Department of Industrial Policy and Promotion. (2016). *('DIPP'), Press Note No. 3*. Series.

DES Cipher. (2022). https://en.wikipedia.org/wiki/Triple_DES

Deshpande, A. (2021, October 6). *'Update your KYC', a new trick adopted by cybercrooks to siphon off the money*. Available at:https://www.thehindu.com/news/national/telangana/update-your-kyc-a-new-fraud-trick-adopted-by-cybercrooks-to-siphon-off-the-money/article36856680.ece

Dhanda, S. S., Singh, B., & Jindal, P. (2020). Lightweight Cryptography: A Solution to Secure IoT. *Wireless Person. Commun.*, 1–34.

Dion, Y. L., Joshua, A. A., & Brohi, S. N. (2017). *Negation of Ransomware via Gamification and Enforcement of Standards*. Academic Press.

Direction Blog. (2020). *Africa, Capacity building, Cyber diplomacy, Digital policy*. https://directionsblog.eu/partnering-with-africa-on-cyber-diplomacy/

Drăgan, C. C., & Manulis, M. (2020). KYChain: User-controlled KYC data sharing and certification. In *Proceedings of the 35th Annual ACM Symposium on Applied Computing* (pp. 301-307). 10.1145/3341105.3373895

Duggal, P. (2016). International Conference on Cyberlaw, Cybercrime & Cybersecurity. *The International Review of Information Ethics, 25*.

Dunlap, C. J. Jr. (2008). Towards a Cyberspace Legal Regime in the Twenty-First Century: Considerations for American Cyber-Warriors. *Nebraska Law Review*, *87*, 712.

ECC. (2022). https://en.wikipedia.org/wiki/Elliptic-curve_cryptography

EFCC and Fraud suspects. (2021, December 6). *Premium Times*. https://www.premiumtimesng.com/opinion/499424-from-taking-it-with-consent-to-hacking-it-with-contempt-by-alex-otti.html

Eugen, P., & Petruț, D. (2018). Exploring the new era of cybersecurity governance. *Ovidius University Annals. Economic Sciences Series*, *18*(1), 358–363.

European Union and Council of Europe Partnership Facility. (2015). *Cybercrime and cyber security strategies in the Eastern Partnership region Results of a regional workshop Chisinau, Republic of Moldova, 12 – 14 November 2014*. www.coe.int/cybercrime

European Union Cyber Direct. (2020). *EU-Africa Cyber Consultations*. https://eucyberdirect.eu/events/eu-africa-cyber-consultations

European Union: Africa the Journey. (2020). *Cyber Security: Challenges*. https://www.euafricathejourney.com/challenge/cyber-security/#toggle-id-1

Europol Cyber Security Intelligence. (2022). *European Cybercrime Centre (EC3)*. Europol.

Faquir, D., Chouliaras, N., Sofia, V., Olga, K., & Maglaras, L. (2021). Cybersecurity in smart grids, challenges and solutions. *AIMS Electronics and Electrical Engineering*, *5*(1), 24–37.

Farahbod, K., Shayo, C., & Varzandeh, J. (2022). Six sigma and lean operations in cybersecurity management. *Journal of Business and Behavioral Sciences*, *34*(1), 99–109.

Fazlida, M. R., & Said, J. (2015). Information security: Risk, governance and implementation setback. *Procedia Economics and Finance*, *28*, 243–248. doi:10.1016/S2212-5671(15)01106-5

FBI, (2021). *Federal Bureau of Investigation, Internet Crime Report 2021*. Internet Crime Complain Center (IC[3]).

FBI. (2017). *2017 Internet Crime Report*. Federal Bureau of Investigation.

FBI. (2018). *2018 Internet Crime Report*. Federal Bureau of Investigation. https://www.ic3.gov/media/annualreport/2018_IC3Report.pdf

Fedele, A., & Roner, C. (2022). Dangerous games: A literature review on cybersecurity investments. *Journal of Economic Surveys*, *36*(1), 157–187. doi:10.1111/joes.12456

Fedosejev, A. (2015). *React.js essentials*. Packt Publishing Ltd.

Feistel Cipher. (2022). https://en.wikipedia.org/wiki/Feistel_cipher

Felten, E. W., Balfanz, D., Dean, D., & Wallach, D. S. (1997). *Web Spoofing: An Internet Con Game* (Technical report 540-96; p. 9). Princeton University.

Ferguson-Boucher, K., & Convery, N. (2011). Storing information in the cloud–A research project. *Journal of the Society of Archivists*, *32*(2), 221–239. doi:10.1080/00379816.2011.619693

Ferrag, M. A., Maglaras, L. A., Janicke, H., & Jiang, J. (2017). Authentication Protocols for Internet of Things: A Comprehensive Survey. *Security and Communication Networks*, 1–41.

Ferreira, A. (2018). Why Ransomware Needs A Human Touch. *2018 International Carnahan Conference on Security Technology (ICCST)*, 1–5.

Finch, W. (2022, 30 June). Exclusive: Cyber-criminals are hacking an average of 330 Britons A Minute: shock new research has suggested as experts warn it has reached 'epidemic proportions. *Daily Mail*. https://www.dailymail.co.uk/news/article-10970571/amp/Cyber-criminals-hacking-average-330-

Fisher, R., Porod, C., & Peterson, S. (2021). Motivating employees and organizations to adopt a cybersecurity-focused culture. *Journal of Organizational Psychology*, *21*(1), 114–131.

Foreign Exchange Management Act, 1999

Frame, W. S., & White, L. J. (2014). *Technological change, financial innovation, and diffusion in banking*. Leonard N. Stern School of Business, Department of Economics.

F-Secure. (2017). *F-Secure State of Cyber Security 2017*. F-Secure Corporation.

Gafni, R., & Tal, P. (2022). Cyberattacks against the health-care sectors during the COVID-19 pandemic. *Information and Computer Security*, *30*(1), 137–150. doi:10.1108/ICS-05-2021-0059

Gallegos-Segovia, P. L., Bravo-Torres, J. F., Larios-Rosillo, V. M., Vintimilla-Tapia, P. E., Yuquilima-Albarado, I. F., & Jara-Saltos, J. D. (2017). Social engineering as an attack vector for ransomware. *2017 CHILEAN Conference on Electrical, Electronics Engineering, Information and Communication Technologies (CHILECON)*, 1–6. 10.1109/CHILECON.2017.8229528

Gangire, Y., Da Veiga, A., & Herselman, M. (2021). Assessing Information Security Behaviour: A self – determination theory perspective. *Information & Computer Security*, *29*(4), 625–646. doi:10.1108/ICS-11-2020-0179

Garg, P. (2020). Cybersecurity breaches and cash holdings: Spillover effect. *Financial Management*, *49*(2), 503–519. doi:10.1111/fima.12274

Gattenio, C. A. (2002). Digitizing finance: Views from the leading edge. *Financial Executive*, *18*(2), 49–51.

Geer, D. E. Jr. (2010). Cybersecurity and national policy. *Harv. Nat'l Sec. J.*, *1*, i.

Georgiadou, A., Mouzakitis, S., Bounas, K., & Askounis, D. (2022). A Cyber-security culture framework for assessing organization readiness. *Journal of Computer Information Systems*, *62*(3), 452–462. doi:10.1080/08874417.2020.1845583

Gercke, M. (2016). *Understanding cybercrime: a guide for developing countries*. Academic Press.

Ghiyamipour, F. (2020). Secure graphical password based on cued click points using fuzzy logic. *Security and Privacy*, *4*(2). Advance online publication. doi:10.1002py2.140

Gomathi, S., Soni, M., Dhiman, G., Govindaraj, R., & Kumar, P. (2021). A survey on applications and security issues of blockchain technology in business sectors. *Materials Today: Proceedings*.

Govender, I., Watson, B. W. W., & Amra, J. (2021). Global virus lockdown and cybercrime rate trends: A routine activity approach. *Journal of Physics: Conference Series*, *1828*(1), 012107. doi:10.1088/1742-6596/1828/1/012107

Graham, C. (2021). Fear of the unknown with healthcare IoT devices: An exploratory study. *Information Security Journal: A Global Perspective*, *30*(2), 100–110.

Greiff, M., & Johansson, A. (2019). *Symfony vs Express: A Server-Side Framework Comparison*. Academic Press.

Grillenmeier, G. (2022). Ransomware–one of the biggest threats facing enterprises today. *Network Security*, *2022*(3). doi:10.12968/S1353-4858(22)70029-3

Grobler, M., Van Vuuren, J., & Leenen, L. (2012). Implementation of a cyber Security Policy in South Africa: Reflection on Progress and the Way Forward. *International Federation for Information Processing*, *386*, 215–225. doi:10.1007/978-3-642-33332-3_20

Gubbi, J., Buyya, R., Murusic, S., & Palaniswami, M. (2013). Internet of Things (IoT): A vision, architectural elements, and future directions. *Future Generation Computer Systems*, *29*(7), 1645–1660.

Guidelines for Smart Grid Cybersecurity, Volume 1 - Smart Grid Cybersecurity Strategy, Architecture, and High-Level Requirements . (2014). National Institute of Standards and Technology (NIST). Retrieved from https://nvlpubs.nist.gov/nistpubs/ir/2014/NIST.IR.7628r1.pdf

Gupta, D. (2020). Digital Platforms and E-Commerce in India–Challenges and Opportunities. *Available at SSRN 3577285*.

Gupta, A., Tripathi, M., Shaikh, T. J., & Sharma, A. (2019, February). A lightweight anonymous user authentication and key establishment scheme for wearable devices. *Computer Networks*, *149*, 29–42.

Gupta, M., Verma, S., & Pachare, S. (2021). An analysis of Conventional and Alternative financing—Customers' perspective. *International Journal of Finance & Economics*, 1–11. doi:10.1002/ijfe.2541

Gyem, F. (2022 September 10). ICT as a colossal symbol of Nigeria's digital economy. *Premium Times*. https://www.premiumtimesng.com/opinion/552586-ict-as-acolossal-symbol-of-nigerias-digital-economy-by-fom-gyem.html

Gyem, F. (2022, August 10). Cyber Security Initiatives for Protecting a Country. *Premium Times*. Retrieved from https://www.premiumtimesng.com/opinion/547973-cyber-security-initaitves-for-protecting-a-country-by-fom-gyem.html

Hacker in front of computer. (2020, October 26). *Forbes Africa*. https://www.forbesafrica.com/technology/2020/10/26/cybersecurity-covid-19-or-not-cybercrime-is-here-to-stay/

Haes Alhelou, H., Hamedani-Golshan, M. E., Njenda, T. C., & Siano, P. (2019). A survey on power system blackout and cascading events: Research motivations and challenges. *Energies*, *12*(4), 682. doi:10.3390/en12040682

Haislip, J., Lim, J. H., & Pinsker, R. (2021). The impact of executives' IT expertise on reported data security breaches. *Information Systems Research*, *32*(2), 318–334. doi:10.1287/isre.2020.0986

Halder, D., & Jaishankar, K. (2021). Cyber governance and data protection in India: A critical legal analysis. In *Routledge Companion to Global Cyber-Security Strategy* (pp. 337–348). Routledge. doi:10.4324/9780429399718-28

Hampton, N., & Baig, Z. A. (2015). *Ransomware: Emergence of the cyber-extortion menace*. Academic Press.

Hampton, N., Baig, Z. A., & Zeadally, S. (2018). Ransomware behavioural analysis on windows platforms. *Journal of Information Security and Applications*, *40*, 44–51. doi:10.1016/j.jisa.2018.02.008

Harbi, Y., Aliouat, Z., Harous, S., Bentaleb, A., & Refouf, A. (2019). A Review of Security in Internet of Things. *Wireless Personal Communications*, *108*, 325–344.

Harbi, Y., Aliouat, Z., Refoufi, A., Harous, S. A., & Bentaleb, A. (2019). Enhanced authentication and key management scheme for securing data transmission in the Internet of Things. *Ad Hoc Networks*, *94*(Nov), 101948.

Harrison, J. (2021, November 30) The UK is The Most Dangerous Country in Europe for Cybercrime. *The Fintech Times*. https://thefintechtimes.com/the-uk-is-the-most-dangerous-country-in-europe-for-cybercrime/?utm_source=dlvr.it&utm_medium=twitter

Haykin, S. (1998). Neural Networks: A Comprehensive Foundation (2nd ed.). Prentice Hall PTR.

Hepfer, M., & Powell, T. C. (2020). Make cybersecurity a strategic asset. *MIT Sloan Management Review*, *62*(1), 40–45.

Hinch, R., Probert, W., Nurtay, A., Kendall, M., Wymant, C., Hall, M., Fraser, C., Lythgoe, K., Cruz, A. B., Zhao, L., Stewart, A., Ferretti, L., Parker, M., Meroueh, A., Mathias, B., Stevenson, S., Montero, D., Warren, J., Mather, N. K., . . . Fraser, C. (2020). Effective configurations of a digital contact tracing app: A report to NHSX (NHSX Report). The Conversation Trust (UK). Available online: https://cdn.theconversation.com/static_files/files/1009/Report_-_Effectiv_App_Configurations.pdf

Hinz, O., Nofer, M., Schiereck, D., & Trillig, J. (2015). The influence of data theft on the share prices and systematic risk consumer electronics companies. *Information & Management*, *52*(3), 337–347. doi:10.1016/j.im.2014.12.006

Hoffman, M. H. (2003). The Legal Status and Responsibilities of Private Internet Users Under the Law of Armed Conflict: A Primer for the Unwary on the Shape of Law to Come. *Wash. U. Global Stud. L. Rev.*, *2*, 415.

Homayoun, S., Dehghantanha, A., Ahmadzadeh, M., Hashemi, S., Khayami, R., Choo, K.-K. R., & Newton, D. E. (2019). DRTHIS: Deep ransomware threat hunting and intelligence system at the fog layer. *Future Generation Computer Systems*, *90*, 94–104. doi:10.1016/j.future.2018.07.045

Hong, Y., & Furnell, S. (2021). Understanding cybersecurity behavioral habits: Insights from situational support. *Journal of Information Security and Applications*, *57*, 102710. doi:10.1016/j.jisa.2020.102710

Horovic, S., Boban, M., & Stipanovic, I. (2021). Cybersecurity and criminal justice in digital society. In *Economic and Social Development: Book of Proceedings*. Varazdin: Varazdin Development and Entrepreneurship Agency (VADEA). https://umasslowell.idm.oclc.org/login?url=https://www-proquest-com.umasslowell.idm.oclc.org/conference-papers-proceedings/cybersecurity-criminal-justice-digital-society/docview/2508649367/se-2?accountid=14575

Hu, Y. C., Perrig, A., & Johnson, D. B. (2003). Packet leashes: A defense against wormhole attacks in wireless networks. In *Twenty-Second Annual Joint Conference of the IEEE Computer and Communications. INFOCOM 2003*. IEEE.

Huang, S. Q., & Zhang, H. M. (2008). Research on Improved MVC Design pattern based on Struts and XSL. In *2008 International Symposium on Information Science and Engineering* (Vol. 1, pp. 451-455). IEEE. 10.1109/ISISE.2008.252

Hull, G., John, H., & Arief, B. (2019). Ransomware deployment methods and analysis: Views from a predictive model and human responses. *Crime Science*, *8*(1), 2. doi:10.118640163-019-0097-9

Humayun, M., Jhanjhi, N., Alsayat, A., & Ponnusamy, V. (2020). *Internet of things and ransomware: Evolution, mitigation and prevention. Egyptian Informatics Journal.* doi:10.1016/j.eij.2020.05.003

Information Technology (Intermediary Guidelines and Digital Media Ethics Code) Rules 2021, Notification no. G.S.R. 139(E), Available at: https://mib.gov.in/sites/default/files/IT%28Intermediary%20Guidelines%20and%20Digital%20Media%20Ethics%20Code%29%20Rules%2C%202021%20English.pdf

Information Technology Act 2000

Insider-related Cybersecurity Incidents in East Africa Increase by 55% in 3 Months. (2020, June 29). *News Security Technology*. https://pctechmag.com/2020/06/insider-related-cybersecurity-incidents-in-east-africa/

Interpol's Cybercrime Directorate. (2021). *African Cyber Threat Assessment Report: Interpol's Key Insight into Cybercrime in Africa*. Interpol Publications.

Interpol's Cybercrime Directorate. (2021). *National Cybercrime Strategy: Guide Book*. Author.

Iyer, S. (2011). Cyber security for smart grid, cryptography, and privacy. *International Journal of Digital Multimedia Broadcasting*, *2011*, 2011. doi:10.1155/2011/372020

Jacqueline, F. (2009). *Cybercrime in South Africa: Investigating and Prosecuting Cyber Crime the Benefits of Public-Private Partnerships*. Price Water House Coopers.

Jain, A. K., & Gupta, B. B. (2018). Rule-based framework for detection of smishing messages in mobile environment. *Procedia Computer Science*, *125*, 617–623. doi:10.1016/j.procs.2017.12.079

Jain, A. K., Sahoo, S. R., & Kaubiyal, J. (2021). Online social networks security and privacy: Comprehensive review and analysis. *Complex & Intelligent Systems*, *7*(5), 2157–2177.

Jamil, Z. (2016). Comparative analysis of the Malabo Convention of the African Union and the Budapest Convention on Cybercrime. Bucharest: Council of Europe.

Janakiraman, R., Lim, J. H., & Rishika, R. (2018). The effect of a data breach announcement on customer behavior: Evidence from a multichannel retailer. *Journal of Marketing*, *82*(2), 85–105. doi:10.1509/jm.16.0124

Jha, S. K., & Kumar, S. S. (2022). Cybersecurity in the Age of the Internet of Things: An Assessment of the Users' Privacy and Data Security. In *Expert Clouds and Applications* (pp. 49–56). Springer. doi:10.1007/978-981-16-2126-0_5

Jideani, P. C. (2018). *Towards A Cybersecurity Framework For South African E-Retail Organisations* [Master's thesis]. Faculty of Informatics and Design at the Cape Peninsula University of Technology, South Africa.

John Wiley & Sons. (2013). *The Ernst & Young Tax Guide 2014*. Author.

Jose, B., & Abraham, S. (2020). Performance analysis of NoSQL and relational databases with MongoDB and MySQL. *Materials Today: Proceedings*, *24*, 2036–2043. doi:10.1016/j.matpr.2020.03.634

Joshi, A. P., Han, M., & Wang, Y. (2018). A survey on security and privacy issues of blockchain technology. *Mathematical Foundations of Computing, 1*(2), 121.

Kalia, P., Arora, R., & Law, P. (2016). Information Technology Act in India: e-Commerce value chain analysis. *NTUT Journal of Intellectual Property Law and Management*, *5*(2), 55–97.

Kamath, N. (2013). Should The Law Beat A Retweet? Rationalising Liability Standards For Sharing Of Digital. *Indian Journal of Law and Technology*, *9*(1), 4.

Karlof, C., & Wagner, D. (2003). Secure routing in wireless sensor networks: Attacks and countermeasures. *Ad Hoc Networks*, *1*(2), 293–315.

Karlsson, O. (2021). *A Performance Comparison Between ASP.NET Core and Express.js for creating Web APIs* (Dissertation). Retrieved from http://urn.kb.se/resolve?urn=urn:nbn:se:hj:diva-54286

Kaspersky. (2022). *What is cybercrime?* https://www.kaspersky.com/resource-center/threats/what-is-cybercrime

Kaspersky. (2022, August 17). *Backdoor Computer Malware in Africa skyrocketed in the second quarter of 2022*. https://kaspersky.africa-newsroom.com/press/backdoor-computer-malware-in-africa-skyrocketed-in-the-second-quarter-of-2022?lange=en

Kasturi, R., & Pachaiyappan, V. (2018). Block Chain Technology (DLT Technique) for KYC in FinTech Domain: A Survey. *International Journal of Pure and Applied Mathematics*, *119*, 259–265.

Kaushik, K., & Dahiya, S. (2018). Security and Privacy in IoT based EBusiness and Retail. *2018 International Conference on System Modeling & Advancement in Research Trends (SMART)*, 78–81. 10.1109/SYSMART.2018.8746961

Kaushik, K., & Singh, K. (2020). Security and Trust in IoT Communications: Role and Impact. In S. Choudhury, R. Mishra, R. Mishra, & A. Kumar (Eds.), *Intelligent Communication, Control and Devices. Advances in Intelligent Systems and Computing, 989*. Springer. doi:10.1007/978-981-13-8618-3_81

Kawoosa, A. I., & Prashar, D. (2021, January). A review of cyber securities in smart grid technology. In *2021 2nd International Conference on Computation, Automation and Knowledge Management (ICCAKM)* (pp. 151-156). IEEE. 10.1109/ICCAKM50778.2021.9357698

Kessler, D. J., Ross, S., & Hickok, E. (2014). A Comparative Analysis of Indian Privacy Law and the Asia-Pacific Economic Cooperation Cross-Border Privacy Rules. *Nat'l L. Sch. India Rev., 26*, 31.

Kharchenko, V., Sklyar, V., Brezhnev, E., Boyarchuk, A., Starov, O., & Phillips, C. (2016, June). University-Industry Cooperation in Cyber Security Domain: Multi-Model Approach, Tools and Cases. In *Proceedings of the University-Industry Interaction Conference: Challenges and Solutions for Fostering Entrepreneurial Universities and Collaborative Innovation* (pp. 265-283). Academic Press.

Khatoun, R and Zeadally, S (2017) Cybersecurity and Privacy Solutions in Smart Cities Enabling Mobile and Wireless Technologies for Smart Cities: Part 2. *IEEE Communications Magazines*.

Khumalo, B. N., & Baloyi, C. (2017). The possible benefits of freedom of information laws to the records management landscape in the ESARBICA region. *Information Development*, 1–5.

Kitchenham, B., & Charters, S. (2007). *Guidelines for performing Systematic Literature Reviews in Software Engineering*. Technical Report EBSE 2007-001. https://www.elsevier.com/__data/promis_misc/525444systematicreviewsguide.pdf

Klared, A. S. (2015). 'Isn't it information assets we're really talking about?' A discourse analysis of a panel discussion on digital archives. *Architectural Record, 36*(2), 167–178. doi:10.1080/23257962.2015.1058245

Klein, D. V. (1990, August). Foiling the cracker: A survey of, and improvements to, password security. *Proceedings of the 2nd USENIX Security Workshop*, 5-14.

Klett, E. (2018). Theory, regulation and practice in Swedish digital records appraisal. *Records Management Journal, 29*(1/2), 86 – 102.

Kostopoulos, G. K. (2017). Cyberspace and Cybersecurity (2nd ed.). Taylor & Francis.

Kotsiantis, S. (2007). Supervised Machine Learning: A Review of Classification Techniques. *Informatica Journal, 31*, 249–268.

Krishnaveni, R., & Meenakumari, J. (2010). Usage of ICT for Information Administration in Higher Education Institutions – A study. *International Journal of Environmental Sciences and Development, 1*(3), 282–286. doi:10.7763/IJESD.2010.V1.55

Kristensen, K. S. (2008). The absolute protection of our citizens: Critical infrastructure protection and the practice of security. In M. Dunn Cavelty & K. S. Kristensen (Eds.), *The politics of securing the homeland: Critical infrastructure, risk and securitisation* (pp. 63–83). Routledge.

Kritzinger, E., & Solms, S. (2012). A Framework for Cyber Security in Africa. *Journal of Information Assurance and Cybersecurity*. http://www.ibimapublishing.com/journals/JIACS/jiacs.html

Kshetri, N. (2016). Cybersecurity and Development, Markets, *Globalization &. Developmental Review, 1*(2). https://digitalcommons.uri.edu/mgdr/vol1/iss2/3

Kshetri, N. (2019). Cybercrime and Cybersecurity in Africa. *Journal of Global Information Technology Management*. Advance online publication. doi:10.1080/1097198X.2019.1603527

Kudo, M., Araki, Y., Nomiyama, H., Saito, S., & Sohda, Y. (2007). Best practices and tools for personal information compliance management. *IBM Systems Journal*, *46*(2), 235–252. doi:10.1147j.462.0235

Kumar, V. V., & Prasad, N. C. (2022). E-Commerce: Problems and Prospects. *Specialusis Ugdymas*, *1*(43), 1621-1628. Available at: https://www.sumc.lt/index.php/se/article/view/183

Kumar, A., & Jha, A. (2022). Information Technology Rules, 2021 of India in dock! A Critical evaluation of the Ã¢ Â Â Guidelines for Intermediaries and Digital Media Ethics Code. *Global Media Journal*, *20*(48), 1–9.

Kumar, M., & Nikhil, P. A. (2020). A blockchain based approach for an efficient secure KYC process with data sovereignty. *Int J Sci Technol Res*, *9*, 3403–3407.

Kumar, N. M., & Mallick, P. K. (2018). Blockchain technology for security issues and challenges in IoT. *Procedia Computer Science*, *132*, 1815–1823.

Kumar, S., Satheesh, N., Mahapatra, A., Sahoo, S., & Mahapatra, K. (2019). Physical unclonable functions for on-chip instruction: Enhancing the security of the internal joint test action group network. *IEEE Consumer Electronics Magazine*, *8*(4), 62–66.

Kundu, I. (2021). The Copyright System Is Unable to Effectively Respond to the Challenges Posed by Digitalization and the Internet. *Supremo Amicus, 27*, 201. Available at: https://www.researchgate.net/profile/Irina-Atanasova-3/publication/339077032_COPYRIGHT_INFRINGEMENT_IN_DIGITAL_ENVIRONMENT/links/5e3c1f89458515072d838a02/COPYRIGHT-INFRINGEMENT-IN-DIGITAL-ENVIRONMENT.pdf

Kundy, E. D., & Lyimo, B. J. (2019). Cyber security threats in higher learning Institutions in Tanzania, A case of University of Ausha and Tumaini University Makumira. Olva Academy – School of Researchers, 2(3).

Kwon, J., & Johnson, M. E. (2018). Meaningful healthcare security: Does meaningful-use attestation improve information security performance? *Management Information Systems Quarterly*, *42*(4), 1043–1067.

Larose, R., Mastro, D., & Eastin, M. S. (2001). Understanding Internet Usage: A Social-Cognitive Approach to Uses and Gratifications. *Social Science Computer Review*, *19*(4), 395–413. doi:10.1177/089443930101900401

Lashkari, A. H. (2014). GPIP: a new graphical password based on image portions. *18th International Conference on Circuits Systems Communications and Computers (CSCC 2014)*.

Lastdrager, E. E. (2014). Achieving a consensual definition of phishing based on a systematic review of the literature. *Crime Science*, *3*(1), 9. Advance online publication. doi:10.118640163-014-0009-y

Le Nguyen, C., & Golman, W. (2021). Diffusion of the Budapest Convention on cybercrime and the development of cybercrime legislation in Pacific Island countries: 'Law on the books' vs 'law in action'. *Computer Law & Security Review*, *40*, 105521. doi:10.1016/j.clsr.2020.105521

Lee, H., Kang, D., Ryu, J., Won, D., Kim, H., & Lee, Y. (2020, June). A three-factor anonymous user authentication scheme for Internet of Things environments. *Journal of Information Security Application.*, *52*, 102494.

Lee, I. (2022). An analysis of data breaches in the U.S. healthcare industry: Diversity, trends, and risk profiling. *Information Security Journal*, *31*(3), 346–358. doi:10.1080/19393555.2021.2017522

Lee, I., & Shin, Y. J. (2018). FinTech: Ecosystem, business models, investment decisions, and challenges. *Business Horizons*, *61*(1), 35–46. doi:10.1016/j.bushor.2017.09.003

Leonhardt, M. (2021). *Online fraud attempt are up 25% in the US - here's why*. Available at: https://www.cnbc.com/2021/06/03/why-online-fraud-attempts-are-up-25percent-in-the-us.html

Lerner, J., & Tufano, P. (2011). The consequences of financial innovation: A counterfactual research agenda. *Annual Review of Financial Economics*, *3*(1), 41–85. doi:10.1146/annurev.financial.050808.114326

Li, J. H. (2018). Cyber security meets artificial intelligence: A survey. *Frontiers of Information Technology & Electronic Engineering*, *19*(12), 1462–1474. doi:10.1631/FITEE.1800573

Lika, R. A., Murugiah, D., Brohi, S. N., & Ramasamy, D. (2018). NotPetya: Cyber Attack Prevention through Awareness via Gamification. *2018 International Conference on Smart Computing and Electronic Enterprise (ICSCEE)*, 1–6. 10.1109/ICSCEE.2018.8538431

Lin, I. C., & Liao, T. C. (2017). A survey of blockchain security issues and challenges. *International Journal of Network Security*, *19*(5), 653–659.

Liu, T., Wang, Y., Li, Y., Tong, X., Qi, L., & Jiang, N. (2020, September). Privacy protection based on stream cipher for spatiotemporal data in IoT. *IEEE Internet Things J.*, *7*(9), 7928–7940.

Li, Y., & Liu, Q. (2021). A comprehensive review study of cyber-attacks and cyber security; Emerging trends and recent developments. *Energy Reports*, *7*, 8176–8186. doi:10.1016/j.egyr.2021.08.126

Li, Z., & Liao, Q. (2022). Preventive portfolio against data-selling ransomware—A game theory of encryption and deception. *Computers & Security*, *116*, 102644. doi:10.1016/j.cose.2022.102644

Lueth, K. L. (2018, August). *State of the IoT 2018: Number of IoT devices now at 7B - Market accelerating*. IOT Analytics. https://iot-analytics.com/product/state-of-the-iot-02-2017/

Luo, X., & Liao, Q. (2007). Awareness Education as the Key to Ransomware Prevention. *Information Systems Security*, *16*(4), 195–202. doi:10.1080/10658980701576412

Madan, S., Sofat, S., & Bansal, D. (2022). Tools and Techniques for Collection and Analysis of Internet-of-Things malware: A systematic state-of-art review. *Journal of King Saud University-Computer and Information Sciences*.

Maiorca, D., Mercaldo, F., Giacinto, G., Visaggio, C. A., & Martinelli, F. (2017). R-PackDroid: API Package-based Characterization and Detection of Mobile Ransomware. *SAC*, 1718-1723.

Manda, T. D. (2018). *Manda Maturity of Cybersecurity initiatives in Malawi: A comparison with the drive for fast and ubiquitous Internet connectivity*. DiploFoundation. www.diplomacy.edu

Maria, E., & Haryani, E. (2011). Audit Model Development of Academic Information System: Case Study on Academic Information System of Satya Wacaa. *Journal of Arts, Science & Commerce*, *11*, 12–24.

Marks & Spencer's V. One-in-A Million (1998) FSR 265

Marsal, J. (2021, July 20). *What is DevSecOps? And what you need to do it well*. Dynatrace. Retrieved from https://www.dynatrace.com/news/blog/what-is-devsecops/#:~:text=DevSecOps%20is%20the%20seamless%20integration,any%20specific%20technology%20or%20techniques

Marutha, N. (2019). The application of legislative framework for the management of medical records in Limpopo Province, South Africa. *Information Development*, *35*(4), 1–13. doi:10.1177/0266666918772006

Masmali, H., & Miah, J. S. (2021). Emergent Insgith of the Cyber Security Management for Saudi Arabia Universities: A Content Analysis. *Pacific. Journal of the Association for Information Systems*, *13*(3), 1–18.

McLoughlin, J. (2018). *J2 Software supports global reports of alarming increase in numbers of e-mail attacks: South Africa is no exception.* https://www.j2.co.za/j2-software-news/294-j2-software-supports-global-reports-of-alarming-increase-in-numbers-of-e-mail-attacks-south-africa-is-no-exception

McLoughlin, M. (2022). *Development of 'smart' university campus is within reach.* University World News. https://www.universityworldnews.com/page.php?page=UW_Mai

Mehta, S., Sharma, A., Chawla, P., & Soni, K. (2021, May). The Urgency of Cyber Security in Secure Networks. In *2021 5th International Conference on Intelligent Computing and Control Systems (ICICCS)* (pp. 315-322). IEEE. 10.1109/ICICCS51141.2021.9432092

Merges, R. P. (2007). Software and patent scope: Report from the middle innings. *Texas Law Review, 85*(7), 1627–1676.

Mihindukulasuriya, R. (2020, March 3). *India was the most cyber-attacked country in the world for three months in 2019.* The Print. Retrieved from https://theprint.in/tech/india-was-the-most-cyber-attacked-country-in-the-world-for-three-months-in-2019/374622/

Mills, A. J., & Plangger, K. (2015). Social media strategy for online service brands. *Service Industries Journal, 35*(10), 521–536.

Mishra, R. C. (2002). *Cyber crime: impact in the new millenium.* Authorspress.

MizrachiA. (2021). https://frontegg.com/author/aviadmizrachi

Modares, H., Salleh, R., & Moravejosharieh, A. (2011). Overview of security issues in wireless sensor networks. *Third International Conference on Computational Intelligence, Modelling and Simulation (CIMSiM)*, 308–311.

Mohan, G., & Mini, S. (2021). *The Various issues in Cyberspace that are not Addressed by the copyright Laws, from the Indian perspective.* Available at: http://14.139.185.167:8080/jspui/bitstream/123456789/448/1/LLM_0220023_CAL.pdf

Moore, C. (2016). Detecting ransomware with honeypot techniques. *2016 Cybersecurity and Cyberforensics Conference (CCC)*, 77–81. 10.1109/CCC.2016.14

Morabito, V. (2017). *Business innovation through blockchain.* Springer International Publishing.

Moskai, J. E. (2015). A model for Establishing a Cybersecurity Centre of Excellence. *Information Systems Education Journal, 13*(6), 97–103.

Mullon, A. P., & Ngoepe, M. (2019). An integrated framework to elevate information governance to a national level in South Africa. *Records Management Journal, 29*(1/2), 103–116. doi:10.1108/RMJ-09-2018-0030

Murugesan, S. (2019), The cybersecurity renaissance: security threats, risks, and safeguards. *IEEE ICNL, 14*(1), 33-40. Available at: http://ieeecs-madras.managedbiz.com/icnl/19q1/p33-p40.pdf

Nappinai, N. S. (2010). Cyber Crime Law in India: Has Law kept pace with emerging trends? An empirical study. *Journal of International Commercial Law and Technology, 5*(1). Available at: https://media.neliti.com/media/publications/28731-EN-cyber-crime-law-in-india-has-law-kept-pace-with-emerging-trends-an-empirical-stu.pdf

Nel, F., & Drevin, L. (2019). Key Elements of an information security culture in organizations. *Information & Computer Security, 27*(2), 146–164. doi:10.1108/ICS-12-2016-0095

Nelson, D. L., Reed, V. S., & Walling, J. R. (1976). Pictorial superiority effect. *Journal of Experimental Psychology. Human Learning and Memory, 2*(5), 523–528. doi:10.1037/0278-7393.2.5.523 PMID:1003125

Newsome, J., Shi, E., Song, D., & Perrig, A. (2004). The sybil attack in sensor networks: Analysis & defenses. *Proceedings of the 3rd International Symposium on Information Processing in Sensor Networks*, 259–268.

Ngila, F. (2021, December 16). Why firms must invest more in cyber security. *Business Daily*. https://www.businessdailyafrica.com/bd/corporate/technology/firms-must-invest-more-cyber-security-3654090?view=htmlamp

Nigeria is experiencing unprecedented cyber attacks. (2021, September 7). *Business Day*. https://businessday.ng/amp/news/article/nigeria-is-experiencing-unprecedented-cyber-attacks

Nikhita, G. R., & Ugander, G. J. R. (2014). *A Study of Cyber Security Challenges and Its Emerging Trends On Latest Technologies*. https://www.researchgate.net/publication/260126665

Ning, W., Liming, L., Yanzhang, W., Yi-bing, W., & Jing, W. (2008). Research on the web information system development platform based on MVC design pattern. In *2008 IEEE/WIC/ACM International Conference on Web Intelligence and Intelligent Agent Technology* (Vol. 3, pp. 203-206). IEEE. 10.1109/WIIAT.2008.64

Nord V. P. N. (2021). *Cybersecurity Risk Index*. nordvpn.com/cri/

Norvill, R., Steichen, M., Shbair, W. M., & State, R. (2019). Blockchain for the simplification and automation of KYC result sharing. In *2019 IEEE International Conference on Blockchain and Cryptocurrency (ICBC)* (pp. 9-10). IEEE. 10.1109/BLOC.2019.8751480

Noura, H., Couturier, R., Pham, C., & Chehab, A. (2019). Lightweight stream cipher scheme for resource-constrained IoT devices. *Proc. Int. Conf. Wireless Mobile Comput., Netw. Commun. (WiMob)*, 1–8.

Nweze-Iloekwe, N. (2022). *The Legal and Regulatory Aspect of International Cybercrime and Cybersecurity: Limits and Challenges* [Dissertation]. The Golden Gate University School Of Law, Department Of International Legal Studies, In Fulfillment Of The Requirement For The Conferment Of The Degree Of Scientiae Juridicae Golden Gate University School of Law.

O'Kane, P., Sezer, S., & Carlin, D. (2018). Evolution of Ransomware. *IET Networks*, 7(5), 321–327. doi:10.1049/iet-net.2017.0207

Oh, S., Karina, S., Johnston, R. B., Lee, H., & Lim, B. (2006). A Stakeholder Perspective on Successful Electronic Payment Systems Diffusion. *Hawaii International Conference on System Sciences (HICSS – 39)*.

Ojha, S. (2021, June 7). *SBI warns of KYC fraud. 3 things you must do to you're your account safe*. Available at: https://www.livemint.com/money/personal-finance/sbi-warns-of-kyc-update-fraud-3-things-you-must-do-to-keep-your-account-safe-11623896065849.html

Okonji, E. (2022, June 8). Rising Trends of Cyber attacks in Nigeria. *Thisdaylive*. https://www.com/amp/s/www.thisdaylive.com/index.php/2022/06/08/rising-trends-of-cyberattacks-in-nigeria-2/amp

Olatunbosun, B. S., Edwards, J. N., & Martineau, D. C. (2018). Capturing The Existential Cyber Security Threats from the Sub- Saharan Africa Zone through Literature Database. KSU *Proceedings on CyberSecurity Education, Research and Practice, 3*. https://digitalcommons.kennesaw.edu/ccerp/2018/research/3

Online impersonation becoming a major threat to businesses on social media-Cyber Security Authority. (2022, July 21). *Joy Business*. https://www.myjoyonline.com/online-impersonation-becoming-a-major-threat-to-businesses-on-social-media-cyber-security-authority/

Onyekpeze, O., Olumide Owolabi, O., & Bisalla, H. I. (2021). Classification of Cybersecurity Incidents in Nigeria Using Machine Learning Methods *Covenant Journal of Informatics & Tongxin Jishu, 9*(2).

Opara, U. E., & Dieli, J.O. (2021). Enterprise Cyber Security Challenges to Medium and Large Firms: An analysis. *I.J of Electroncis and Information Engineering*, *13*(2), 77 – 85.

Padhy, N. P., & Jena, P. (2022). *Introduction to Smart Grid (MOOC)*. NPTEL. https://nptel.ac.in/courses/108107113

Pal, K. (2019). Algorithmic Solutions for RFID Tag Anti-Collision Problem in Supply Chain Management. *Procedia Computer Science*, 929-934.

Pal, K. (2021a). Privacy, Security and Policies: A Review of Problems and Solutions with Blockchain-Based Internet of Things Applications in Industrial Industry. *Procedia Computer Science*.

Pal, K. (2021b). A Novel Frame-Slotted ALOHA Algorithm for Radio Frequency Identification System in Supply Chain Management. *Procedia Computer Science*, 871-876. 10.1016/j.procs.2021.03.110

Pal, K. (2022a). Application of Game Theory in Blockchain-Based Healthcare Information System. In Prospects of Blockchain Technology for Accelerating Scientific Advancement in Healthcare. IGI Global.

Pal, K. (2022b). A Decentralized Privacy Preserving Healthcare Blockchain for IoT, Challenges and Solutions. In Prospects of Blockchain Technology for Accelerating Scientific Advancement in Healthcare. IGI Global.

Pal, K. (2022b). Semantic Interoperability in Internet of Things: Architecture, Protocols, and Research Challenges. In Management Strategies for Sustainability, New Knowledge Innovation, and Personalized Products and Services. IGI Global.

Pal, K. (2022d). Cryptography and Blockchain Solutions for Security Protection of Internet of Things Applications. In Information Security Practices for the Internet of Things, 5G, and Next-Generation Wireless Networks. IGI Global.

Pal, K., & Yasar, A. (2020b). Semantic Approach to Data Integration for an Internet of Things Supporting Apparel Supply Chain Management. *Procedia Computer Science*, 197 - 204.

Pal, K., & Yasar, K. (2020a). Internet of Things and Blockchain Technology in Apparel Manufacturing Supply Chain Data Management. *Procedia Computer Science*, 450 - 457.

Palmieri, M., Shortland, N., & McGarry, P. (2021). Personality and online deviance: The role of reinforcement sensitivity theory in cybercrime. *Computers in Human Behavior*, *120*, 106745. doi:10.1016/j.chb.2021.106745

Panagiotis, T., Georgios, C., Silvia, P., Prokopios, D., Lauri, P., Dimitra, L., & Andrea, D. (2017). *Cybersecurity in the EU Common Security and Defence Policy (CSDP) Challenges and risks for the EU: Study EPRS/STOA/SER/16/214N*. European Union.

PanditN. (2021). https://www.c-sharpcorner.com/article/what-and-why-reactjs

Papadopoulos, T. N., Durmus, E., & Memon, N. (2017). Illusion (2017). PIN: Shoulder-surfing resistant authentication using hybrid images. *IEEE Transactions on Information Forensics and Security*, *12*(12), 2875–2889. doi:10.1109/TIFS.2017.2725199

Parimala, S., & Ramachandran, M. (2022, May). A study on E-consumer awareness towards E-commerce Consumer Protection Act, 2019. In AIP Conference Proceedings: Vol. 2393. *No. 1* (p. 020110). AIP Publishing LLC.

Parra Moyano, J., & Ross, O. (2017). KYC optimization using distributed ledger technology. *Business & Information Systems Engineering*, *59*(6), 411–423. doi:10.100712599-017-0504-2

Patel, D., Suslade, H., Rane, J., Prabhu, P., Saluja, S., & Busnel, Y. (2021). KYC as a Service (KASE)—A Blockchain Approach. In *Advances in Machine Learning and Computational Intelligence* (pp. 795–803). Springer. doi:10.1007/978-981-15-5243-4_76

Patent Act Trademark Act 1999

Patil, J. (2022). Cyber Laws in India: An Overview. *Indian Journal of Law and Legal Research*, *4*(01), 1391–1411.

PC Technology. (2020). *News insider-related Cybersecurity Incidents in East Africa Increase by 55% in 3 Months*. https://pctechmag.com/2020/06/insider-related-cybersecurity-incidents-in-east-africa/

Peachey, K. (2021). *Fraudsters steal £4m a day as crime surges*. BBC News. Available at: https://www.bbc.com/news/business-58649698

Phiri, J. M., & Tough, G. A. (2018). Managing university records in the World of Governance. *Records Management Journal*, *28*(1), 47–61. doi:10.1108/RMJ-11-2016-0042

Pipikaite, A., Gretchen, B., Akshay, J., & Jurgens, J. (2022). *Global Cybersecurity Outlook 2022: Insight Report*. World Economic Forum.

Pisoni, G., Molnár, B., & Tarcsi, A. (2021, February). Comparison of two technologies for digital payments: Challenges and future directions. In *International Conference on Remote Engineering and Virtual Instrumentation* (pp. 478-484). Springer.

Playboy Enterprises, Inc. v. Frena (1993) 839 F. Supp. 1552 M.D. Fla.

Pop, D. P., & Altar, A. (2014). Designing an MVC Model for Rapid Web Application Development 24th DAAAM International Symposium on Intelligent Manufacturing and Automation, 2013. *Procedia Engineering*, *69*, 1172–1179. doi:10.1016/j.proeng.2014.03.106

Posthumus, S., & Von Solms, R. (2004). A framework for the governance of information security. *Computers & Security*, *23*(8), 638–646. doi:10.1016/j.cose.2004.10.006

Potgieter, P. (2019). The Awareness Behaviour of Students On Cyber Security Awareness by Using Social Media Platforms; A Case Study at Central University of Technology. *Kalpa Publications in Computing*, *12*, 272–280. doi:10.29007/gprf

Prakash, G. A., Sundaram, A., & Sreeya, B. (2021). Online exploitation of children and the role of intermediaries: An Indian legislative and policy perspective. *International Review of Law Computers & Technology*, 1–22.

Prasad, R., & Rohokale, V. (2020). Artificial intelligence and machine learning in cyber security. In *Cyber Security: The Lifeline of Information and Communication Technology* (pp. 231–247). Springer. doi:10.1007/978-3-030-31703-4_16

Principles for Financial Market Infrastructures . (2012). BIS. Retrieved from https://www.bis.org/cpmi/publ/d101a.pdf

Priya, G. J., & Saradha, S. (2021, February). Fraud detection and prevention using machine learning algorithms: a review. In *2021 7th International Conference on Electrical Energy Systems (ICEES)* (pp. 564-568). IEEE. 10.1109/ICEES51510.2021.9383631

Prokofyeva, N., & Boltunova, V. (2017). Analysis and practical application of PHP frameworks in development of web information systems. *Procedia Computer Science*, *104*, 51–56. doi:10.1016/j.procs.2017.01.059

Purba, J., Samuel, S., & Budiono, S. (2021). Collaboration of digital payment usage decision in COVID-19 pandemic situation: Evidence from Indonesia. *International Journal of Data and Network Science*, *5*(4), 557–568. doi:10.5267/j.ijdns.2021.8.012

Radanliev, P., De, R. D., Van, K. M., Uchenna, A., Pete, B., Eirini, A., & Nurse, J. R. (2020). Dynamic real-time risk analytics of uncontrollable states in complex Internet of Things systems: Cyber risk at the edge. *Environment Systems & Decisions*, *41*(2), 236–247. doi:10.100710669-020-09792-x PMID:33251087

Raghav, M., & Dewani, N. D. (2020). Intellectual Property Rights Protection in Cyberspace: An Indian Perspective. In *Impact of Digital Transformation on Security Policies and Standards* (pp. 169-182). IGI Global. Available at: https://www.igi-global.com/chapter/intellectual-property-rights-protection-in-cyberspace/251954

Ramadan, R. A., Aboshosha, B. W., Jalawi, S. A., Alzahrani, A. J., El-Sayed, A., & Dessouky, M. M. (2021). Cybersecurity and countermeasures at the time of pandemic. *Journal of Advanced Transportation, 2021*, 1–19. doi:10.1155/2021/6627264

Ramanna, A. (2002). Policy Implications of India's Patent Reforms: Patent Applications in the Post-1995 Era. *Economic and Political Weekly*, 2065–2075.

Rankhambe, B. P., & Khanuja, H. (2021). Hassle-Free and Secure e-KYC System Using Distributed Ledger Technology. *International Journal of Next-Generation Computing*, 74-90.

Rao, A. (2019). *Cyber Security-a New Secured Password Generation Algorithm with Graphical Authentication, and Alphanumeric Passwords Along with Encryption* [Doctoral dissertation]. Old Dominion University.

Report, S. (2018). *Africa Cybersecurity Report and Cybersecurity Skill Gaps*. Bostwana.

Ribeiro, J. V. A. (2022). A brief overview of ransomware behavior analysis challenges. *Brazilian Journal of Development, 8*(5), 38275–38280. doi:10.34117/bjdv8n5-365

Ricart, R. J. (2020). *European Union's foreign policy and technology in Africa*. Real Instituto Elcano Global Presence. https://www.realinstitutoelcano.org/en/european-unions-foreign-policy-and-technology-in-africa/

Ringhoff, J., & Torreblanca, J. I. (2022). *Policy Brief: European Power: The geopolitics of technology: How the EU can become a global player*. https://ecfr.eu/publication/the-geopolitics-of-technology-how-the-eu-can-become-a-global-player/?amp

RSA. (2022). https://en.wikipedia.org/wiki/RSA

Rugo, A., Ardagna, C. A., & Ioini, N. E. (2022). A Security Review in the UAVNet Era: Threats, Countermeasures, and Gap Analysis. *ACM Computing Surveys, 55*(1), 1–35. doi:10.1145/3485272

Russian hacker group Killnet claimed responsibility for the attacks. (2022, August 18). *Aljazeera*. https://www.aljazeera.com/amp/news/2022/8/18/estonia-says-it-repelled-cyber-attacks-claimed-by-russian-group

Rutter, K. (2018). If at First You Don't Succeed, Try a Decentralized KYC Platform: Will Blockchain Technology Give Corporate KYC a Second Chance? *R3 Reports, 3*.

Sadhukhan, D., Ray, S., Biswas, G. P., Khan, M. K., & Dasgupta, M. (2021). A lightweight remote user authentication scheme for IoT communication using elliptic curve cryptography. *The Journal of Supercomputing, 77*(2), 1114–1151.

Saeed, M., & Osakwe, S. (2021). *Are African Countries doing enough to ensure Cybersecurity and Internet Safety*. The International Telecommunication Union. https://www.itu.int/hub/2021/09/are-african-countries-doing-enough-to-ensure-cybersecurity-and-internet-safety/

Saha, A., & Khanna, S. R. (2021). Evolution of consumer courts in India: The Consumers Protection Act 2019 and emerging themes of consumer jurisprudence. *IJCLP, 9*, 115.

Salih, A., Zeebaree, S. T., Ameen, S., Alkhyyat, A., & Shukur, H. M. (2021, February). A survey on the role of artificial intelligence, machine learning and deep learning for cybersecurity attack detection. In *2021 7th International Engineering Conference "Research & Innovation amid Global Pandemic" (IEC)* (pp. 61-66). IEEE. 10.1109/IEC52205.2021.9476132

Salvi, M. H. U., & Kerkar, M. R. V. (2016). Ransomware: A cyber extortion. *Asian Journal for Convergence in Technology, 2*.

Samtani, S., Chai, Y., & Chen, H. (2022). Linking exploits from the dark web to known vulnerabilities for proactive cyber threat intelligence: An attention-based deep structured semantic model. *Management Information Systems Quarterly, 46*(2), 911–946.

Sarkar, M. P. (2019). Literature review on adoption of digital payment system. *Global Journal of Enterprise Information System, 11*(3), 62–67.

Sarker, I. H., & Apu, K. (2014). Mvc architecture driven design and implementation of java framework for developing desktop applications. *International Journal of Hybrid Information Technology, 7*(5), 317–322. doi:10.14257/ijhit.2014.7.5.29

Sarvari, S., Sani, N. F. M., Hanapi, Z. M., & Abdullah, M. T. (2020). An efficient anomaly intrusion detection method with feature selection and evolutionary neural network. *IEEE Access: Practical Innovations, Open Solutions, 8*, 70651–70663. doi:10.1109/ACCESS.2020.2986217

Satoshi, T., Makoto, K., Kunihiko, M., & Yasuko, F. (2014). Trends in Cybersecurity and Latest Countermeasures. *Hitachi Review, 63*(5), 264–269.

Scaife, N., Carter, H., Traynor, P., & Butler, K. R. B. (2016). CryptoLock (and Drop It): Stopping Ransomware Attacks on User Data. *2016 IEEE 36th International Conference on Distributed Computing Systems (ICDCS)*, 303–312.

Schwartz, M. (2021, November 12). *Pace of Cybercrime Evolution Is Accelerating, Europol Warns.* Bank Info Security. Retrieved from https://www.bankinfosecurity.com/pace-cybercrime-evolution-accelerating-europol-warns-a-17902?utm_source=Twitter&utm_medium=CollateralSM&utm_campaign=editorial_post

Schweigert, C. T., & Johnson, R. A. (2021). Testing the susceptibility of employees to phishing emails. *International Journal of Information, Business and Management, 13*(3), 190–203.

Scott, E. D., Chris, K. W., & Stanley, G. S. (2018). *Understanding Security Issues.* Walter de Gruyter Incorporated.

Sega Enters. v MAPHIA (1996) 948 F.Supp. 923, 41 (1705) USPQ2d

Seger, A. (2017). *Enhancing regional and international cooperation to improve the rule of law in cyberspace Being a paper delivered Regional Conference On Cybercrime 27 – 29 June 2017 Cebu City, Philippines organized by the Philippine Department of Justice in cooperation with the Council of Europe under the GLACY+ project.* Academic Press.

Sengupta, J., Ruj, S., & Bit, S. D. (2020). A comprehensive survey on attacks, security issues and blockchain solutions for IoT and IIoT. *Journal of Network and Computer Applications, 149*, 102481.

Serianu Report. (2017). *Demystifying Africa's Cyber Security Poverty Line.* Africa Cyber Security Report.

Seth, K. (2010). IT Act 2000 vs 2008-Implementation, Challenges, and the Role of Adjudicating Officers. *National Seminar on Enforcement of Cyberlaw.* Available at: https://www.sethassociates.com/wp-content/uploads/2011/07/IT-Act-2000-vs-20083.pdf

Sgandurra, D., Muñoz-González, L., Mohsen, R., & Lupu, E. C. (2016). *Automated Dynamic Analysis of Ransomware: Benefits, Limitations and use for Detection.* https://arxiv.org/abs/1609.03020

Shahzadi, R., Anwar, S. M., Qamar, F., Ali, M., & Rodrigues, J. P. C. (2019). Chaos based enhanced RC5 algorithm for security and integrity of clinical images in remote health monitoring. *IEEE Access: Practical Innovations, Open Solutions, 7*, 52858–52870.

Shaikh, A. N., Shabut, A. M., & Hossain, M. A. (2016). A literature review on phishing crime, prevention review and investigation of gaps. *2016 10th International Conference on Software, Knowledge, Information Management & Applications*, 9–15. 10.1109/SKIMA.2016.7916190

Shalika, C. (2019). Online Copyright Infringement and the Liability of Internet Service Providers. *Available at SSRN 3464140*.

Shankar, R., & Ahmad, T. (2021). Information Technology Laws: Mapping the Evolution and Impact of Social Media Regulation in India. *DESIDOC Journal of Library and Information Technology*, *41*(4).

Shannon, C. E. (1949). Communication Theory of Secrecy Systems. *The Bell System Technical Journal*, *28*(4), 656–715. doi:10.1002/j.1538-7305.1949.tb00928.x

Sharafi, M., Fotouhi-Ghazvini, F., Shirali, M., & Ghassemian, M. (2019). A low power cryptography solution based on chaos theory in wireless sensor nodes. *IEEE Access: Practical Innovations, Open Solutions*, *7*, 8737–8753.

Sharma, S. (2022). Cybersecurity as a service: A freedom movement to defeat cybercrime August 15, 2022. *Times of India* https://timesofindia.indiatimes.com/blogs/voices/cybersecurity-as-a-service-a-freedom-movement-to-defeat-cybercrime/?source=app&frmapp=yes

Sharma, S. (2022). Cybersecurity as a service: A freedom movement to defeat cybercrime August 15, 2022. *Times of India*. https://timesofindia.indiatimes.com/blogs/voices/cybersecurity-as-a-service-a-freedom-movement-to-defeat-cybercrime/?source=app&frmapp=yes

Sharma, S., Kumar, R., & Krishna, C. R. (2020). RansomAnalysis: The Evolution and Investigation of Android Ransomware. In M. Dutta, C. R. Krishna, R. Kumar, & M. Kalra (Eds.), *Proceedings of International Conference on IoT Inclusive Life (ICIIL 2019), NITTTR Chandigarh, India* (Vol. 116, pp. 33–41). Springer Singapore. 10.1007/978-981-15-3020-3_4

Sharma, G., & Kalra, S. (2018, October). A lightweight multi-factor secure smart card based remote user authentication scheme for cloud-IoT applications. *Journal of Information Security Applications*, *42*, 95–106.

Sharma, R., & Arya, R. (2022). Security threats and measures in the Internet of Things for smart city infrastructure: A state of art. *Transactions on Emerging Telecommunications Technologies*, 4571. doi:10.1002/ett.4571

Sharma, S., Mate, G. S., Pawar, M., Patil, S., & Gole, S. (2017). *Cued Click Point (CCP) Algorithm For Graphical Password To Authenticate Shoulder Surfing Resistance*. Savitribai Phule Pune University Tathawade.

Sheelagh, B., & Caitriona, H. (2020). Cybercrime: Current Threats and Responses. *A Review of the Research Literature*.

Sheen, S., & Yadav, A. (2018). Ransomware detection by mining API call usage. *2018 International Conference on Advances in Computing, Communications and Informatics (ICACCI)*, 983–987. 10.1109/ICACCI.2018.8554938

Shen, J., Chang, S., Shen, J., Liu, Q., & Sun, X. (2018, January). A lightweight multi-layer authentication protocol for wireless body area networks. *Future Generation Computer Systems*, *78*, 956–963.

Shi, E., & Perrig, A. (2004). Designing secure sensor networks. *IEEE Wireless Communications*, *11*(6), 38–43. doi:10.1109/MWC.2004.1368895

Shnain, A. H., & Shaheed, S. H. (2018). The use of graphical password to improve authentication problems in e-commerce. In. AIP Conference Proceedings: Vol. 2016. *No. 1* (p. 020133). AIP Publishing LLC. doi:10.1063/1.5055535

Shushaanth, S., & Prakash, G. A. (2018). A Study on Copyright Infringement in Cyberspace with Special Reference to the Liability of the Internet Service Provider for Infringement. *International Journal of Pure and Applied Mathematics*, *119*(17), 1503–1516. https://papers.ssrn.com/sol3/papers.cfm?abstract_id=3553588

Sicari, S., Cappiello, C., Pellegrini, F. D., Miorandi, D., & Coen-Porisini, A. (2014). A security-and quality-aware system architecture for Internet of Things. *Information Systems Frontiers*.

Siegel, B. (2022, January 24). *Ransomware payments up 33% in Q1 2020*. Coveware. Retrieved from https://www.coveware.com/blog/q1-2020-ransomware-marketplace-report

Signé, L., & Signé, K. (2021). *How African states can improve their cyber security*. https://www.brookings.edu/techstream/how-african-states-can-improve-their-cybersecurity/

Singer, J. B. (2014). User-generated visibility: Secondary gatekeeping in a shared media space. *New Media & Society*, *16*(1), 55–73.

Singer, P. W., & Allan, F. (2014). *Cybersecurity and Cyber war: What you Need to Know*. Oxford University Press.

Singh, K., Kaushik, K. A., & Shahare, V. (2020). Role and Impact of Wearables in IoT Healthcare. In *Proceedings of the Third International Conference on Computational Intelligence and Informatics*. Springer.

Singhal, N., Sharma, M. K., Samant, S. S., Goswami, P., & Reddy, Y. A. (2020). Smart KYC using blockchain and IPFS. In *Advances in Cybernetics, Cognition, and Machine Learning for Communication Technologies* (pp. 77–84). Springer. doi:10.1007/978-981-15-3125-5_9

Skeldon, P. (2021, December 10). Analysis: What is the reality of real-world and cybercrime in Europe? *Telemedia*. https://www.telemediaonline.co.uk/analysis-what-is-the-reality-of-real-world-and-cybercrime-in-europe/

Smith, K. J., & Dhillon, G. (2020). Assessing blockchain potential for improving the cybersecurity of financial transactions. *Managerial Finance*, *46*(6), 833–848. doi:10.1108/MF-06-2019-0314

Smith, R. E. (1997). *Internet Cryptography*. Addison Wesley.

Solms, E., & Strous, L. A. (2002, November). Information security: A corporate governance issue. In *Working Conference on Integrity and Internal Control in Information Systems* (pp. 115-133). Springer.

Soni, S. (2019). Navigating E-Commerce Marketplace in India: A Study of Impact from Indian Regulations. *Available at SSRN 3435488*.

Sonowal, G., & Kuppusamy, K. S. (2018). Smidca: An anti-smishing model with machine learning approach. *The Computer Journal*, *61*(8), 1143–1157. doi:10.1093/comjnl/bxy039

Spence, A., & Bangay, S. (2022). Security beyond cybersecurity: Side-channel attacks against non-cyber systems and their countermeasures. *International Journal of Information Security*, *21*(3), 437–453. doi:10.100710207-021-00563-6

Sri, K. H., Vardhan, M. V., Nikitha, K., Kiran, K. M., & Saritha, A. K. (2020). Graphical Password Authentication. *Journal of Xi'an University of Architecture & Technology*, *12*(4), 1006–7930.

Srinivas, N., & Biswas, A. (2012). Protecting patient information in India: Data privacy law and its challenges. *NUJS L. Rev.*, *5*, 411.

Statista Research Department. (2021). *Number of bank fraud cases across India between from financial year 2009 to 2021*. Available at: https://www.statista.com/statistics/1012729/india-number-of-bank-fraud-cases/

Steichen, M., Fiz, B., Norvill, R., Shbair, W., & State, R. (2018). Blockchain-based, decentralized access control for IPFS. In 2018 IEEE International Conference on Internet of Things (iThings) and IEEE Green Computing and Communications (GreenCom) and IEEE Cyber, Physical and Social Computing (CPSCom) and IEEE Smart Data (SmartData) (pp. 1499-1506). IEEE. doi:10.1109/Cybermatics_2018.2018.00253

Stratton, G., Powell, A., & Cameron, R. (2017). Crime and justice in digital society: Towards a 'digital criminology'? *International Journal for Crime. Justice and Social Democracy*, *6*(2), 17–33. doi:10.5204/ijcjsd.v6i2.355

Stuart, K., & Bromage, D. (2010). Current State of Play: Records management and the Cloud. *Records Management Journal, 20*(2), 217–225. doi:10.1108/09565691011064340

Subramaniam, R., Singh, S. P., Padmanabhan, P., Gulyás, B., Palakkeel, P., & Sreedharan, R. (2021). Positive and Negative Impacts of COVID-19 in Digital Transformation. *Sustainability, 13*(16), 9470. doi:10.3390u13169470

Sugandhi, R., Soumya, V., Jha, M., Sanyasi, A. K., Adhikari, A., & Awasthi, L. M. (2021). Development of electronic record-keeping software for remote participation in Large Volume Plasma Device upgrade using Angular 2 and NodeJS web technologies. *The Review of Scientific Instruments, 92*(7), 075102. doi:10.1063/5.0049037 PMID:34340411

Suganya, S., & Prema, E. (2021). Authorship of Copyrightable Works Created by Artificial Intelligence. *IUP Law Review, 11*(1). Available at: https://papers.ssrn.com/sol3/papers.cfm?abstract_id=3829579

Sumanjeet, D. (2010). The state of e-commerce laws in India: A review of Information Technology Act. *International Journal of Law and Management, 52*(4), 265–282.

Sundareswaran, N., Sasirekha, S., Paul, I. J. L., Balakrishnan, S., & Swaminathan, G. (2020). Optimised KYC Blockchain System. In *2020 International Conference on Innovative Trends in Information Technology (ICITIIT)* (pp. 1-6). IEEE.

Sunil, S. S., Prakash, D., & Shivaji, Y. R. (2014). Cued click points: Graphical password authentication technique for security. *International Journal of Computer Science and Information Technologies, 5*(2).

Suo, X., Zhu, Y., & Owen, G. S. (2005). Graphical passwords: A survey. In *21st Annual Computer Security Applications Conference*. IEEE.

Sutherland, E. (2017). Governance of Cybersecurity: the case of South Africa. *The African Journal of Information and Communication,* (20), 83-112. doi:10.23962/10539/23574

Świątkowska, J. (2020). Tackling cybercrime to unleash developing countries' digital potential. Pathways for Prosperity Commission Background Paper Series no. 33.

Swift, O., Colon, R., & Davis, K. (2020). The impact of cyber breaches on the content of cybersecurity disclosures. *Journal of Forensic and Investigative Accounting, 12*(2), 197–212.

Symantec Report. (2016). *Cyber Crime and Cyber Security Trends in Africa*. Author.

Symantec. (2015). *Android.Lockdroid.E.* https://www.symantec.com/security-center/writeup/2014-103005-2209-99

Taha, M. (2016, March 10). *Cybercriminals target millions of bank app users*. https://www.abc.net.au/news/2016-03-10/cybercriminals-target-millions-of-bank-app-users/7237220

Tal, G., & Nayia, B. (2020). *Insight Report: Partnership against Cybercrime Shaping the Future of Cybersecurity and Digital Trust*. World Economic Forum.

Tandon, A., & Nayyar, A. (2019). A Comprehensive Survey on Ransomware Attack: A Growing Havoc Cyberthreat. In V. E. Balas, N. Sharma, & A. Chakrabarti (Eds.), *Data Management, Analytics and Innovation* (Vol. 839, pp. 403–420). Springer Singapore. doi:10.1007/978-981-13-1274-8_31

Tasnim, N., & Sarker, I. H. (2022). Ransomware family classification with ensemble model based on behavior analysis. Preprints. () doi:10.20944/preprints202201.0454.v1

Terebey, S. (2016, September 22). *African Union Cybersecurity Profile: Seeking a Common Continental Policy*. https://jsis.washington.edu/news/african-union-cybersecurity-profile-seeking- common-continental-policy/

Terebey, S. (2016). *African Union Cybersecurity Profile: Seeking a Common Continental Policy.* The Henry M. Jackson School of International Studies, University of Washington.

the Consumer Protection (E-Commerce) Rules, 2020

The European Union Agency for Cybersecurity. (2022). *Towards a Trusted and Cyber Secure Europe.* https://www.enisa.europa.eu/about-enisa

The European Union Institute for Security Studies. (2021). *Cyber Conflict Prevention on the EU-Africa Security Agenda.* https://www.iss.europa.eu/content/cyber-conflict-prevention-eu-africa-security-agenda

The European Union Institute for Security Studies. (2021). *Regionalized multilateralism? EU-Africa cooperation in cyberspace.* https://www.iss.europa.eu/content/regionalised-multilateralism-eu-africa-cooperation-cyberspace

The future of cyber survey 2019 . (2019). Deloitte. Retrieved from https://www2.deloitte.com/content/dam/Deloitte/us/Documents/finance/us-the-future-of-cyber-survey.pdf

The Global Forum on Cyber Expertise. (2021). *AUC-GFCE Collaboration: Enabling African countries to identify and address their cyber capacity needs.* https://thegfce.org/auc-gfce-collaboration-enabling-african-countries-to-identify-and-address-their-cyber-capacity-needs/

The Information Technology (Amendment) Act 2008.

The Information Technology. (2011). *reasonable Security Practices And Procedures And Sensitive Personal Data Or Information.* Rules.

The Times of India. (2022). *KYC Frauds.* Available at: https://timesofindia.indiatimes.com/topic/kyc-fraud(accessed on 16August, 2022)

Thomas, R. (2014). *The rise of cyber-diplomacy: the EU, its strategic partners and Cybersecurity.* Working Paper No. 7. Madrid: European Strategic Partnership Observatory and Fride.

TinyOS. (2022). https://en.wikipedia.org/wiki/TinyOS

Tomar, S. (2013, August 26). *National Cyber Security Policy 2013: An Assessment.* IDSA. Retrieved from https://www.idsa.in/idsacomments/NationalCyberSecurityPolicy2013_stomar_260813

Tomas, M., & Audrey, G. (2022). *Internet Infrastructure Security Guidelines for Africa Unveiled by the African Union.* https://ccdcoe.org/incyder-articles/internet-infrastructure-security-guidelines-for-africa-unviled-by-african-union/

Topping, C., Dwyer, A., Michalec, O., Craggs, B., & Rashid, A. (2021). Beware suppliers bearing gifts!: Analysing coverage of supply chain cyber security in critical national infrastructure sectorial and cross-sectorial frameworks. *Computers & Security, 108,* 102324. doi:10.1016/j.cose.2021.102324

Torres, P. E. P., & Yoo, S. G. (2017). Detecting and neutralizing encrypting Ransomware attacks by using machine-learning techniques: A literature review. *International Journal of Applied Engineering Research: IJAER, 12*(18), 7902–7911.

Townsend, C. (2019). *A Brief and Incomplete History of Cybersecurity.* https://www.uscybersecurity.net/history/

Toyin, F. (2022, August 18). Cut soap for me. *Premium Times.* https://www.premiumtimesng.com

Tranfield, D., Denyer, D., & Smart, P. (2003). Towards a Methodology for Developing Evidence-Informed Management Knowledge by Means of Systematic Review. *British Journal of Management, 14*(3), 207–222. doi:10.1111/1467-8551.00375

Tsen, E., Ko, R. K. L., & Slapnicar, S. (2022). An exploratory study of organizational cyber resilience, its precursors and outcomes. *Journal of Organizational Computing and Electronic Commerce*, *32*(2), 153–174. doi:10.1080/109193 92.2022.2068906

Turianskyi, Y. (2020). *Africa and Europe: Cyber Governance Lessons. African Perspectives Global Insights*. South African Institute of International Affairs.

U.S. Embassy Ghana. (2021). *Remarks by Chargé d'Affaires Nicole Chulick on Protection of Critical Information Infra-structure Directive held on October 1, 2021 during the Cybersecurity Awareness Month Launch*. United State Government.

United Nations Office on Drugs And Crime. (2013). *Draft: Comprehensive Study on Cybercrime*. United Nations.

United Nations Office on Drugs and Crime. (2017). *Capacity-building on cybercrime and E-evidence: the Experience of EU/Council of Europe Joint Projects, 2013-2017 Non-Paper Submitted by European Union*. Council of Europe. Document No. CCPCJ/EG.4/2017/CRP.2/6.

Usman, M., Ahmed, I., Aslam, M. I., Khan, S., & Shah, U. A. (2017). *SIT: A lightweight encryption algorithm for secure Internet of Things*. Available: https://arxiv.org/abs/1704.08688

Van der Meulen, N., Jo, E. A., & Soesanto, S. (2015). *Cybersecurity in the European Union and beyond: exploring the threats and policy responses*. Academic Press.

Van Raemdonck, N. (2021). *Africa as a Cyber Player*. https://eucyberdirect.eu/research/africa-as-a-cyber-player

Verma, A. (2014). Data protection law in India: A business perspective. *Journal of Commerce & Accounting Research*, *3*(1).

Villegas-Ch, W., Ortiz-Garces, I., & Sanchez-Viteri, S. (2021). Proposal for an Implementation Guide for a Computer Security Incident Response Team on a University Campus. *Computers*.

Vindele, L., & Cane, R. (2022). The role of intellectual property rights in the technological age. *Acta Prosperitatis*, 183. Available at: https://www.turiba.lv/storage/files/ap-13-makets-www_1.pdf#page=177

von Krogh, H., Haefliger, Spaeth, & Wallin. (2012). Carrots and Rainbows: Motivation and Social Practice in Open Source Software Development. *Management Information Systems Quarterly*, *36*(2), 649. doi:10.2307/41703471

Von Solms, B. (2006). Information security–the fourth wave. *Computers & Security*, *25*(3), 165–168. doi:10.1016/j.cose.2006.03.004

Von Solms, B., & Von Solms, R. (2005). From information security to… business security? *Computers & Security*, *24*(4), 271–273. doi:10.1016/j.cose.2005.04.004

von Solms, B., & von Solms, R. (2018). Cybersecurity and information security - what goes where? *Information and Computer Security*, *26*(1), 2–9. doi:10.1108/ICS-04-2017-0025

Von Solms, R., & von Solms, S. B. (2006). Information Security Governance: A model based on the direct–control cycle. *Computers & Security*, *25*(6), 408–412. doi:10.1016/j.cose.2006.07.005

Von Solms, R., & von Solms, S. B. (2006). Information security governance: Due care. *Computers & Security*, *25*(7), 494–497. doi:10.1016/j.cose.2006.08.013

Wahdani, F. (2021). The legal character of domain names'cybersquatting. *Law, Society & Organisations*, *10*(1), 23-41. Available at: https://dea.lib.unideb.hu/dea/bitstream/handle/2437/326329/FILE_UP_5_LSO_10_2.pdf?sequence=1

Wang, E. K., Lin, C. W., Wu, T. Y., Chen, C. M., & Ye, Y. (2015, September). Privacy protection framework in social networked cars. In *International Conference on Multidisciplinary Social Networks Research* (pp. 553-561). Springer. 10.1007/978-3-662-48319-0_46

Wang, Z., Wu, X., Liu, C., Liu, Q., & Zhang, J. (2018). RansomTracer: Exploiting cyber deception for ransomware tracing. *2018 IEEE Third International Conference on Data Science in Cyberspace (DSC)*, 227–234. 10.1109/DSC.2018.00040

Wazid, M., Das, A. K., Odelu, V., Kumar, N., Conti, M., & Jo, M. (2017, February). Design of secure user authenticated key management protocol for generic IoT networks. *IEEE Internet Things J.*, *5*(1), 269–282.

Wertheim, S. (2019). The willingness not to believe. *Certified Public Accountant. The CPA Journal*, *89*(12), 86–87.

Wertheim, S. (2020a). When is a business 'shielded' from financial harm? *Certified Public Accountant. The CPA Journal*, *90*(2), 70–71.

Wertheim, S. (2020b). Tips for fighting off cybercrime in 2020. *Certified public accountant. The CPA Journal*, *90*(3), 64–66.

Wiedenbeck, S., Waters, J., Birget, J. C., Brodskiy, A., & Memon, N. (2005). Authentication using graphical passwords: Effects of tolerance and image choice. In *Proceedings of the 2005 symposium on Usable privacy and security* (pp. 1-12). 10.1145/1073001.1073002

Wiedenbeck, S., Waters, J., Birget, J. C., Brodskiy, A., & Memon, N. (2005). PassPoints: Design and longitudinal evaluation of a graphical password system. *International Journal of Human-Computer Studies*, *63*(1-2), 102–127. doi:10.1016/j.ijhcs.2005.04.010

Wikipedia Contributors. (2022, January 26). National Cyber Security Policy 2013. In *Wikipedia, The Free Encyclopedia*. Retrieved 18:22, October 14, 2022, from https://en.wikipedia.org/w/index.php?title=National_Cyber_Security_Policy_2013&oldid=1068035612

Wilding, E. (Ed.). (1990). *Virus Bulletin*, 20.

Wilson, B. (2010). Data Privacy in India: The Information Technology Act. *Available at SSRN 3323479.*

Wood, A., & Eze, T. (2020). The Evolution of Ransomware Variants. *9th European Conference on Cyber Warfare and Security.* https://chesterrep.openrepository.com/handle/10034/623242

World Bank and United Nations. (2017). Combating Cybercrime: Tools and Capacity Building for Emerging Economies. Washington, DC: World Bank License.

World, E. F. F. S. R. (2020). *Cybersecurity, emerging technology and systemic risk.* University of Oxford.

Wu, F., Li, X., Sangaiah, A. K., Xu, L., Kumari, S., Wu, L., & Shen, J. (2018, May). A lightweight and robust two-factor authentication scheme for personalized healthcare systems using wireless medical sensor networks. *Future Generation Computer Systems*, *82*, 727–737.

Xenofontos, C., Zografopoulos, I., Konstantinou, C., Jolfaei, A., Khan, M. K., & Choo, K.-K. R. (2022). Consumer, commercial, and industrial IoT (In)security: Attack taxonomy and case studies. *IEEE Internet of Things Journal*, *9*(1), 199–221. doi:10.1109/JIOT.2021.3079916

Yahoo.com V. Akash Arora (1999) PTC (19) 201

Yang, L., Lau, L., & Gan, H. (2019). Investors' perceptions of the cybersecurity risk management reporting framework. *International Journal of Accounting and Information Management*, *28*(1), 167–183. doi:10.1108/IJAIM-02-2019-0022

Yang, T. Y., Shamala, P., Chinniah, M., & Foozy, C. F. M. (2021, February). Graphical Password Authentication For Child Personal Storage Application. *Journal of Physics: Conference Series*, *1793*(1), 012065. doi:10.1088/1742-6596/1793/1/012065

Yan, S. Y. (2019). Offensive Cryptography. In *Cybercryptography: Applicable Cryptography for Cyberspace Security*. Springer. doi:10.1007/978-3-319-72536-9_9

Yokohama, S. (2017). Business Management and Cyber Security. *NTT Corporation Journal*, *1*(1), 123.

Young, A. L., & Yung, M. (2017). Cryptovirology: The birth, neglect, and explosion of ransomware: Recent attacks exploiting a known vulnerability continue a downward spiral of ransomware-related incidents. *Communications of the Association for Information Systems*, *60*(7), 24–26.

Young, A., & Yung, M. (1996). Cryptovirology: Extortion-based security threats and countermeasures. *Proceedings 1996 IEEE Symposium on Security and Privacy*, 129–140. 10.1109/SECPRI.1996.502676

Yu, B., Yang, M., Wang, Z., & Gao, C. S. (2006). Identify Abnormal Packet Loss in Selective Forwarding Attacks. *Chinese Journal of Computers*, *9*, 1540–1550.

Zadeh, A. H., Jeyaraj, A., & Biros, D. (2020). Characterizing cybersecurity threats to organizations in support of risk mitigation decisions. *e-Service Journal*, *12*(2), 1–34, 65–66. doi:10.2979/eservicej.12.2.01

Zhang, H., Xiao, X., Mercaldo, F., Ni, S., Martinelli, F., & Sangaiah, A. K. (2019). Classification of ransomware families with machine learning based on N-gram of opcodes. *Future Generation Computer Systems*, *90*, 211–221. doi:10.1016/j.future.2018.07.052

Zhao, H., Zhang, H., & Chen, Q. (2014). The research of dynamic statistics chart based on MVC design pattern. In *2014 IEEE International Conference on System Science and Engineering (ICSSE)* (pp. 56-59). IEEE. 10.1109/ICSSE.2014.6887904

Zia, T., & Zomaya, A. (2006). Security issues in wireless sensor networks. In *International Conference on Systems and Networks Communications, ICSNC'06*. IEEE.

Zimba, A. (2017). *Malware-Free Intrusion: A Novel Approach to Ransomware Infection Vectors*. Academic Press.

Zimba, A., & Chishimba, M. (2019). Understanding the Evolution of Ransomware: Paradigm Shifts in Attack Structures. *International Journal of Computer Network and Information Security*, *11*(1), 26–39. doi:10.5815/ijcnis.2019.01.03

Zimba, A., & Mulenga, M. (2018). A dive into the deep: Demystifying WannaCry crypto ransomware network attacks via digital forensics. *International Journal on Information Technologies & Security*, *4*(2).

Zimba, A., Wang, Z., & Chen, H. (2017). Reasoning crypto ransomware infection vectors with Bayesian networks. *2017 IEEE International Conference on Intelligence and Security Informatics (ISI)*, 149–151. 10.1109/ISI.2017.8004894

Zuech, R., Hancock, J., & Khoshgoftaar, T. M. (2021). Detecting web attacks using random undersampling and ensemble learners. *Journal of Big Data*, *8*(1), 1–20. doi:10.118640537-021-00460-8 PMID:33425651

About the Contributors

Suhasini Verma is Associate Professor in the Department of Business Administration at School of Business & Commerce, Manipal University Jaipur. She is also: Research supervisor. Course Coordinator; Course instructor; Chairperson-BoS- Department of Business Administration.

Vidhisha Vyas is a faculty of Economics and Business Analytics at IILM. She comes with an enriching experience of 10+ years and has been teaching at IILM, for over 8 years. Dr Vyas has a keen interest in Industrial organization, mergers and acquisitions and research on pharmaceutical industry and has published various research papers in this area. Additionally, she has worked on research papers such as IPOs, banking, corporate governance and sustainability. She has also conducted management development/training programs for corporate executives for organisations such as Concentrix, Engineers India Ltd. Pullman Hotel, etc.

Keshav Kaushik is an experienced educator with over eight years of teaching and research experience in Cybersecurity, Digital Forensics, and the Internet of Things. He is working as an Assistant Professor (Senior Scale) in the systemic cluster under the School of Computer Science at the University of Petroleum and Energy Studies, Dehradun, India. He has published 60+ research papers in International Journals and has presented at reputed International Conferences. He is a Certified Ethical Hacker (CEH) v11, CQI and IRCA Certified ISO/IEC 27001:2013 Lead Auditor, Quick Heal Academy Certified Cyber Security Professional (QCSP), and IBM Cybersecurity Analyst. He acted as a keynote speaker and delivered 50+ professional talks on various national and international platforms. He has edited over ten books with reputed international publishers like Springer, Taylor and Francis, IGI Global, Bentham Science, etc. He has chaired various special sessions at international conferences and also served as a reviewer in peer-reviewed journals and conferences.

* * *

G. V. Chiranjeevi Adari graduated from Chaitanya Engineering college, Visakhapatnam in 2007 from Electrical and Electronics Engineering. Completed post Graduation from JNTUK college of Engineering(A), JNTUK Kakinada in the year 2012 from the same stream. Started Ph.D. research work at JNTUK College of Engineering, JNTUK under the supervision of Prof. M. Ramalingaraju from the year 2019. Formerly Associated with Aditya Group of Engineering colleges, Vignan's institute of Information technology and Raghu Educational Institutions, Andhra Pradesh. Currently he is associated with MallaReddy Engineering College for women, Hyderabad, since 2022.

Sunita Bangal is working as an Assistant professor with Indira Institute of Management Pune. expertise is in Databases, Algorithms, and Programming, Machine learning analytics.

Abubakar Bello is a Lecturer in Cyber security and Behaviour at Western Sydney University in the School of Social Sciences: Criminology and Policing discipline. Abubakar and his team are currently researching on Ransomware, Internet of Things, Brain-Inspired Algorithms for Network Anomaly and Intrusion Detection, Smart Cities, Payment Diversion Fraud, BYOD Security and Privacy, and Cyber Sextortion. They have undertaken consultancy work around cyber security across several corporations, privately held entities and government organisations where they provided security and privacy risk management services.

Kirti Raj Bhatele is working as an Assistant Professor in the Department of CSE in RJIT, Border security Force Academy, Tekanpur, Gwalior, Madhya Pradesh, India. He has about 9 years of teaching and research experience. He has published many research papers in many peer reviewed International journals and Conferences. He has also published ten Book Chapters. He has received three Government research fellowships from the Madhya Pradesh Council of Science and Technology, Bhopal, M.P, India. His research interest lies in Image Processing, Medical Image Processing, Machine Learning, etc.

Edward T. Chen is a professor of Management Information Systems in the Operations and Information Systems Department at the University of Massachusetts Lowell. Dr. Chen has published numerous research articles in scholarly journals such as Information & Management, Journal of Computer Information Systems, Project Management, Comparative Technology Transfer and Society, Journal of International Technology and Information Management, and International Journal of Innovation and Learning. Dr. Chen has been served as vice-president, journal editor, board director, editorial reviewer, track chair, and session chair of many professional associations and conferences. Professor Chen has received the Irwin Distinguished Paper Award at the Southwestern Federation of Administrative Disciplines conference, the Best Paper Award at the International Conference on Accounting and Information Technology, and the Best Paper Award at the Annual Meeting of Northeast Decision Science Institute. His main research interests are in the areas of Project Management, Machine Learning, and Healthcare IT.

Prince Dawar is working in Poornima Group of Colleges, Jaipur. Dr. Prince Dawar did his Ph.D. from Malaviya National Institute of Technology (MNIT) Jaipur. He has more than 16 years of research and teaching experience. He has published several research papers in national and international journals.

Sunny Dawar holds Ph.D., MBA and M.COM degrees. Dr. Sunny Dawar is working at Faculty of Management & Commerce, Manipal University Jaipur, Rajasthan, India. Dr. Dawar is having 12 years experience of teaching and research. He has published many research papers in refereed journals. He has also presented several research papers in national and international conferences.

Vijaya Geeta Dharmavaram is a Doctorate in Computer Science from Andhra University. She has been in the academics for the last 19 years. Her research interests are Machine Learning, Cyber Security and Information Systems. She is currently working at GITAM School of Business in the area of Business Analytics.

Anand Jha is an assistant professor in the department of information technology, Rustamji Institute of Technology, BSF Academy, Tekanpur, Gwalior, Madhya Pradesh, India. He has 18 years of academic experience. He has published research papers in many peer reviewed international journals and conferences. His areas of interest include image processing, machine learning, deep learning, web applications development, usage of technology in education, etc.

Amit Kashyap is working as Assistant Professor, Institute of Law, Nirma University Ahmedabad.

Pallavi Kudal is a certified Data Analyst and Data Science Trainer with 12+ years of experience in academics and training and 3+ years of experience in interpreting and analyzing data in order to drive successful business solutions. She holds a BSc. in Statistics, an MBA in Finance and Marketing and Ph.D. in Finance. She has Proficient knowledge in statistics, mathematics, and analytics. Dr. Pallavi is at present associated DYPIMS, Pune as Faculty- Business Analytics. In the past she has been associated with prestigious universities like Christ University, Bangalore and Amity University, Noida.

Ramalinga Raju Manyala did his B. Tech in Electrical Engineering from J.N.T.U. College of Engineering, Kakinada in 1986 and M. Tech in Electrical Machines and Industrial Drives from Regional Engineering College, Warangal, India in 1989. He did his Ph.D. from J.N.T.U., Hyderabad, India in the year 2004. Professor Raju handled several academic positions at JNTUK Kakinada. His areas of interest are Energy Management, Power Electronics, etc.

Alana Maurushat is Professor of Cybersecurity and Behaviour at Western Sydney University where she holds a joint position in the School of Computers, Data and Mathematical Sciences, and in the School of Social Sciences. Alana is the Associate Dean International in the SCDMS and is Director of a Level 1 Cyber Incident Response Centre, Western CACE (mycace.org). She is currently researching on Payment Diversion Fraud and Ransomware, Cyber Reputation Risk Management, Tracking Money-Laundering through Bitcoin Blenders, distributed extreme edge computing for micro-clustered satellites, and Ethical Hacking. She has recently become the Director for a new cyber incident response centre assisting small business with cyber attacks. Western Centre for Cybersecurity Aid and Community Engagement (WCACE) will open its doors to assist the public in 2021 post lock-down. She previously was Senior Lecturer in Law, Key Researcher on the CRC Data to Decisions – Big Data in National Security, and Senior Fellow with the Australian CyberSecurity Centre for Research and Education all at UNSW. She is the Cyber-Ambassador for the NSW Cybersecurity Node with AusCyber and sits as an expert reviewer in cybersecurity and big data with the Australian Research Council. She is Special Advisor for the cybercrime investigation company IFW Global and Cybertrace. She lectures & researches in Cybersecurity, Privacy and Security by Design, Cyber Risk Management, and Artificial Intelligence across the disciplines of law, criminology, business, political science and information communications technology. Alana has done consultancy work on cyber security, open data, big data, technology and civil liberties for both the Australian and Canadian governments, industry and NGOs. Alana has done media with 60 Minutes, the New York Times, The Wall Street Journal, Insight, ABC, and 730 Report, and is the author of many books and articles.

Oly Mishra is a Doctorate in Business Management from Andhra University. She is a researcher in the field of consumer behavior and has been in academics for the last five years. She is currently working at the Indian Institute of Foreign Trade in the area of Marketing.

Nkholedzeni Sidney Netshakhuma completed PhD Information Science at UNISA. He is currently a Deputy Director of Records and Archives at the University of Mpumalanga, South Africa. He worked as Senior Manager at South Africa National Park and various public services.

Smita Pachare is a full-time academician working with Symbiosis Skills and Professional University Pune. Research area in Fintech and Digital Payments and Finance.

Kamalendu Pal is with the Department of Computer Science, School of Science and Technology, City, University of London. Kamalendu received his BSc (Hons) degree in Physics from Calcutta University, India, Postgraduate Diploma in Computer Science from Pune, India, MSc degree in Software Systems Technology from the University of Sheffield, Postgraduate Diploma in Artificial Intelligence from Kingston University, MPhil degree in Computer Science from the University College London, and MBA degree from the University of Hull, United Kingdom. He has published over eighty international research articles (including book chapters) widely in the scientific community with research papers in the ACM SIGMIS Database, Expert Systems with Applications, Decision Support Systems, and conferences. His research interests include knowledge-based systems, decision support systems, teaching and learning practice gamification, blockchain technology, software engineering, service-oriented computing, ubiquitous computing, and supply chain management. He is on the editorial board of an international computer science journal and is a member of the British Computer Society, the Institution of Engineering and Technology, and the IEEE Computer Society.

Pranav Saraswat is working as Associate Professor, Institute of Commerce, Nirma University Ahmedabad.

Jeevesh Sharma has an experience with 5 years in teaching and presently working as Assistant Professor, Faculty of Management and Commerce, Manipal University Jaipur. She has has done MBA and cleared the UGC-NET. She has presented research papers in various national and internal conference and also awarded with best paper. Her research papers are published in Scopus, Web of Science and ABDC listed journals and also authored book chapters in Taylor & Francis. FinTech and application of FinTech, Financial inclusion are the interest area of her research.

Digvijay Singh is a B. Tech Graduate from BML Munjal University. He received his bachelors degree in computer science. His current research interest includes Malware Analysis and he has worked on Digital Forensics research projects in past. His research aims to make a successful career ahead by contributing in reducing malware attacks.

Rajesh Yadav has more than a decade's experience in teaching various Computer Science and Engineering courses. He has an extensive academic and administrative experience along with being involved in various sports-related activities during his previous assignment. His central focus of research is Cyber Security and Blockchain.

Index

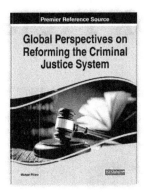

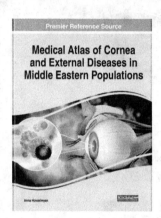

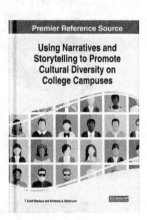

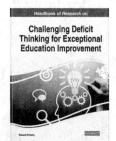

Printed in the United States
by Baker & Taylor Publisher Services